The Inclusive Museum Leader

AMERICAN ALLIANCE OF MUSEUMS

The American Alliance of Museums has been bringing museums together since 1906, helping to develop standards and best practices, gathering and sharing knowledge, and providing advocacy on issues of concern to the entire museum community. Representing more than thirty-five thousand individual museum professionals and volunteers, institutions, and corporate partners serving the museum field, the Alliance stands for the broad scope of the museum community.

The American Alliance of Museums' mission is to champion museums and nurture excellence in partnership with its members and allies.

Books published by AAM further the Alliance's mission to make standards and best practices for the broad museum community widely available.

The Inclusive Museum Leader

*Edited by Cinnamon Catlin-Legutko
and Chris Taylor*

ROWMAN & LITTLEFIELD
Lanham • Boulder • New York • London

Published by Rowman & Littlefield
An imprint of The Rowman & Littlefield Publishing Group, Inc.
4501 Forbes Boulevard, Suite 200, Lanham, Maryland 20706
www.rowman.com

6 Tinworth Street, London, SE11 5AL, United Kingdom

British Library Cataloguing in Publication Information Available

Library of Congress Cataloging-in-Publication Data

Names: Catlin-Legutko, Cinnamon, editor. | Taylor, Chris James, 1973-
    editor. | American Alliance of Museums.
Title: The inclusive museum leader / edited by Cinnamon Catlin-Legutko and
    Chris Taylor.
Description: Lanham : Rowman & Littlefield, [2021] | Includes
    bibliographical references and index. | Summary: "The Inclusive Museum
    Leader offers insights and perspectives from two recognized museum
    leaders who have joined together to offer practical solutions and
    opportunities responding to the call for museums to play an active
    social justice role"—Provided by publisher.
Identifiers: LCCN 2021006301 (print) | LCCN 2021006302 (ebook) | ISBN
    9781538152249 (cloth ; alk. paper) | ISBN 9781538152256 (paper ; alk.
    paper) | ISBN 9781538152263 (electronic)
Subjects: LCSH: Museums and minorities—United States. | Museums—United
    States—Management. | Museums and community—United States. |
    Museums—Social aspects—United States. | Social integration—United
    States. | Social justice—United States. | Social action—United States.
Classification: LCC AM7 .I343 2021 (print) | LCC AM7 (ebook) | DDC
    069/.0680973—dc23
LC record available at https://lccn.loc.gov/2021006301
LC ebook record available at https://lccn.loc.gov/2021006302

Contents

Preface

Museums have been hurtling toward this difficult year for decades now. Leading into this infamous year of 2020, the structure and nature of museums and museum work were under the microscope. Academics, antiracist practitioners, and decolonizers were pushing leadership to upend the status quo and make radical change. We could see that in relation to the sea change that museums need to experience, leaders were only offering miniscule droplets of change in the face of a boiling workforce and constituency. This certainly influenced our interest in joining forces to work on a book like this, but we felt urgently compelled to write and edit this book after George Floyd was murdered on camera by a Minneapolis police officer on May 25, 2020.

For Chris, living and working in the Twin Cities as a biracial man where the global phenomenon ignited by the death of George Floyd began, made him exceptionally interested in this topic of inclusive museum leadership. And of course, this murder follows a succession of murders of Black bodies at the hands of law enforcement and vigilantes. Whether it's Ahmaud Arbery, Breonna Taylor, or the shooting of Jacob Blake, the horror is the same and unending, but museums have a role to play in helping to change the future. In May and June, we saw museums respond with solidarity statements that were trying to express how they empathize or sympathize. These were important to note and observe (and those who were quiet), but we were really looking for statements of apology and action. Ideally, the statement would describe how the museum is part of the problem and that they are committing to making fixes. It would also state that they were going to examine how they play a role in supporting the status quo and supporting the systemic racism that is visible to Black, Indigenous, and People of Color (BIPOC) and a few White people. Leadership is key to how these statements are written and released. We are in a pivotal time for museums.

Adding to this, we were compelled to create this book after observing, or not observing, how leaders are shaping their leadership styles and toolkits. Adding equity and social justice to their learning regimen seems more critical now than ever. For example, a few years ago Cinnamon was participating in a facilitated dialogue training (to better engage around difficult topics and to learn how to meet people "where they are at"), and she heard from the trainer how leaders were never in the room when she taught these courses across the United States and sometimes globally. It's important for leaders to learn alongside their teams to reveal humility, transparency, and authenticity. There are hallmarks of inclusive practice that you'll see peppered throughout this book.

Then later with MASS Action's[1] first convening, Cinnamon was the only director in the room; this number barely changed in the consecutive convenings. Movements like this focus the gaze on leadership, and leadership has to opt in or the board has to push leaders into change (or get one who is willing to change). We followed up on this observation by asking colleagues for examples and monitoring to see if this was the norm. It became clear to both of us that we have a serious problem in this field because leadership seems to think they don't have a role or learning opportunity in inclusive practice, or that they don't have a need to learn antiracism methodology.

We then started thinking about where leaders are engaging in professional development and expanding their skill sets, and we couldn't recall when we'd ever sat next to museum leaders who are engaging in antiracism and social justice training. We could count on maybe . . . maybe . . . two hands the number of White museum leaders who are actively and visibly on a personal journey of inclusion and are showing up in shared learning spaces in order to lead the critical change museums are being asked to do. Now, one could argue that directors are pulled in other directions and their learning about inclusive practice happens elsewhere, but we're not finding those rooms either.

To be honest and transparent, the book is a call out to museum leaders. Throughout the book, leaders and inclusive practitioners share their attitudes, commitments, and practices. This book can be a catalyst for personal change and understanding. For us, this book felt like something we could do in 2020, a time when we felt powerless. With this publication we can amplify voices for change as we all prepare for the future.

Moving into post-2020, museums will be faced with increased pressure around racial justice and equity. They will also be faced with pressure to keep the doors open during and after this pandemic. Can the field face both pressures? Can we take time to retool and shift toward equity and anti-oppression? All eyes are on museum leadership at this moment, and having the right kind of leadership is critical.

Inclusive practice needs to be a function of museum work and a skill set of museum leaders. We think that the authors who contributed to this book help by sharing their perspectives of what inclusive leadership looks like through their skill-building processes and the skills they use every day. These leaders and practitioners know, "It's not just because my staff needs that training. I need that training. I set the tone in this institution." Whether it's equity, justice, or however you describe antiracism and social justice in museums, inclusive leadership is a skill set.

It is our hope that you read the book in the order outlined, but that you also can read individual chapters for reference and inspiration from time to time. Each section follows an order of progression. Part 1, "Setting the Stage," gives background for the need for inclusive museum leadership and offers core understandings about what is needed and what is at the core of inclusive thinking and action. The next part, "Change Is Required," illustrates the urgency and timeliness of this book and offers some guidelines about making changes that lead to inclusive practice. The third section, "Inclusive Leadership," shares personal perspectives from museum leaders who have leaned into the practice of inclusion and have effectively stayed with the work. Part 4, "Values and Action," demonstrates how values can guide an institutional response. In the next section, "Choosing Your Environment," readers are encouraged to look at organizations from the outside and consider if it's a model to follow or join and whether it is a place for belonging. Finally, in part 6, "Looking Ahead," we ask leaders to think ahead, receive the call to action, and make a plan. Throughout the book are activities designed to help leaders situate themselves in their leadership journey, identify areas of growth, and structure a plan of action that will help them and their organizations navigate an inclusive future.

We have taken great care throughout to standardize language, embracing the most inclusive standards we know and understand. Any errors are truly ours, and when found, we'll be sure to learn from it and find a better pathway. We also wanted our readers to understand who is writing and thinking for this book. Author biographies are certainly helpful, and you'll find those at the end, but they don't typically convey the lenses and experiences we use to view the world and the museum field. For that we've asked each author to describe their identities in open and honest language that is comfortable to them. Each author agreed to this, and we are grateful. You will see this right at the beginning in the table of contents.

Both of us have a long list of people to acknowledge because our learning is collaborative and our commitments to this work are public. This invites heartfelt conversations that move us and shake us. It is also fair to say that every person who wrote for this book or sat for a recorded conversation inspires us both. They are all at the top of our acknowledgments list.

We are also deeply grateful to Laura Lott, president and CEO of the American Alliance of Museums (AAM), and Dean Phelus, AAM editor in chief, for enthusiastically responding to our proposal and for agreeing that this needs to be a fast-track project. We thank you, Charles Harmon with Rowman & Littlefield, for setting us free to create and for giving us the green light to move as fast as we were comfortable. Finally, we each have a list of good people to thank. To do this, we'll shift voice.

From Chris: I am deeply grateful for my partner, Kelly C. Weiley, who continues to teach me how to be inclusive every day. The support I received from her and my family on this project was invaluable. The many nights that I worked late, or the weekends that I spent trying to make deadlines caused you all to make sacrifices. And you did so willingly so that I could complete this project. Thank you!

I want to thank my colleagues who worked with me in the Department of Inclusion and Community Engagement: Kyle Parsons, Coral Moore, Jessica Hobson, Amber Annis, Maren Levad, Amber Jones, and Xia Bell. Such a powerful team. I am lucky to have had such a phenomenal staff to provide a safe place for me to learn how to be a leader.

I also want to thank my professional colleagues who have been agitators, activists, conveners, and change agents. Many of them have contributed to this book, but there are many of you out there. I want to thank you for setting the standard and blazing trails for this work with a fierce passion that is truly creating foundational change within the field. You know who you are.

To my mentors, people who have taught me and made time for me—people who have been working in this field for longer than I and have opened the doors that allow me to do my work—thank you. I will mention two here: Lonnie G. Bunch III and Joanne Jones-Rizzi. Thank you. You motivate me to continue in the work.

And to Cinnamon Catlin-Legutko: You have been such a gracious coconspirator on this project. Thank you for asking me to be a part of it. But more than that, thank you for trusting me to create change with you as a consultant and friend. You continue to make change every day in this field. I am honored that you thought of me for this work. This has been so much fun!!

From Cinnamon: Much love and gratitude goes to my Professional Muse group of women museum leaders. We bound ourselves to each other during the pandemic, making sure we are OK and felt support and love. Our weekly meetings have been some of the only bright moments in the really dark weeks of 2020. You also helped me see how this book could take shape, giving it clarity and dimension. I also want to thank my colleagues in my New Orleans Leadership Roundtable. Hearing from your examples and how you grappled with difficult decisions and moments during 2020 has been inspirational and heartbreaking.

Several people served as readers for my chapter "The Three-Body Problem of Museums," and I am grateful for your patience and your gift of feedback. Thank you to Melanie Adams, Scott Stroh, Ashley Rogers, Darren Macfee, Noelle Trent, Sarah Jencks, Dina Bailey, and Larry Legutko.

Laughter and friendship always gets me through difficult times, and during the year of the pandemic, I lost my mother. The people who helped me cry, laugh, and move forward must be acknowledged: Martha Searchfield, Jennifer Judd-McGee, Jen Hughes, Susan Reed, Sandy Alter, Tony Loudermilk, Ted Donosky, Courtney McGovern, Kristen Watson, Lance and Samantha Tawzer, Robyn Clark, and Joanna Rigby-Jones. The time to write and the energy to do it well is possible because of my loving family, my husband Larry Legutko and son Jacob Legutko; my brother Carson and his wife Julie Catlin and their children Anna, Jasper, and Stella; and my fabulous family through marriage, the Lees and Guests. While we haven't been together as much as we wanted to this year, your love is felt, and we'll be together soon.

Thank you, Chris Taylor. You've helped me understand what is asked of me as a museum leader, working inclusively to reduce harm and creating a new museum reality. I am grateful that you said yes to this adventure.

Cinnamon Catlin-Legutko	Chris Taylor
Springfield, Illinois	St. Paul, Minnesota

December 6, 2020

Note

1. MASS Action, launched in 2016, is committed to creating resources for and dialogue about museums that are aligning with equitable and inclusive practice. You can read more about this project at www.museumaction.org. Formed in 2015, Museums & Race is also of note and is committed to challenging and transforming structural racism and oppression in museums. You can read more about their efforts at www.museumsandrace.org.

Epigraph

This can't be all. No one survives this way, not long term. This can't be the purpose of our species, to constantly identify each other as "other," build walls against us, and engage in both formal and informal wars against each other's bodies.

—adrienne maree brown, *Emergent Strategy* (2017)

Every generation leaves behind a legacy. What that legacy will be is determined by the people of that generation. What legacy do you want to leave behind?

—John Lewis, *Across That Bridge: A Vision for Change and the Future of America* (2012)

Part I
Setting the Stage

Chapter 1

With Fierce Intention

Joanne Jones-Rizzi

I write from my home in South Minneapolis, Minnesota, in the midst of a global pandemic and a heightened, racialized nation that is experiencing a toxic threat to our democracy. Museums and other cultural entities have been impacted by these harsh realities. Survival for many museums is in question, and the demand for equity, dismantling White supremacy culture, denouncing racial injustice, and being held accountable have altered the culture and leadership dynamics within our institutions. Our ability to control and to lead within these tectonic shifts taking place within our field bring new, exciting, and daunting challenges.

Since March 15, 2020, I've been working from home. I have joked with my senior leadership colleagues that we are running our museum from our homes, but it's actually not a joke, it's our current reality. Since March 15, I've been to my museum office only twice. On my last visit, I was aware of my own sadness. The museum office space where I used to work was silent, no office bustle and sounds of humans involved in their work, no click-click-clicking of computer keyboards, no animated voices of colleagues sitting in meetings. All the activity of our work has vanished from the site of our museum. We've moved that activity to our individual homes and Google Hangout meetings. I've become accustomed to this way of work, which is both comforting and frightening. I am so thankful that we have the benefit of communication technologies that allow for this new adaptation to human interaction and leadership. I conduct my one-on-one meetings with staff on Google Hangout, I meet with my division leaders on Google Hangout, and meet with senior leadership multiple times per week in the same way. This new reality has, in many ways, caused me to be more intentional, focused, and driven. All of us are working longer and harder. There are no more casual conversations that happen interstitially and no more walking from meeting rooms in one part of the building to another; now I just click on a new link to attend my next meeting. It is an instantaneous transition. Leading my division this way is as far away from my approach to leadership that I can imagine, and yet I have adapted. We all have.

For the purposes of this chapter, I have been reflecting on the past few years and my personal development as a leader. I have been reflecting on how that is manifested within the context of equity, inclusion, liberation, broadening participation, decolonization, decentering Whiteness, dismantling White supremacy culture, addressing educational disparities, and meeting our division goals and metrics. I could share with you strategies that we've used within our museum to move us forward. I could relay logistical information, positional statements that reflect our museum values and intentions. I could present the questions we used for a racial equity survey we ask staff to take annually. I could advise you to develop a theory of change focused on equity and inclusion for your institution, and I could recount how groups that I've been active in have shaped larger conversations within the field. The things I have listed are all critical and essential to leadership that advances equity and inclusion. Rather, I've been reflecting on the factors and events that led me to this work and why I've stayed in it despite the isolation and erasure I've often felt. I continue to reflect on how to best support my colleagues just beginning their careers, particularly those colleagues who identify as Brown, Black, or Indigenous women. I am thinking about mentors, in particular, one, and how her unique style inspired, grounded, and supported me. Her mentoring is not the sole reason for my staying in the field, but it made a difference and it's what I want to focus on here. Leading in this field at this moment is challenging, particularly for those Black, Indigenous, and People of Color (BIPOC) women and individuals who are passionate about museum work, yet bear the burden of representing, educating, being counted, and touted, in the midst of a radical time in our field.

I have been thinking about Claudine, Claudine Brown. When I first became aware of Claudine, she was the deputy assistant secretary at the Smithsonian Institution. I was in Washington, DC, in residence at the Experimental Gallery at the Smithsonian working on an exhibition I codeveloped at the Boston Children's Museum. The Smithsonian Institution Traveling Exhibition Services (SITES) was touring *The Kids Bridge* exhibition. The first stop was the Experimental Gallery. At the opening, Claudine made a few remarks; I think I was introduced to her there, but I don't have a clear memory. For me as a young Black woman, I had an awareness that she was unique, and as I learned more about her, I both revered and feared her. She seemed intense, and she clearly had an important, highly visible role. I had an awareness too, that she was one of the few Black women I met within the field. I was new to museums then, having joined the Boston Children's Museum seven years earlier. After our initial introduction, I would see Claudine at conferences, usually the annual American Alliance of Museums (AAM) conference, and we would talk for a few minutes; it was very surface. She wasn't particularly friendly or warm, but I did have the sense that she was watching me, maybe even looking out for me. I looked forward to those conversations each year even though they lasted only ten to fifteen minutes. She would ask me about what I was working on, what my ideas were about this or that. She would share a little bit about herself and her projects. She often made recommendations about who or what I should meet, hear, or read, or which sessions I should attend. During that time, I was always tenuous around her; she was hard for me to read. A shift in our interactions came when her son Ebon was accepted into the yearly cohort of the interpreter program at the Children's Museum in Boston. Claudine called and e-mailed me frequently then to check in on Ebon. She was worried about him living in Boston; she understood Boston as a place that was dangerous for her son, a young Black man. These conversations shifted our dynamic; it suddenly became easier, and there was a rapport.

When Ebon finished the program and our frequent communication stopped, I continued to be in touch with Claudine. We saw each other yearly at AAM, and when she left the Smithsonian to move back to New York to work at Nathan B. Cummings Foundation, we stayed in touch. She was working at the foundation and teaching in the museum studies program at Bank Street College of Education. She was co-teaching a class in the museum studies program, and I was asked to be a thesis advisor to one of the students. I agreed and advised a student through the ten-month process of developing and writing her thesis. This experience created yet another shift. I heard back from Claudine and her colleague that the thesis was wonderful and amazing. I actually believed then and still do that this student would have written a fantastic thesis without me, but I felt a new appreciation from Claudine that I had not experienced. Working as a thesis advisor helped me see the power of working with someone engaged in a formative and pivotal moment, supporting them in their work, in their process. I was different from Claudine, but I now understood, reflecting on my experiences knowing her, that the interactions that she and I had over the years was a form of mentoring. I wanted to be able to provide this student and others with the support and connection that I felt I had with Claudine.

One of the last times I saw Claudine was in New York. We met for breakfast, and we checked in as usual about our lives. By then I had moved to Minnesota and was working at the Science Museum. We had just opened the *RACE: Are We So Different?* exhibition. She had a lot of questions about my experiences in Minnesota, working at a Science Museum and the exhibition itself. Claudine suggested I research the Shannon Leadership Institute.[1] She said it had changed her, her views, and how she moved through the world.

Fast forward several years, I spoke with Claudine after she returned to the Smithsonian as director of education. She called me to learn about the education programs we developed to support educators and students visiting the *RACE: Are We So Different?* exhibition. She wanted resources for how to talk with educators and how to talk about the exhibition in general since the exhibition had been booked by the Smithsonian. I remember her telling me that in her role she would have to talk about it and she was looking for tips from me. She asked if I had checked out Shannon; I hadn't yet, and she urged me to consider it. That was our last conversation; she died in 2016. Claudine and I never discussed whether she was a mentor to me or what our connection was. We were opportunistic about meeting and getting together; it was often happenstance, but for me it was always instructive.

I have tried to carry that tradition forward by meeting with colleagues, offering myself and my experiences as a learning resource. These relationships are informal, and formal to the extent that they are scheduled. Beyond that we have conversations and respond to what we each are thinking. I offer suggestions, just as Claudine did with me, of people and places to see, hear, and visit. I never refuse a request from a young person within the field, a museum studies student, or a colleague who wants to talk. These individual, hour-long conversations, mostly on the phone, give my museum equity work deep meaning. They give me energy, new perspectives, and new colleagues, and they might mean more to me than to the individuals I am supporting. These meetings and conversations do, in so many ways, add value to my life and are central to who I am as a leader and how I want to lead.

When I was promoted and became a vice president at the Science Museum of Minnesota, I remembered Claudine's urging me to consider the Shannon Leadership Institute. The museum had a new president and CEO, Alison Rempel Brown, who supported and encouraged professional development. Alison understood that to become strong leaders we needed resources that would support our own growth and development. She understood that even natural leaders needed development, and she too urged me to find a program or coach to support my ongoing growth. Coincidentally, someone else nominated me for the Shannon Leadership Institute program. I don't know who it was, but this time I responded to the invitation. I attended the informational meeting and decided to apply. When I was selected as a participant in the next cohort, my museum supported me to attend, both financially and with an acknowledgment of the value placed on my participation personally, professionally, and institutionally. When I sent a request for vacation time in order to participate in the multiday Shannon sessions, Alison denied my request. She followed up with an e-mail that conveyed an unequivocal message of affirmation: this is work, not vacation.

When contemplating the Shannon Leadership Institute program, I wondered if maybe my understanding of leadership and how to be a strong leader was wrong. I wasn't interested in learning how to run meetings or develop spreadsheets or strategic plans. My interests were focused on how to lead in alignment with my own personal values, to be vulnerable, and to recognize vulnerability as a strength. I wanted to lead in a way that was congruent with who I am and the things—the issues—that I am most passionate about. I wanted the people I work with to be colleagues and not regarded, in a diminishing way, as just staff. This seemed to me to be fundamental to being an inclusive leader, to create an environment where my colleagues feel validated and supported even in the face of conflict. The idea of not bringing politics, or the personal to work, does not fit with how I imagine leadership. I want staff to bring their full selves to work, whether they are Black, gay, Jewish women, straight, White, cis men, or whether they identify as nonbinary individuals. The values inherent in each of us are directly linked to our institutions. Who we are and the things we care about form the lifeblood of our institutions.

I have always been committed to my conviction about the importance of bringing our whole selves to work. However, the contexts in which I have worked have often intentionally or unintentionally attempted to filter my capacity for embodying my wholeness. In these too-numerous-to-recount situations, my capacity has been prejudged based on norms embedded in White corporate cultural behaviors and standards. This has taken many forms. Some of these filters judged my competence in learning through dialogue to be so far from the expected norm of silently sitting at a desk, or in a cubicle, that my substantial, though casual in style, conversations with colleagues in all areas of the museum were perceived not as generative and purposeful activity but, rather, unproductive socializing. The expectation of compartmentalization has been another exceedingly powerful filter, particularly the notion that being conversant in contemporary popular culture and talking about interpersonal dynamics was somehow incompatible with the intellectual power of a person who is also a voracious reader engaged in deep reflection and discussion. Early on, my commitment to collaboration veered far away from the prevailing notion of a singular individual, one person solely responsible for the work produced, such that many of my contributions were relegated to the invisible, not legible as catalytic contributions to a collaborative process. Recognition was given to the loudest voice, often a dominant rephrasing of my ideas. As I write this now, I am reminded of the hierarchy of value placed on oral and written communication. With little effort, I can recount the numerous instances in which the ideas that I have shared verbally with colleagues—my insights, emerging theories, observations, and acts of making connections between normative ideas and structural assumptions—have been related, without attribution or without an acknowledgment of me. And then there is the shift that happens when a conversation becomes a text, and the text gains authority, and the ideas do not refer to the context and people who produced them as situated knowledge. This lived experience, the practice of my belief that it is essential that I bring my whole self to work and that I create a space with permeable and elastic boundaries that include and support each person as they bring their whole selves to work, remains a central tenet of my leadership values.

Unexpectedly, I learned that my goals and the process of Shannon were in alignment. The program focused on core values, purpose, developing personal strategies to become a more effective leader, and examining ourselves to better identify how we can improve our focus, thus deepening our commitment to our work. The ideas emphasizing that focus and commitment bring energy and satisfaction to our lives resonated with me, and I felt I could get with that program. When people ask me about my participation in Shannon and what it did for me, I say it's a program that focuses on the whole leader. By identifying our values and having a clarity of purpose, we are made stronger leaders. If we have that clarity about ourselves, we can be effective transformational leaders. It is with that lens that I approach my work as a leader. During Shannon, we took a variety of assessments from the Meyers-Briggs. I am an ENFP (extraverted, intuitive, feeling, and perspective) personality type to values inventory assessments. I learned that my values are *love, creativity*, and *broadmindedness*. I took those assessments multiple times, and I resisted the notion of *love* being part of my leadership style; it challenged how I wanted to be seen. It felt mushy and lacked my perception of strength. At the end of the year-long program, we had to develop and present a *Renewal Plan*, based on our values, in any format that we selected. It could be a performance, poem, presentation, PowerPoint—whatever. There were no constraints, only a time limit. I worked on my *Renewal Plan*, calling it my strategic plan for life, ironic since I identified this as a traditional leadership task that I devalued. After we each gave our presentation, our fellow Shannons, in my cohort seventeen other leaders, had the opportunity to inquire about (not critique) our values presentation.

By the time I was finished with my *Renewal Plan*, I understood the *love* value and how I wanted to use it within my leadership role moving forward. I shared my written *Renewal Plan* with Alison, and when I have wavered or questioned a decision, she has reminded me, "Remember your Shannon." I wish I had completed the program while Claudine was alive; I would like to know how it changed her and what her values were. It's been two years since I participated in Shannon and have since nominated and urged several colleagues to take it, much in the way Claudine urged me. I've even been invited back to introduce new cohorts as part of their introductory session. I've come to terms with my own values, especially the *love* value. I can still be a fierce leader and do it with love.

By the way, I am not in the habit of telling my colleagues that I love them, but I do want my actions to come from a loving place and not a place of frustration or anger. It's not that I don't experience anger, frustration, and annoyance at times—I do. I try hard to not lead with those emotions. The science, equity, and education work that we do requires love, creativity, broadmindedness, patience, and fierceness. The majority of my colleagues are White identified. We do not share a common life experience, but we do share a vision that is focused on equity and inclusion and on decentering Whiteness and dismantling White supremacy culture. It's a constant practice and one that we discuss frequently. How we center equity within science and education is core to our work. We consider and recognize that audience, relevancy, cultural appropriation, cultural representation, and cultural perspectives are embedded in and active in science.

It would be disingenuous for me to cite success without honest reflection about my mistakes. When in the moment of living my mistakes, I've been in pain and shame, and I've found it hard to shake. I wish I could say that I have had the clarity to know that my mistakes have helped me learn and that the painful lessons gained from them have helped me to never ever repeat them. I wish I could say that, since I've had so many years in the field doing this work, that I had the wisdom to not stumble, but I still do. We do stumble, and in service of working in a learning environment, we take advantage of those mistakes. My colleagues are smart, thoughtful, and inclusive leaders. They know that making mistakes, mishaps, and stumbles are part of the learning process. Not to diminish the actual pain when stumbles occur, we try to use them as learning opportunities, not at the expense of those hurt but in service of learning. Thinking about the future, I don't expect to see equity and inclusion and true liberation within our museums in my lifetime. I know it's not an uplifting assessment, but I want to offer honesty. We live and work in the context of a country that is still grappling with the aftermath of slavery. There is still no clarity on confederate flags, monuments, and tributes. There are still large swaths of the population that don't understand why "Black Lives Matter" is critical and assert that Black Life Matters somehow negates White lives. I sound dire. There are many museums actively working to undo decades, centuries of wrong, through decolonization and intentional work. I recognize that I am a part of this system and that most museums are grounded in White supremacy culture. I understand that my institution is nowhere near where we want to be and where some of us know we should be. This work is painstakingly slow, and some are impatient. The awareness alone of where we should be, but are not yet, speaks volumes. You can't address a problem if there's no awareness that a problem exists. I am committed to leading using my practice of *love, creativity*, and *broadmindedness* as my guides to lead with fierceness and intention.

Thank you for listening.

Note

1. In December 2020, the Shannon Leadership Institute sadly closed due to organizational restructuring of the Wilder Foundation. I urge people to find other opportunities to build their leadership skills through immersive leadership experiences.

Chapter 2

The Three-Body Problem of Museums

Cinnamon Catlin-Legutko

This chapter shares historical accounts of museum practices that have harmed Indigenous people. As such, the author recognizes that the contents may be upsetting to Indigenous readers.

The museum field is experiencing a critical gaze that is both "of the moment" and long overdue. Looking back on 2020, museums will see that the economic disruptions were considerable and, for some, not survivable. For all museums, it is a year where the history of museum practice and its supremacist origins connect sharply with the present, demanding change. Museums were built as colonial enterprises and are slow to awaken to the harm caused by their actions, which are not limited to the capturing and keeping of Indigenous ancestors; the exclusion and erasure of Black voices, bodies, and creativity; and the positioning of White power in the C-suite and boardrooms. Collective rooms of action where museum practitioners are talking about making substantiative change in the industry are heavy with museum educators, millennials and younger, and the disenfranchised; these rooms of action rarely see museum directors in the mix. This year has seen protests in the media and online, public actions by boards and directors with many directors losing their jobs, numerous statements of solidarity that reflect little to no evidence of authentic change, and hundreds more museums that said nothing at all when George Floyd was murdered and social unrest filled streets across the nation. A museum reckoning is underway—how will museums emerge on the other side? Which ones will survive?

This is a problem constructed over time in three parts. This first problem rests with the history of museums; they are laden with oppression, racism, and static structures. This freight created a legacy that influences modern museums of every kind. The second problem relates to the people working in museum spaces—galleries, office spaces, or boardrooms. They are predominantly White people. Black, Indigenous, and People of Color (BIPOC) are significantly underrepresented, and as a consequence, their stories and perspectives are not told and shared and BIPOC audiences have largely stayed away from the museum experience. When there are BIPOC working in the museum, they primarily hold service-related positions in security, housekeeping, and facilities. The third problem is the nature of museum leadership. In addition to being primarily White, whether they are the top executive or a board member, museum leadership tends to separate itself from the impacts of these historical and contemporary problems. Additionally, a trend of the last twenty-plus years is the hiring of non-museum workers by boards for leadership roles, recruiting from the for-profit world to run a nonprofit like a business. These leaders have a thin relationship to museum history and practice when they take the helm and have little incentive to learn more.

Borrowing from astrophysics, the museum field has a three-body problem. Nearly 350 years ago, Sir Isaac Newton outlined the laws of motion in relation to the earth's orbit of the sun, but when solving for the moon's motion in relation to the sun, the math becomes elusive. A gravitational power struggle develops when two or more bodies of unequal weight and mass orbit a fixed point. It is a chaotic system.[1] For this analogy, albeit a stretch for the astrophysicists but logical to me, the history of museum practice is the portion of the third-body problem that cannot be solved because it has already happened. But, when we solve two parts of the three, the system change we want becomes predictable. We can't change history, but we can recognize it, name harmful practices, and make positive changes. That solution rests with the people and leaders working in museums today. This three-body problem can arrive close to solution if we solve two problems— leadership and the nature of museum workers and goers. When these are addressed and solved, the weight of oppressive history is lighter and slows the perpetuation of exclusion and harm, creating a more predictable future.

Problem One: Oppressive Histories and Visible Legacies

For the purposes of this chapter, the following discussion focuses on anthropology/natural history museums as their histories include some of the greatest atrocities and human rights violations the museum field has ever committed. To be fair, art museums have determined what is beautiful and artistic through selective lenses and have privileged subject matter that is sometimes violent and oppressive in the name of mastery. Science museums rely on Westernized ways of understanding the world and have been slow to welcome diversity in their scientist ranks. BIPOC stories and experiences are underrepresented in exhibits, collections, programming, and research across the museum field. This list continues, but for the scope of this chapter, the focus is on anthropology/natural history museums and the harm they've caused to Indigenous people. These harms, or sins, sit at the heart of modern museum practice and provide a powerful object lesson for other museum disciplines. This history must be understood and addressed in order to change the present-day museum field and help us solve the three-body problem.

Public museums were created, in great part, to showcase and celebrate the colonial power, providing a place where objects came to rest: the spoils of war, collections of the strange and unusual, and the "other." Visitors came alone and in groups; children were often frowned upon in galleries.[2] Visitors were from the highest strata of society, coming to gaze upon these treasures, marvel at their personal ability to be curious, and be prideful about their nation and its colonial might. This colonial enterprise arrives as early as the 1700s in Europe and later in the United States, arriving at their colonial heyday during the nineteenth and early twentieth centuries. "The private collections of the intellectual elite were transformed into public spaces for 'improvement' of a population seen as the bearers and practitioners of national cultures."[3] Some of the big US collecting museums of the time are the Smithsonian (1846), the Peabody Museum of Archaeology and Ethnology at Harvard (1866), New York's American Museum of Natural History (1869), and the Metropolitan Museum of Art (1870), officially entering American museums into the global mainstream.[4]

By their nature, museum systems and perspectives were built in exclusive, oppressive, and colonizing ways. As Ho-Chunk scholar Amy Lonetree writes, "Museums can be very painful sites for Native peoples, as they are intimately tied to the colonization process."[5] The interpretation of Indigenous peoples in museum spaces is rooted in the development of anthropology as a field of study. Starting in the late nineteenth century, anthropologists launched fields of study while vigorously collecting for museums in major cities across the United States. It is important to understand that, concurrently, federal Indian policies were focused on forced removal and genocidal practices. US policies were taking land, destroying families, and denying religious practice. Added to this, disease continued to ravage tribal communities. Anthropologists thought they were in a race against time and began looting like pirates.[6]

In her book, *Decolonizing Museums: Representing Native America in National and Tribal Museums*, Lonetree writes about these collecting practices and the harmful impact misrepresentations have for Indigenous people. While much has changed over the past twenty years in exhibition practices and Indigenous collaboration, some museums still perpetuate this formula, and others have the vestiges lingering in gallery spaces.

- Exhibitions tend to reinforce a view of static, unchanging Indigenous cultures that is scientifically incorrect. Certainly, the museum diorama supports this by depicting Indians as frozen in time and by displaying them near dinosaurs and extinct animals and other zoological presentations. Exhibit techniques fail to show the connection between living peoples or to address an object's cultural relevance to a community.

- Objects are presented and defined by Western scientific categories and not by Indigenous categories of culture, worldview, and meaning. The human story is often removed from the material culture on exhibit; the context is removed.

- Native communities are homogenized into one Native American community, disregarding the complexity and difference that 574 Indigenous nations represent.[7]

Static, isolated, and homogenized representations of Indigenous people are not limited to museums. These harms can be found in many places—in classrooms, in advertising, at sports venues, at the movies . . . almost everywhere. These misrepresentations are forms of cultural appropriation that reenforce invisibility and erasure by limiting and removing Indigenous voice and agency. Instead of adding to these harms, museums have the responsibility to change their practices through collaboration and relationship building with tribal communities.

There is more to this problem. As museums were gathering collections in the late nineteenth and early twentieth centuries, they were also collecting the physical bodies and belongings of Native people—from massacres, executions, traditional burials, and battlefields. Modern anthropology, archaeology, and museum practice was founded in great part by violating human rights.[8]

The White "Founding Fathers" of modern anthropology were instrumental to these collecting efforts. Samuel G. Morton, known as the "father of physical anthropology," actively collected human remains for studies. He paid soldiers, settlers, and government agents to desecrate Native American graves. Many of these were mass graves due to disease, murder, and massacres, making graves more plentiful.[9] Collecting for his study at the Army Medical Museum, Morton's collection of more than thirty-seven hundred individuals were ultimately transferred to the Smithsonian in 1864.[10]

Franz Boas, one of the "fathers of cultural anthropology," was a grave robber, too. He is most known for his research among the Northwest Coast tribes, collecting oral histories and documenting cultural practices. He was also collecting the bodies of the ancestors along the way, robbing graves after dark and noting it in his field journals.[11] During his early field days, he collected roughly one hundred complete skeletons and two hundred skulls that he mostly sold to the Field Museum in Chicago and European collectors.[12]

Collecting crania was a popular activity for White scholars attempting to relate intelligence, personality, and character to skull and brain size (phrenology). And, of course, the measurement of cranial capacity and skull shape was used to further theories of White supremacy, the study of eugenics, which was widely in practice in scientific circles from the late nineteenth century through World War II.[13]

The amassing by museums of the ancestors and their belongings is the result of discriminatory practices that viewed Native people as less than human, perceptions of the vanishing Indian fueled by anthropologists and adventurers, and unmitigated genocidal government policies. Approximately 90 percent of the human remains in North American museum collections are Native American while less than 2 percent of the US population today identifies as Indigenous.[14] The bodies of enslaved people, Indigenous and Aboriginal people from around the world, as well as White settlers, are also found in museum collections, but in vastly far fewer numbers. (Their return is primarily negotiated through ethical considerations and precedents set by peer museums.)

Morton and Boas are only two members of a long list of White scientists and museum workers who preyed upon Indigenous trauma and death to competitively build bone collections for American museums. By the time the Native American Graves Protection and Repatriation Act (NAGPRA) passed in 1990, it was estimated that museums, federal agencies, and private collectors held half a million Native American bodies and untold millions of cultural objects; an equal number of Native American ancestors are held in collections in Europe.[15] Thirty years after NAGPRA's passage, museums are slow to repatriate with only 20 percent of the ancestors returned.[16]

As I write this, it is important for me to share where the Illinois State Museum (ISM), my institution, lands in this mix.[17] A 2020 review of NAGPRA data found that 56 percent of the ancestors held in collections, museum or university, are held by thirteen institutions.[18] The ISM is number five on this list of thirteen, holding close to seven thousand ancestors in our collections. Repatriation processes initiated quickly after the passage of NAGPRA: "In-person consultation occurred with 37 representatives from six tribes once resident in Illinois (the Peoria, Miami, Ho-Chunk/Winnebago, Sac & Fox, Kickapoo, and Potawatomi), remote consultation took place with Pueblo tribes on ethnographic items, and letters were sent to 184 tribes to consult on potentially sacred objects. An 18-volume report was generated documenting collections subject to NAGPRA."[19] While these early efforts resulted in a co-curation partnership with the Peoria Nation for their ancestors' belongings, since 1996 the ISM has only repatriated 2 percent of the ancestors.[20] The slow pace of repatriation is likely due to academic privilege—anthropologists committed to holding the ancestors for their own and future scientific pursuits—coupled with disruption. In 2015, the ISM was shut down by Governor Bruce Rauner, and top museum leadership was removed and numerous staff fled the institution. The museum was reopened in less than a year. It was an ill-advised budget-saving maneuver that devastated the functionality of the museum and derailed critical activities such as NAGPRA compliance. This rate of return is unacceptable.

In fall 2020, we took action to change the narrative by dedicating ourselves to repatriation processes that are guided by Indigenous leaders. Cultural affiliation will be determined through consultation with tribal members and not by museum staff. We will make available, if requested, state land for reburial. We are also working to add staffing to the repatriation process so that we can move faster over the next five years to return the ancestors.

In addition, we will continue global repatriation efforts. In October 2019, the ISM was the first in the world to repatriate forty-two sacred and culturally significant objects to the Aranda and Bardi Jawi people as part of the Australian government's Return of Cultural Heritage Project, which aims to return Australian Indigenous materials from overseas. In 2006, the ISM repatriated a sacred Kenyan *kigango* that came to the museum through another museum's closure. This particular *kigango* was found to be stolen, and by working with the National Museum of Kenya (NMK), it was reconnected with the appropriate village. However, there remain thirty-seven *vigango* in the ISM collection. We will follow the example set by Stephen Nash at the Denver Museum of Nature and Science and secure their repatriation as well, working with the NMK staff to do so.[21]

The work ahead of us is significant, and it will be emotional and painful for the communities impacted. To be effective in this work and to be sensitive to the issues and anticipated experiences ahead, the ISM team is working to better understand decolonizing museum practices, NAGPRA, and diversity, equity, accessibility, and inclusion (DEAI). Learning how they intersect in museum work is critical and essential for our future as an inclusive museum.

The ISM offers one example of the urgent museum work in front of all museum workers to recover from this history and move toward a reparative future. With this history as its foundation, museums today determine how their audiences see and learn about culture, science, and creativity through a prescribed academic and "best practice" set of lenses. Who is determining these practices? Further, who is deciding what goes into the collections for future generations? Who is deciding what goes on gallery walls and what is shared in educational programs?

Problem Two: A Homogenous Workforce

The aspiring museum worker rarely finds an easy pathway to a museum job, and for a BIPOC trying to get in, the path is often completely blocked or the journey never begins. Getting a job in museums already takes several small miracles and privilege. Room after room of White people make the majority or all decisions about exhibitions, programming, collecting, fundraising, governance—the whole gamut of museum work. The audience responds to this Whiteness and mirrors it back. The second problem of the three-body problem is White people—who gets the jobs, who stays in the jobs (and they tend to stay their entire careers), and who visits the museum in response. Unlike the previous problem of history, this problem can be solved.

This second problem goes unsolved when museum leadership and management doesn't recognize its role in addressing this disparity and creating organizational change. This requires a close examination of hiring practices and work culture. Funding internship programs and ensuring a livable wage for workers helps as well.

Once the workforce is diverse—meaning there is a significant number of BIPOC employed by museums and at all levels—there also need to be access to decision making and leadership. If diversity exits at all in a museum, it coalesces at the entry level and front line, the lowest paid salaries and the most dispensable when economic crises hit.

Managers and leaders need to address unconscious bias and micro-aggressions as well as systemic racism and White supremacy. This requires a sea change for the work environment, carefully guided by well-trained museum leaders who are actively and transparently on their inclusion journeys. In the absence of this kind of change, country club mentality prevails. People who act alike and look alike are hired over and over again, pushing out experience and opportunity and certainly marginalizing and excluding BIPOC.

The data confirms this reality. Pulling from multiple research projects and data sources to draw a clear picture—American Alliance of Museums (AAM), Pew Research, Association of Art Museum Directors, Wilkening Consulting, and the US Census—we can see this problem in stark detail.[22]

The current US population is one-third non-White, heading toward majority non-White. In twenty-five years, the United States will be 54 percent White, and this trend will only grow. Museum participation numbers (employees, boards, and museum-goers) are out of step with this trend. Approximately 20 percent of museum employees are BIPOC, and 9 percent of museum core audiences are non-White. Looking at only art museums, 72 percent of staff are White; 28 percent are BIPOC, and 60 percent are female.

Where the power rests, museum boards and leaders are the least diverse in the bunch—46 percent of museum boards surveyed stated they were 100 percent White. In science centers and children's museums, nearly 97 percent of CEOs are White, and 84 percent of staff leadership positions in art museums are White. African Americans hold only 4 percent of the leadership positions in US art museums while Latinx people hold only 3 percent of the total leadership jobs in the sector.

When asked if they were satisfied with the racial and ethnic diversity of the board, 12 percent of board members said yes. Fewer than one-third of museum leaders or boards have prioritized diversity strategies; 32 percent have evaluated and modified recruitment efforts; and 14 percent have conducted diversity training.

When looking at who holds the most power in museums, 93 percent of both museum directors and board chairs identify as White. However, 77 percent of museum directors and 66 percent of board chairs believe diversity and inclusion are important to advancing their missions. Only 10 percent of boards have developed a plan of action to become more inclusive. As AAM president and CEO Laura Lott writes, "There is a real disconnect between perception and urgent action."[23]

This litany of percentages spotlights that in addition to the oppressive history of museum formation and operation, the people working in museum offices, conference rooms, classrooms, and galleries are mostly White. This leaves little room for divergent ideas and perspectives to develop, grow, and shape an organization. How does this affect museum performance? A recent study of eighteen major US art museums found that 85 percent of artists represented in their collections are White, and 87 percent are men.[24] Although a comprehensive study of all museum collections types is unavailable, it's safe to assume that over the past 150-plus years, museum collections have grown using narrow lenses of White dominant society, colonialism, and curiosity. Previously you read how traditional gallery interpretations of Indigenous lifeways contribute to Indigenous erasure and invisibility. From the encyclopedic museums to the historic sites and historical societies, most have neglected the full, dynamic stories of American history, culture, and experience in exhibits and educational programs. When we bring museum-goers into the story, Wilkening Consulting's 2020 survey tells us that 88 percent of them are White.[25]

While there are outstanding examples of inclusive practices in many museums (trust me, I see you and you're amazing!), the majority of museums present a White story of the United States and the globe for White donors, volunteers, and audiences.

Collectively the museum field can solve this second-body problem by transforming the museum workforce. Talented museum leaders have shown us that inclusive change begins in a variety of ways. It begins with recognizing how White the field is and making changes to recruitment and retention strategies. It begins with a comprehensive plan of action to engage staff and boards in DEAI, antiracism, and social justice practices.

Problem Three: Exclusive Leadership

The third problem of this three-body problem analogy is museum leadership, the focus of this book. It is a solvable problem just as the second. Leaders arrive at their posts from a variety of directions and with, hopefully, relevant skills and experiences. How they get these posts is determined by community volunteers—board members. Many of these board members are the museum's highest giving donors and wield great power in their own lives and communities. This often transmits to the boardroom, centralizing power and control. This should be noted and considered. For the sake of this discussion and to aid my analogy, this third-body problem focuses on top museum leadership—the director.

Leading a museum requires vision, strategy, and the ability to gather resources. The director holds the line between the board and staff, working both sides of the same coin. Not often discussed, but painfully clear to anyone who serves in this role, is the reality that it is a lonely job. When it is going well, the director works in lockstep with their board chair and in collaboration with their leadership team. When it is not going well, difficult decisions and conversations fill your days. In these ups and downs, the director is essentially alone without peers in the organization. There is usually some form of leadership team structure that the director relies on for thought partnership, strategic planning, and management, but she is still the only individual wearing the director's shoes. Sometimes a director will have a partner in his board chair, and when they are in sync, a great deal of change can be orchestrated. However, the director is there for career reasons (and is making a living doing it), and the chair is a volunteer who is serving because she has a passion for the mission. The consequences are very different for the director when something goes awry or gets neglected; the loneliness of the gig can be overwhelming.

This isolation, if not recognized and addressed, also creates blind spots that will affect the work culture and the fulfillment of the museum's mission and purpose. These blind spots can limit the ability to act inclusively and favor exclusive thinking and action. As mentioned earlier, a contributing factor is that many directors are not trained in museum work but, rather, are hired from other nonprofits or the corporate sector for their experience in generating income and managing expenses and for other universal leadership skills. Some boards don't consider museum-specific training as a critical criterion for selecting a director.

Add to the situation another frank reality: the job requires a healthy ego or no one would do the job. There's a purpose for a healthy ego because the stress and intensity of the role requires a strong psyche, but when the ego is unchecked and doesn't fuel action or success for the museum, the magnitude of harm is profound. Directors need to regularly use a mirror to reflect and check egos. This mirror can take the form of executive coaching, working with accountability partners and peer roundtables, and seeking formal counseling and training.

The director position holds incredible power and influence. While they can define and fuel a work culture, some directors can also navigate board conversations and meetings like a smooth operator, bending them to her will. This can keep the director in a protective bubble and prevent toxic relationships from being easily revealed. Because they have power and influence, leaders must be avidly self-aware and actively work to recognize their positionality and privilege and how this systemically affects and operates in museum spaces.

I have found from observing my peers and documenting my experiences that, when museum leaders reach the top, many of them move professional development to the back burner and don't join staff-wide training sessions. Directors avoid being vulnerable in front of their staff, but when fundamental museum practices need to be reshaped and reenvisioned for an inclusive future, a different expectation is needed. Directors need to refresh their approach to professional development. How many museum directors have spent time in antiracism training to arrive at their new leadership gig ready to dismantle racism in the museum? Not many.

Actively committing to professional development, peer learning, or executive coaching is important and should be a time commitment the director makes—*and* the director needs to join his colleagues in the classroom. Doing this makes his learning visible and communicates that this learning is important and essential to the museum's future and communities.

Directors are the gatekeepers of museum inclusion and, as such, need to vigorously work a plan and stay on their journey toward change so that the museum field can transition to a new reality. If the director is not introspective and actively working a journey of inclusion, their leadership can make a museum exclusive, out of step, and isolated from community. Directors also need to find kinship in each other. They can be notoriously unfriendly to their peers, and elitism across museum types and sizes is prevalent. Daily work and connection among leaders can accelerate a solution for the third problem of this chapter's analogy, making a new framework from the chaos.

How to Solve the Three-Body Problem

Museums may tell different stories and use different strategies to meet their missions, but most of them follow a model or carry a history that is rife with racism and colonization. The players, the decision makers, and the operators of museum spaces need to authentically understand this and begin to make change. If we don't, we are complicit and become knowing perpetrators of harm.

Numerous BIPOC and White museum academics and practitioners have raised countless calls to action for years now. As Critical Race Scholar and museologist Porchia Moore writes, using the analogy of cartography, "We have maps for days. We have been speaking out about structural racism in museums for years."[26] Why is the field not using the well-designed and expertly researched "maps," or tools and strategies? To help us solve the third-body problem, each of us can pick up a "map" and learn to read it. Until leadership is using the tools and strategies that scholars and practitioners have carefully developed for them (many of which are identified throughout this book, such as MASS Action), the problem will resist solution.

The year 2020 has illuminated for many the violence of now, and it is manifesting by creating loud and effective protests. Very publicly museum leaders are losing their jobs because their boards decided, seemingly overnight, to sleuth and learn about the racism raging in their museums. For me, those boards are not to be rewarded or heralded for these decisions. Very rare is the board that has engaged in antiracist training and learning in order to dismantle White supremacy and structural racism in museums. The problem is systemic, and they contribute to the problem as board members. As they are removing their directors, they should also work to remove themselves. This can be done by securing a committed team of staff members and community members who are empowered by a public body, public leaders, or membership to appoint a new board.

While it may take longer to accomplish the solutions provided here, a radical rethinking of governance structures is needed. Without it, there will always be a power differential among the board, director, and staff, which does not breed equitable and inclusive practice. None of us has a crystal ball, but those of us who have seen the pain museums cause are looking for that kind of vision.

Museum leaders can be the individuals our present and future need when they study museum history and comprehend the bedrock of harm that our origin story has created. With this understood, museum leaders can impact what can be changed. They can begin to transform their organizations by changing out exclusive hiring practices and policies for more inclusive systems. Directors can lead transformation by working on themselves.

I have heard it whispered and shouted in virtual rooms, chats, online, and in person—there is a museum reckoning underway. What does it look like when an entire industry is turned on its ear? Chaos. When we solve two of the museum industry's problems—the demographics of museum workers and the practices of leaders—we can navigate the weight and mass of museum history and begin to create a brighter and predictable future for museums.

Notes

1. Hebrew University of Jerusalem, "Researchers Crack Newton's Elusive '3-Body' Problem That Has Baffled Scientists for Centuries," *SciTechDaily*, January 5, 2020, https://scitechdaily.com/researchers-crack-newtons-elusive-3-body-problem-that-has-baffled-scientists-for-centuries/; and Caroline Delbert, "Why Is the Three-Body Problem Unsolvable?," *Popular Mechanics*, November 6, 2019, https://www.popularmechanics.com/science/a29714375/three-body-problem-unsolvable/
2. British prime minister Benjamin Disraeli, in a report to the trustees of the National Gallery, presented his case: "it must be a dangerous thing to admit children; they do mischief in mysterious ways." See "Report from the Select Committee on the National Gallery," 1850, 6.
3. Ian S. Fairweather, "Colonialism and the Museum," in *The International Encyclopedia of Anthropology*, ed. Hilary Callan (Hoboken, NJ: Wiley Blackwell, 2018), 999–1004.
4. Amy Lonetree, *Decolonizing Museums: Representing Native America in National and Tribal Museums* (Chapel Hill: University of North Carolina Press, 2012), 10; and Edward P. Alexander, Mary Alexander, and Juilee Decker, *Museums in Motion: An Introduction to the History and Functions of Museums* (Lanham, MD: Rowman & Littlefield, 2017), 7.
5. Lonetree, *Decolonizing Museums*, 1.
6. Lonetree, *Decolonizing Museums*, 9–11.
7. Lonetree, *Decolonizing Museums*, 14.
8. While numerous sources spell this out for academics and practitioners, the United Nations Declaration on the Rights of Indigenous Peoples makes it crystal clear in Article 12: "1) Indigenous peoples have the right to manifest, practice, develop and teach their spiritual and religious traditions, customs and ceremonies; the right to maintain, protect, and have access in privacy to their religious and cultural sites; the right to the use and control of their ceremonial objects; and the right to the repatriation of their human remains. 2) States shall seek to enable the access and/or repatriation of ceremonial objects and human remains in their possession through fair, transparent and effective mechanisms developed in conjunction with indigenous peoples concerned." See "United Nations Declaration on the Rights of Indigenous Peoples," United Nations, accessed December 5, 2020, https://www.un.org/development/desa/indigenouspeoples/declaration-on-the-rights-of-indigenous-peoples.html.

9. Lonetree, *Decolonizing Museums*, 12–13.
10. Samuel J. Redman, *Bone Rooms: From Scientific Racism to Human Prehistory in Museums* (Cambridge, MA: Harvard University Press, 2016), 35.
11. Redman, *Bone Rooms*, 45–46.
12. Lonetree, *Decolonizing Museums*, 13.
13. Lonetree, *Decolonizing Museums*, 12–13.
14. Stephen E. Nash, "The Skeletons in the Museum Closet," *Sapiens*, October 29, 2018, https://www.sapiens.org/column/curiosities/natural-history-museum-human-remains/.
15. Megan J. Highet, "Body Snatching and Grave Robbing: Bodies for Science," *History and Anthropology* 16, no. 4 (2005): 454.
16. Shannon O'Loughlin, "Repatriating Human Rights," Native News Online, October 14, 2020, https://nativenewsonline.net/sponsored-content/repatriating-human-rights?fbclid=IwAR2Csg1S-aHznVsE-FbXYctcJPpCh4XpsNo41L_olUCW1sYDoAwGQhEmK9E.
17. I joined the ISM as its new director in September 2019. I identify as White/female/straight/cisgender/middle class/no known disabilities and bring my own privilege to this new role. It is critical that I understand my bias and how it can affect decision-making strategies and places where I hold power and authority. To act inclusively and to effectively respond to those harmed by the ISM's history and current practice, I continue to engage in daily personal work and regular courses of structured antiracism and leadership training.
18. Anne Amati, "NAGPRA Data," University of Denver Museum of Anthropology, August 7, 2020, https://liberalarts.du.edu/anthropology-museum/news-events/all-articles/nagpra-data.
19. Illinois State Museum, *Technical Report No. 96-983-8* (Springfield: ISM, 1996); and Brooke Morgan and Duane Esarey, "NAGPRA and the ISM (1993–2020): Process and Promise," working paper (Springfield: Illinois State Museum, 2020).
20. Since 1996, 136 human remains have been returned to seven tribes and traditional governments, and 32,821 associated funerary objects have been returned to the Peoria. The ISM repatriated sacred objects to Hopi and Odawa communities. Beyond NAGPRA processes, the ISM has returned culturally significant objects to Kenyan and Australian communities. See Morgan and Esarey, "NAGPRA and the ISM (1993–2020)."
21. Stephen E. Nash, "A Curator's Search for Justice," *Sapiens*, May 14, 2020, https://www.sapiens.org/column/curiosities/vigango-repatriation/.
22. American Alliance of Museums, *Facing Change: Insights from AAM's Diversity, Equity, Accessibility, and Inclusion Working Group* (Arlington, VA: AAM, 2018); BoardSource, *Museum Board Leadership 2017: A National Report* (Washington, DC: BoardSource, 2017); and Mariët Westermann, Roger Schonfeld, and Liam Sweeney, *The Andrew Mellon Foundation: Art Museum Demographic Survey 2018* (New York: Andrew W. Mellon Foundation, 2019); and Wilkening Consulting and American Alliance of Museums, *Illinois State Museum 2020 Annual Survey of Museum-Goers*, commissioned report, 2020; and U.S. Census Bureau, "QuickFacts," December 6, 2020, https://www.census.gov/quickfacts/fact/table/US/PST045219.
23. Laura Lott, "The Leadership Imperative: Diversity, Equity, Accessibility, and Inclusion as Strategy," in *Diversity, Equity, Accessibility, and Inclusion in Museums*, ed. Johnnetta Betsch Cole and Laura Lott (Arlington, VA: AAM, 2019), 38.
24. Eileen Kinsella, "An Estimated 85 Percent of Artists Represented in US Museum Collections Are White, a New Study Claims," *Artnet News*, February 19, 2019, https://news.artnet.com/market/new-study-shows-us-art-museums-grappling-with-diversity-1467256.
25. Wilkening Consulting and American Alliance of Museums, *Illinois State Museum 2020 Annual Survey of Museum-Goers*.
26. Porchia Moore, "Cartography: A Black Woman's Response to Museums in the Time of Racial Uprising," *The Incluseum* (blog), June 10, 2020, https://incluseum.com/2020/06/10/cartography-a-black-womans-response-to-museums-in-the-time-of-racial-uprising/.

Bibliography

Alexander, Edward P., Mary Alexander, and Juilee Decker. *Museums in Motion: An Introduction to the History and Functions of Museums*. Lanham, MD: Rowman & Littlefield, 2017.

Chapter 2

Amati, Anne. "NAGPRA Data." University of Denver Museum of Anthropology, August 7, 2020. https://liberalarts.du.edu/anthropology-museum/news-events/all-articles/nagpra-data.

American Alliance of Museums. *Facing Change: Insights from AAM's Diversity, Equity, Accessibility, and Inclusion Working Group.* Arlington, VA: AAM, 2018.

BoardSource. *Museum Board Leadership 2017: A National Report.* Washington, DC: BoardSource, 2017.

Delbert, Caroline. "Why Is the Three-Body Problem Unsolvable?" *Popular Mechanics*, November 6, 2019. https://www.popularmechanics.com/science/a29714375/three-body-problem-unsolvable/.

Fairweather, Ian S. "Colonialism and the Museum." In *The International Encyclopedia of Anthropology*, edited by Hilary Callan, 999–1004. Hoboken, NJ: Wiley Blackwell, 2018.

Hebrew University of Jerusalem. "Researchers Crack Newton's Elusive '3-Body' Problem That Has Baffled Scientists for Centuries." *SciTechDaily*, January 5, 2020. https://scitechdaily.com/researchers-crack-newtons-elusive-3-body-problem-that-has-baffled-scientists-for-centuries/.

Highet, Megan J. "Body Snatching and Grave Robbing: Bodies for Science." *History and Anthropology* 16, no. 4 (2005): 415–44.

Illinois State Museum. *Technical Report No. 96-983-8.* Springfield: ISM, 1996.

Kinsella, Eileen. "An Estimated 85 Percent of Artists Represented in US Museum Collections Are White, a New Study Claims." *Artnet News*, February 19, 2019. https://news.artnet.com/market/new-study-shows-us-art-museums-grappling-with-diversity-1467256.

Lonetree, Amy. *Decolonizing Museums: Representing Native America in National and Tribal Museums.* Chapel Hill: University of North Carolina Press, 2012.

Lott, Laura. "The Leadership Imperative: Diversity, Equity, Accessibility, and Inclusion as Strategy." In *Diversity, Equity, Accessibility, and Inclusion in Museums*, edited by Johnnetta Betsch Cole and Laura Lott, 33–40. Arlington, VA: AAM, 2019.

Moore, Porchia. "Cartography: A Black Woman's Response to Museums in the Time of Racial Uprising." *The Incluseum* (blog), June 10, 2020. https://incluseum.com/2020/06/10/cartography-a-black-womans-response-to-museums-in-the-time-of-racial-uprising/.

Morgan, Brooke, and Duane Esarey. "NAGPRA and the ISM (1993–2020): Process and Promise." Working paper. Springfield: Illinois State Museum, 2020.

Nash, Stephen E. "A Curator's Search for Justice." *Sapiens*, May 14, 2020. https://www.sapiens.org/column/curiosities/vigango-repatriation/.

———. "The Skeletons in the Museum Closet." *Sapiens*, October 29, 2018. https://www.sapiens.org/column/curiosities/natural-history-museum-human-remains/.

O'Loughlin, Shannon. "Repatriating Human Rights." Native News Online, October 14, 2020. https://nativenewsonline.net/sponsored-content/repatriating-human-rights?fbclid=I wAR2Csg1S-aHznVsE-FbXYctcJPpCh4XpsNo41L_oIUCW1sYDoAwGQhEmK9E.

Redman, Samuel J. *Bone Rooms: From Scientific Racism to Human Prehistory in Museums*. Cambridge, MA: Harvard University Press, 2016.

United Nations. "United Nations Declaration on the Rights of Indigenous Peoples." Accessed December 5, 2020. https://www.un.org/development/desa/indigenouspeoples/declaration -on-the-rights-of-indigenous-peoples.html.

U.S. Census Bureau, "QuickFacts," December 6, 2020. https://www.census.gov/quickfacts/fact /table/US/PST045219

Westermann, Mariët, Roger Schonfeld, and Liam Sweeney. *The Andrew Mellon Foundation: Art Museum Demographic Survey*. New York: Andrew W. Mellon Foundation, 2019.

Wilkening Consulting, and American Alliance of Museums. *Illinois State Museum 2020 Annual Survey of Museum-Goers*. Commissioned report, 2020.

Chapter 3

Creating the Just Leader

Inclusive Leadership and Organizational Justice

Chris Taylor

Justice is the notion of fairness and equity. Lee Anne Bell writes that social justice is both a goal and a process: "The goal of social justice is full and equitable participation of people from all social identity groups in a society that is mutually shaped to meet their needs."[1] She adds that the process to achieve social justice should be inclusive, participatory, and respectful of human diversity and group differences.[2] The events of the spring and summer 2020 have initiated an awakening and a desire for many leaders in museums to strive for justice.

During spring 2020, museums across the country issued statements about standing in solidarity with George Floyd, Black Lives Matter, and other social justice movements. Quite often, these museum statements were challenged by staff and community members as being performative because museums lacked diversity within their staffs and equity in their actions. While museum leaders strive to have a social justice impact in their external environment, the lack of justice within museums paints a picture of talking the talk, but not walking the walk. Museum leaders may be better served to prioritize organizational justice within their museums.

The concept of organizational justice is concerned with application of fairness and equity within organizations, and it can support museum leaders in their desire for justice. There are three facets to organizational justice. First, distributive justice is concerned with fairness within resource distributions, such as pay, rewards, promotions, and the resolution of disputes. Next, procedural justice relates to the decision-making processes that promote or inhibit distributive justice. Finally, interactional justice refers to the interpersonal treatment that individuals experience within an organization, particularly interactions with those with key organizational roles. This framework provides opportunities to interrogate the systems within the organization. Museum leaders can work toward justice in their museums by examining the level of justice embedded within the systems of their own museums.

Justice as a process is inclusive, participatory, and respectful of diversity and differences. Leadership that works to eliminate injustice must therefore be inclusive, invite participation, and respect diversity and difference. This chapter will define and describe the characteristics of inclusive leadership. Next, an examination of the barriers to inclusive leadership will highlight some of the areas where museum leaders are challenged to exhibit more inclusive leadership. The benefits of inclusive leadership and the impact on individuals and the organization are also discussed. The chapter then explores the development of inclusive leadership at multiple levels and the impact it can have on organizational justice.

Inclusive Leadership Defined

Strong leadership within museums is necessary to envision a more just and inclusive museum and then create the necessary change to realize that vision. Applying the "justice as a process" model to leadership means that leaders must become more inclusive in how they lead. Leaders set the tone for organizations, based on their beliefs and values. As leaders become more inclusive, organizations become more inclusive. Although leaders, due to their power within the organization, typically feel included, they also determine whether others will feel included within an organization. What is more important for leaders is to understand and practice inclusive leadership. The type of leadership necessary for museums focuses on justice and fairness, as well as creating an environment where all staff can achieve their definition of success. Lize Booysen writes, "Inclusive leadership extends our thinking beyond assimilation strategies or organizational demography to empowerment and participation of all, by removing obstacles that cause exclusion and marginalization.[3]

This type of leadership ensures a culture respectful of human diversity and group differences. Inclusive leadership leads to organizations where diverse talent is fostered and in which diverse teams operate to their highest potential. Inclusive leadership becomes a practice where leaders constantly question which voices are missing and if actions and outcomes are truly just and fair. Leaders who proactively ask these types of questions begin to understand that they may be privileging certain groups over others, thereby perpetuating the status quo, and see how their actions may intervene to disrupt this cycle of oppression.

Characteristics of Inclusive Leadership

Change for inclusion requires strong leaders with the ability to challenge dominant organizational paradigms and evolve practices that have long been held as "best practices." The leadership paradigm in museums must move away from the dominant perspective that focuses on a unidirectional relationship between leaders and those they lead to one that is relationship based. Inclusive leaders must develop a deep sense of their own cultural awareness and challenge their own norms and assumptions. They must develop the ability to acquire new behaviors and skills to adapt to new cultural situations. There are many characteristics of inclusive leadership, including being authentic, having emotional intelligence, and developing good relationships with those you lead.

Inclusive Leaders as Authentic Leaders

Authenticity is an important element of inclusive leadership. Authentic leaders have a genuine desire to serve others, they know themselves, and they feel free to lead from their core values. Inclusive leaders who are authentic prioritize equity and justice in their value systems and act accordingly. Leaders who have equity and justice as core values promote inclusion by administering all functions of the institution fairly, supporting and promoting distributive and procedural facets of organizational justice.

Authentic leadership is also relational, created by leaders and those they lead together. Inclusive leaders who are authentic exhibit emotional intelligence, humility, and transparency toward staff. The ability to tend to the needs of self and others simultaneously is difficult but critical for leaders who are creating change within their museum. Change increases anxiety, and inclusive leaders must be able to sense this anxiety and behave in ways that can influence staff to persevere through the change process.

It is critical for leaders to understand that they "don't know what they don't know." Inclusive leaders must be equally aware of their weaknesses as they are with their strengths. Understanding limitations, particularly as they relate to inclusion and cultural knowledge, allows leaders to develop an openness to learning. Cultural humility is the lifelong process of developing an interpersonal stance that is other oriented rather than self-focused, characterized by respect and lack of superiority toward an individual's cultural background and experience.[4] Personal learning and development helps leaders continue on a journey to develop more intercultural competence.

Inclusive leadership, as a relational process between leaders and those they lead, hinges on the development of trust between both parties. Followers must be able to anticipate that leaders will act consistently in uncertain situations. Inclusive leaders must be consistent in their practice of inclusion, even when being inclusive is challenging. Leaders need to make their own positions on justice and inclusion clearly known and stand by them consistently.

Leaders who incorporate the skills and characteristics of inclusive leaders and build trust within their teams and organizations foster the interactional facet of organizational justice. When staff experience interpersonal interactions with leaders that are facilitated by transparency, cultural humility, and trust, their sense of fairness and belonging within the organization increases.

Out with the Old and in with the New

Leadership styles must be less hierarchical and more inclusive for justice to become embedded within museums. Inclusive leadership requires that leaders inspire and enable others, rather than commanding and controlling them. Welcoming input from all levels of the institution must become the new normal. As museums strive to develop a more diverse workforce, Gallegos cautions that "[w]e require a paradigm shift in our frameworks of leadership to incorporate how dimensions of diversity shape our understanding of leadership and influence styles of leadership and followership, and how bias influences the exercise of leadership."[5] Self-awareness is crucial to inclusive leadership, and leaders who cannot recognize their blind spots will fail to create inclusive organizations.

Museums have long underserved diverse communities. Museums must not remain negligent in their responsibilities to a wider spectrum of society. Leaders have the ability to elevate fairness and inclusion as critical factors within organizational planning. As creators of the vision for organizations, leaders must be cognizant of the desires and input from various units in the organization, but it is the leader who synthesizes the input into the direction of the organization. Embedding inclusion into the vision creates the road map for museums to keep pace with our changing external environment.

Simply understanding opportunities for increased relevance and value to our audiences and embedding inclusion into the institutional vision is not enough. Leaders must align the culture of the organization to be inclusive and model the desired behaviors for the rest of the staff. Organizations in the corporate sector have realized that the best companies today are composed of a wide range of people. Creating an inclusive culture increases the likelihood for a museum to increase and retain a more diverse workforce. As museum staffs increase levels of diversity, they are in a better position to serve a more diverse audience. Diversity in the workplace provides more insight into how to serve diverse communities, and that insight can be reflected in a museum's priorities, mission, vision, strategies, and resource allocations. As a result, museums are better prepared to be relevant to diverse audiences. It is not enough to just increase the numbers of diverse staff, though. Employees who perceive they are being treated fairly are more likely to be retained within an organization. Leaders must focus on becoming successful in integrating procedures that promote organizational justice within the values, beliefs, and practices of their museum.

Barriers to Inclusive Leadership

While inclusion has been a slow process in museums, leaders have the level of influence to increase the pace of change. However, the ability of the leader to be inclusive and to create change are key factors in creating an inclusive museum. Leaders encounter several barriers related to justice and inclusion, such as an individual's dominant norms, unconscious biases, and lack of experience with creating change that addresses the need for inclusion within museums. Often, a leader's mental models or norms are a barrier to creating change for inclusion. A leader whose cultural norms are based on dominant culture ideologies will, in turn, embed those norms into the culture of the museum. These become actions and behaviors that are seen as normal.

Another barrier to inclusive leadership is unconscious bias. When leaders are blind to injustice and exclusion within their museums, they continue to perpetuate the status quo within organizations. Leaders who do not address unconscious bias "allow their organizations to bury their inclusion blind spots. . . . Blind spots can lead to underestimating or overestimating our cultural abilities and to truly understanding what needs to be done regarding culture and diversity."[6] Exploring your blind spots is both personal work and organizational work. As individuals explore their blind spots, they are able to see how their bias influences their practices and begin to interrupt personal patterns of unjust or exclusive actions. Developing these skills on an individual level creates opportunities for leaders to expand their scope to look for institutional blind spots and develop new operating norms that promote organizational justice and inclusion.

Similar to the norms discussed earlier, unconscious bias creates in-group and out-group dynamics within the culture of an organization. The perception of interactional justice is very different between the two groups. Those in the in-group are likely to feel included and have access to power and resources within the organization. Those in the out-group are going to feel alienated and excluded. While members of the in-group may not recognize the privileges of being in the in-group, members of the out-group see the disparities and perceive them as unjust. This type of exclusion already exists within most museums; it is the failure to recognize it as an obstacle to creating inclusive work cultures and work practices that is the barrier to moving forward. Leaders who can increase the members of the in-group by expanding and diversifying the requisite membership characteristics can promote a higher sense of justice within their organizations.

In addition to norms and unconscious bias, museum leaders may lack experience with changing the direction of their organization to be inclusive. When addressing intercultural situations, most museum leaders lack the ability to address the deeper cultural issues and problems that lie below the surface level. The tendency is to address symptoms rather than deeper issues. The inability to address the deeper issues and provide opportunities for staff to develop the necessary skills and capabilities to be inclusive can have the opposite impact, creating anxiety in staff and failing to sustain change.

Developing Inclusive Leadership

For museums to successfully evolve into inclusive organizations, inclusive leaders must be developed within institutions. Museum leaders need to develop individual human capacity (knowledge, skills, attitudes) and grow their social capital (relationships and networks).[7] Leadership is a continuous learning journey, and leaders who have not exhibited inclusive leadership must learn a new skill set and integrate it into their leadership philosophy and style. This continuous process requires self-reflection, honesty, and a commitment toward change on the part of the leader. This can include training, but it goes beyond formal training settings. Leaders must have genuine conversations about inclusion to continue to push themselves to deeper levels of learning. Mai Moua identifies three principles for inclusive leadership. First, knowledge is a central tenet in intercultural training and is essential for all people, leaders in particular. "You must know how cultures are created, interpreted, and shared, as well as how cultural interpretations, meaning, and symbols can impact behaviors and attitudes."[8] Next, Moua writes, "Strategic thinking is important because it is how you think about, or make sense of, the knowledge and use it in a way that helps you better perform and interact with different cultures."[9] Learning new knowledge is useless unless you understand how to apply the knowledge. Thinking strategically about how to integrate new knowledge into the vision and behaviors of leaders helps actualize the benefits of learning new information. Finally, according to Moua, leaders need to "pay attention to [their] surroundings as well as [their] responses to unfamiliar situations."[10] This requires leaders to reflect on their own interests, drive, and motivation, as well as their level of willingness to work through difficult cultural situations.

A general model for developing inclusive leaders integrates assessment, challenges, and support to help leaders grow. Assessment provides an individual leader with an understanding of where they are now in terms of inclusive practices, and it provides a baseline of their current performance and can serve as a benchmark to measure future progress. Challenges provide opportunities for leaders to push themselves outside their comfort zone to try and apply new knowledge and behaviors. There is anxiety in applying new knowledge in the face of a challenge. The risk of failure is real, but inclusive leadership encourages leaders to have humility. Leaders are not required to have all of the answers. Support becomes critical to provide encouragement to leaders who are addressing challenges in new ways with the goal of creating inclusive organizations. Support can come from multiple directions. It can come from above, when a supportive Board of Directors understands the need for change and the need to address adaptive challenges with new ways of working. It can come from below, when staff help leaders reflect on the way a challenge was addressed and create space for all to learn from the results. This requires suspending judgment and allowing leaders to be vulnerable.

Leadership development is a systemic process as well. Leaders must expand capabilities to embed inclusion into the organization at individual, group, and organizational levels of the system. Booysen writes, "[T]o enable the organization as a system to continually learn and develop, formal and informal learning mechanisms must be established on all three levels."[11]

Individual Level

Applying Bell's notion of justice, leaders must demonstrate and promote respect for human diversity and group differences. Essentially, cultural intelligence is your ability to adapt to unfamiliar cultural settings.[12] Learning how to adapt to various cultural settings, rather than reacting to them from a fixed perspective rooted in dominant norms, allows a leader to be flexible and inclusive. While learning cultural knowledge is important, it is impossible to know all the important information about every culture. Learning how to adapt within cultural situations is a capability that allows leaders to be open to learning and to sense when they need to adjust behaviors.

Self-awareness deals with how well we know ourselves. It requires that we understand our various identities and that leaders are self-reflective in order to begin to understand their basic assumptions, norms, and values. It also means that we must be aware of how we process information, particularly in different cultural settings. Self-reflection is an important tool to develop a deeper awareness of self. Self-reflection can help an individual better understand how they identify with various dimensions of diversity—and how those identities may or may not have privilege attached to them—and help them understand personal biases.

Self-efficacy is also important for inclusive leaders to develop. Self-efficacy represents your perception of your abilities to meet a goal you have set for yourself. Self-efficacy determines how you think, feel, and behave in cultural situations. It concerns your beliefs about what is acceptable in different situations, your confidence level in intercultural situations, and the ability to adapt to another culture. Once leaders understand their biases and become more self-aware, self-efficacy provides them the catalyst to put themselves into different cultural settings and learn new behaviors.

In addition to developing themselves on an individual level, inclusive leaders also help those they lead develop on the individual level. This happens through exhibiting transformational leadership. In contrast to transactional leadership, which focuses on exchanges between leaders and followers, transformational leadership requires building relationships with followers and leading in ways that inspire and motivate them. For inclusion efforts to be successful, leaders must motivate followers to continue to challenge themselves to be more inclusive in their day-to-day work. Helping others understand and shift values and beliefs is critical to developing inclusive work practices. Leaders must help staff see beyond their anxiety to change and challenge themselves to develop.

Team/Group Level

Bell's concept articulates that justice is participatory. The interactional facet of organizational justice supports the participatory nature of organizations. At the team or group level, it is important for leaders to foster a climate and work norms within groups that is inclusive of difference. This applies both to in-group/out-group dynamics as well as inviting diverse perspectives and input from staff.

As mentioned earlier, in-groups and out-groups exist in organizations. Those with stronger relationships with leaders tend to be in the in-group, while those who have weaker relationships with leaders fall into the out-group. Interactional justice requires a leader to develop relationships across difference within the organization so that the in-group becomes as diverse as possible. Leaders must understand their biases and conduct an audit of those who are close to them as a self-reflective practice to identify whether their in-group is homogenous. If it is, it requires intentionality on the part of the inclusive leader to increase diversity in those close to them.

Once the leader has created a diverse network of relationships, leaders must become less authoritarian and be willing to seek input from across all levels of the organization. Inclusive leaders understand that they can leverage radically different viewpoints to create better solutions for organizational and work challenges. They recognize and resist group think, demonstrating higher levels of ease with diversity and realizing that the different viewpoints drive innovation within the organization. The perspectives can come from people both internal and external to the organization. What is most important is that the leader develops the capacity to listen to those who are giving the input. Soliciting input from others, and intentionally incorporating it into vision and strategy can be an effective way for leaders to create inclusion within their museums.

Organizational Level: Procedural Justice and Distributive Justice

Inclusive leadership at this level concerns the vision of the leader and how that shapes the direction of the museum. First, a leader must make sure there is alignment between espoused values and the behaviors within the organization. While museums continue to espouse inclusion as a value, most museums struggle with putting inclusion into action within their museums. Leaders who are developing themselves at the individual level are better equipped to actualize inclusion as a practice within museums by creating inclusive systems and expectations at the organizational level. When a leader has a deeper understanding of how justice and inclusion influence their personal values, it provides an opportunity to imprint those values within the organizational vision. Incorporating procedural and distributive justice into the operating values and procedures of the organization ensures alignment between espoused values and behaviors.

In addition, organizations often have competing priorities. Inclusion, as the business imperative, can be a powerful frame to achieve just outcomes. It is about relevance and sustainability of museums in the long term. Leaders must understand the future of museums hinges on the ability for museums to shift to more inclusive organizations that a more diverse array of communities will see as a valuable asset.

Inclusive leaders inspire others to stay engaged in difficult work by creating a culture where difficult, controversial, or sensitive topics are discussed, rather than these types of conversations being seen as disruptive or uncomfortable. If inclusion is core to the work, then everyone must engage the work head on. This requires staff to move beyond their comfort zone and try new practices. Inclusive leaders must create an atmosphere that supports staff taking risks and learning by doing. If staff feel that they may be punished, they will remain in their comfort zone and avoid participating in inclusion work.

Inclusive leaders can begin to create and communicate this vision in several ways. They can frame the change in a positive way. Leaders who create the understanding that this work will be hard, also understand moving to eliminate injustice in the organization far outweighs the anxiety of the work. It helps more people remain engaged, supported, and motivated to change. Inclusive leaders can help articulate a vision of success and help staff move in that direction. Inclusive leaders must also take a critical look at their own practices and the organization as a whole. Leaders must model the change they want to see. The inclusive leaders must also understand the ways that the culture of the organization will either support change or make it impossible, including examination of current practices. For example, talent acquisition and talent management systems are crucial to creating a more diverse workforce. Inclusive leaders will first recognize that the current systems are not supporting organizational justice, and then help shift these systems to be more inclusive. Most important of all, inclusive leaders can develop and support other inclusive leaders. Working to create inclusive leadership practices as the norm for all leaders within an organization sets this practice as the new norm for the organization.

More specifically, activities that can support inclusive leadership development include coaching and mentoring programs, formal training, informal training, practice fields, and support groups. Leaders would benefit from cross-cultural coaching. Finding a role model at a similar level who can help a developing inclusive leader in a one-on-one relationship allows for discussion of difficult topics, honesty, and transparency; additionally, the developing leader will have the benefit of learning from someone who has a different perspective or background. Formal training programs can include targeted topics on recognizing bias, cultural competency, cross-cultural communication, and other skills necessary for emerging inclusive leaders. Informal training consists of putting oneself into situations that will challenge beliefs and norms and learning through observation and interaction. Opportunities for informal learning may be various community festivals or situations where the leader is in the minority group. This is an opportunity to develop emotional and cultural intelligence—or the ability to sense and feel difference—and use that information to adapt actions. Practice fields are opportunities for emerging inclusive leaders to apply learning from formal and informal situations and coaching relationships to work responsibilities. These are judgment-free zones where leaders can experiment and take risks to learn by doing. Feedback in these situations is critical for emerging inclusive leaders. Support groups provide opportunities for leaders to communicate, receive feedback and encouragement, and renew motivation for learning.

Conclusion

The practice of justice and inclusion in museums goes well beyond programs and exhibitions. Museums must undergo core changes to the identity of the organizations in order to become just and inclusive organizations. These changes require strong leadership. Leaders must develop themselves as individuals, while supporting the development of others throughout the organization. In addition, it is the leader's responsibility to create the vision of an inclusive organization, and then help align the institutional values with the new vision. This is tough work. It will not be an easy shift, but for leaders who are not working to create an inclusive organization, the legacy you will leave for your organization is a legacy of irrelevance. This work must start now. The business model of museums—who we serve and how we serve them—is not sustainable. Leaders, above all others, are the ones that can be the catalysts for change within their organizations and within the larger field as a whole.

Notes

1. Lee Anne Bell, "Theoretical Foundations for Social Justice Education," in *Readings for Diversity and Social Justice*, ed. Maurianne Adams, Warren J. Blumenfeld, D. Chase J. Catalano, Keri "Safire" DeJong, Heather W. Hackman, Larissa E. Hopkins, Barbara J. Love, Madeline L. Peters, Davey Shlasko, and Ximena Zuniga (New York: Routledge, 2018), 34–41.
2. Bell, "Theoretical Foundations," 34.
3. Lize Booysen, "The Development of Inclusive Leadership Practice and Processes," in *Diversity at Work: The Practice of Inclusion*, ed. Bernardo M. Ferdman and Barbara R. Deane (San Francisco: Jossey-Bass, 2014), 298.
4. Joshua N. Hook, Don E. Davis, Jesse Owen, Everett L. Worthington, and Shawn O. Utsey, "Cultural Humility: Measuring Openness to Culturally Diverse Clients," *Journal of Counseling Psychology* 60, no. 3 (2013): 353–366, https://doi.org/10.1037/a0032595.

5. Placida V. Gallegos, "The Work of Inclusive Leadership: Fostering Authentic Relationships, Modeling Courage and Humility," in *Diversity at Work: The Practice of Inclusion*, ed. Bernardo M. Ferdman and Barbara R. Deane (San Francisco: Jossey-Bass, 2014), 178.
6. Mai Moua, *Culturally Intelligent Leadership: Leading through Intercultural Interactions* (New York: Business Expert Press, 2010), 115.
7. Booysen, "The Development of Inclusive Leadership Practice and Processes," 300.
8. Moua, *Culturally Intelligent Leadership*, 62.
9. Moua, *Culturally Intelligent Leadership*, 62.
10. Moua, *Culturally Intelligent Leadership*, 62.
11. Booysen, "The Development of Inclusive Leadership Practice and Processes," 306–307.
12. Moua, *Culturally Intelligent Leadership*, 59.

Bibliography

Bell, Lee Anne. "Theoretical Foundations for Social Justice Education." In *Readings for Diversity and Social Justice*, edited by Maurianne Adams, Warren J. Blumenfeld, D. Chase J. Catalano, Keri "Safire" DeJong, Heather W. Hackman, Larissa E. Hopkins, Barbara J. Love, Madeline L. Peters, Davey Shlasko, and Ximena Zuniga, 34–41. New York: Routledge, 2018.

Booysen, Lize. "The Development of Inclusive Leadership Practice and Processes." In *Diversity at Work: The Practice of Inclusion*, edited by Bernardo M. Ferdman and Barbara R. Deane, 296–329. San Francisco: Jossey-Bass, 2014.

Gallegos, Placida V. "The Work of Inclusive Leadership: Fostering Authentic Relationships, Modeling Courage and Humility." In *Diversity at Work: The Practice of Inclusion*, edited by Bernardo M. Ferdman and Barbara R. Deane. San Francisco: Jossey-Bass, 2014.

Hook, Joshua N., Don E. Davis, Jesse Owen, Everett L. Worthington, and Shawn O. Utsey. "Cultural Humility: Measuring Openness to Culturally Diverse Clients." *Journal of Counseling Psychology* 60, no. 3 (2013): 353–366. https://doi.org/10.1037/a0032595.

Moua, Mai. *Culturally Intelligent Leadership: Leading through Intercultural Interactions*. New York: Business Expert Press, 2010.

Chapter 4

Two Change Agents, Two Cups of Coffee

A Conversation between Cinnamon Catlin-Legutko and Chris Taylor

The following conversation was recorded in September 2020. As coeditors and authors for The Inclusive Museum Leader, *we felt it was important to examine our experiences in and around inclusive practice and our motivations for making this book happen. Transparency is a hallmark of inclusive practice, and we wanted to demonstrate it by recording and sharing one of the many conversations we have around our own practices and the world we'd like to see in museum practice. Normally a conversation like this would have happened in a conference hallway or over dinner with colleagues. This year, we had Zoom and strong coffee.*

Cinnamon: Can you talk a little bit about how you came to museum work?

Chris: I started my career in museums as a museum educator doing community outreach. I went through a museum fellows program when I was a junior in an undergrad program that was about increasing diversity in the field. It was a life-changing experience for me and introduced me to the Minnesota Historical Society. It was a program that we brought back at the MNHS and I was fortunate to lead it. The program consisted of coursework, an internship, and a travel experience. As I was developing the syllabus for the class, I really started to dig into research around equity in museums. It dawned on me that there are some systemic issues that have been embedded in my environment because we rely on tradition and museum best practices to steer us.

Leadership across the field is woefully, woefully White. I don't say *woefully* meaning White people can't lead. What I'm saying is it is not representative of the people that we are trying to engage. It's not representative of the stories and the cultures that we're representing. Why is that? Is it because only folx who are White and predominantly men possess leadership qualities? Clearly, no. I think our traditional perspectives around leadership skew in that direction. How do we redefine leadership characteristics and qualities that will help reshape who we see as leaders in museums? At MNHS, I made the argument that we needed a department related to this work. This was really underscored by the fact that, in my opinion, when diversity is everybody's job, it's nobody's job because everybody is just tacking it onto what they already do.

The creation of this department gave me space to start to work within organizational systems to create change for equity. I should also note that even with the formation of a department an organization's leader still sets the tone for the museum. How leaders embody the values of a museum is what becomes accepted practice and behavior for other people. Departments like this and the leader must work together.

I think this book is going to be critical because leaders have the biggest sphere of influence at the museum. I've seen so many colleagues working hard at lower levels of the museum to the point of burnout for this work. If a leader would have picked up the torch, that burden would have been shifted. I think that's critical.

I think your story is important, too. I think with the work that you created around decolonization is important, and I'd love to hear more about how that developed because I think it's very similar. It's the recognition that museums support Whiteness and systemic racism. I think that realization is key. I'd love to hear your story.

Cinnamon: I wanted to work in museums from day one. My parents were active learners. Vacations always included visits to museums. As one of those kids that was in and around museum spaces, I just thought everybody went to museums. I had no idea when I was younger that museums were colonial enterprises and would be harmful to certain groups of people. That was lost on me. I pursued a college education, then graduate work, and focused on getting a museum job. It never came up that museums were complicated spaces. It never came up until I was in grad school, in an anthropology program not long after NAGPRA[1] was passed.

I remember at the time learning about NAGPRA and realizing that I never considered, or had to consider, what it meant to have ancestors held by museums. It wasn't visible when you went to museums in the way that it would be for an Indigenous person. I didn't have the literacy around this. I remember in grad school, too, not really even knowing the human rights issues around it. I just had this training that was coming into me from very traditional, anthropologically focused museum workers making sure we document what we have in the collection before it is gone forever. That was the mind-set. Then fast forward, seven years later, when I finally do get the museum gig and start really forming my leadership style, I didn't end up working in anthropology museums. I ended up more in history-related museums.

This necessary learning kept eluding me. I never returned to it. Never questioned museum work until I got to the Abbe Museum. I'll admit, I was super naïve. I always felt like I was this activist kid and activist adult because I was really involved with Amnesty International in college. Ha! I had my little things that I did in the name of social justice, but I didn't really understand the transformation that was needed in all of us to do better. I was given that opportunity when I joined the Abbe Museum in 2009, which isn't that long ago when you think about it. I'd skipped along blissfully, living my life and making a career and not really having to ask hard questions about the place I worked in or my role in the narrative.

When I arrived for the job, I thought I was well equipped. I had known Indigenous people my whole life. I had no idea how my lack of preparation and work around understanding colonization and antiracism methodologies could be harmful. Of course it was. You and I have talked about this. I'm still haunted at times about things I've said or things that I've done when I didn't know better. My blind spots were so huge. They're not gone, and it was several years at the Abbe before I really understood I had to make a change. We had to make a change.

A catalyzing moment at the Abbe really forced me into changing. I was asked to look at how Indigenous people would like to serve on the board, which, at the time, was a traditional governance model of middle- to upper-class White people. There hadn't been much representation on the board by Wabanaki people, and the museum is about Wabanaki history, art, and culture. When I arrived, there were two. Then at one point there was one. The White people on the board were really stumped as to why Native people didn't want to be on a board. It was completely lost on them. Fortunately for me, there was a lot of opportunity for conversation with Wabanaki community members to find out what their interests were. The recommendation from our newly formed Native Advisory Council that was for board members to be appointed by tribal leadership.

Great idea! I took this recommendation to the next board meeting, asking to begin the conversation with tribal leaders, and there was considerable pushback from the board. There was anger at the boardroom table. There was concern and fear. Some of the questions asked were really upsetting. "What if tribal chiefs appoint people to the board we don't like?" Not sure that is a realistic scenario. "Five Native people on a board could create a voting bloc." Well, if five Native people want you to do something, you should do it. Just these simple questions were really harmful and confusing and caused me to take a huge pause. I remember my ears were still ringing two days later because it was such a strange space where everything felt upside down.

It was one of those moments where I thought I knew one thing and realized I really know very little. I felt powerless. But I had enough of a commitment in my leadership style to begin the learning. I think that's the little moment of opportunity that many leaders fail to take the next step and get lost or never start their learning journey.

I think it is important to feel powerlessness and know that I couldn't lead an organization any further unless I did that personal work and the organizational work. I remember very purposely going back and rethinking everything I was taught in anthropology because it was not OK. It was not OK. I'm still unlearning that. And I'm still figuring that out. I often ask myself, "How do I know that?"

Now that I work at the Illinois State Museum with this gigantic anthropological mission, in addition to other mission areas, I'm still reminding myself that if it looks that way, it doesn't mean it's good for others. I came to the museum world very traditionally—I wanted the job. I got the schooling. I figured it out. I networked. I finally got the job. I thought I knew what it was all about. Then suddenly I knew differently. I had to do something about it. That's my pathway.

Chris: You used the word *unlearn*. I think that's such a powerful word. To me it underscores this indoctrination—how we're trained and what's missing in that training. I think it connects to what I often say is that this is a skill set. As a leader, you were in this place where you recognized you needed an additional set of skills to do this work. You asked yourself, "How do I go and do that?" You then pushed yourself to go and learn those skills and get that knowledge.

Another thing I want to point out is the questioning of assumptions. Unlearning what you learned in anthropology and the assumptions that this is the way we do things. I think questioning assumptions can help us start to deconstruct where these Eurocentric or Westernized principles govern the work that we do. This is incredibly critical. I think when leaders are doing that, one, they have the biggest sphere of everyone. They can create bigger change when they question their assumptions. And, two, it models behavior, and it makes it okay for other people to question those assumptions, too. It was powerful what you said. I just wanted to underscore those two things.

Cinnamon: It definitely reveals the complexity that the world does not allow you to see a lot of times. There's a lot of people in workplaces, work cultures that are very black and white, rigid thinkers because they are under performance evaluations or job descriptions that ask them to do X, Y, Z and stay in their box. If you are a collaborative leader or you're somebody really committed to teamwork, you can shake things up a lot, but people still revert back to these places because they're worried about job security and other things. The museum field is so nasty, to be frank, about job security.

There are very few jobs. The is a culture of scarcity, and it's a really privileged workplace. When I was trying to get a museum job, you either had to know somebody or somebody had to die to create a space for you. That is not a healthy workplace if that is the only way you can get in. And to be fair, that's only for the White people. Everyone else has a mountain to climb or even a door that can't be opened. I think that will embed in your colleagues this kind of rigid thinking system because it is so privileged and designed.

I'd love to hear what your catalyzing moment was that put you on the path to inclusive leadership.

Chris: I have a couple that I'll share. There's one moment that ignited my passion for DEAI [diversity, equity, accessibility, and inclusion] work, and it was an incredibly embarrassing moment. I'm going to model vulnerability to tell it. Then I'll share about another moment that helped me understand leadership without title and courage.

My first example was when I was doing workshops for teachers, helping them deliver Indigenous content better in the classroom. Essentially, it was how to bring more culturally relevant material into your history classes. We were at a site in southern Minnesota, which is connected to the Dakota peoples' history. It is called the Lower Sioux agency, and all kinds of terrible things had happened there. I was impressed with the site and moved by the history.

I'm introducing the site manager to the group. His name was Tom Sanders, one of the most gracious people I've ever met and a wonderful colleague and mentor. Tom is very light skinned, he had blond hair and blue eyes, and I was holding Tom up as an example of someone who does not have to be Indigenous to run an Indigenous site well. Tom, very understated, got up in front of the group of teachers and said, "Hi, I'm Tom Sanders. I'm an enrolled member of the Cherokee Nation." I didn't hear what he said after that because I wanted to crawl into a hole and disappear. What that did for me was exactly what I was just talking about. It was a crystal-clear example of how I need to do my own homework and check my own assumptions. This experience put me on a journey to better understand myself and how I show up in spaces. That was one catalyzing moment! I remember that day clearly, vividly. I point to this as an experience, as painful as it was, that needed to happen and I'm really happy it did.

Here's a second catalyzing moment for me. I was accepted into a program called the Shannon Leadership Program as I was coming into the leadership ranks at MNHS. It was funny because I was really looking for a leadership program that was really like command and control, "Teach me the leadership skills that I need to have" kind of thing. A colleague of mine had gone through this and he was someone I had a lot of respect for, so I applied to the program and was accepted. They introduced it as this values-based leadership program. And I'm like, "I don't understand what that means." By the end of the program, I had done some interpersonal work around my values and how my values show up in my leadership style—values around ethics, authenticity, and honesty. These values floated to the top.

Then I had to ask myself, "How do I exhibit these values in my leadership style?" I mentioned the word *courage* before; courage helped me to speak up in my organization. When I saw things that I just could not tolerate, or I knew were just ethically wrong or things that we had been doing as best practices or traditions that needed to change, I knew I needed to speak up. The Shannon Leadership Program brought this clarity for me. I knew what I needed to do and how I needed to show up. It also helped me see that when I didn't step up and step in, I was not living up to my potential. I was not honoring myself. I was not honoring all those people who mentored me. I have a responsibility.

I meant it when I say it was crystal-clear to me now. I understood that I was trying to emulate leadership examples that I have been seeing and that's not what I need. What I need is to lead from my heart and lead from who I am. This shifted how I showed up in my organization. I could no longer sit on the senior leadership team meetings and be silent. When I saw something, I said something. It was no longer about could I keep my job or how people might receive me in those spaces. It was now about how I have to live with myself when I go home at the end of the day. Will

I be able to feel like I did the right thing each day? It was an incredible transformation for me. I can point to those two as catalyzing moments, both in the DEAI space and for my leadership journey.

Cinnamon: I think you hit on something that is a thread throughout this book. Inclusion requires heart-centered and emotional thinking and systems and a commitment to leadership development. I don't know of a leader in this inclusive space who isn't thinking that way. With inclusive leadership, the whole person comes together and shows up in all rooms. I passionately believe that and I say it again and again to the colleagues I work with—I need your whole self to show up. I don't need half of you. I want all of you, and all of you matters and everything that you bring to this workplace matters. And if you're feeling marginalized, if you're feeling invisible, I want you to feel like you can tell this to someone and you'll be heard. This is opposite of what's been traditionally expected from employees: "Leave your personal stuff at home."

I think we are seeing a change in who shows up in museum leadership. The boards for so long were scavenging for these corporate models of leaders, because they felt that it was a business bottom line, and that's how we figure out our sustainability. And, oh, by the way, guess what, folx with big hearts can also balance the books. You don't have to have a corporate leader to do that. But you do need people in that C-suite who are mindful of the human potential around them and mindful of the oppression of the structure they've inherited, and work in the in-between to make it happen. I think a heart-centered leadership model is 100 percent where we need to go.

Chris: I have been fortunate to see and be surrounded by museum colleagues, or maybe I have been attracted to museum colleagues, who wholly subscribed to that, and you being one of them. And it's interesting to see the work that they've done in their field, particularly around equity. You're right; it is a consistent theme in this book and in the work of inclusion.

When I realized I didn't have to follow somebody else's path and that I can make my own way as a museum leader, it was such a freeing moment for me. There's a little bit of anxiety, because now I have to make it up as I go along, but there's also a kind of independence that comes with it.

Tell me more about your catalyzing moment. When did you know?

Cinnamon: Definitely that boardroom moment of not understanding how things work set me on a path. But I think the die was cast when I was doing some leadership training. I was in Maine at the time, and the Maine Association of Nonprofits had this leadership institute where we met once a month for a year. It was a great design because you have this cohort you come back to and have a lot of time for things to play out in between. The curriculum they subscribed to was from *The Leadership Challenge* by James Kouzes and Barry Posner's book, and it offered an incredible assessment process.

The structure of the learning offers five practices for exemplary leadership. The one that showed me the most opportunity to improve was "Encourage the heart." This practice recommends that leaders need to create ways to celebrate each other and our successes and create a workplace that is joyful and human centered. It was my lowest score, and I remember sitting with that for a long time. It still comes back to me. They offered examples of how you might do it is, "Well, maybe in the workplace, you could have pizza Fridays or hire a clown to come in." I'm like, "Yeah, I'm not hiring a clown." But the exercise really helped me understand that I was missing something.

I'm very driven. I'm project management oriented and I am 100 percent about solutions. Please come to my office with solutions. I'm naturally a hard ass. I don't need to see all these broken parts. I need to focus on moving the organization. I need everybody else to put the parts together and let's go. And I'm very fast minded (which means I miss a lot of details). I move really fast and that is problematic for everybody else around me. As it turns out it's not popular. Fortunately, I caught that early in my tenure at the Abbe and realized that I need to listen more closely to the heart. I still grapple with these tendencies every day.

Chris: Self-reflection and self-awareness are so critical. Until you can believe it about yourself or be aware of it about yourself, you're not going to wind up changing that.

I want to follow up on something that you had mentioned before. You talked a bit about barriers. You have a ton of museum experience, and you're exposed to leaders through so many different avenues. What do you feel is causing the most resistance to leaders exhibiting more inclusive leadership?

Cinnamon: Identity. I think museum workers are so passionate about the job they do (I think this is also the case with academia, by the way). We have to work really hard to have a job in this field and network constantly. This job requires everything from you. It is a time-consuming labor of "love," and it is easy to wrap an identity into it.

I remember as a young person in the field, having those moments where people ask about my work-life balance. I am a mom, and I have this really wonderful husband who is supportive. I never felt like I was cheating on the family with work. I remember saying to myself, "It's okay, this is who I am. Museum work is my identity. Other people have ways of framing their life. I framed my life through museum work. It's my passion." That's not okay. That's ridiculous. No, it's my profession, it's not my identity. And I don't think I came out of that belief system until fairly recently. It's really stuck with me.

I think about other leaders I know. Believe it or not, just because you're a leader in the museum field doesn't mean you're nice to other leaders. Some of them are unkind to other leaders, because, I think, of competition, that scarcity mentality, but also their identity is compromised if they see so-and-so leader who has this style, "Well, that's not my style. Is my board going to want that style?" That dynamic of working for a board puts a threat level that's totally different and particular. (And we hear a lot about bad board behavior.) What you end up doing is fusing it to your identity, and it's the only thing you know. That means you don't know who you are, and by extension, you miss the mark on how you show up and affect the people who work for you and with you.

Chris: That's really interesting. I see that a hundred percent. I hadn't thought about it in that way, though, in terms of the scarcity mentality, "What if my board wants that kind of leadership style?" Consider the power of boards . . . if boards were to signal more that they want inclusive leaders, how would that impact behavior of not only current leaders, aspiring leaders or emerging leaders as well? That's such a powerful question.

Could you talk about the importance of self-reflection to be an inclusive leader and your process? Or share any tools that you use or how you create space for self-reflection? I think this has to be an intentional practice.

Cinnamon: It does. I have to say as much as I talk about the importance of self-reflection, I don't think I'm very good at it. I guess that's helpful though—knowing when you're not good at it. I am really bad at receiving feedback. I have a horrible time with it, and you've got to be able to do that. I don't know what that is, who knows, it's probably my parents, I don't know. It sometimes feels like a character flaw. For me, what I've been doing most recently is bullet journaling. Bullet journaling not only helps you organize your life, but it creates space for you to record thoughts and ideas about what else is happening in your life. It really helps me see myself as a whole person.

I am cognizant of how I'm feeling on a given day. How did everything go today? When I have a difficult conversation I need to have with a colleague, I will sit with it and really think about how

I want to show up in that conversation. I don't have that conversation if I'm feeling off. I'll let it wait a day or two, if nobody's life's in danger. I want to feel really strong and centered during a difficult conversation.

I'm also really good at checking in with folks who know me and letting myself be seen. They can usually see stuff that I can't see. I think I've become better at that. I am part of a group of women working in museums that meets every Friday by Zoom. We're really purposeful about checking in with each other and seeing how we're doing. It's taught me how to check in with myself. In return, I make sure I do that with colleagues at work and using the language of the moment and recognizing that something traumatic is going on, like the pandemic or the violence that we're seeing on the news. I really, really want my team to have their feelings validated.

Chris: I think these questions are important to ask. How did I show up? How am I feeling right now? I don't check in with myself as much as I should. And so even posing this question, it's like, "Oh, I hope I don't have to answer it too!" And then we have to ask, "Did the outcome align with my intent?" These are things are incredibly important because oftentimes our intent does not align with our impact. Reflecting on that and asking yourself, "What could I have done differently?"

I do this with my partner a lot, asking her what questions I should ask or reviewing with her if I asked the question in the right way. I think those are all activities that could be fantastic for a journal and just keeping track of that in a way that I can measure that arc over time.

One of the activities readers will see in the book is the Johari Window. It's essentially a conversation where, if you can find somebody that you trust, they can help you see those blind spots or understand better how other people are perceiving you. It is valuable to have somebody who you trust, preferably somebody from a different cultural background. Or it can be someone who is different enough from you that they will help you see things in a different perspective or a different light. It's dependent on having a relationship where you both be very honest with each other. Not honest to the point where all of that hurts, but honest to the point where you acknowledge that you sharing this with love and from a developmental mind-set. It's a way to help you get better.

Like you said, feedback is hard. Nobody wants to be told they failed at something or acted less than ideal, particularly leaders. Nobody wants to be told you're not doing a good job. It doesn't feel good. I think that's part of the work that we need to do and part of the shift that needs to happen. It's not a shift to feeling good, but it is a shift to using feedback as a motivating factor, particularly with this work. Having someone to call you out and process blind spots with you is critical. Ask the questions: What am I not seeing? Is my ego getting in the way? Did I not seem prepared? Did I just get up and nail that?

I feel like I know my area of expertise backwards and forwards and I can just get up and do a panel. I can get up and run a team meeting. One thing that I love is when people call me out on words that I use because that helps me. It helps me understand how I'm showing up in a space, but more importantly, it helps me be better at modeling what I'm expecting other people to do. As a leader, this is fantastic. In regard to self-reflection, I think having people that can bring actions to your attention in a way that is supportive is critical. A little bit of a hint here, if you can't find that person that is different enough from you, that might be a great place to start.

Cinnamon: I agree with that! I'm also thinking back to your question about barriers. I would say the other barrier that compounds the identity issue is the power differential between leaders and staff and boards. I've been hearing from some leaders who say they need to do this personal work, develop their cultural competency, learn antiracism methodologies, but that they really don't want the staff to hear about their weaknesses or the racist things they may have unknowingly said.

For me, I think my filter's pretty thin around that. I've thought about things I've said in a staff setting that maybe I shouldn't have shared with them about what's going on at the board level or some pressures I'm experiencing. I think that's backfired on me at times because all sides don't understand that power differential, or even recognize that it's happening or that we all are human in this. We all need help. You've asked me to lead, but I don't have all the answers. I know I am a decisive person and I know that's a trait I have, but my position of power has put me in a place where I'm not hearing all the things I need to hear. I think that's also why it can be hard to receive feedback, the differential.

Chris: I'll add to that because we've heard this in spaces like MASS Action and Museums & Race. There is a problematic power differential when the leader is not invested or truly understands that oppression or racism is an issue in the institution. Folx who are doing the work, whether it's your educators or it's your staff of color or whoever it is that's doing the work, get minimized. It is such a terrible feeling. Whether it's intentionally minimized or unconsciously minimized, that work gets minimized and the power differential is what causes it. We've heard countless times from colleagues who will participate in a national convening like that and everyone's all in for making change at home. Then they go back to their institutions and their leaders minimize the experience and knowledge. It's so frustrating.

Cinnamon: I wonder if we could spend a little bit of time talking about practical changes. I think we hear a lot about why we need to do this work. And some people arrive at that space a little quicker than others, but I think all of us benefit from seeing what it looks like when inclusion is in action. What does the workplace look like? What are the internal hallmarks of an inclusive museum? How do we recognize it even from the outside, if we're looking to work there? We do well for ourselves when we seek healthy workplaces. When you think back to when you created the Department of Inclusion and Community Engagement (DICE) at Minnesota Historical Society, can you talk a little about what that launch phase looked like and what was your first-things-first mentality? What were some of those first changes that really felt tangible?

Chris: In creating the department, communicating that it happened was the biggest thing. It was interesting. I'll give a shout out to Wendy Jones, who was my boss at the time. DICE was created within the education department, and at first, all we cared about was just getting it created. She had the ability as the director of education to restructure her area and create the department. We weren't even created on an institutional level at first, but all we said was give us some real estate and we'll make the rest happen. From the get-go, we had the mind-set that even though we were in education, and Wendy was completely on board with this, we were an institutional resource.

We started reaching out to other departments saying, "Hey, here's who we are, here's what we do, here's what we can help you do. Here's our network of community folx that we're very protective of and we can be an asset to you." I think one of the things we did, I think by accident, is we used the words of the institution in the work that we were doing. As we have value statements and vision statements that talked about inclusion, we were saying, "We're here to help realize that thing that you've already stated that you wanted to do; we're here to help realize that." That was beneficial early on because if we encountered pushback we could say we've had something related to inclusion in our mission, vision, and values the whole time and nothing has really moved forward on this. What is stopping you?

It goes back to that when it's everyone's job, it's no one's job. I'll give you an example. I was sitting in a meeting, and there was a number of our senior leadership team members in this meeting. I was feeling courageous that day, and I posed the question, "How many of you wake up in the morning and your first work-related thought is around diversity and inclusion?" Nobody answered. I followed up with, "This is exactly why we need to have a unit that is focused on developing a strategy around this and pushing the rest of the institution." Very much like our marketing and communications department, very much like our human resources department, very much like our finance department, it needed to be a core function, a core support unit for the rest of the institution.

It wasn't up to us to do programs or do community engagement for the sake of community engagement. It was for us to help the rest of the institution do that work. It was very critical that we established that up front.

I'll share one story about the second half of that question about understanding some of the tangible ways that we operated differently and how we shared that with the rest of the institution. Kyle Parsons was my right-hand guy. I mean from day one, we were in this together. We had a climate in my department where everybody's voice was critical to decision making, to strategy development, all of it. I got the final say as the head of the department, but it was a collaborative process in the iteration of the ideas.

Kyle and I were in a meeting where several departments were represented on a project that we were working on. I was sharing ideas and observations, and Kyle was pushing back on me in the meeting. We got into an exchange where you could see heads looking around the table concerned about the exchange. We knew we were fine. Kyle knew he was well within his accepted methods of operation or behavior, but other people around the table got uncomfortable because he was pushing back on me and they knew I was his boss.

I thought it was interesting that we were modeling this inclusive culture for the rest of our colleagues; we circled back to them and talked about that moment. We let them know that this is acceptable in DICE. This is how we roll. This is why we do things, in my opinion, better than a lot of the other departments in the historical society. It is because we have this collaborative nature, and we know that collaborative decision making and diversity lead to better outcomes. The research is solid on that. We were actually putting our practice into behavior. I think that it caught a lot of people off guard. I won't say it caught on like wildfire, but we tried. It was one way that we would live in our values and showing them to other departments in the institution.

Cinnamon: I think one of my biggest lessons as we were becoming more inclusive at the Abbe, and it will certainly be the case where I am now at the Illinois State Museum, is that when this commitment is an action and when people are doing their internal work and preparing for the external and making changes, it becomes a new way of working. That to me is the biggest tangible outcome. This then attracts people who want to work in inclusive spaces. The words you use to promote a job description and a job announcement get noticed. The way that you conduct the interview, that gets noticed. The way you make selections for public programming changes. These changes get noticed.

People who are hungry for it, will pick up on it pretty fast. One of the reasons why I came to the Illinois State Museum is because I want to scale up that dynamic and see how this way of working changes and expands across a museum system and state agency. I've learned from people like you that it can happen, but it's a precarious place because people change, roles change, and funding sources change. What do you think one of the biggest vulnerabilities of work like this might be once it gets rooted in an organization? What can really take it off its path?

Chris: I think what comes to mind initially is that we're talking about a long-term change, right? We may not see or realize the true benefits for years. Either the change doesn't go deep enough or there's a perception that we did do that deep level work and it didn't take. We need to check how we're doing the changes. So that's one. The second is that it's complex and it's messy and we're not seeing the instant return on our investment in this. People just give up.

When we talk about the amount of time that it has taken to fully entrench these practices in our process to where it's now taught in our training programs, this is the level where we need to be patient to see this change really take root. Then we can assess. My fear is that whether it's an institution or a field or a training program or whatever, we'll do it for a couple of years and decide that it's too hard and no real change is being seen. Folx will want to go back to what they were doing in the past. How about you?

Cinnamon: I think the vulnerabilities hinge on size of the organization. I think we had a real concern when we got going at the Abbe around this. Some folx thought that if I left, things might roll backwards or not go anywhere, which I think was a false fear. I mean, everybody sitting at the table has responsibility. Yes, I had a role in driving the bus, but we all have a responsibility to affect change.

I think a smaller institution has a greater chance of holding onto the momentum because a bigger institution can easily sweep it into dark corners as it churns forward on other practices. It might not be so visible because of all of those moving parts and that's especially why leadership has to keep on top of it. It's also why boards have to then replace that leader with someone who's going to take them further and not manage the status quo. But unfortunately, boards, to be frank, are not equipped for that. There's some early work going on around board mindedness around inclusion, but they are light-years away from being the body that museums need to help them go further. I think that's where that big power differential really comes home to roost. Look, if a board is built because they can give five- and six-figure donations, it's almost a nonstarter at times for inclusive conversation to permeate. That is definitely not the case for all boards, but there still is a mentality that's embedded in board service that they hold all of the purse strings.

It's so obvious right now that we need something different in our leaders—as we weather this pandemic and we navigate really important conversations about race in our museum spaces, and as more open letters are written and more really public call-outs. When Change the Museum on Instagram and other vehicles out there [are] making impact, it's going to be hard for boards to ignore it, really difficult. I think the vulnerabilities are changing, but definitely there's a difference in organizational size.

I'm really happy to say that as I left the Abbe, they hired someone who is perfect to take it to the next step. They didn't hire someone who's going to do what I did. They hired someone who's going to take it even further as an Indigenous person and as a museum leader. I think that's one way the board can head off failure and backsliding—recognize where you're at and build from new places of learning and change, not the status quo.

Chris: I feel like the size of the institution is critical, but I feel like it's not insurmountable. I push. I thought the scope of my job working at the largest historical society in the country was big. When I shifted jobs and I now work with twenty-four cabinet-level agencies for state government, it's monumental. What I see is our governor and our lieutenant governor publicly stating that this is the work that we're doing and this is the work we will be held accountable for . . . here's no equivocal. It is a commitment.

It puts a little pressure on me and other people who are doing the work, but behind the scenes, I get support. I'm asked, what do I need? I am asked, where do you need me to show up as the governor or the lieutenant governor to have your back? I think that is the type of leadership that we all need to have. I didn't have that before; I felt like I was in a position where I was constantly making suggestions and hoping while I built coalitions of support, rather than being recognized for my expertise in this area. As a part of the leadership team, I should be driving that work. I think structure plays a big role in what we're doing.

For directors, there are so many things that they have to be focused on. I'm seeing diversity and inclusion officers being hired more and more. I applaud that because you need to have somebody who can advise the leader on these matters, but who also has a sphere of influence in the institution that can actually make change. I split the responsibility with MNHS 50/50 in that I don't think we went as far or as fast as we could have. There are things I could have done differently in terms of pointing some things out and advocating maybe a little bit harder; it's not all on leadership.

In the typical museum work culture, the director of exhibitions called the shots on exhibitions. The chief financial officer called the shots on the finances. The chief inclusion officer needs to be able to offer new ideas, challenge assumptions, and push the envelope. Until we get to that point where we have these high-level positions that are dictating inclusive practices and setting expectations and promoting accountability, I'm not sure that we're really going to go to the next level. But I do love the fact that I'm seeing more and more museums have these C-suite-level diversity positions. That is continuing to trend forward and it's phenomenal.

Now let me ask my last question, and I'm happy to offer my thoughts, but I think it will be important as leaders who will be reading this book are going to be predominantly White. What can White leaders contribute to a shift toward inclusive leadership in museums? What can their contribution be to this work?

Cinnamon: There's so much. I think it's essential to get ready for the contribution, because if you don't do the personal work, you stand to cause more harm. Making sure there's a readiness within each of us, whether it's the intensive training or active learning, is critical. We all need to know what readiness looks like and have ways to checking in with trusted colleagues.

Equally important is that we need to purposely change who's in the workplace, who's at the table. Make that table bigger. It can always be bigger. There can always be more voices and perspectives at that table.

We also need to rethink how museum work is done. This is something I'm spending a lot of brainpower around right now. We talked about this at the beginning, about the structures of best practices and how museum work is designed. You've got this department for this and this department for that. Curatorial practice in general, that solo curatorial mind-set, is problematic. Period. How do you create space for curators to understand that they need to take a different approach to exhibition work and research? It has to come from the top. It's going to be a big battle for a lot of particular museum types like art museums. There is a lot of pride in that curatorial title.

I think one of the biggest shifts we had at the Abbe was curatorial thinking became more about facilitation. They were certainly content specialists, but they also navigate multiple perspectives. They had to be able to catch ideas, people, designs that were coming and going. For a new core exhibit that we did, *People of the First Light*, we worked with more than Wabanaki scholars and artists and cultural leaders to create exhibition texts and designs, guided by an interpretive plan that was cocreated with the Native Advisory Council. Something that everybody will tell you can't be done, lo and behold, it can be done. The person at the core has to have that mind-set and not be that person who lords with misplaced authority.

I think White leaders can really call out those best practices and ask, is it really best? What do we mean by that? Is this going to get us where we need to go? Is this going to help us live in our values, live through our values? Is this going to create the community engagement that we want? If we concentrate authority and power in these little dominions, these areas of work, the answer is always going to be no. If we're working toward inclusive space, I think White leaders can challenge the field rigorously around that. And do it transparently 100 percent of the time.

I think there are some leaders doing this work, but they're not telling anybody about it. It's not like they need to be bragging. They need to be writing. They need to be sharing. They need to be bringing people into their conversation. They need for folx to know this work is going on because when they do, it helps everyone else. We can all see those tangible examples and learn collaboratively. It will break down those scarcity models and ultimately change that boardroom dynamic. The more we show it transparently, different types of people, new audiences, will be attracted to us. And, guess what, if your measurement in charitable giving, there are people on the planet who think inclusively, who also have money. You're not throwing one out without the other, if that's your standard. Those folks do exist.

Chris: When I think about that question, I also wonder if leaders understand how they are creating the tone and the culture in their organizations. Do they understand their museum's culture? What lens do they see the world through, and what are those norms? How does that permeate how they expect people to operate in museums? Inclusive leaders recognize when they come from a culture of Whiteness and can see the dominant norms around Whiteness. Hopefully, leaders will start to interrupt harmful patterns and make tables bigger. Putting people in the conversation that can help disrupt that, I think, is key.

There are so many people out there who are doing good work that would love that opportunity to be able to disrupt. Leaders provide access to the leadership process. They are also comfortable sharing power and influence and trusting those who may not have the longevity of experience and may not have the title. They understand that these are not indicators of ability or intellect. I think that that is one of the biggest contributions that White leaders could make to this process.

In turn it will be a learning process, and it's going to shift or impact their leadership style. This will be very interesting to see over time.

Note

1. Passed in 1990, the Native American Graves Protection and Repatriation Act (NAGPRA) is human rights legislation that requires museums, universities, local governments, and state agencies that receive federal funding to repatriate ancestral remains, their belongings, and objects of community significance. You can learn more here: https://www.nps.gov/subjects/nagpra/index.htm.

ACTIVITY

Examining Implicit Bias

To complete the activity, you'll need paper or a journal, your favorite pen, access to the internet, and a computer with a keyboard. A paper journal such as a bullet journal or some other bound book is optional but recommended.

For the first part of this exercise, you will go online and take a short test that helps reveal hidden biases that we all have.

1. Using a web browser, visit Harvard's Office for Diversity, Inclusion, and Belonging, which hosts the Implicit Association Test: https://dib.harvard.edu/implicit-association-test-iat.

   a. From there, select "Learn More."

   b. At the menu bar, select "Take a Test."

   c. Read the privacy and disclaimer info and then click "I wish to proceed" at the bottom of the page.

   d. From the buttons on the left, click "Race IAT" and begin the test. This test will take you ten minutes or less to complete.

2. Once you reach the end of the test with your score, it is recommended that you keep that page for your records either by printing it out or taking a screen grab. Your scores can change over time, and it's good practice to check in every now and then.

3. Now take some time for reflection. Were you surprised by the test and the outcome? What actions will you take to understand bias and your role as a leader? Take time to record your thoughts in a way that you can refer back to in the future.

4. Now that you have read part 1, spend some time to reflect on what you read. What are your expectations of the book?

If you decide to take additional IATs, be sure to take time after to be reflective.

Thanks for reading so far and for investigating implicit bias. We all have blind spots, and it's important to regularly look for them, ask questions, and make changes.

Keep going. We need you.

Part Two

Change Is Required

Chapter 5

Anatomy of a Movement

Armando Perla

I have never known what it feels like not to be Othered. I was born queer in a homophobic country. The path to where I am today has not been easy. That will never change. I fled El Salvador to seek refuge in Canada. Yet, no country will ever feel completely safe for me. Since I can remember, I have experience homophobia, at different levels, wherever I have lived. After I arrived in Canada, I also learned what racism feels like and how it can permanently scar you. This is the most painful lesson museums have taught me. For those of us living the colonial difference, demanding to be included and seeking equity is not a choice. Fighting to be recognized as full humans is a means of survival. It is the reality under which we are born.

This chapter illustrates how those of us who have been historically excluded are now leading the way, inside and outside of museum spaces, pushing to create a museum sector that is diverse, equitable, accessible, and inclusive of all.

Soon after the killing of George Floyd on May 15, 2020, museums joined institutions around the world making public statements of solidarity with the Black Lives Matter (BLM) movement. Most of the statements from museums were not backed up by any record of antiracist work; many in fact were covering up a culture of human rights abuses and discrimination that has plagued these institutions for far too long. Institutional racism and the upholding of White supremacy are structural problems that are pervasive in the museum sector. Those of us who are either Black, Indigenous, and People of Colour (BIPOC) and exist in museum spaces know this firsthand and have started to publicly call out institutions for creating environments where racism, homophobia, transphobia, sexism, and other forms of oppression did harm.

Many of us attempted time and again to create a dialogue with all levels of an overwhelmingly White, heterosexual, cisgender, able-bodied leadership only to have our claims constantly dismissed. When we dared to speak, we were chastised, vilified, and pushed out of institutions. Frustrated and heartbroken by the small gains coming from the inside, we grew tired of waiting. This led many of us to use digital direct action to expose how museums have harmed us and to seek change. Direct action is defined by BLM-Toronto cofounder Janaya Khan as an "effort to leverage, seize, or demonstrate power against oppressive systems."[1] Direct action, she argues, is used when negotiations or opportunities for those in power to do the right thing have failed or go unacknowledged. It is about "forcing people with decision-making power to respond" to public demands instead of ignoring them.[2] Some among us chose open letters[3] as the way to expose these abuses. Others used social media campaigns to further our mobilizations. Airing museums' dirty laundry in public was not our first choice, but it has proven to be the most effective strategy in a long history of resistance and activism we have carried out in the sector. Speaking publicly brings the transparency that many in the field have historically avoided, allowing for toxic abuse to become ingrained in institutions.

The double combination of museums' lack of diversity in leadership positions and the absence of institutional self-reflection on embedded White supremacy and other ways of privilege favoring dominant groups has enabled colonial thought, institutional racism, and other forms of oppression to harm those of us living in margins. Jamaican scholar and philosopher Charles W. Mills argues that White supremacy is "the unnamed political system that has made the modern world what it is today."[4] A system of European global domination, bringing into existence Whites and non-Whites, full persons and sub-persons. Prominent Maori lawyer and Indigenous rights expert Moana Jackson affirms that the idea that White people are inherently superior to everyone else is the "founding presumption" of colonialism. He elaborates:

> Some of Europe's greatest thinkers contributed to the development of this presumption, and it eventually encompassed everything from the superiority of their form of government to the greater reason of their minds and even the beauty of their bodies. They were merely warped fantasies posing as fact, but they were eventually learned as the "truths" that enabled Europeans to assert that they had the right to take over the lands, lives, and power of those they had decided were the "lesser breeds." The consequent dispossession of indigenous peoples was a race-based process that led to the genocide and deaths of millions of innocent men, women and children around the world.[5]

This process of European invasion, social classification based on the idea of race, establishing a system of White supremacy, dispossession of land and wealth, policies of genocide and enslavement is what we know as colonialism.[6] Colonization created privilege based on a false belief of White supremacy that dominates and shapes all aspects of our society. Museums and universities validated and advanced these ideas. In her book *Decolonizing Museums: Representing America in National and Tribal Museums*, Amy Lonetree argues that museums are inherently colonial institutions and are thus very painful sites for Indigenous peoples.[7] This argument is also reflected in museum professionals and scholars Bernadette Lynch and Samuel Alberti's words:

> Consciously or not, many who staff museums and galleries have been trained and socialised to think and know in those ways, a reminder that museums are not set apart from global injustices and the realities of racial conflict and prejudice. . . . Encounters between museum professionals and external individuals, particularly those from Diaspora communities, still bear traces of coloniser meeting colonised.[8]

An overwhelming White representation in museums' leadership represents a problem because White people have a specific White frame of reference and a White worldview. Whiteness is not a universal human experience. White sociologist Robin DiAngelo argues that Whiteness represents one particular type of experience and one framework of reference in a society where race matters profoundly because it is deeply separate and unequal by race.[9] This privileging of a dominant way of knowing within societal structures leads to institutional racism—a concept that Stokely Carmichael defined in his book *Black Power: The Politics of Liberation in America* as a form of racism that is subtler and less identifiable than overt racism.[10]

In the report out of the investigation on the racially motivated assassination of Stephen Lawrence in the United Kingdom, William McPherson further unpacks the concept, stating that institutional racism is

> [t]he collective failure of an organisation to provide an appropriate and professional service to people because of their colour, culture, or ethnic origin. It can be seen or detected in processes, attitudes and behaviour which amount to discrimination through unwitting prejudice, ignorance, thoughtlessness and racist stereotyping which disadvantage minority ethnic people.[11]

He also observes:

> Unwitting racism can arise because of lack of understanding, ignorance or mistaken beliefs. It can arise from well-intentioned but patronising words or actions. It can arise from unfamiliarity with the behaviour or cultural traditions of people or families from minority ethnic communities. . . . Often this arises out of uncritical self-understanding born out of an inflexible police ethos of the "traditional" way of doing things.[12]

Those of us who have invested emotional resources in showing our White colleagues how they can, consciously or not, be part of the problem, have often faced defensiveness and retaliation. This can be attributed to "White fragility," a concept coined by DiAngelo, which describes "a state in which even a minimum amount of racial stress becomes intolerable, triggering a range of defensive moves. These moves include the outward display of emotions such as anger, fear, and guilt, and behaviors such as argumentation, silence, and leaving the stress-inducing situation. These behaviors, in turn, function to reinstate White racial equilibrium."[13] Many of these ideas, power structures, behaviors, and dynamics have defined the approach of many museums, where White supremacy, implicit bias, and privilege have historically gone unchallenged and have been allowed to cause harm. Hence, resistance has taken many shapes and forms in different parts of the world. Those of us on the front line continue to raise our voices in our efforts to dismantle a system that has repeatedly failed us. We persist in pushing the sector to adopt a more inclusive way of thinking and doing.

In Canada, starting in summer 2020, we have exposed organizations like the Canadian Museum for Human Rights (CMHR), the Art Gallery of Mississauga (AGM), the Art Gallery of Ontario (AGO), the Vancouver Art Gallery (VAG), Contemporary Calgary (CC), the Royal Alberta Museum (RAM), the Gardiner Museum (GM), Lakeshore Arts (LSA), and the Royal British Columbia Museum (RBCM) for their abuses against historically marginalized communities and their lack of representation in leadership positions.

On June 5, 2020, Breonna Taylor's birthday, a rally organized by #Justice4BlackLives[14] in Winnipeg saw thousands of people march from the Manitoba Legislature to the CMHR.[15] During a radio interview with CBC Manitoba, Nampande Londe, a Black Canadian woman who was present, explained that a lot of non-Black people thought of this march as a form of solidarity with the protests in the United States, "as if this wasn't a problem that also exists here in Canada."[16] As a reaction, she created the #ItHappensInWinnipeg[17] social media campaign for Black people to share their stories and to serve as a record that "racism is alive and well here in Canada."

On June 7, 2020, Thiané Diop, former program interpreter at the CMHR, shared her own story of anti-Black racism at the institution using Londe's #ItHappensInWinnipeg.[18] Her leadership prompted other current and former Black employees at the CMHR to do the same. Diop then created the hashtag #CMHRStopLying,[19] encouraging other BIPOC individuals to share their experiences of racism and to hold the museum accountable. The CMHR responded with a public statement[20] that appeared disingenuous to many of us, triggering dozens of past and present employees to come forward with their experiences using the hashtag #CMHRStopLying. As the only curator from a visible minority ever hired by the museum, I shared too.

The personal accounts of racism,[21] homophobia,[22] and sexual harassment[23] that employees were exposed to under the museum's overwhelming White leadership produced a persistent media frenzy that lasted months. Our stories forced the museum to acknowledge some of its wrong-doings,[24] to launch an independent investigation,[25] and to compel the chief executive officer to step down.[26] During an investigation—led by Black, Queer, Winnipeg lawyer Laurelle Harris and a team of LGBTTQI+ BIPOC individuals—we spent hours reliving the trauma experienced at the CMHR. This produced a seventy-two-page report titled "Rebuilding the Foundation," where they found that racism is "pervasive" and "systemic" in the institution.[27]

At the same time, in other parts of the country other BIPOC and LGBTTQI+ leaders were raising their voices. In early June, Sharada Eswar, a former AGM's community activator published an open letter on Twitter accusing the institution of bullying, gaslighting, and upholding patriarchy and White supremacy.[28] Others joined in creating a website[29] articulating their demands to hold the gallery accountable. They received an outpouring of support on Instagram comments when the institution tried to label their activism a "smear campaign."[30] Around the same time, Rea MacNamara, who oversaw public programming initiatives at the Gardiner Museum in Toronto, wrote an open letter discussing the institutional racism she experienced and witnessed while working there.[31] In mid-June, Devyani Saltzman, director of public programming at the AGO wrote a piece where she spoke about the physical pain experienced by BIPOC individuals in the cultural sector trying to reflect the community while also "not being too political."[32] This was followed by a powerful article by visual artist, community activist, scholar, and member of BLM-Toronto Syrus Marcus Ware. Here, he not only recounts his experiences of anti-Black racism while working at the AGO but also challenges Art institutions in Canada to end it.[33]

Toward the end of June, Indigenous women Paulina Johnson, Judy Half, and Miranda Jimmy, who were involved under different capacities with the Royal Alberta Museum, spoke about both in-stitutional racism and individual instances of racism they experienced there.[34] Additionally, in an interview for the Institute for Canadian Citizenship, the student-run organization Museum Professionals of Colour (MPOC) at the University of Toronto spoke about their work aimed at remediating an "emphatically White and Eurocentric" curricula and academic staff within the Master of Museum Studies.[35] To end the month, on June 30, in support of BLM, a group of seven Asian American women artists publicly canceled an event at the VAG due to the lack of Black representation at its board and executive levels.[36] The event was rescheduled to take place at Contemporary Calgary, but the women pulled out days later after citing similar issues there.[37]

In Québec, starting in July, the Montreal Museum of Fine Arts became embroiled in controversy surrounding the firing of its former director and chief curator Nathalie Bondil.[38] Almost a month after her departure, an open letter signed by almost one hundred current and former employees affirmed that she created a toxic environment rife with intimidation and psychological harass-ment.[39] In August, Natasha Morris, former operations manager at LSA, penned an open letter addressed to the gallery's Board of Directors; she was supported by several Black artists from the community. In her letter, Morris denounced the appointment of another White director as "rooted in White supremacy culture."[40] She also questioned the institution's commitment to identifying and dismantling White supremacy as well as embedding an antiracism and anti-oppression lens in its hiring practices.[41] In mid-September, the *Globe and Mail*, one of Canada's most widely read newspapers, published an article about Lucy Bell's resignation as head of the First Nations Department and Repatriation Program at the Royal British Columbia Museum and Archives in Victoria. The article stated that in her goodbye speech Bell told her coworkers "she was leaving for her personal well-being and cultural safety"[42] after she had called out staff and executives for the racist behaviors she had experienced and witnessed.

Why are these issues so widespread in the museum sector in Canada? Why are we vilified and reprimanded, and why do we end up paying the consequences when we speak out? In her CBC interview, Londe states that some people believe that racism is a question of ignorance; yet she argues that racism is a matter of "willful blindness."[43] In Canada, the museum sector has deliberately chosen to ignore the prevalence of systemic racism and to actively uphold the status quo, as demonstrated by Sean O'Neill's study on the lack of diversity in Canada's four major art museums.[44] This study found that all the museums' directors and all board presidents are White; additionally, all but one of the senior executives are also White. The day after the study was published, the VAG announced the hiring of a new *White* CEO.[45] Discouragingly, there seems to be no intention of addressing the crisis in the museum sector in Canada, which is why our work leading the struggle to make the sector more inclusive is needed.

In 2017, Michael Maranda published a similar study on Canadian art galleries where he found that, out of 184 senior positions, 92 percent were occupied by White people, less than 4 percent by Indigenous people, and just more than 4 percent by visible minorities.[46] No specific data was collected regarding how many were/identified as Black. This study focused exclusively on art galleries that receive public funding. These numbers are all the more shocking when compared to the figures from the 2016 Canadian census, where 7,674,580 people—or 22.3 percent—identified as belonging to the visible minority category.[47] More comprehensive studies conducted in England (2017–2018)[48] and the United States (2015[49] and 2018[50]) have revealed that diversity in leadership positions in the art gallery and museum sector in those two countries has had a very slow increase. A 2018 study commissioned by the Canadian Parliament titled "Moving Forward—towards a Stronger Museum Sector," actively encourages museums to increase their diversity so that all Canadians can see themselves represented in the sector.[51] Given the recent outpouring of BIPOC people sharing their experiences, there remains a major disconnect between this recommendation and its implementation.

The BLM movement's impact goes beyond Canadian arts and heritage institutions; it has galvanized inclusive museum leaders/activists worldwide. South of the border, BIPOC individuals have exposed dozens of institutions that have been individually covered by the mainstream media regarding their harmful treatment of historically marginalized groups. Similarly, the Instagram account @changethemuseum[52] seeks to amplify these experiences of discrimination in cultural institutions.[53] In a *Vulture* article in July, founders are quoted saying that "the goal of the account is to pressure U.S. museums to move beyond lip-service proclamations of anti-racist missions by amplifying anonymously-shared, crowdsourced tales of unchecked racism."[54] @changethemuseum has provided a platform for hundreds of cultural workers exposing harmful behaviors in almost every major art museum in the United States[55] to more than thirty-five thousand followers. Other remarkable mobilizations led by BIPOC individuals in the United States include the Metropolitan Museum of Art (MET),[56] the San Francisco Museum of Modern Art (SFMOMA),[57] the New Orleans Museum of Art (NOMA),[58] the Guggenheim Museum,[59] the Getty Museum,[60] the Smithsonian African Museum of Art,[61] the Museum of Contemporary Art of Detroit (MOCAD),[62] and the Whitney Museum of Art.[63]

In the United Kingdom, the Tate Modern,[64] the British Museum, and the Southbank Centre have been criticized for their performative antiracist public statements. The posting of a solidarity statement by the British Museum prompted thousands of Twitter users[65] to bring up the hollowness of this gesture in light of the museum's past refusal to address its colonial past and its lack of diversity.[66] Visual artist and activist Bayryam Mustafa Bayryamali also blamed the museum for promoting racist and colonial stereotypes for decades.[67] In an open letter by the employees of the Southbank Centre, they accused it of allowing "disturbing instances of racism" including active resistance against the formation of a network of Black, Asian, and Minority Ethnic (BAME) staff in 2019.[68] The Southbank Centre tried to disband the network, and a board member affirmed that she did not believe in "victimhood."[69]

In a recent piece focused on the International Council of Museums (ICOM), the *New York Times* stated that "museums are having an identity crisis."[70] Headquartered in Paris, ICOM represents museums around the world. It works to protect their interests, including the development of a museum definition and a code of ethics that member institutions must follow. The current definition has not been significantly updated in almost fifty years. It serves as an ode to the status quo and a tool of unchallenged preservation. This has enabled the overwhelmingly White leadership of museums in the "West" to erroneously assert that institutions must remain neutral and apolitical. It has also disregarded the voices of the historically marginalized while also creating toxic and unsafe environments for those who dare challenge this fallacy.

The growing number of museums being held accountable is a testament to the inefficiency of a definition that does not challenge injustice when it stares it in the face. This inefficiency does a great disservice to the museum sector. ICOM's meeting in Kyoto in fall 2019, Japan was meant to culminate in a vote to redefine the museum as an institution more receptive to our heterogeneous realities.[71] Instead, we saw a long parade of predominantly White European countries ask for more time to analyze and discuss the proposed redefinition before holding the vote.[72] Some non-European countries also argued more time was needed. I watched in shame when Canada's own commitment to diverse representation and its ability to adapt to a field in flux were challenged when Canadian delegates pointed fingers at Danish curator Jette Sandahl, the chair of the standing committee on the Museum Definition, Prospects and Potentials (MDPP). They shamefully accused her of creating a false division between ICOM members. But this proposed new definition did not create division; it only exacerbated already-existing issues.

What suggestions could possibly require so much consideration and incite such tension among members?

The new proposed definition actively calls on institutions to democratize museums, including having critical dialogues about the past and addressing the conflicts and challenges of the present.[73] It also talks about equal rights, equal access, and contributing to human dignity, social justice, and global equality.[74] But in Kyoto, delegate after delegate from the prominent and powerful nations affirmed how they did not need a new definition to continue doing what they were *already doing.*

Still, the accounts by BIPOC, LGBTTQI, and other historically marginalized people working in museums are getting louder. Our harrowing testimonies in summer 2020 have further proven how equal rights, respect for human dignity, social justice, and equality are still a distant reality for many museums. Inclusive leaders like Lonnie Bunch—the first African American to hold the position of secretary general of the Smithsonian Institution—are tired of waiting. He spoke about how he has repeatedly been told throughout his life to be patient and keep waiting. "The time is now," he said during the plenary session "The Museum Definition—the Backbone of ICOM." Indeed, it is only easy to keep waiting when you are the one benefiting from the status quo.[75]

Many in Kyoto referred to the public consultations on the museum definition as the most democratic and open process ICOM had ever embarked on. The MDPP met with 850 ICOM members and other museum professionals worldwide asking them what a more relevant museum definition for the twenty-first century would look like.[76] Yet, in Kyoto, the organization refused to hold the vote to make progressive values and equal rights for all a priority. Those of us who strived to steer museums in a new direction and supported voting for the new definition were outnumbered in an ICOM heavily dominated by White European states set on maintaining the status quo.

In the aftermath, former president Suay Aksoy—a Turkish woman—suddenly resigned from her position.[77] Other high-profile departures followed.[78] Many cited disagreements over the proposed new definition as the main reason behind these resignations. Her replacement by a White European man, however, not only reflects a Eurocentric organization that refuses to include different frames of reference and embrace a more progressive approach to the museum sector but also is a symptom of deeper structural and organizational issues that go beyond the museum definition debates. This prompted those of us on the executive board of ICOM's International Committee on Ethical Dilemmas to hold an extraordinary meeting to determine our course of action. On June 22, 2020, we released an open letter to ICOM's president, executive board, and general director, where we requested that the organization release Aksoy's letter of resignation[79] as well as give more transparency into the events that led to her leaving the institution and the designation of a new president.[80] We knew that we needed to act quickly if we wanted to set a precedent. Other national and international ICOM committees followed soon after.[81]

The refusal to cast a vote on a more progressive definition and the events surrounding Aksoy's resignation are especially disconcerting considering that many of us have recently exposed many of the abuses committed by museums against historically marginalized communities in different parts of the world.

But how can museums be more responsible to and inclusive of the communities they intend to serve? Since I started to work in the museum sector, I have promoted the use of participatory and more accountable ways of working by applying a human rights–based approach (HRBA) to museum practice. This approach prioritizes the empowerment of historically marginalized voices, allowing them to participate in all decision-making processes and to permeate every level of museum governance. Empowering members from historically excluded communities to participate in policy formulation also contributes to hold cultural institutions accountable and to promote project sustainability. I first started to advocate for an HRBA to museum practice at the CMHR. This was met with resistance in a museum that understood human rights only as a philosophical concept and not as a method of work. Yet, I used this approach in my own curatorial work at the museum. Almost ten years later, when I moved to Sweden to work in a pilot project for a new national museum on migration and democracy, I also used an HRBA to museum practice to develop a vision premised in the meaningful participation of historically marginalized communities. I am cognizant that an HRBA is not the only way of implementing participatory and inclusive practices. I am also aware of its shortcomings. However, being trained as a human rights lawyer, this is the approach I have chosen to follow. And, as needed, I have used it and modified it to frame and articulate my own type of inclusive museum practice.

An "HRBA is not about making human rights one element or dimension in mainstream processes,"[82] legal scholars John Packer and Slava Balan insist. "It is about making them the foundational framework and basis for the entire process of socio-political organisation and development."[83] Critical frameworks such as antiracism and anti-oppression as well as decolonial practice add additional layers needed in an HRBA. This approach means anchoring respect for human dignity, nondiscrimination, equity, participation, and inclusion at the heart of museum work. Grounding museum practice in this way would help museums embody values they already claim to implement but are not living up to.

Meaningful BIPOC leadership and community participation means ensuring genuine ownership and control over all museum processes in all phases of a project: assessment, analysis, planning, implementation, monitoring, and evaluation. Adopting ethical guidelines created in partnership with historically marginalized communities to help museums anchor their practice must be a priority for institutions wanting to become more inclusive, transparent, democratic, and accountable. For instance, at the Museum of Movements (MoM), I led the development of a set of ethical guidelines to promote inclusion and to address the institutional racism and the unequal distribution of power embedded in museums. This project also complemented my international work on ethics as a member of ICOM's IC-Ethics. In fall 2019, I organized a workshop on ethics that brought to Sweden thirty-five experts from three different sectors: community, academia, and museums. These experts also belonged to and worked with historically marginalized communities around oral history, community participation, and ethics. They represented the MoM's neighborhood, the city of Malmo, Sweden, and countries spanning five different continents. They shared their knowledge and experiences over three days, resulting in the first draft of the ethical guidelines that would guide the MoM's work. Museums wanting to become more inclusive would benefit from adopting similar models of policy development helmed by staff belonging to historically excluded groups.

Since my return to Canada due to the COVID-19 pandemic, I have focused on my writing to amplify several mobilization campaigns led by historically marginalized people against institutional racism and other forms of abuse in museums. Along with Thiané Diop and Julie White, I have also been one of the three main organizers behind the #CMHRStopLying social media campaign. I continue to organize and participate in digital conferences in Europe, North America, and Latin America, and I also continue to work inside and outside museum spaces. Throughout these actions, my message continues to be the same: not prioritizing the inclusion of historically marginalized perspectives and talent in leadership roles in museums allows for the status quo to go unchallenged. This preservation of the old ways of knowing and doing furthers tokenistic, victimizing, and stereotypical representations of those of us living the colonial difference, while also exposing us to racial violence and other forms of oppression inside museums. It is time for those who have held the power in the sector for far too long to start listening to new perspectives and to make the necessary changes for museums to redress past wrongs and truly reflect the societies and communities they intend to serve. For a long time, many of us have felt isolated in our work dismantling a system that has oppressed and harmed us. But, if something has become clear during this historic moment, it is that we are not alone. Our leadership is collective and relies in our communities. This is the museum leadership of the future. We are here, we exist, and we are not going away.

Notes

1. Rodney Divelrus, Sandy Hudson, and Syrus Marcus Ware, *Until We Are Free: Reflections on Black Lives Matter in Canada* (Regina, SK: University of Regina Press, 2020), 118.
2. Divelrus, Hudson, and Ware, *Until We Are Free*, 119.

3. Aaron Randle, "'We Were Tired of Asking': Why Open Letters Have Become Many Activists' Tool of Choice for Exposing Racism at Museums," *Artnet News*, July 15, 2020, https://news.artnet.com/art-world/museum-open-letters-activism-1894150.

4. Charles W. Mills, *The Social Contract* (Ithaca, NY: Cornell University Press, 1997), 1.

5. Moana Jackson, "The Connection between White Supremacy and Colonisation," E-Tangata, March 24, 2019, https://e-tangata.co.nz/comment-and-analysis/the-connection-between-white-supremacy/.

6. Walter D. Mignolo and Catherine E. Walsh, *On Decoloniality: Concepts, Analytics, Praxis* (Durham, NC: Duke University Press, 2018), 16.

7. Amy Lonetree, *Decolonizing Museums: Representing Native America in National and Tribal Museums* (Chapel Hill: University of South Carolina Press, 2012), 1.

8. Bernadette T. Lynch and Samuel J. M. M. Alberti, "Legacies of Prejudice: Racism, Co-production and Radical Trust in the Museum," *Museum Management and Curatorship* 25, no. 1 (2010): 13, https://doi.org/10.1080/09647770903529061.

9. Robin DiAngelo, *White Fragility: Why It's So Hard for White People to Talk about Racism* (Boston: Bacon Press Boston, 2018), 7.

10. Stokley Carmichael, *Black Power: The Politics of Liberation in America* (New York: Random House, 1967), 20.

11. William McPherson, *The Stephen Lawrence Inquiry* (London: Secretary of State for the Home Department by Command of Her Majesty, 1999), 6.34.

12. McPherson, *"The Stephen Lawrence Inquiry*, 6.17.

13. Robin DiAngelo, "White Fragility," *International Journal of Critical Pedagogy* 3, no. 3 (2011): 54–70.

14. Justice 4 Black Lives, https://www.instagram.com/justice4blackliveswinnipeg/?hl=en.

15. Nicholas Frew, "Thousands Gather in Peaceful Protest at Manitoba Legislature to Demand Justice 4 Black Lives," *CBC News*, CBC/Radio Canada, June 5, 2020, https://www.cbc.ca/news/canada/manitoba/justice-4-black-lives-petition-abolish-winnipeg-police-1.5601130.

16. Canadian Broadcasting Corporation (CBC), "It Happens in Winnipeg: Social Media Account Sharing Racist Experiences Faced by Black People in the City," *Up to Speed*, June 30, 2020, https://www.cbc.ca/listen/live-radio/1-111-up-to-speed/clip/15785058-it-happens-in-winnipeg.-social-media-account-sharing-racist-experiences-faced-by-black-people-in-the-city.

17. It Happens in Winnipeg, https://www.instagram.com/ithappensinwinnipeg/.

18. It Happens in Winnipeg, June 7, 2020, https://www.instagram.com/p/CBH73ivnvLi/.

19. CMHR Stop Lying, https://www.instagram.com/cmhrstoplying/?utm_source=ig_embed&utm_campaign=loading.

20. CMHR (Canadian Museum for Human Rights), June 8, 2020, https://www.facebook.com/canadianmuseumforhumanrights/posts/10158566122555513.

21. Sam Thompson, "Canadian Museum for Human Rights under Fire after Allegations of Racism, Discrimination Surface," CJOB, *Global News*, June 11, 2020, https://globalnews.ca/news/7053839/canadian-museum-for-human-rights-allegations-racism-discrimination/.

22. Danton Unger, "'Just Appalling': Pride Winnipeg Cuts Ties with Human Rights Museum over LGBTQ2+ Censorship," *CTV News*, Winnipeg, June 24, 2020, https://winnipeg.ctvnews.ca/just-appalling-pride-winnipeg-cuts-ties-with-human-rights-museum-over-lgbtq2-censorship-1.4998605.

23. Austin Grabish, "Canadian Museum for Human Rights Employees Say Sex Harassment Complaints Dismissed by Human Resources," *CBC News*, CBC/Radio Canada, June 25, 2020, https://www.cbc.ca/news/canada/manitoba/cmhr-sexual-harassment-1.5625684.

24. CMHR, "Apology from the Executive Team of the CMHR," June 19, 2020, https://humanrights.ca/share/apology-from-the-executive-team-of-the-cmhr.

25. Carol Sanders, "CMHR Announces Workplace Review after Multiple Complaints of Racism," *Winnipeg Free Press*, June 10, 2020, https://www.winnipegfreepress.com/special/arts-editors-picks/cmhr-announces-workplace-review-after-multiple-complaints-of-racism-571175732.html.

26. CMHR, "CMHR Board Announces Immediate Departure of CEO," June 25, 2020, https://humanrights.ca/news/cmhr-board-announces-immediate-departure-of-ceo.

27. Laurelle Harris, "Rebuilding the Foundation: External Review into Systemic Racism and Oppression at the Canadian Museum for Human Rights," Canadian Museum for Human Rights, August 5, 2020, https://humanrights.ca/sites/prod/files/2020-08/A-FullReport_EN.pdf.

28. Ashley Newport, "Art Gallery of Mississauga Responds to Allegations of Racism, Calls for the Gallery to Cease Operations," *Insauga*, August 25, 2020, https://www.insauga.com/art-gallery-of-mississauga -responds-to-allegations-of-racism-calls-for-the-gallery-to-cease-operatio.

29. Hold AGM Accountable, "We Must Hold the AGM Accountable," https://holdagmaccountable.word press.com/.

30. Art Gallery of Mississauga, "A Statement," August 7, 2020, https://www.instagram.com/p/CDmy l1YA_w6/.

31. Rea McNamara, "Why Your Museum's BLM Letter Isn't Enough," Medium, June 9, 2020, https://medium.com/@rea.mcnamara/why-your-museums-blm-letter-isn-t-enough-33841b31b9ae.

32. Patel Brown, "Some Thoughts on Culture: Devyani Saltzman," *PatelBrown* (blog), June 16, 2020, https://www.patelbrown.com/blog/some-thoughts-on-culture?fbclid=IwAR3phXLrxdsPWIMZruw5Ay5 _UOILdeeaZyjCjjkGUcuuyZZJom9RPdawh10.

33. Syrus Marcus Ware, "Give Us Permanence-Ending Anti-Black Racism in Canada's Art Institutions," *Canadian Art*, June 24, 2020, https://canadianart.ca/features/give-us-permanence-ending-anti -black-racism-in-canadas-art-institutions/.

34. Omar Mosleh, "'I'm Not Your Token': Indigenous Employee Accuses Alberta Museum of Systemic Racism," *Toronto Star*, June 27, 2020, https://www.thestar.com/news/canada/2020/06/27 /im-not-your-token-indigenous-employee-accuses-alberta-museum-of-systemic-racism.html.

35. Institute for Canadian Citizenship, "Interview with Museum Professionals of Colour," June 30, 2020, https://www.inclusion.ca/article/interview-with-museum-professionals-of-colour-mpoc/?fbclid=I wAR2Lq6tfmD9ZHddfLLOTR5Hhb_cE6sTod5887eBTCp_fANvfKKSY5PPj5AM.

36. Elisa Wouk Almino, "Seven Asian Women Artists Discuss Racism and Tokenism in the Art World," Hyperallergic, July 7, 2020, https://hyperallergic.com/575433/hyperinvisibility-panel-contempo rary-calgary/.

37. Contemporary Calgary, June 30, 2020, https://www.instagram.com/p/CCEipfspB2-/.

38. Julia Jacobs, "Firing of Museum Director Stirs Debate and an Official Inquiry," *New York Times*, July 22, 2020, https://www.nytimes.com/2020/07/22/arts/design/montreal-museum-nathalie-bondil.html.

39. Eileen Kinsella, "Over 100 Current and Former Staff Sign a Letter Supporting the Controversial Firing of the Montreal Museum's Director," *Artnet News*, August 12, 2020, https://news.artnet.com/art-world /open-letter-employees-montreal-museum-firing-1901465.

40. Natasha Adiyana Morris, "An Open Letter to the Board of Directors of Lakeshore Arts," August 18, 2020, https://www.instagram.com/p/CEC6-v6Fill/.

41. Morris, "An Open Letter."

42. Marsha Lederman, "Royal B.C. Museum Responds to Accusations of Racism," *Globe and Mail*, September 12, 2020, https://www.theglobeandmail.com/arts/article-royal-bc-museum-responds-to-accusa tions-of-racism/.

43. CBC, "It Happens in Winnipeg."

44. Sean O'Neill, "A Crisis of Whiteness," *Canadian Art*, June 23, 2020, https://canadianart.ca/features /a-crisis-of-whiteness/.

45. John Mackie, "Vancouver Art Gallery Appoints New Director," *The Province*, June 25, 2020, https://theprovince.com/news/vancouver-art-gallery-appoints-new-director/wcm/d379d22a-d44c-4cf5 -998c-4dfb51dc45dc.

46. Michael Maranda, "Hard Numbers: A Study on Diversity in Canada's Galleries," *Canadian Art*, April 5, 2017, https://canadianart.ca/features/art-leadership-diversity/.

47. Statistics Canada, "Focus on Geography Series, 2016 Census," https://www12.statcan.gc.ca/census -recensement/2016/as-sa/fogs-spg/Facts-can-eng.cfm?Lang=Eng&GK=CAN&GC=01&TOPIC=7.

48. Arts Council England, "Equality, Diversity and the Creative Case: A Data Report, 2017–2018," January 2019, https://www.artscouncil.org.uk/sites/default/files/download-file/Diversity_report_1718.pdf.

49. Roger Schonfeld, Mariët Westermann, and Liam Sweeney, "The Andrew W. Mellon Foundation Art Museum Staff Demographic Survey," Andrew W. Mellon Foundation, July 28, 2015, https://mellon.org

/media/filer_public/ba/99/ba99e53a-48d5-4038-80e1-66f9ba1c020e/awmf_museum_diversity
_report_aamd_7-28-15.pdf.

50. Mariët Westermann, Roger Schonfeld, and Liam Sweeney, "Art Museum Staff Demographic Survey 2018," Andrew W. Mellon Foundation, January 28, 2019, https://mellon.org/media/filer_public
/b1/21/b1211ce7-5478-4a06-92df-3c88fa472446/sr-mellon-report-art-museum-staff-demographic
-survey-01282019.pdf.

51. Julie Dabrusin, "Moving Forward—towards a Stronger Museum Sector," Parliament of Canada—Standing Committee on Canadian Heritage, September 2018, https://www.ourcommons.ca/Content/Committee
/421/CHPC/Reports/RP10011476/chpcrp12/chpcrp12-e.pdf.

52. Change the Museum, https://www.instagram.com/changethemuseum/.

53. Valentina Di Liscia. "An Instagram Account Is Amplifying Anonymous Testimonies of Racism in Museums," Hyperallergic, June 30, 2020, https://hyperallergic.com/574189/change-the-museum
-instagram/.

54. Trupti Rami, "The Instagram Account 'Change the Museum' Is Doing Just That," *Vulture*, July 15, 2020, https://www.vulture.com/2020/07/change-the-museum-instagram.html.

55. Rami, "The Instagram Account 'Change the Museum.'"

56. Robin Pogrebin, "Upheaval over Race Reaches MET Museum after Curator's Instagram Post," *New York Times*, June 24, 2020, https://www.nytimes.com/2020/06/24/arts/design/met-museum-staff-letter
-racism.html.

57. Daria Harper, "SFMOMA Employees Call Out the Institutional Racism and Censorship in Open Letter," *Artsy*, June 24, 2020, https://www.artsy.net/news/artsy-editorial-sfmoma-employees-accused-insti
tution-racism-censorship-open-letter.

58. Alex Greenberger, "Alleging 'Plantation-Like Culture,' Former Workers Accuse New Orleans Museum of Art of Racism and Hypocrisy," *ARTnews*, June 24, 2020, https://www.artnews.com/art-news/news
/new-orleans-museum-of-art-racism-open-letter-1202692299/.

59. Helen Holmes, "The Guggenheim's First Black Curator Is Denouncing the Museum's Treatment of Her," *Observer*, June 5, 2020, https://observer.com/2020/06/guggenheim-museum-chaedria-labouvier/.

60. Daria Harper, "Current and Former Staff Complain of Racial Bias at the Getty Museum in Open Letter," *Artsy*, July 20, 2020, https://www.artsy.net/news/artsy-editorial-current-staff-members-com
plained-racial-bias-getty-museum-open-letter.

61. Peggy McGlone, "Smithsonian's National Museum of African Art Accused of Culture of Racism," *Washington Post*, July 15, 2020, https://www.washingtonpost.com/entertainment/museums/smith
sonians-national-museum-of-african-art-accused-of-culture-of-racism/2020/07/15/7d63ff48-c6d8
-11ea-a99f-3bbdffb1af38_story.html.

62. MOCAD Resistance, "Former Staff Letter," *MOCAD Resistance* (blog), https://www.mocadresistance
.com/blog/former-staff-letter.

63. Josephine Livingstone, "The Whitney Museum's Careless Attempt to Curate a Summer of Black Uprising," *New Republic*, August 25, 2020, https://newrepublic.com/article/159078/whitney-muse
ums-careless-attempt-curate-summer-black-uprising.

64. Sofia Elk, "UK's Tate Faces Heat over Racist Mural in Gallery Restaurant," *Jakarta Post*, August 6, 2020, https://www.thejakartapost.com/life/2020/08/06/uks-tate-faces-heat-over-racist-mural-in-gallery
-restaurant.html.

65. Catherine Hickley, "'Time to Give Back the Swag, Guys!' British Museum Unleashes Twitter Storm with Statement on Black Lives Matter," *Art Newspaper*, June 9, 2020, https://www.theartnewspaper.com
/news/british-museum-unleashes-twitter-storm-with-statement-on-black-lives-matter.

66. Kate Brown, "'This Is Performative': Critics Mock the British Museum for Its 'Hollow' Statement of Solidarity with Black Lives Matter," *Artnet News*, June 9, 2020, https://news.artnet.com/art-world
/british-museum-black-lives-matter-1882296.

67. Bayryam Mustafa Bayryamali, "Addressing the British Museum's Colonial History and Hollow Solidarity with Black Lives," Hyperallergic, June 16, 2020, https://hyperallergic.com/570591/letter-to-british
-museum-hartwig-fischer/.

68. Damian Jones, "London Southbank Centre Workers Pen Open Letter Protesting against Redundancies and 'Institutional Racism,'" *NME Music News*, August 4, 2020, https://www.nme.com/news/music

/london-southbank-centre-workers-pen-open-letter-protesting-against-redundancies-and-institu
tional-racism-2721040.

69. Save Our Southbank, "An Open Letter on Southbank Centre's Brutal Redundancies, Their Impact on the Diversity of Our Workforce, and the Future of Southbank Centre," https://saveoursouthbank.com/.

70. Alex Marshall, "What Is a Museum? A Dispute Erupts over a New Definition," *New York Times*, August 6, 2020, https://www.nytimes.com/2020/08/06/arts/what-is-a-museum.html.

71. ICOM (International Council of Museums), "The Challenge of Revising the Museum Definition," November 24, 2017, https://icom.museum/en/news/the-challenge-of-revising-the-museum-definition/.

72. Suse Anderson and Ed Rodley, "Museopunks Episode 39: A New Definition of 'Museum'?" American Alliance of Museums, October 10, 2019, https://www.aam-us.org/2019/10/10/museopunks-episode-39-a-new-definition-of-museum/.

73. ICOM, "Museum Definition," https://icom.museum/en/resources/standards-guidelines/museum-definition/.

74. ICOM, "Museum Definition."

75. ICOM, "Museum Definition."

76. Jette Sandahl, "Report and Recommendations Adopted by the ICOM Executive Board," Standing Committee for Museum Definition, Prospects and Potentials, December 2018, https://icom.museum/wp-content/uploads/2019/01/MDPP-report-and-recommendations-adopted-by-the-ICOM-EB-December-2018_EN-2.pdf.

77. Suay Aksoy, "Farewell Note from President Suay Aksoy," ICOM, June 21, 2020, https://icom.museum/en/news/farewell-note-from-president-suay-aksoy%E2%80%A8/.

78. Jonathan Knott, "Icom in Turmoil after Resignations," Museums Association, July 17, 2020, https://www.museumsassociation.org/museums-journal/news/2020/07/icom-museum-definition-row-rumbles-on/.

79. IC-Ethics (International Committee on Ethical Dilemmas) Executive Board, "Open Letter to the President, Executive Board, and General Director of ICOM," IC-Ethics, June 22, 2020, https://www.facebook.com/ICEthics/photos/a.461450331007345/879861389166235/.

80. IC-Ethics Executive Board, "Open Letter."

81. Suay Aksoy, "Resignation," June 19, 2020, http://comcol.mini.icom.museum/wp-content/uploads/sites/9/2020/07/Resignation-of-President-Suay-Aksoy.pdf.

82. Slava Balam and John Packer, "A Genuine Human Rights–Based Approach for Our Post-Pandemic Future," Open Global Rights, July 29, 2020, https://www.openglobalrights.org/genuine-human-rights-based-approach-for-post-pandemic-future/?lang=English.

83. Balam and Packer, "A Genuine Human Rights–Based Approach."

Bibliography

Aksoy, Suay. "Farewell Note from President Suay Aksoy." ICOM, June 21, 2020. https://icom.museum/en/news/farewell-note-from-president-suay-aksoy%E2%80%A8/.

———. "Resignation." June 19, 2020. http://comcol.mini.icom.museum/wp-content/uploads/sites/9/2020/07/Resignation-of-President-Suay-Aksoy.pdf.

Almino, Elisa Wouk. "Seven Asian Women Artists Discuss Racism and Tokenism in the Art World." Hyperallergic, July 7, 2020. https://hyperallergic.com/575433/hyperinvisibility-panel-contemporary-calgary/.

Anderson, Suse, and Ed Rodley. "Museopunks Episode 39: A New Definition of 'Museum'?" American Alliance of Museums, October 10, 2019. https://www.aam-us.org/2019/10/10/museopunks-episode-39-a-new-definition-of-museum/.

Arts Council England. "Equality, Diversity and the Creative Case: A Data Report, 2017–2018." January 2019. https://www.artscouncil.org.uk/sites/default/files/download-file/Diversity_report_1718.pdf.

Balam, Slava, and John Packer. "A Genuine Human Rights–Based Approach for Our Post-Pandemic Future." Open Global Rights, July 29, 2020. https://www.openglobalrights.org/genuine-human-rights-based-approach-for-post-pandemic-future/?lang=English.

Bayryamali, Bayryam Mustafa. "Addressing the British Museum's Colonial History and Hollow Solidarity with Black Lives." Hyperallergic, June 16, 2020. https://hyperallergic.com/570591/letter-to-british-museum-hartwig-fischer/.

Brown, Kate. "'This Is Performative': Critics Mock the British Museum for Its 'Hollow' Statement of Solidarity with Black Lives Matter." Artnet News, June 9, 2020. https://news.artnet.com/art-world/british-museum-black-lives-matter-1882296.

Brown, Patel. "Some Thoughts on Culture: Devyani Saltzman." PatelBrown (blog), June 16, 2020. https://www.patelbrown.com/blog/some-thoughts-on-culture?fbclid=IwAR3phXLrxdsPWIMZruw5Ay5_UOlLdeeaZyjCjjkGUcuuyZZJom9RPdawh10.

Canadian Broadcasting Corporation (CBC). "It Happens in Winnipeg: Social Media Account Sharing Racist Experiences Faced by Black People in the City." Up to Speed, June 30, 2020. https://www.cbc.ca/listen/live-radio/1-111-up-to-speed/clip/15785058-it-happens-in-winnipeg.-social-media-account-sharing-racist-experiences-faced-by-black-people-in-the-city.

Canadian Museum for Human Rights (CMHR). "Apology from the Executive Team of the CMHR." June 19, 2020. https://humanrights.ca/share/apology-from-the-executive-team-of-the-cmhr.

———. "CMHR Board Announces Immediate Departure of CEO." June 25, 2020. https://humanrights.ca/news/cmhr-board-announces-immediate-departure-of-ceo.

Carmichael, Stokley. Black Power: The Politics of Liberation in America. New York: Random House, 1967.

Dabrusin, Julie. "Moving Forward—towards a Stronger Museum Sector." Parliament of Canada—Standing Committee on Canadian Heritage, September 2018. https://www.ourcommons.ca/Content/Committee/421/CHPC/Reports/RP10011476/chpcrp12/chpcrp12-e.pdf.

DiAngelo, Robin. "White Fragility." International Journal of Critical Pedagogy 3, no. 3 (2011): 54–70.

———. White Fragility. Why It's So Hard for White People to Talk about Racism. Boston: Bacon Press Boston, 2018.

Di Liscia, Valentina. "An Instagram Account Is Amplifying Anonymous Testimonies of Racism in Museums." Hyperallergic, June 30, 2020. https://hyperallergic.com/574189/change-the-museum-instagram/.

Divelrus, Rodney, Sandy Hudson, and Syrus Marcus Ware. Until We Are Free: Reflections on Black Lives Matter in Canada. Regina, SK: University of Regina Press, 2020.

Elk, Sofia. "UK's Tate Faces Heat over Racist Mural in Gallery Restaurant." *Jakarta Post*, August 6, 2020. https://www.thejakartapost.com/life/2020/08/06/uks-tate-faces-heat-over-racist-mural-in-gallery-restaurant.html.

Frew, Nicholas. "Thousands Gather in Peaceful Protest at Manitoba Legislature to Demand Justice 4 Black Lives." *CBC News*, CBC/Radio Canada, June 5, 2020. https://www.cbc.ca/news/canada/manitoba/justice-4-black-lives-petition-abolish-winnipeg-police-1.5601130.

Grabish, Austin. "Canadian Museum for Human Rights Employees Say Sex Harassment Complaints Dismissed by Human Resources." *CBC News*, CBC/Radio Canada, June 25, 2020. https://www.cbc.ca/news/canada/manitoba/cmhr-sexual-harassment-1.5625684.

Greenberger, Alex. "Alleging 'Plantation-Like Culture': Former Workers Accuse New Orleans Museum of Art of Racism and Hypocrisy." *ARTnews*, June 24, 2020. https://www.artnews.com/art-news/news/new-orleans-museum-of-art-racism-open-letter-1202692299/.

Harper, Daria. "Current and Former Staff Complain of Racial Bias at the Getty Museum in Open Letter." *Artsy*, July 20, 2020. https://www.artsy.net/news/artsy-editorial-current-staff-members-complained-racial-bias-getty-museum-open-letter.

———. "SFMOMA Employees Call Out the Institutional Racism and Censorship in Open Letter." *Artsy*, June 24, 2020. https://www.artsy.net/news/artsy-editorial-sfmoma-employees-accused-institution-racism-censorship-open-letter.

Harris, Laurelle. "Rebuilding the Foundation: External Review into Systemic Racism and Oppression at the Canadian Museum for Human Rights." Canadian Museum for Human Rights, August 5, 2020. https://humanrights.ca/sites/prod/files/2020-08/A-FullReport_EN.pdf.

Hickley, Catherine. "'Time to Give Back the Swag, Guys!' British Museum Unleashes Twitter Storm with Statement on Black Lives Matter." *Art Newspaper*, June 9, 2020. https://www.theartnewspaper.com/news/british-museum-unleashes-twitter-storm-with-statement-on-black-lives-matter.

Holmes, Helen. "The Guggenheim's First Black Curator Is Denouncing the Museum's Treatment of Her." *Observer*, June 6, 2020. https://observer.com/2020/06/guggenheim-museum-chaedria-labouvier/.

IC-Ethics (International Committee on Ethical Dilemmas) Executive Board. "Open Letter to the President, Executive Board, and General Director of ICOM." IC-Ethics, June 22, 2020. https://www.facebook.com/ICEthics/photos/a.461450331007345/879861389166235/.

ICOM (International Council of Museums). "The Challenge of Revising the Museum Definition." November 24, 2017. https://icom.museum/en/news/the-challenge-of-revising-the-museum-definition/.

———. "Museum Definition." https://icom.museum/en/resources/standards-guidelines/museum-definition/.

Institute for Canadian Citizenship. "Interview with Museum Professionals of Colour." June 30, 2020. https://www.inclusion.ca/article/interview-with-museum-professionals-of-colour -mpoc/?fbclid=IwAR2Lq6tfmD9ZHddfLLOTR5Hhb_cE6sTod5887eBTCp_fANvfKKSY5 PPj5AM.

Jackson, Moana. "The Connection between White Supremacy and Colonisation." E-Tangata, March 24, 2019. https://e-tangata.co.nz/comment-and-analysis/the-connection-between -white-supremacy/.

Jacobs, Julia. "Firing of Museum Director Stirs Debate and an Official Inquiry." *New York Times*, July 22, 2020. https://www.nytimes.com/2020/07/22/arts/design/montreal-museum -nathalie-bondil.html.

Jones, Damian. "London Southbank Centre Workers Pen Open Letter Protesting against Redun-dancies and 'Institutional Racism.'" *NME Music News*, August 4, 2020. https://www.nme.com /news/music/london-southbank-centre-workers-pen-open-letter-protesting-against-redun dancies-and-institutional-racism-2721040.

Kinsella, Eileen. "Over 100 Current and Former Staff Sign a Letter Supporting the Controversial Firing of the Montreal Museum's Director." *Artnet News*, August 12, 2020. https://news.artnet .com/art-world/open-letter-employees-montreal-museum-firing-1901465.

Knott, Jonathan. "Icom in Turmoil after Resignations." Museums Association, July 17, 2020. https://www.museumsassociation.org/museums-journal/news/2020/07/icom-museum -definition-row-rumbles-on/.

Lederman, Marsha. "Royal B.C. Museum Responds to Accusations of Racism." *Globe and Mail*, September 12, 2020. https://www.theglobeandmail.com/arts/article-royal-bc-museum -responds-to-accusations-of-racism/.

Livingstone, Josephine. "The Whitney Museum's Careless Attempt to Curate a Summer of Black Uprising." *New Republic*, August 25, 2020. https://newrepublic.com/article/159078 /whitney-museums-careless-attempt-curate-summer-black-uprising.

Lonetree, Amy. *Decolonizing Museums: Representing Native America in National and Tribal Museums.* Chapel Hill: University of South Carolina Press, 2012.

Lynch, Bernadette T., and Samuel J. M. M. Alberti. "Legacies of Prejudice: Racism, Co-production and Radical Trust in the Museum." *Museum Management and Curatorship* 25, no. 1 (2010): 13–35. https://doi.org/10.1080/09647770903529061.

Mackie, John. "Vancouver Art Gallery Appoints New Director." *The Province*, June 25, 2020. https:// theprovince.com/news/vancouver-art-gallery-appoints-new-director/wcm/d379d22a-d44c -4cf5-998c-4dfb51dc45dc.

Maranda, Michael. "Hard Numbers: A Study on Diversity in Canada's Galleries." *Canadian Art*, April 5, 2017. https://canadianart.ca/features/art-leadership-diversity/.

Marshall, Alex. "What Is a Museum? A Dispute Erupts over a New Definition." *New York Times*, August 6, 2020. https://www.nytimes.com/2020/08/06/arts/what-is-a-museum.html.

McGlone, Peggy. "Smithsonian's National Museum of African Art Accused of Culture of Racism." *Washington Post*, July 15, 2020. https://www.washingtonpost.com/entertainment /museums/smithsonians-national-museum-of-african-art-accused-of-culture-of-racism /2020/07/15/7d63ff48-c6d8-11ea-a99f-3bbdffb1af38_story.html.

McNamara, Rea. "Why Your Museum's BLM Letter Isn't Enough." Medium, June 9, 2020. https:// medium.com/@rea.mcnamara/why-your-museums-blm-letter-isn-t-enough-33841b31b9ae.

McPherson, William. *The Stephen Lawrence Inquiry*. London: Secretary of State for the Home Department by Command of Her Majesty, 1999.

Mignolo, Walter D., and Catherine E. Walsh. *On Decoloniality: Concepts, Analytics, Praxis*. Durham, NC: Duke University Press, 2018.

Mills, Charles W. *The Social Contract*. Ithaca, NY: Cornell University Press, 1997.

MOCAD Resistance. "Former Staff Letter." *MOCAD Resistance* (blog). https://www.mocadresis tance.com/blog/former-staff-letter.

Mosleh, Omar. "'I'm Not Your Token': Indigenous Employee Accuses Alberta Museum of Systemic Racism." *Toronto Star*, June 27, 2020. https://www.thestar.com/news/canada/2020/06/27 /im-not-your-token-indigenous-employee-accuses-alberta-museum-of-systemic-racism .html.

Newport, Ashley. "Art Gallery of Mississauga Responds to Allegations of Racism, Calls for the Gallery to Cease Operations." *Insauga*, August 25, 2020. https://www.insauga.com/art-gal lery-of-mississauga-responds-to-allegations-of-racism-calls-for-the-gallery-to-cease -operatio.

O'Neill, Sean. "A Crisis of Whiteness." *Canadian Art*, June 23, 2020. https://canadianart.ca /features/a-crisis-of-whiteness/.

Pogrebin, Robin. "Upheaval over Race Reaches MET Museum after Curator's Instagram Post." *New York Times*, June 24, 2020. https://www.nytimes.com/2020/06/24/arts/design /met-museum-staff-letter-racism.html.

Rami, Trupti. "The Instagram Account 'Change the Museum' Is Doing Just That." *Vulture*, July 15, 2020. https://www.vulture.com/2020/07/change-the-museum-instagram.html.

Randle, Aaron. "'We Were Tired of Asking': Why Open Letters Have Become Many Activists' Tool of Choice for Exposing Racism at Museums." *Artnet News*, July 15, 2020. https://news.artnet .com/art-world/museum-open-letters-activism-1894150.

Sandahl, Jette. "Report and Recommendations Adopted by the ICOM Executive Board." ICOM, Standing Committee for Museum Definition, Prospects and Potentials, December

2018. https://icom.museum/wp-content/uploads/2019/01/MDPP-report-and-recommen dations-adopted-by-the-ICOM-EB-December-2018_EN-2.pdf.

Sanders, Carol. "CMHR Announces Workplace Review after Multiple Complaints of Racism." *Winnipeg Free Press*, June 10, 2020. https://www.winnipegfreepress.com/special/arts -editors-picks/cmhr-announces-workplace-review-after-multiple-complaints-of-racism -571175732.html.

Save Our Southbank. "An Open Letter on Southbank Centre's Brutal Redundancies, Their Impact on the Diversity of Our Workforce, and the Future of Southbank Centre." https://saveour southbank.com/.

Schonfeld, Roger, Mariët Westermann, and Liam Sweeney. "The Andrew W. Mellon Founda- tion Art Museum Staff Demographic Survey." Andrew W. Mellon Foundation, July 28, 2015. https://mellon.org/media/filer_public/ba/99/ba99e53a-48d5-4038-80e1-66f9ba1c020e /awmf_museum_diversity_report_aamd_7-28-15.pdf.

Statistics Canada. "Focus on Geography Series, 2016 Census." https://www12.statcan.gc.ca /census-recensement/2016/as-sa/fogs-spg/Facts-can-eng.cfm?Lang=Eng&GK=CAN&G C=01&TOPIC=7.

Thompson, Sam. "Canadian Museum for Human Rights under Fire after Allegations of Rac- ism, Discrimination Surface." CJOB, *Global News*, June 11, 2020. https://globalnews.ca /news/7053839/canadian-museum-for-human-rights-allegations-racism-discrimination/.

Unger, Danton. "'Just Appalling': Pride Winnipeg Cuts Ties with Human Rights Museum over LGBTQ2+ Censorship." *CTV News, Winnipeg*, June 24, 2020. https://winnipeg.ctvnews.ca /just-appalling-pride-winnipeg-cuts-ties-with-human-rights-museum-over-lgbtq2-censor ship-1.4998605.

Ware, Syrus Marcus. "Give Us Permanence—Ending Anti-Black Racism in Canada's Art Insti- tutions." *Canadian Art*, June 24, 2020. https://canadianart.ca/features/give-us-permanence -ending-anti-black-racism-in-canadas-art-institutions/.

Westermann, Mariët, Roger Schonfeld, and Liam Sweeney. "Art Museum Staff Demographic Survey 2018." Andrew W. Mellon Foundation, January 28, 2019. https://mellon.org/media /filer_public/b1/21/b1211ce7-5478-4a06-92df-3c88fa472446/sr-mellon-report-art-muse um-staff-demographic-survey-01282019.pdf.

Chapter 6

How Should Inclusive Museum Leadership Respond to COVID-(16)19?

Omar Eaton-Martinez

A Special Acknowledgment

We stand on the shoulders of freedom fighters who have been leading us through critical moments since the beginning of the colonial project we call museums. During this time of COVID-(16)19,[1] our field has seen responses from organizations like Museums & Race, MASS Action, the American Alliance of Museum's DEAI Facing Change initiative, the Association of African American Museum's regional discussions around COVID-19, and the thoughtful response by #MuseumWorkersSpeak in creating the Museum Workers Relief Fund, which has raised roughly $70,000 to support the economic loss of museum workers impacted by the financial threat posed by the pandemics.

Additionally, I would like to acknowledge the contributions of two African American women, Adrianne Russell and Dr. Aleia Brown, who used the hashtag #MuseumsRespondToFerguson to facilitate critical discussions interrogating the role of museums in their response to racial violence by police. They hosted monthly Twitter chats that allowed people who care about our institutions to express rage and frustration at the lack of response to these heinous acts that stem from systemic inequities.

Intersecting Pandemics Have Exposed Our Social Inequities

> COVID acts just like a spotlight
> That highlights inequities that we know are not right

—Papo Moreno

These precarious times have illuminated the impact of systemic oppression in the United States. The false premise that American exceptionalism is a foundational truth has been exposed. American exceptionalism, as a principal proposition or "cornerstone" for the United States, has multiple cracks, and the newest wave of highly publicized racial injustices, COVID-19, and climate change have been the storms that have caused the cracks to become bigger and easier to see. This moment has left our country in a weakened state. Some of us want it to return to "normal," not fully acknowledging that what was normal was also inequitable. As chaotic as life is during this moment, it was chaotic for us who lived on the margins of dominant culture before COVID-19.

An article written by Samantha Artiga, Bradley Corallo, and Olivia Pham for the Kaiser Family Foundation asserts, "Multiple analyses of available federal, state, and local data show that people of color are experiencing a disproportionate burden of COVID-19 cases and deaths."[2] Additionally, other research has consistently concluded that "Black Americans continue to experience the highest actual COVID-19 mortality rates nationwide—two or more times as high as the rate for Whites and Asians, who have the lowest actual rates."[3] Systemic inequities that impact access to wealth, health care, and education are some of the many reasons why we are seeing these disproportionate numbers of cases and deaths.

"In 2019 data of all police killings in the country compiled by Mapping Police Violence, black Americans were nearly three times more likely to die from police than White Americans," writes Willem Roper in an article he wrote for Statista. Black people make up 24 percent of police killings in the United States but only 13 percent of its population.[4] These asymmetric statistics not only represent quantitative evidence of systemic racism but also serve as a metaphor that there are those of us who are Afro Latinx, African American, Latinx, and Indigenous who experience a lived reality that is marked by unsteadiness.

The intersecting pandemics of COVID-1619 (racial injustice), COVID-19, and climate change impart a disproportionate burden on those who are valued less (or not at all) because of their race, ethnicity, gender, class, and a host of identities that are marginalized in our society. We must consider the impact of intersectionality, a concept derived from Critical Race Theory (CRT), which describes the interconnected nature of social categorizations such as race, class, and gender as they apply to a given individual or group, regarded as creating overlapping and interdependent systems of discrimination or disadvantage. For example, the oppressive burden of black women existing in this space becomes exponentially worse.[5]

For some White people, these last several months have caused a "pricking" in ways they were not prepared for, personally or professionally. Pricking usually happens when a person is presented a new truth or a new perspective on an existing truth. This experience can give people new insight, which allows them to develop a conviction that did not exist before. For example, as a black Puerto Rican, I grew up like many Puerto Ricans *de aquí o de allá*,[6] with the false premise that Puerto Rico is a racial democracy. As I began my investigative journey to make meaning of my blackness, I started to discover that Puerto Rico has a history of racism, which still permeates the island and its culture today. For me, the pricking happened when I was visiting family and doing research in Puerto Rico in 1998. My great-uncle took me to the island of Vieques, which is where my maternal side of the family lived before they came to the San Juan metropolitan area of Puerto Rico. During that trip, my great-uncle showed me places on the island where my Black grandfather and White grandmother had to sneak around during their courtship for fear of my grandmother's family finding out that she was being courted by a black man. That "aha" moment caused me to be convicted to understand that there are variations of racism and they all have a traumatic impact on our humanity.

For other White people, it has sparked a combative nature rooted in White fragility[7] and a false urgency toward a scarcity mind-set. This type of thinking begets stress and anxiety, which compromise people's ability to empathize and share space with others they perceive as different or "lesser than." Predominantly White museums have made decisions about layoffs and furloughs that disproportionately affect people of color. This did not necessarily happen because there were White leaders singling out Black, Latinx, Asian American, or Indigenous employees. However, it did happen because systemic racism influences who and how we hire and for which types of labor we hire them for in our museums. In some cases, this means that the jobs that people of color tend to hold are the most vulnerable for reduction in pay, furloughs, or layoffs.

Skills and Knowledge That Help Me Work through These Chaotic Times

Empathy

This term literally means to be "in your feelings." The ability for a museum leader to empathize allows them to understand and share the feelings of another. Empathy is an interpersonal skill and a key element of Emotional Intelligence.[8] According to www.SkillsYouNeed.com, there are three types of empathy (cognitive, emotional, and compassionate).[9]

1. Cognitive empathy is when a person takes the time to think of another person's perspective. This type of empathy does not imply connecting with a feeling. It is possible for a museum leader to think about what it is like for their frontline staff to have their jobs taken away without developing an emotional connection. Cognitive empathy can also be described as the skill exercised during a game of chess. You want to see the board from your opponent's perspective so that you can move your pieces and achieve your objective of checkmate.

2. Emotional empathy is when you connect with the other person's emotions as if they were your own. This also has been described as "catching" another person's emotions, which promotes a deeper understanding of their feelings. The negative side of emotional empathy is when these connections engulf you and create what is called empathy overload. Museum leaders must exercise self-care in order to maintain emotional and mental health. Additionally, they must empathize with members of their staff who do not have the ability to take personal leave and find new ways to support their health. Many of us view our work as critical in supporting social justice and racial equity in our communities, and with all that is going on in the world today, we can feel burned out.

3. Compassionate empathy is being connected to someone's emotions in a way that convicts you to take action. As museum leaders, we must not only understand other perspectives and connect emotionally but also be pricked to do something. According to Bryan Stevenson, the founding director of the Equal Justice Initiative, this type of empathy takes proximity. In a lecture Stevenson gave at the 2016 Carnegie Summit, he said, "You cannot be an effective problem-solver from a distance. There are details and nuances to problems that you will miss unless you are close enough to observe those details."[10]

In a futuristic article I wrote for the Museum 2040 edition of AAM's *Museum* magazine, I wrote imaginatively about a high tech solution to build compassionate empathy,

> [A] team of computer scientists named We Are Wakanda (WAW) developed an advanced immersive virtual technology to support a program they called "Take a Walk in My Shoes" (TAWIMS). This now-familiar program allows the user to explore a virtual world as a person with a different ethno-racial, gender, or sexual orientation. As museums nationwide began to reorganize missions, visions, and governance to more evenly distribute power and privilege, WAW decided that TAWIMS would be most effectively deployed in museums.[11]

As museum leaders we must envision our institutions as spaces where different people can be proximate to encourage compassionate empathy.

Humility

Dominant culture behavior does not privilege humility. Let me be even clearer: the society we live in rarely privileges a humble leader. However, we as community members—and more specifically, museum leaders—have an opportunity to model behaviors of modesty and meekness during these pandemics. These times are unprecedented, and even the most seasoned and savvy leaders are going to be wrong in addressing some of these issues. Museum leaders must be reminded that there is strength in admitting they're wrong about a decision. If you look at the etymology of the word *humble*, it literally means "on the ground," which is a reminder for leaders to step down from their proverbial ivory towers and lock arms with their staff and communities in which we serve and are co-stewards. This requires self-awareness that comes from periodic self-reflection and the type of listening that produces cooperative conversation.

Exercising humility can be difficult for museum leaders. We are all socialized to believe that the "squeaky wheel gets the oil." As a cisgendered black Puerto Rican man, I have certainly felt the pressure to have to constantly prove my worth to my employers. The asymmetric binary of black excellence versus White mediocrity has been the lived experience for many people of color. However, it is crucial that we find ways to rebuke this racist norm by remembering that there is strength in acknowledging your shortcomings. It is an opportunity for you as a leader to then lift someone else's work so that they can be recognized exemplifying the importance of collaborative work. I am reminded that there were people of different races, ethnicities, and genders who lifted my work up in an exercise of humility. Our call to action as museum leaders is to pay those acts of kindness forward.

These intersecting pandemics have revealed our blind spots. It is incumbent upon us as museum leaders to make humility our "superpower." Drafting organizational #BlackLivesMatter statements are meaningless without being honest and humble about your workplace culture, the demography of your museum and the content of your exhibitions and programs. Instead of drafting statements from the top floor for the public image of a museum, let us write them from "on the ground" floor expressing your museum's conviction to take a stand for our collective humanity. This positionality allows museums to remove the proverbial "beam from their own eye" so that they can be active about their own shortcomings, making their social advocacy statements more genuine.

Coalition Building

In order to increase our capacity to deal with the intersecting pandemics, we must build and sustain coalitions with community members. As stated earlier, these intersecting pandemics have had a disproportionate impact on people of color and other intersectional identities on the margins of dominant culture. However, everyone has been impacted at some level. This means that these intersecting pandemics represent a common oppressor. If we recognize this collectively, then it becomes an impetus to seek community members out to be in "locked arm" in rebuke of these systems of oppression.

History has shown that it is possible for communities to work across boundaries to take a stand for their humanity. There was an uprising in the colony of Virginia in 1676 that involved the enslaved,

White indentured servants and Indigenous people in opposition to a White planter elite. In the 1960s, we have the Poor People's Campaign, which was initiated by Dr. Martin Luther King Jr. before he was murdered in Memphis, Tennessee. This campaign brought poor people from every hue to the National Mall in Washington, DC, to build Resurrection City to address poverty as a national issue. This preceded the Occupy movement.[12] The Poor People's Campaign was a six-week, live-in demonstration in Washington, DC, that attracted protesters nationwide to mark a new era in American history.[13] The 1960s also birthed the original Rainbow Coalition, which was a coalition active in the late 1960s and early 1970s, founded in Chicago, with members from the Black Panther Party, Young Patriots Organization, and the Young Lords as a civil and human rights movement. It later expanded to include various radical socialist groups. These grassroots organizations represented the diversity of the African descendant, Latino/a/x, Indigenous, Native American, and Asian American communities. They also found a common oppressor in poverty, police brutality, access to public health, and fair housing.

A great example of coalition building in the museum field was the formation of Museums & Race: Transformation and Justice, a movement to challenge and reimagine institutional policies and systems that perpetuate oppressions in museums. The movement began with a convening that was supported by The Museum Group (TMG)[14] with the help of Dr. Porchia Moore and nikhil trivedi in January 2016. The convening brought together approximately two dozen museum professionals, representing diversity across race, gender, sexuality, experience, type of museum, and job title. I was included in this group and attended the convening. Later on, in 2016, Museums & Race became an independent movement united against systems of oppression in museum spaces. I was part of its all-volunteer steering committee, which modeled a pluralistic leadership from May 2016 to January 2020. This model increased our capacity to effect radical change in our field. It produces an environment that values diversity, draws on the collective voices and resources from our field. This type of coalition building better positioned this movement to fully integrate multiple perspectives so it could tackle the complexities of systems of oppression that tend to intersect organically. In the last four years, Museums & Race has produced a menu of critically acclaimed programming, organizational tools, and a virtual conference that are all a result of coalition building.

Dr. Johnnetta Betsch Cole, an iconic leader and a mentor to many of us in the museum sector, always quoted the African proverb that states, "If you want to go fast, go alone. If you want to go far, go together." As inclusive leaders, we must remember that dismantling systemic oppression is a marathon, not a sprint. It takes patience, but more important, it takes long-suffering. The difference between the two is that long-suffering is the exercise of patience despite troubles that you may experience. This work is not for the weary, which is why it is imperative that we build coalitions to hold each other up in times like we are experiencing now.

Our Response to the Murders of Ahmaud Arbery, Breonna Taylor, and George Floyd

Currently, I work for the Department of Parks and Recreation, Prince George's County. Our department is part of the larger Maryland–National Capital Parks and Planning Commission (M-NCPPC). The division I work for is the Natural and Historical Resources Division, which oversees the historic preservation, natural conservation, and interpretation of historic sites, archaeological parks, museums, natural parks, and nature centers. I am the assistant division chief for historic resources, so I support the great work of this history side of our division.

One of the units that falls under my supervision is the M-NCPPC Black History Program, which provides year-long programming on the black experience as well as the management of three historic sites. One of their signature programs is our annual Juneteenth[15] Festival, which for the last few years has been held at Watkins Regional Park with attendance that has reached six thousand people! The festival has served as a type of homecoming for local communities and the region at large. The experience is a mixture of hands-on history, arts and crafts, food vendors, nonprofit exhibitors, and a live stage filled with musical performances. In the recent years, we have used Juneteenth as a platform to celebrate black culture as an expression of the freedom the holiday signifies.

Like many organizations in 2020, our programs have been making the virtual pivot to online programming. The Black History Program, led by Dr. Dennis Doster, has an internal and external committee that it collaborates with to organize the event. We knew there was interest from our communities to be able to develop a Virtual Juneteenth in lieu of not being able to come together physically. However, managing this transition to virtual was not the only thing on the top of our minds. Many of us on the Juneteenth Committee are of African descent, and our White colleagues have been allies to us in this work for years. We were feeling the burden of the intersecting pandemics in planning for the Virtual Juneteenth program. The committee recognized this as an opportunity to take our programming beyond the celebration of black culture. This is where our *compassionate empathy* convicted us to something different to acknowledge the murders of Ahmaud Arbery, Breonna Taylor, and George Floyd, as well as countless other murders that were more local to our communities.

I put together a proposal for a panel titled "I Can't Breathe"[16] that would be the opening program for Virtual Juneteenth 2020 to the Juneteenth Committee. The purpose of the panel was to examine the history of racial violence and the interconnections between enslavement, lynching, and twenty-first-century police killings. The committee reviewed the proposal and decided to move forward with producing the panel. When I put together the proposal, I was thinking about how to invite panelists who would lift up the voices of historians, mental health professionals, and activists. My idea was to elevate these voices in order to create an interdisciplinary connection concerning the consistent anti-black racial violence in this country. The creation of this panel was also amid the newest wave of the call to defund the police. Initially, I did not have a member of the panel representing law enforcement. This was a blind spot[17] for me. As a black Puerto Rican man, I have experienced racial profiling by the police. Having those negative experiences influenced how I view police. I had to *humble* myself by acknowledging that shortcoming so that this panel could bring forth the voice of law enforcement to this timely discussion. I invited our Park Police chief, an African American man, who gave incredible voice to the need to support defunding the police and more accountability for law enforcement's role in violence toward people of color. Without that exercise of humility, I could have silenced this important voice that our communities really needed to hear.

We also enacted our ability to *build coalitions* with organizations like the Maryland Lynching Truth and Reconciliation Commission, Prince George's County Memorial Lynching Group, StandUp! (student activists), and M-NCPPC Park Police. The amalgamation of these organizations produced historical truths, awareness of trauma-informed care, grassroots activism, and empathy from law enforcement. One of the components of the program that I am most proud of was a spoken-word poem written and recited by my then sixteen-year-old daughter Sanai titled "I Can't Breathe."[18] This poem was a national finalist for the national "I Matter" spoken-word competition organized by the National Youth Foundation. Here is an excerpt of the poem:

I haven't been able to breathe since I was born

*When society decided the melanin in my skin was not something
to be uplifted but a tragedy to be mourned*

I'm still struggling to breathe

Her poem is a metaphorical uprising, which signifies that the intersectionality of her race, ethnicity, gender, and age are not being heard. As inclusive museum leaders, it is absolutely essential that we are proactive with our "hearing." If we continue to fail in this capacity as leaders, these cries will only become louder and more frequent.

As inclusive museum leaders we must affirm the following:

- We must believe that our museums are conveners of social action that allow people to see the humanity in one another.
- We must believe that our work informs the conscience of the communities we serve.
- We must be able to decrease allowing others to increase in the spirit of humility and meekness.
- We must dismantle the colonial project of museums centering empathy while cultivating cocreation with our communities through strategic coalitions.

These affirmations have helped me think about being a museum leader during these chaotic times. Septima Poinsette Clark, an African American educator and civil rights activist, talked about how she dealt with chaos in her work in the often-quoted statement, "I have great belief in the fact that whenever there is chaos, it creates wonderful thinking. I consider chaos a gift."[19]

Let's do something radically different and embrace the chaos as a gift so that we can create wonderful thinking!

Notes

1. *COVID-(16)19* is a term to describe the intersecting pandemics of racial injustice and COVID-19. The year 1619 marks the landing of the first enslaved Africans in English-occupied North America in August 1619 at Virginia's Point Comfort. In 2019, the 1619 Project led by Nikole Hannah-Jones, *New York Times* journalist, aims to reframe the country's history by placing the consequences of slavery and the contributions of black Americans at the very center of national narrative.
2. Samantha Artiga, Bradley Corallo, and Olivia Pham, "Racial Disparities in COVID-19: Key Findings from Available Data and Analysis." Kaiser Family Foundation, August 17, 2020, https://www.kff.org/racial-equity-and-health-policy/issue-brief/racial-disparities-covid-19-key-findings-available-data-analysis/.
3. APM Research Lab, "The Color of Coronavirus: COVID-19 Deaths by Race and Ethnicity in the U.S.," October 15, 2020, https://www.apmresearchlab.org/covid/deaths-by-race.
4. Willem Roper, "Black Americans 2.5X More Likely Than Whites to Be Killed by Police," Statista, June 2, 2020, https://www.statista.com/chart/21872/map-of-police-violence-against-black-americans/.
5. Intersectionality was made popular by Kimberlé Crenshaw, an African American woman, lawyer, civil rights advocate, and scholar.
6. *De aquí o de allá* (from here or from there) is a Puerto Rican euphemism describing the binary of Puerto Ricans on the island and the Puerto Rican diaspora.
7. The term *White fragility* refers to the defensive reactions White people have when their racial worldviews, positions, or advantages are questioned or challenged. This term was coined by Robin DiAngelo, a White American woman and educator.

8. Emotional Intelligence is the measure of an individual's abilities to recognize and manage their emotions, and the emotions of other people, both individually and in groups. See https://www.skillsyouneed.com/general/emotional-intelligence.html.
9. "Types of Empathy," https://www.skillsyouneed.com/ips/empathy-types.html.
10. Leandra Fernandez, "Empathy and Social Justice: The Power of Proximity in Improvement Science," *Carnegie Commons Blog*, April 21, 2016, https://www.carnegiefoundation.org/blog/empathy-and-social-justice-the-power-of-proximity-in-improvement-science/.
11. Omar A. Eaton-Martínez, "Truth + Reconciliation: Museums as Advocates for Human Rights and Healing," *Museum*, November/December 2017.
12. The Occupy movement is an international progressive sociopolitical movement that expresses opposition to social and economic inequality and to the lack of "real democracy" around the world. It aims primarily to advance social and economic justice and new forms of democracy.
13. Smithsonian National Museum of African American History and Culture, "Welcome to Resurrection City!," Public Program, May 12, 2018, https://nmaahc.si.edu/event/welcome-resurrection-city.
14. The Museum Group is a consortium of museum consultants founded in 1995 by independent professionals who had held leadership positions in museums. Their mission is to work with museums to help them achieve their greatest potential in an ever-changing world.
15. Juneteenth is the oldest nationally celebrated commemoration of the ending of slavery in the United States. Dating back to 1865, it is also called Freedom Day or Jubilee Day.
16. This is a slogan associated with the Black Lives Matter movement in the United States. Most recently the slogan has been associated with the murders of George Floyd and Eric Garner who were put in a choke hold by police, but it has historical connections to lynching in the United States as well.
17. The term *blind spot* describes the act of recognizing the impact of biases on the judgment of others while failing to see the impact of biases on one's own judgment. The term was created by social psychologist Emily Pronin.
18. Sanai R. Eaton-Martínez, "I Can't Breathe," *Freedom's Plow* (blog), July 4, 2020, https://www.freedomsplow.org/blog/i-cant-breathe-sanai-eaton-martinez.
19. Read the Spirit, "Septima Clark," accessed March 13, 2021, https://readthespirit.com/interfaith-peacemakers/septima-clark/.

Bibliography

APM Research Lab. "The Color of Coronavirus: COVID-19 Deaths by Race and Ethnicity in the U.S." October 15, 2020. https://www.apmresearchlab.org/covid/deaths-by-race.

Artiga, Samantha, Bradley Corallo, and Olivia Pham. "Racial Disparities in COVID-19: Key Findings from Available Data and Analysis." Kaiser Family Foundation, August 17, 2020. https://www.kff.org/racial-equity-and-health-policy/issue-brief/racial-disparities-covid-19-key-findings-available-data-analysis/.

Eaton-Martínez, Omar A. "Truth + Reconciliation: Museums as Advocates for Human Rights and Healing." *Museum*, November/December 2017.

Eaton-Martínez, Sanai R. "I Can't Breathe." *Freedom's Plow* (blog), July 4, 2020. https://www.freedomsplow.org/blog/i-cant-breathe-sanai-eaton-martinez.

———. "I Can't Breathe." In *I Matter*, edited by Isabella Hanson, 8. Chadds Ford, PA: National Youth Foundation, 2020.

Fernandez, Leandra. "Empathy and Social Justice: The Power of Proximity in Improvement Science." *Carnegie Commons Blog*, April 21, 2016. https://www.carnegiefoundation.org/blog/empathy-and-social-justice-the-power-of-proximity-in-improvement-science/.

Read the Spirit. "Septima Clark." Accessed March 13, 2021, https://readthespirit.com/inter
faith-peacemakers/septima-clark/.

Roper, Willem. "Black Americans 2.5X More Likely Than Whites to Be Killed by Police." Statista,
June 2, 2020. https://www.statista.com/chart/21872/map-of-police-violence-against-black
-americans/.

Smithsonian National Museum of African American History and Culture. "Welcome to Resurrection City!" Public Program, May 12, 2018. https://nmaahc.si.edu/event/welcome-resurrec
tion-city.

Chapter 7

Hope Is Not a Metaphor

An Annotated Guide to Twenty-Five Essential Skills
for Museum Leaders

Lisa Yun Lee

I sit at my desk waiting for the reminder alarm for the next online staff meeting, trying to finish this chapter as the night air is filled with protest chants about defunding the police and armed militia and curfews are commonplace. At this moment as the twin viruses of COVID-19 and racism ravage communities, with global uprisings making demands for racial and economic justice, what are the necessary skills for museum leaders?

"The role of the cultural worker," Toni Cade Bambara suggests, "is to make the revolution irresistible."[1] This idea always resonates with me, and it is one of the reasons why I chose to become a museum worker. Cultivating spaces for collective joy, finding ways to unleash people's radical imaginations, and communicating knowledge through art, artifacts, and material culture is enthralling work. It requires one's full self, because it demands the emotional and affective labor of cultivating care, compassion, and empathy in visitors. The best museums encourage people to think differently, feel deeply, and act with conviction.

My work as the executive director of the National Public Housing Museum (NPHM) is filled with joy. The work includes overseeing the renovation of the last remaining building of the Jane Addams Homes, a three-story brick 1938 Works Projects Administration housing project that was home to thousands of America's working poor. NPHM is an unapologetically activist museum, and our expansive and capacious vision to serve as a community anchor includes exhibits, education, and creative programming that harness the power of place and memory to address questions around housing insecurity. Our mission is to preserve, promote, and propel the right of all people to a place where they can live and prosper—a place to call home.

As a member of the International Coalition of Sites of Conscience, NPHM fervently believes that, in order to solve today's most pressing social issues, we need to go back in time and ask: What have we yet to learn from history? Our methodology includes a commitment to bridging history, arts, culture, and public policy in order to create a more inclusive process for addressing housing insecurity. We emphasize the deep interconnected threads between storytelling, accepting individual and collective accountability, and the equitable distribution of resources. Through an effort to collect the oral histories of public housing residents, NPHM is expanding the nation's foundation of stories that are preserved and told in order to unleash the radical imaginations of visitors and to be a catalyst for action. NPHM's efforts include the development of a cultural workforce training program as a part of a community benefits agreement with the neighborhood, a commitment to prevent gentrification and displacement as we grow, and a museum store that will be a cooperative owned with public housing residents.

In these strange and precarious times, I am also planning an online memorial for a board member who passed during the pandemic, and sending flowers to another, whose husband may need to be put on a respirator. I have made notations to the Oral History Archive about narrators who have died from COVID-19. I redo budgets over and again, trying to forecast for every possible scenario, and I have made decisions about who is the bossiest and most officious staff member to serve as our COVID-19 safety officer. On top of all this, I am fielding late-night calls from city officials asking if the museum would be interested in accessioning a statue of Columbus that has finally been taken down after several weeks of peaceful protests that were met with extreme police violence.

In order to navigate these times, I have depended on skills and knowledge acquired through a mixture of formal education and on-the-job training from the past two decades, ever since my first institutional leadership position as the director of the Jane Addams Hull-House Museum. But honestly, the skills that I rely on, over and again, are those learned from activists, artists, and organizers. My chosen family includes radical intellectuals informed by Black feminist thought and a cadre of movement builders committed to remaking this broken world into a better place for all of us. They are my "beloved community," and I trust them to hold me accountable to vision, mission, and values as a human being, rather than just a museum director.

In these past months of sheltering at home with my parents, I have also spent long evenings listening to my mother share stories of my ancestors, and her experiences *táo luàn* (逃难)—the mandarin phrase for fleeing as a refugee during war. I have come to realize how much I am informed by the resilience and artful survival strategies of the matriarchs of my family. They were Chinese women, who survived foot-binding, leapt into peanut bushes to hide from bombing raids, and bore witness to the rape of Nanjing. My mother immigrated to the United States and gave up her dreams of becoming a poet because she didn't speak the language, and she managed to find community, open and run a family business, and create a safe home for me and my sisters, all while enduring the traumas of racism and discrimination. My ancestors (see figure 7.1) taught me, by example and with encouragement, how to find my voice and speak truth to power when those in power would rather silence you or would rather you be invisible. The theme of the 2020 American Association of State and Local History conference this year asked: What kind of ancestor will you be? It is a question that my friend and colleague Omar Eaton-Martínez asks whenever I see him. Omar never fails to remind us that, as museum professionals, we should strive to be the types of ancestors that changed the course of history by how we steward it. What will future generations say about us?

Figure 7.1 A photo of my ancestors, with my mother in the center, and my grandmother seated in the dark dress. Lisa Yun Lee

In many ways, the skills for now have nothing to do with trends or newness. They are informed by old-fashioned knowledge handed down through generations. Below is a partially annotated list (marked by an asterisk) of the skills and knowledge for museum leaders in these times:

1. The largest artifact in your collection is your building. Acknowledge that it is on stolen land. Recognize the Indigenous people who occupied, and continue to steward, that land.*
2. Go ahead. Make election day and Juneteenth paid holidays.
3. Cherish Maxine Greene's maxim: *"The most important questions are those without answers."*
4. At some point, the history of your institution will disappoint you. Tell this history, and take responsibility for the past. Begin to make amends and restore justice.
5. Honor this truth: "It's always someone else's story first," Rebecca Solnit has written, "and it never stops being their story too, no matter how well you tell it, how widely you spread it."[2]
6. Acknowledge #MuseumsAreNotNeutral.*
7. Remember that listening is not waiting for your turn to talk.
8. Ella Baker's movement-building philosophy is also true for institutions: "Strong people do not need strong leaders."
9. Invest in a modern Human Resources Department.*

10. Everything worth doing is done with others.
11. Share authority with community members, and recognize that you never had the authority in the first place.*
12. Instead of promoting self-care, facilitate collective care.
13. Fiction and poetry are useful devices for interpreting history.*
14. Recognize that if you aren't engaging in relevant contemporary social justice struggles, you are not doing your job.
15. Love, imagination, and play will be as important to your daily work as any museum-specific skill.
16. Cultivate spaces for collective joy.
17. If you run a historic site, don't forget that somebody's labor, often unacknowledged, helped build the site. This history is important to tell.
18. Value the dedicated people who clean and care for any museum. They do the work that makes all other work possible.
19. Create a Community Benefits Agreement with your neighbors.*
20. The shortest difference between two people is a story.
21. Diversity is a fact. Insist on racial equity.
22. Welcome all visitors with radical hospitality and critical generosity.*
23. Never forget that every archive, and any collection, is incomplete.
24. If you are really paying attention, you will need to redo your wall text to be more inclusive, over and again, because the struggle is eternal. If you are successful, you will always need to become more capacious in your definition of who your audience includes.
25. Practice hope as a discipline.*

Annotations on the preceding list:

#1. Although land acknowledgments have become a part of a larger #DecolonizeMuseums effort, it is important for museum leaders to grapple with what is most "unsettling" about decolonization. In this respect, the work of Eve Tuck and K. Wayne Yang is profoundly important. Tuck and Yang argue that our understanding of decolonization should be firmly situated in the repatriation of Indigenous land and life.[3] This means that decolonization is not a metaphor for other important goals that we may aspire to in order to improve museums and societies, like hiring Indigenous curators, or including more Indigenous artists in our collections, or paying fair wages. Tuck and Yang convincingly argue that the easy adoption of decolonizing discourse turns decolonization into a metaphor, and this metaphorization makes possible a set of evasions, or what they describe as "settler moves to innocence." These evasive efforts, even if well intended with social justice as an aim, problematically attempt to reconcile settler guilt and complicity, and rescue settler futurity. Instead, they argue for "an ethic of incommensurability" that recognizes what is distinct and what is sovereign about Indigenous life and land.

#3. I never had the privilege of meeting the great Maxine Greene, who was the founder and director of the Center for Social Imagination, the Arts and Education at Teachers College, Columbia University. My mentor and friend Bill Ayers, also at the forefront of educational philosophy, is so fond of quoting her that I feel I have learned so much from her. She had another favorite saying: "I don't want to save the world. I just want to start a conversation."

#6. Arundhati Roy has famously said: "The trouble is that once you see it, you can't unsee it. And once you've seen it, keeping quiet, saying nothing, becomes as political an act as speaking out."[4] Too many museums have been complicit in reinscribing power and privilege under the cover and claims of neutrality throughout history. #MuseumsAreNotNeutral is a global advocacy initiative coproduced by La Tanya S. Autry and Mike Murawski to expose the myth of museum neutrality. The initiative began in August 2017 through an online T-shirt campaign and the social media hashtag, and it has engaged more than one million people across social media platforms to demand equity-based transformation across institutions.

#9. One of the most important things that museum leaders can do for their organizations is to strengthen from the inside by investing in a full-fledged and modern Human Resources (HR) Department. HR has ever-expanding responsibilities and priorities during economic uncertainty and the pandemic, and the need to ethically respond to issues of sexual harassment, racial equity, and accessibility, while always important, has never been so urgent as now. Instead of regarding HR as the henchmen for the chief financial officer, as prurient compliance officers, or simply a first-line of defense for crisis management, HR could be the moral compass for an institution, and a safe place to acknowledge and help negotiate power and privilege in institutions committed to justice in an unjust world.

#11. One of the best handbooks for sharing authority is *Letting Go? Sharing Historical Authority in a User-Generated World*, an anthology edited by Bill Adair, Benjamin Filene, and Laura Koloski.[5] Through thought pieces, case studies, conversations, and artworks by nineteen leading cultural practitioners (Jack Tchen, Nina Simon, Fred Wilson, and many others), the contributors deftly explore the implications of twenty-first-century audiences who can become active cocreators of knowledge, rather than passively receive information.

#13. Jules Prown makes this point beautifully in his important essay, "The Truth of Material Culture: History or Fiction," where he suggests that artifacts may reveal deeper truths when interpreted as fictions rather than as history. Prown suggestively argues "in one sense history consistently uses small untruths to build large untruths. . . . On the other hand, literature can weave small fictions into profound and true insights regarding the human condition."[6] This is not a license to play fast and loose with historical fact but, instead, a reminder that artistic license, poetry, and literature can play a role in the work of interpretation. At the Jane Addams Hull-House Museum, we worked with writer Terri Kapsalis to develop a book-length label for Jane Addams's travel medicine kit that captivated visitors.[7] Terri partnered with pharmacists and forensic experts at the University of Illinois at Chicago to test the pills in Jane Addams's travel medicine kit, and paired observations about this scientific investigation with a meditation on rest and restlessness, antagonism and peace, and domesticity and social justice.

#19. NPHM is proud to have signed a Community Benefits Agreement (CBA) with public housing residents. Our agreement includes a commitment to inclusive hiring practices, paid internships for public housing youth, and engaging resident voices in exhibits and programming, and it extends to monitoring gentrification in the surrounding neighborhood and advocating against displacement, in recognition of the possible long-term impact of successful cultural institutions in previously economically depressed areas. One of the most high-profile museums to negotiate a CBA is the Obama Presidential Center (OPC), which, after a long-protracted struggle, finally agreed to some of the demands around six areas of concern: economic development, education, employment, housing, sustainability, and transportation.[8] Recommendations of the coalition include the following: 30 percent of profits set aside for affordable housing for new and rehab construction, freezing of property taxes for longtime residents, local hiring for all jobs connected to the OPC, and a creation of a Black business corridor.

Hope Is Not a Metaphor

79

#22. Radical hospitality moves beyond simply being "friendly" to a concerted effort to make all people feel truly welcome. I first encountered this captivating notion in the work of poststructuralist philosopher Jacques Derrida while in graduate school. In his poetic text, *Of Hospitality*, Derrida focuses on breaking down barriers that prevent people from participating in an effort, campaign, or community.[9] Derrida demands a lot from the reader, so I will try to efficiently explain his approach to hospitality that can be so useful for reimagining the relationship between museum and visitor. Derrida deconstructs the relationship between a "Host" and the guest, who he refers to as a "foreigner, or a stranger" (the French term *étranger* covers both concepts). Derrida distinguishes between two kinds of hospitality. The first is conditional hospitality, where the guest is forced to ask for hospitality, and must faithfully answer according to the law: What is your name? Where do you come from? In this form, the host recognizes and tolerates the guest but also reminds the guest that she is not in her own house. In contrast, Derrida describes an unconditional form of hospitality, which does not depend on a guest's identity or status but, instead, relies on the host to commit to a relationship of radical openness to an absolute, indistinguishable other. In this way, the host breaks with the law, in one sense, and is able to most fully realize their identity as a host. Derrida argues that the stranger is then a liberator that allows the host to most fully become free. Although poststructuralist theory can be difficult and outlandish at times, I have found this idea illuminating regarding the relationship between museum and visitor.

Critical generosity is an idea that I came across through the theater scholarship of Jill Dolan[10] and David Román.[11] They both make the case for an ethic of critique or criticism that can be generative, rather than antagonistic or agonistic. For example, when you encounter someone with a different point of view or belief, instead of dismissing, judging, berating, or convincing them to be otherwise, you seek to understand how and where they came to that belief. The effort is directed toward understanding and developing an ongoing social relationship and committing to a larger project of collective world making. It is harder to do this in practice than in principle.

#25. Abolitionist Mariame Kaba eloquently insists, "Hope is a discipline."[12] In this philosophy, hope doesn't preclude feeling sad, frustrated, or angry—and/or any other emotion. But hope, itself, isn't a feeling. And it isn't blind optimism. It is a practice. Hope is something that we practice every day. It involves organizing with others—and the belief that there is always a potential for transformation and for change. Practicing hope as a museum leader in these times is essential. Listen to episode 19 of the podcast *Beyond Prisons*.[13] It is revelatory.

Notes

1. Thabiti Lewis, *Conversations with Toni Cade Bambara* (Jackson: University Press of Mississippi, 2012), 35.
2. Rebecca May Solnit, "To Break the Story, You Must Break the Status Quo," Literary Hub, March 26, 2019, https://lithub.com/to-break-the-story-you-must-break-the-status-quo/.
3. Eve Tuck and K. Wayne Yang, "Decolonization Is Not a Metaphor," *Decolonization: Indigeneity, Education and Society* 1, no. 1 (2012): 1–40.
4. Arundhati Roy, *Power Politics* (Cambridge, MA: South End Press, 2002), 7.
5. Bill Adair, Benjamin Filene, and Laura Koloski, *Letting Go? Sharing Historical Authority in a User-Generated World* (Philadelphia: Pew Center for Arts & Heritage, 2011).
6. Jules David Prown, "The Truth of Material Culture: History or Fiction?," in *History from Things: Essays on Material Culture*, ed. Steven D. Lubar (Washington, DC: Smithsonian Institution Press, 2000), 1–19.
7. Terri Kapsalis, *Jane Addams' Travel Medicine Kit* (Chicago: UIC College of Architecture & the Arts, 2011), http://cdn.flipsnack.com/iframehtml5/embed.html?hash=fzc30utd&fullscreen=1&startIndex=0&previous_page=true&startPage=1&t=13603557341360356177&bwd=1&pbs=1&v=4.8.

8. Chicago City Council, "Obama CBA Residential Area Affordable Housing Pilot Ordinance," Community Benefits Agreement (CBA) for the area around the Obama Center, July 24, 2019, http://www.obama cba.org/ordinance.html.
9. Jacques Derrida and Anne Dufourmantelle, *Of Hospitality* (Stanford, CA: Stanford University Press, 2000).
10. Jill Dolan, "Critical Generosity," *Public: A Journal of Imagining America* 1, nos. 1 and 2 (2013), https://public.imaginingamerica.org/blog/issues/volume-1-issue-1/.
11. David Román, *Acts of Intervention: Performance, Gay Culture, and AIDS* (Bloomington: Indiana University Press, 1998).
12. Mariame Kaba, quoted in Brian Sonenstein and Kim Wilson, "Hope Is a Discipline," episode 19 of *Beyond Prisons* (podcast), January 5, 2018, https://podcasts.google.com/feed/aHR0cHM6Ly9iZXlvbmR wcmlzb24ubGlc3luLmNvbS9yc3M/episode/OGY4NjFjMzQ5NjJjYzljMmFjMjVjY2QwZjZhNDg5Z TU?sa=X&ved=0CAUQkfYCahcKEwiAvfWO8dPuAhUAAAAAHQAAAAAQAQ.
13. Sonenstein and Wilson, "Hope Is a Discipline."

Bibliography

Adair, Bill, Benjamin Filene, and Laura Koloski. *Letting Go? Sharing Historical Authority in a User-Generated World*. Philadelphia: Pew Center for Arts & Heritage, 2011.

Chicago City Council. "Obama CBA Residential Area Affordable Housing Pilot Ordinance." Community Benefits Agreement (CBA) for the area around the Obama Center, July 24, 2019. http://www.obamacba.org/ordinance.html.

Derrida, Jacques, and Anne Dufourmantelle. *Of Hospitality*. Stanford, CA: Stanford University Press, 2000.

Dolan, Jill. "Critical Generosity." *Public: A Journal of Imagining America* 1, nos. 1 and 2 (2013). https://public.imaginingamerica.org/blog/issues/volume-1-issue-1/.

Kapsalis, Terri. *Jane Addams' Travel Medicine Kit*. Chicago: UIC College of Architecture & the Arts, 2011. http://cdn.flipsnack.com/iframehtml5/embed.html?hash=fzc30utd&fullscreen=1&startIndex=0&previous_page=true&startPage=1&t=13603557341360356177&bwd=1&pbs=1&v=4.8.

Lewis, Thabiti. *Conversations with Toni Cade Bambara*. Jackson: University Press of Mississippi, 2012.

Prown, Jules David. "The Truth of Material Culture: History or Fiction?" In *History from Things: Essays on Material Culture*, edited by Steven D. Lubar, 1–19. Washington, DC: Smithsonian Institution Press, 2000.

Román, David. *Acts of Intervention: Performance, Gay Culture, and AIDS*. Bloomington: Indiana University Press, 1998.

Roy, Arundhati. *Power Politics*. Cambridge, MA: South End Press, 2002.

Solnit, Rebecca May. "To Break the Story, You Must Break the Status Quo." Literary Hub, March 26, 2019. https://lithub.com/to-break-the-story-you-must-break-the-status-quo/.

Sonenstein, Brian, and Kim Wilson. "Hope Is a Discipline." Episode 19 of *Beyond Prisons* (podcast), January 5, 2018. https://podcasts.google.com/feed/aHR0cHM6Ly9iZXlvbmRwcmlzb24ub

Glic3luLmNvbS9yc3M/episode/OGY4NjFjMzQ5NjJjYzljMmFjMjVjY2QwZjZhNDg5Z
TU?sa=X&ved=0CAUQkfYCahcKEwiAvfWO8dPuAhUAAAAAHQAAAAAQAQ.

Tuck, Eve, and K. Wayne Yang. "Decolonization Is Not a Metaphor." *Decolonization: Indigeneity, Education and Society* 1, no. 1 (2012): 1–40.

Chapter 8

2020: A Harsh Teacher for Leaders

Terri Lee Freeman

In November 2014, I made the decision to take on a career challenge and accept the position of president of the National Civil Rights Museum at the Lorraine Motel in Memphis, Tennessee. The Lorraine Motel was the assassination site of Dr. Martin Luther King Jr. The National Civil Rights Museum is accredited by the American Alliance of Museums and a member of the International Coalition for the Sites of Conscience. The motel, which was being auctioned by the City of Memphis, was saved by Memphis businessmen and supported by the state of Tennessee to become the nation's first museum devoted to the American civil rights era and movement.

I came to the museum with a sense of both adventure and commitment—adventure because I was stepping into an entirely new sector and commitment to work toward Dr. King's legacy, not of racial harmony but of equity for Black folks in the United States. I was on a mission to use the museum as a platform to discuss the issues of the day, for dialogue on difficult topics like race, equity, and othering, and to provide a place of learning that connected the incredible history told on the walls and through the twenty-four exhibits at the museum to the contemporary, everyday issues and challenges Black, Indigenous, and People of Color (BIPOC) have to wrestle with every day. Most important, my desire was for the museum to be viewed as a public square, a place where people could gather to discuss, debate, and dialogue about issues and be inspired to create solutions. And for the past six years, that is what our museum has done, and it has brought a different energy to the museum and certainly created a different level of expectation of the National Civil Rights Museum.

As a cultural institution that is devoted to telling the story of the very difficult history of oppression, terrorism, and second-class citizenship of Black people, fast forwarding to 2020 and the issues that seemed to be an epiphany to many other cultural institutions was not a difficult transition. From the murder of Trayvon Martin, to the uprisings in Ferguson, Missouri, and Baltimore, Maryland, and from the slaughter of nine members of the Mother Emmanuel Church to the White supremacist murder of Heather Heyer in Charlottesville, Virginia, we were steeped in these issues of racial discrimination and social injustice. Helping our guests and visitors better understand the history of a successful citizen movement and the very long, very real tail of racism became integral to our mission of chronicling the history of the American civil rights movement.

And we would not have it any other way. We hope our guests leave the National Civil Rights Museum having more empathy and a better understanding of the tragedies that were turned into triumphs as well as the hard work yet to be done.

What has been interesting is the realization that, until recently, many arts and cultural organizations have not embraced their role as public squares, trusted community spaces that have a responsibility to chronicle and tell the truth, the good, the bad and the ugly. Even more disturbing is the understanding of how cultural institutions themselves can and have been purveyors of a false narrative that does not recognize their own history of oppression and discrimination against BIPOC communities. These institutions have not been welcoming nor have they included representation of these communities in their collections. Or worse, they have included those artifacts but have not accurately interpreted their story or included those populations in their institutions to tell their own story.

So we continue on this journey to create equity and provide inclusive environments that don't simply represent different races, ethnicities, and abilities but also include those voices. As much as I would like to profess that I am totally and fully there and am always an inclusive leader, I think it is more accurate to say that I always seek to be an inclusive leader. But I admit sometimes I must be reminded to be more expansive in my approach. Leading a museum that focuses on civil rights history we sometimes interact with guests who ask our non-Black employees why they work at the museum. This is particularly true for our non-Black tour guides. My response: what a short-sighted question! But I guess that is where we have been in our society. Women's history can only be presented by women, Latinx history can only be interpreted by those with Latinx heritage. Native and Indigenous history requires individuals from that group to discuss that proud and extensive history. It is exactly this line of thought that has us thinking and acting in specific buckets that continue to isolate us as opposed to uniting us. Our institutions should represent us, the holistic us. Thus, our first step needs to ensure representation throughout our organizations. And as we expand representation, we must provide space for those voices to not just have a seat at the table but also help create the table.

I've always strived to have an inclusive and collaborative approach to work and management, but the pandemic has made me question if I've been inclusive enough of all levels of the organization. While the social injustice issues that have been revealed over the course of spring and summer 2020 have made many organizations question their commitment to equity, the COVID-19 pandemic has clearly illustrated how, even in a museum structure, there are those who have more options (privilege) than others.

Nothing has tested my leadership as much as 2020. In my previous role, I had the responsibility of developing a philanthropic response for survivors of the 9/11 attack at the Pentagon. That work was hard. It required a very collaborative response. And it pushed my staff to work hard during a time when other people could get away from what happened while we spent basically every hour of every day for the next six weeks focused intently on what we named the Survivors' Fund. Work on that fund continued for seven years. But it was not 2020.

On March 17, 2020, the doors of the National Civil Rights Museum closed due to COVID-19. The Board of Directors agreed that the museum would maintain all staff at full salary through mid-April. As the weeks progressed, we were able to secure a Paycheck Protection Program loan. It became painfully obvious that the museum would need to be closed for longer than hoped and that employee furloughs were inevitable. While there was a cross-section of employees who were affected by the furlough, the majority of them worked on the floor of the museum. They were guest services, retail, and tour guides. These were jobs that could not work remotely; they required the facility to be open for them to complete their jobs. Recognizing the hardship and the shock of being furloughed, we applied for unemployment for each employee affected. As CEO, I personally talked with each employee furloughed along with our human resources manager and gave them the opportunity to ask any questions. It was stressful all-around. I could not help thinking about those employees who were working parents trying to home-school their kids, protect themselves and their families from the virus, and now going on unemployment. The enriched unemployment cash benefits made it easier to think about valued employees out of work, but I knew that each of those folks wanted to be assured that they would have a job to come back to.

Meanwhile, our administrative staff continued to work, I think harder than ever, from their remote locations. It was clear that this crisis shone a light on the "we/they" dynamic that I worked so hard to eliminate during our usual operations. But clearly, there was a level of "privilege" to be able to work from home remotely versus losing your job to furlough. That said, everyone was still receiving a paycheck. Managing through this crisis would need to be a collaborative and inclusive process; it could not simply be me putting my head down and making decisions. In this instance, inclusion was the entire senior team and the Board of Directors.

It was proven that nothing brings out creativity like a good crisis. Our goal was to maintain relevance during the shutdown, like so many organizations using the virtual world as our canvas. And we needed to bring in some funding given our doors were closed. And then George Floyd happened. Not only were we relevant, but we became a central meeting point for local protests. The National Civil Rights Museum was in the middle of an active civil rights movement in the middle of a global pandemic!

Every decision that was made was a management group decision. Leadership could not be concentrated in one person; it had to be dispersed among the group. There was no time to micromanage; we had to believe in our people. I had to believe in my direct reports. So we multitasked, hosting protest gatherings, encouraging people to wear masks and to social distance, lifting our institutional voice and communicating about the obvious systemic injustices that were occurring, broadcasting virtual programs, and reminding people that we had an election coming up and voting would be paramount. Oh, and we raised money, significant amounts that really helped us with general operating and programming costs.

It was now time to plan for our reopening, which was frankly scarier than closing during a pandemic. While my loyalties were to the organization, I had serious concerns for the staff who would have to work on the floor of the museum and interact with people from various locations. Our local jurisdiction required us to submit a plan to the city; once approved, we would be able to reopen to the public. Our reopen date was July 1, 2020. Prior to reopening, we held a face-to-face socially distanced staff meeting with the 50 percent of furloughed staff we were able to bring back to the museum. We explained our new protocols, the changes to the facility and the exhibits, and the requirements for returning staff and visiting guests. There were obvious concerns about reopening and having to interact with people. Despite the masks, sanitation stations, increased cleaning of the exhibits, plexiglass barriers and the planned timed, online ticketing, returning staff were concerned for their health and the health of their families. I encouraged employees to make known their concerns to their direct supervisor or me. In the end, three employees asked to delay their return. One decided not to continue their employment at the museum.

At this writing, we have brought back a few additional employees, but one-quarter of the staff remains on unemployment. What I've learned during these four months is that transparency requires intentionality. Demonstrating your vulnerability during trying times is equally important. Just because we sit in the seat of leadership does not give us all the answers. I have continued to thank employees for helping me build this airplane while in the air. There is no playbook for leading through a pandemic. Maybe we are writing it now. But currently, we must try things and make course corrections as we go. It requires staff to trust leadership and leadership to be honest, open, and timely with their communication to staff. It requires executive leadership to talk directly with line staff, and you need to have a thick skin. I thought I was doing everything right. I was monitoring our numbers and sticking to our stated ticket maximums. But as time went on, we began overselling our admissions to accommodate our guests. That decision was not always weighed against the concerns and anxiety of the staff. That decision was often made by employees privileged to not have to work on the museum floor every day. That meant the decision makers were not the ones coming face to face with guests who didn't always socially distance appropriately.

One of the best moves I made was to invite a psychiatrist to a staff meeting. It was a Zoom meeting, and it really leveled the playing field. Staff let us know about their concerns and anxieties. They let us know that sometimes guests are inappropriate and often get too close to staff on the floor. They let us know that the museum sometimes gets too crowded for comfort during a pandemic. And they let us know that they didn't feel like they were being heard. It also allowed our senior team to express their concerns, fears, and anxieties and help the line staff understand that we feel and bleed just as they do and we truly are in this together. This meeting served as the impetus for me to meet with each department individually, gather more information, and express to them that I wanted to listen and act appropriately. I have expressed, as I did in 2001 working on the Survivors' Fund, that self- care is a necessity to help us get through these stressful times. What good is it if we save the world but lose ourselves in the process? Sometimes it is OK to not be OK. We just have to let someone know.

These meetings are continuing. We will have a second meeting with the psychiatrist in January 2021. I am sure we will have new concerns, fears, and anxieties post-election, but we will have gotten through 2020. That must be worth something!

So, here are my leadership takeaways from a year that has thrown one challenge after another at us.

1. Evaluate the situation and identify your team.
2. Keep abreast of the relevant news. Not everything is important.
3. Balance solutions that benefit the organization and benefit employees.
4. Communicate, communicate, communicate.
5. Understand that transparency requires honesty and the ability to ask for forgiveness.
6. Recognize that the crisis is not just happening to "them" but also to you.
7. Have a thick skin; be prepared for people to challenge your leadership and your decisions. That will come from both staff and board.
8. Understand that your team wants to make it work. Take advantage of their skills and creativity. Move out of their way!
9. Let staff experience the leader as human being. Be a storyteller to help people get through the most difficult times.

10. Be willing to get dirty and understand the job that line employees are performing. Spend some time walking in their shoes.
11. Remember the crisis will pass.

The year 2020 has made me a better leader. It has also shown me how important our institutional role is as a public square. The museum, being open, provides a safe place for people to go in a time where safe places seem to be limited. But more important, during an awakening to social injustices that persist, to help people understand the historic roots of today's issues is very gratifying. Not everyone agrees with the truth we present, but we do just that—present the truth. We can't make people accept it, but we certainly make people think about it and challenge their long-held beliefs.

In 2018, we worked ourselves nearly to death to present a fiftieth commemoration of the assassination of Dr. King for the world. Similarly, we will look back on 2020 and be proud of the contributions we made helping people understand the times and appreciate the importance of knowing the full story of what has made our nation, our nation—while also inspiring them to act and help build a more perfect union!

Chapter 9

Doing the Work

Because Checking the Box Isn't Enough

Dina A. Bailey

I am a list maker. Though, let's be real, I don't just make lists. I am an *Olympic-level* list maker. For example, I ensure that I literally have little boxes next to my color-coded action items so that I can check them off. It feels true to say that those little check boxes give me a sense of accomplishment, a feeling of success, an affirmation that I am *doing* something, and (self)recognition that I have done that something *well*. Cool. Cool, cool, cool. Except . . . what happens when I want to check off items on my list titled, "Inclusive Leader," and what action items would I even have on that list? I felt a little bubble of anxiety just writing that. You may have felt one just by reading it. Most of us can admit, on an intellectual level, that it is impossible to actually become an inclusive leader by creating a list and checking off action items; and, on an instinctual level, that the force is strong—like Jedi strong—to hold onto the idea of a list like your life and career depend on it. Of course, two things can be true at the same time. It can be impossible to create a comprehensive list, check things off, and be an inclusive leader just by following those actions; *and* it can be possible to create an infinite list—a list that is a never-ending road map on a lifelong journey. Pause for a second to get comfortable with that idea—the list you crave is actually *a never-ending road map on a lifelong journey*. This chapter will help shift the emphasis from that check mark of completion to the satisfaction felt in actually doing the work—and the desire to continue to do it.

Progress through Shared Understandings

An aspect of this emphasis shift comes with working toward shared understandings. First, we may not know exactly where we are going, but we can have a shared understanding of where we do *not* want to go. As an individual, and the leader of an organization, do you already see some of the potential pitfalls and hazard signs on your road map? Do you already know where there might be resistance? Do you feel like some people you work with are saying the right things, but you aren't convinced that they really know what the words mean? Do you say the right things but (if you're honest with yourself) haven't prepared as much as you should have before proclaiming that you've been awake the whole time? Sometimes we learn what we do want as we name what we don't want.

In the work of diversity, equity, accessibility, inclusion, antiracism, decolonization (and so many others), a shared understanding of language is essential. And that does not mean sharing out a glossary of terms—and checking it off your list. Having a shared understanding of language means knowing the words; what they mean generally; what they mean to your organization; how the words will be practically applied within the spaces that you control or influence; and then intentionally, accurately, and consistently using the language in connection to the concepts they embody. For example, diversity is a state of being—we are all diverse—while inclusion is a state of action. Diversity is not a euphemism for Black individuals or People of Color or "the other people." We find buy-in, and responsibility, in what we feel a part of. You are a part of that ideal "diverse organization" that people keep talking about. Inclusion requires intentional, ongoing action. It recognizes both current contexts and past exclusions in ensuring a context where a diverse group of people have the opportunities and access needed to share power/authority, genuinely listen, actively learn, make equitable decisions, and take positive actions.

To continue this emphasis shift, it is essential to have an understanding of where we are so that we know where we have been and where we need to move next. I am aware of both how easy that sounds and how difficult it is in reality. As an inclusion and antiracism consultant, this is where I always begin with a client. We are individuals who are on individual journeys. Each person's path is unique—sometimes we cross, sometimes we run parallel, and sometimes we become inextricably interwoven with others' paths. We are, by nature, social creatures, and our individual experiences can also be part of the makeup of collective experiences. For example, as an individual, you have your own lived experiences and patterns of knowledge that are unique to you. Your experiences are currently being influenced by your board, your staff, and members of the communities in which your organization sits. You are also impacted by the legacies of historical events (broadly and institutionally) and the historical and contemporary harms done—intentionally or unintentionally—to you, by you, around you, or within you.

As you begin (or continue) inclusion work, you need to hold up a mirror and acknowledge what is reflected back. There are a number of ways to do this. We will get to practical application later in the chapter; for now, just know that there is a pattern that repeats over and over on an inclusion journey: finding, assessing, reflecting, acknowledging/truth-telling, and addressing to ensure non-recurrence. In terms of awareness of inclusion/exclusion in theory and in practice: Where are you as a leader? Where is your board? Where is your staff? and, when you mix all of those together, Where is your organization when it comes to societal, local, organizational, and individual work that needs to be done?

And, finally, in preparing to set out (again) on an inclusion journey, what have been some of your catalyzing moments? What is your *why* for committing to this journey? As an individual, and as a leader, you will need to have answers to those two questions if you want to sustain yourself for the long term. Your answers might change from life/career season to season, but you should always have that conscious awareness of your reasons for doing this work—especially in the moments when it is hard or uncomfortable or exhausting. One of my most consistent whys has become consolidated in my mind over time; it came to me when I went through the Greater Cincinnati YWCA's leadership program. The short version is, "Lift as we climb." The longer version comes from Mary Church Terrell, who stated:

And so, lifting as we climb, onward and upward we go, struggling and striving, and hoping that the buds and blossoms of our desires will burst into glorious fruition ere long. With courage, born of success achieved in the past, with a keen sense of the responsibility which we shall continue to assume, we look forward to a future large with promise and hope. Seeking no favors because of our color, nor patronage because of our needs, we knock at the bar of justice, asking an equal chance.[1]

This is one of my essential whys; it is at the heart of my purpose. There is no significant separation for me between "work" and "life" in this. As I continue my journey, I always come back to this—especially in the moments when I would rather check something off the list and set my sights on the next section of my path. What are your whys? Take a moment to pause here. Breathe deep. Recenter yourself.

Centering Yourself aka Getting Control of Your Checklist

In *Emergent Strategy: Organizing for Social Justice*, adrienne maree brown has named core principles that we may use to center ourselves.[2] They include the following:

- Small is good, small is all (the large is a reflection of the small).
- Change is constant (be like water).
- There is always enough time for the right work. There is a conversation in the room that only these people at this moment can have. Find it.
- Never a failure, always a lesson.
- Trust the people (if you trust the people, they become trustworthy).
- Move at the speed of trust.
- Focus on critical connections more than critical mass—build the resilience by building the relationships.
- Less prep, more presence.
- What you pay attention to grows.

As a consultant, I work with leaders, and their organizations, to take this list (which is acceptable in theory) and ensure that the practical application is interwoven throughout the organization. For example, what did it mean to "be like water" when you had just checked off the last item on your "Gala Prep" Checklist—including having signed a lot of contracts—and then the entire country's path shifted to one of working from home, social distancing, and worrying about how to pay for groceries (let alone all of the other bills)? Or how do you focus on "less prep, more presence" when you were focused on finalizing aspects of your annual Juneteenth event in the moment that George Floyd was murdered in Minneapolis, Minnesota, and your community rose up in anger and pain and mourning? Center yourself in your whys and the whys of your institution; don't be controlled by your checklist.

Leadership and trust are inextricably connected. They require vulnerability and honesty with yourself and with others. What answers do you have to these questions:

- How do you define, and exemplify, inclusion?
- How have inclusion and exclusion been structured (formally or informally) in your institution?
- What are the greatest obstacles to DEAI (diversity, equity, accessibility, and inclusion), decolonization, and antiracism efforts within your organization?
- How do you move at the speed of trust when involved in DEAI, decolonization, and antiracism efforts?

- What does it mean to be an inclusive leader in practice; and how do we imagine this practice spreading throughout the organization?
- What do you need to learn about yourself, others, and your organization?

Many leaders start with good intentions. There is a desire to lead in a way that moves forward DEAI, decolonization, and antiracism. However, good intentions aren't enough. And, even with the best of intentions, the impact can still be harmful. That acknowledgment often leads to fear. That fear often leads to spinning. . . . And spinning can lead to anger, frustration, sadness, and uncertainty.

In centering yourself as a leader, and the work that you and your organization need to do, be courageous in honestly reflecting on historic and current harms. Learn more about DEAI, decolonization, and antiracism so that you are able to make informed decisions and take more effective actions. Every organization is unique. As the leader of your organization, take into account how quickly your board, staff, and community are prepared to move. We are, at heart, social creatures. You can't lose your focus on the "quiet middle;" those who are neither at the front of the trend (who believe you aren't moving fast enough) or those at the back of the trend (who believe you are moving way too fast). Move at the speed of trust.

In essence, it is important to ensure that you feel confident in an understanding of your beliefs, convictions, and philosophies. It is necessary to have clarity about your personal insecurities, uncertainties, and passion points—and how those connect to you as a leader of your organization. Embrace this as a season of both learning and action. Be self-aware, be curious, be humble. Be kind to people who are trying to figure all of this out, encourage people to keep moving, and hold yourself and others accountable. There are many museums, and workers in them, that don't see any egregious or obvious problems or exclusions in their museums. What are the signs? Where should you start? What is the difference between "needs" and "desires" in this work? It is, perhaps, instinctive to make lists upon lists as you determine what needs to happen. As we move from philosophy/intention to practical application/impact, find your "heart center"—the core of your being (individually and as an organization), the home of your sense of self.

Moving from Theory to Practice

What skills do you need for this moment? Transformation often becomes sustainable when we recognize the journey as a marathon rather than a sprint. Preparation is essential. Pacing will make or break you. Rehydration is life sustaining. And celebrating smaller accomplishments can lead to celebrating bigger wins. The development of a strategic action plan for your DEAI, decolonization, and antiracism efforts should be just as collaborative, detailed, and measurable as your organizational strategic plan. It is your road map.

As you consider best practices, recognize the value of having a guide for your journey. Many leaders believe that they can change the organization by themselves when it comes to DEAI, decolonization, and antiracism. It is not uncommon for this to lead to heightened tensions and harm. Some leaders have the knowledge and emotional intelligence already; others will need to grow these two aspects. Regardless, inclusion efforts are exceptionally delicate when it comes to

- mandatory versus voluntary participation;
- top-down- versus bottom-up-driven change; and
- performative versus authentic actions.

Perhaps the most obvious directional indicator on your road map is assessment. Create a baseline that you can use for comparison in the future. Analyze individual, organizational, and community readiness. Determine strengths, challenges, opportunities, and threats. Review what knowledge gaps are prevalent. Clarify the current landscape in connection to past actions and inactions. Acknowledge where you need help and ask for it. Intentionally move forward; sometimes that first movement feels like the most difficult one.

The Board

While inclusive organizations recognize the importance of leadership at all levels, there is an acknowledgment that success is highly influenced by the board and their interest in and capacity for movement. Board members should participate in the individual and organizational assessment. They should center themselves and develop a shared understanding of terms, concepts, and accountability. Many times, this includes training. Some leaders just want to ensure that the board will not be a barrier while others want the board to take active and visible roles in the process. Expectations should be set, and roles and responsibilities should be negotiated and agreed upon before too much time has taken place and the board and staff are in drastically different mind-sets.

We must also recognize that board members are volunteers. And while there may be (seemingly or real) differentiations in power dynamics between board members and other organizational volunteers, there may be similar approaches in encouraging collaboration, participation, expectations, and accountability. Similarly, the foundational themes for training are the same: shared language, theory, contextualization, and agency/call to action.

Staff

In many ways, those foundational themes remain the same for staff as well. In addition, there is often a greater depth and breadth in terms of training. Staff have more diverse ways to move the organization forward in terms of practical application, for example, asking curators to review all of the permanent and temporary exhibitions through the lens of equity. That has been done, or not done, when we ensure that exhibitions not only include a diversity of stories but also are equitable in levels of interpretation, inclusive in decision making about the changes that need to be made, and accessible regarding cost, physical accessibility, psychological/emotional triggers, and such.

Training for the organization is important. Knowing what training is right for you during this moment of your journey can help you move more effectively and more efficiently. There is, of course, a difference in DEAI training, decolonization training, and antiracism training. In some ways, they are like a Venn diagram—distinct and yet overlapping. If you are hiring a consultant, be clear in what you are asking for. Don't ask for antiracism training and then be upset that you didn't get to talk about sexism, homophobia, or ageism. Don't ask for DEAI training if the moment is really calling for your organization to talk about White supremacy, racism, and antiracism. Don't search out training on decolonization if you aren't ready to acknowledge that colonization continues today. At the same time, the three that I've named are "on trend" right now, but really reflect on how leadership/management, communication, transparency, resilience, and organizational culture all significantly influence DEAI, decolonization, and antiracism efforts.

I'll add two notes, here, specific to staff: First, organizations naturally lean on their education and programmatic teams to fulfill institutional needs for DEAI, decolonization, and antiracism. While these teams may have more comfort and may have been doing this work pretty naturally, it is not solely the responsibility of these teams. DEAI, decolonization, and antiracism should be woven throughout every aspect of the organization; only then will you be able to confidently say that you are an inclusive organization. Second, organizations also lean on human resources (HR) departments. Many leaders believe that putting DEAI, decolonization, and antiracism efforts in the care of HR is a natural fit. However, holding these efforts within the HR department can create barriers in vulnerability—because effort will be seen as directly connected to job security.

The Director

Fragility often causes particular strain for leaders. They don't want to admit that they don't know, or are uncomfortable, or are not prepared to lead an organization on this particular journey. For example, is it OK for a director to emote during a meeting about past harms done to him? Does it depend on how he identifies? Is crying in the presence of your staff/board OK? Showing emotion is not bad. At the same time, leaders should remain aware of the power dynamics and emotional labor this activates in others.

How does one have difficult conversations about aspects connected to DEAI, decolonization, and antiracism? It's the same way that you would have difficult conversations about other aspects of your individual and organizational work. Know your thoughts, come from a place of curiosity, create spaces that are at least safe (ensure no recrimination) and ideally spaces where bravery is embraced, and be open to changing your mind. If there is a hint that you or your staff are not prepared, then please don't try to facilitate these conversations yourselves. Note, I am not encouraging you to *not* have a conversation; I am encouraging you to find the correct support. Similarly, if you get into a conversation and it is going downhill fast, don't keep going. I am not encouraging you to stop forever; I am encouraging you to pause in order to recenter yourself and provide time and space for others to do the same.

The Organization

Organizations are made up of individuals. The journey is an individual journey where people are moving (hopefully) in the same direction in order to present a collective transformation. As you consider what authentic inclusion looks like from an organizational perspective, review what extractive practices look like. Have you intentionally or unintentionally been extractive in connection to individual staff members, the entire staff as a whole, or members of the community? What does extraction look like in your particular context? And, along this line of thought, now would also be the moment to focus in on what the norms are within your organization. How do traditional/normalized forms have to change? It is not just about bringing in new/different staff members or board members or community partnerships. It is about fundamentally adapting how people work together (inclusion).

Why Checking the Box Isn't Enough

People check boxes. It's a thing. It helps us celebrate wins. As a fellow checklist maker, I can empathize. It isn't so much that checking the box is the problem. It's the mind-set behind that check mark. DEAI, decolonization, and antiracism work is "generational work," meaning you may not see the ripples of your efforts for seven generations or more. Still, generational work should be part of your why. It is an understanding that what you do now, the decisions you make and don't make, will have an impact, and you want to make sure that it is the most positive/constructive impact that you can make.

Do the work. Start with yourself. Recognize what you can control, what you can influence, and what you have a vested interest in. Those are not always the same. Keep the faith. This work is collective in that each person brings a unique perspective and value to what needs to be done. Feel free to make small moves, but keep moving forward. Build confidence and trust, and you will be able to make bigger moves faster. If you succumb to a barrier, practice resilience. And, perhaps my best advice . . . make the courageous choice over and over again.

Notes

1. Terrell, Mary Church, "What Role is the Educated Negro Woman to Play in the Uplifting of Her Race? (1902)," in *Twentieth-Century Negro Literature*, ed. Daniel Wallace Culp, (New York: Arno, 1969).
2. brown, adrienne maree, *Emergent Strategy: Shaping Change, Changing Worlds* (Chico: AK Press, 2017), 41.

Bibliography

brown, adrienne maree. *Emergent Strategy: Shaping Change, Changing Worlds*. Chico: AK Press, 2017.

Terrell, Mary Church. "What Role is the Educated Negro Woman to Play in the Uplifting of Her Race? (1902)." In *Twentieth-Century Negro Literature*, edited by Daniel Wallace Culp. New York: Arno, 1969.

Chapter 10

To Be of Use and Beloved

A Conversation with Kelly McKinley

As coeditors of The Inclusive Museum Leader, *we recorded a conversation with Kelly McKinley in October 2020, in the midst of the coronavirus pandemic, just a mere eight months after she'd started her new position as the CEO of the Bay Area Discovery Museum (BADM) in Sausalito, California. Kelly is a well-established museum leader known for her commitment to community engagement, and this is her first turn at the helm. When we talked, we found her grappling with what it means to serve the community as a children's museum and survive as an organization. While doing so, she is clear-eyed about her purpose and her vision for the BADM.*

Cinnamon Catlin-Legutko: When you think about children's museums, what societal values show up in museum spaces? How do you see values show up in the kids and their families? Do these values align with the organization's values?

Kelly McKinley: I think children's museums come out of a fundamental belief that when you invest in children, when you invest in their earliest years, you will have better long-term outcomes for families and communities. There are very few places where children from different walks of life can gather and make sense of their world together. As schools become increasingly segregated, there are less and less places for children to do that. I think that's one way I see societal values showing up in the foundation of children's museums. But, then I'm struck by the precarity of children's museums, particularly now in this pandemic moment. Children's museums, on one hand, manifest society's understanding of, and commitment to, play-based learning and childhood development, and how that sets children up for a life of well-being. Yet, at the same time, children's museums are so poorly funded. How is it that these organizations that are powerful complements to formal education in those early years can be left to flounder so quickly? Their missions are built on this visionary idea for the potential of investing in children and ultimately the well-being of communities, but their business models are heavily reliant on ticket sales and earned revenue. They're not understood or invested in as part of the larger ecosystem of essential community services and infrastructure serving the well-being of children and their caregivers.

Chris Taylor: It's such a tough conundrum. Because, as we're talking about values, there's stated values, and there's lived values, and actions speak louder than words.

Kelly: I am also thinking about the privilege of play. Who gets to play, and who gets to be lined up at the front of our museum at 8:30 on a Saturday morning with their children in tow? How might we create opportunities for all different kinds of people to experience play, not just those who have the luxury and privilege of a nine-to-five job and ample leisure time?

What will it take for children's museums to be able to fully embrace their foundation, setting children up for success in their lives by giving them access to intentional and joyful play-based experiences to make sense of their world? What would it mean to make that available to all children?

Chris: It's a big question. Let's talk a bit about your Board of Trustees because they also influence the responses to these questions you are asking your team. Your board is engaging in Facing Change: the American Alliance of Museums' national board diversity and inclusion program.[1] Can you tell us how this initiative is structured, and how the board is engaged? And what do you hope comes out of that work, in terms of some type of change, or direction, or support for you as you move forward?

Kelly: Our board has just joined the program. We have a large and committed board of thirty-four people, and for many of them this is their first formal board experience or large board experience. This is different in comparison to other museum boards across the country who tend to be older, and more established donors and philanthropists. Similar to other museum boards nationally, our board is predominantly White, I along with our board's executive committee, felt that Facing Change would be a really powerful learning opportunity, not just for the cohort and the organization but also for individual board members. It is also an important step in creating the foundation for the museum's DEAI [diversity, equity, accessibility, and inclusion] work, making the change on the inside in order to think about serving the community in new ways.

We have just participated in our first retreat. The first year of the Facing Change program is about looking at the personal mind shifts required to communicate and build relationships across difference. The second year is really focused on the interpersonal and structural shifts that have to occur in order to be a more inclusive organization, and to govern in a more inclusive and equitable way.

My hope is that the board will understand that having a more diverse array of voices—and life experiences—around the governance table will make us a more sustainable organization on both sides of our bottom line. On the mission side, and the money side. And it is the right thing to do; it is the moral thing to do. If we're claiming to serve the full diversity of the community then our board should represent the full diversity of the community. In order to be able to have the kinds of community impacts that we desire as an organization, we need to have the voices of those communities around the table. We will not be able to sustain ourselves on both sides of the double bottom line if we are not more inclusive and representative of the full diversity of perspectives, needs, and desires of our community.

Chris: So, let's say the board representation changes, how will this impact you in the director role in terms of articulating and implementing your vision? How critical is that to your success?

Kelly: I'll start with my vision. I'm interested in what it takes for a museum to be both beloved and of use to its community, truly of use. Having a board that is bringing all of the dimensions of the community experience, their needs and wants to the table, will help us understand how we might be both of use, and beloved. This is really interesting to me. Board composition is an important first step in building deep understanding of the needs and composition of the community you serve. It allows you to have different kinds of conversations and make different kinds of choices around how best to deploy all of your resources (your money, expertise, power, facilities) for community benefit.

Our museum serves almost four hundred thousand people a year on-site and off-site, which is a strong success indicator for an organization of our size. But, when you look at who they are, and where they're coming from, you get a more nuanced picture of our success. Despite many programs designed to remove financial barriers to participation, we tend to serve a very particular demographic, one that is largely White and affluent. We clearly have more work to do to not just remove barriers to participation but also more clearly align with the interests and needs of low-income communities and communities of color. I think museums have a very powerful role to play in making our communities better places for everyone to live. We can't do that if we don't have the full breadth of experience represented around the governance table.

Cinnamon: Your museum is well established in the Bay Area community and widely known. But do you have a foundation to build on for diversity, equity, accessibility, inclusion work? Has there been action that precedes you that you're building on, or do you feel like you're starting at square one?

Kelly: I would say that there is a foundation. There have definitely been conversations about the urgency and need to address DEAI, but I don't think there has been a real concerted effort to dig into what that means for this institution in this place. So, what do I mean by that? The institution has invested intensely and successfully in programs that go out into the community. We're a museum, by the ocean, in a National Park, with no public transit, in Marin County. Marin County is predominantly a wealthy, and White, county. The psychological and geographic barriers to participation are pretty significant for our organization, and there has been a concerted effort and investment over many years to bring the museum into the community. For example, we have the *Try-It-Truck*, a mobile engineering studio that goes to community festivals, libraries, and schools across the nine Bay Area counties, at either no cost, or highly subsidized. We rely on trusted, years-long partnerships with local school districts and county libraries to support teachers and librarians to integrate play-based and hands-on learning into their curriculum and programming.

The museum has also built a robust program to remove financial barriers to participation. For example, we have a Family Access Membership. For $35 low-income families can have all the same benefits and unlimited access to the museum as someone who pays the full membership (which is $159.95). In addition, we have an open-door policy. Anybody who shows up at the museum and balks at the ticket price, we let them in (ticket prices start at $14.95). We are also participating in the Museums for All program. In partnership with the Institute for Museum and Library Services (IMLS) and the Association of Children's Museums, families with EBT [electronic benefit transfer] cards can get into the museum for a dollar each.

Cinnamon: This is a really important goal and important transition. It's not a simple fix. Can you identify what kind of skills and strategies you're bringing with you from your career to help begin this work? What is top of mind as you're thinking about implementing strategies? You've been working in inclusive spaces for a while, and I'm wondering, what telegraphs over?

Kelly: I would say first and foremost the skill to paint a vivid and compelling picture of what's possible. And not just what's possible, but also why it's important coupled with a sense of urgency to start the journey to get there. I think that's the most important thing because it takes years of work on many people's parts to be an inclusive, diverse, and community-engaged organization. Having most recently worked at the Oakland Museum of California, an organization that has been committed throughout its fifty-year history to doing this work, I have direct experience with what happens when you commit the time and the resources to doing this work. I have seen the concrete payoffs of this work on both sides of the double bottom line. I think in any process of change where the road is long and challenging, and requires the participation of lots of people along the way, being able to paint a vivid picture of the destination, and the outcomes associated with that destination, is so important. It's important for focus and for inspiration.

I have also learned that the path to that destination, to be being a more beloved and useful museum, has to be shaped by the players both inside and outside the organization, and the particular context within which you work. The path needs to shift and adapt as people come and go and new opportunities and challenges present themselves. Growing up as a leader in more traditional and hierarchical museum contexts, like art museums, and then going to a place like the Oakland Museum of California (OMCA) and working for Lori Fogarty,[2] I learned a lot about the role of personal courage and conviction in leading this work. More specifically, given that there is no one, set path to being a more relevant and inclusive museum, I learned you need to be crystal clear on why you're doing the work, to be open about what you don't know, find strength in the vulnerability of not having all the answers, and to ask for lots of help. So I guess what I brought to this new role is a sense of what's possible, some experience on the path, and knowing some of the people who could potentially help guide us along that path.

Chris: Now, I have three different questions that I want to ask all at the same time! I want to ask about the number of programs that are reducing barriers and access into the museum, which I consider external work, but am also thinking about the internal work that needs to happen. Do you have a sense of what has happened prior to you, or what you see as that work moving forward to balance that external effort with the internal shifts that need to happen as well?

Kelly: I would say BADM was just getting started on the internal work, including the beginning of conversations about what DEAI might mean to BADM. They had drafted a DEAI statement and had engaged a consultant to develop tools and a series of staff training workshops around the socially constructed dynamics of diversity. This work has also been included into our staff onboarding training. They had also started a program where each month a different department would share a video, a book, or an article related to DEAI with the whole staff. Staff would discuss insights and implications for their work at departmental meetings, then share out key takeaways at all staff meetings. Additionally, the HR team had started reviewing and revising job descriptions to eliminate bias.

We're now taking the next step to get the board connected to this work through the AAM [American Alliance of Museums] Facing Change initiative. I've also launched what we're calling the DEAI Alliance. This is a staff team drawn from across the organization (self-nominated or nominated by peers) who will partner with the leadership team to think about and plan on an annual basis where we want and need to go next in our DEAI work. The idea is that we need to chart a path forward together, to determine what our internal DEAI work is going to look like, and what are the desired outcomes. To commit to this work means trade-offs and choices, so how can we partner across the organization to navigate those together? We're doing this at the same time as we're working on our strategic plan.

It's really those three things that have to happen in tandem to put down the micropiles, or the foundations, to be able to sustain the change over time: first, the board coming to terms with what it will take to govern a diverse and inclusive museum; second, the strategic plan that describes how we're going to resource and advance our mission; and third, the culture and competencies we need as a staff to be a more relevant and inclusive organization. Before we can create a sense of welcome and belonging for our whole community, we first need to ensure that BADM is a place where staff of all backgrounds and identities feel like they belong and is a place where they can bring their whole self to work every day. We also need to start growing new skills and capacity to be more responsive to the most pressing and evolving needs of the families we serve.

We're early, early on, and we've got our foot on all three of those pedals. I don't think they're going to move in sync by any stretch—that would be impossible to pull off. Now that we're open to the public again, and we understand what our budget is for next year with a reduced head count, we're coming back to this work. We now have two cochairs for the DEAI Alliance. Together with the leadership team and the board, our first job will be articulating our shared DEAI north star or why we are doing this work.

Chris: I'm wondering if you've thought about the power dynamic between the [DEAI] Alliance and the senior leadership team. What is the role you might play in mitigating that, or setting that power balance between the two?

Kelly: I know it's there. I've identified it and named it. And, I've identified it and named it with the two staff that are going to cochair the alliance in this first year. We're now in the process of recruiting the rest of the group. Watching for how power shows up and how it plays out, we've agreed to build the kind of working relationship that will allow us to talk in an open and safe way about how power shows up and plays out. It's one of those things that I might never have gotten started if I had had to spell out in advance how I and we would navigate those issues. We have agreed with the cochairs to start with developing our shared north star and agreements for working together, get started on the work, and address issues as they arise. We've acknowledged that this can be risky, that we'll have to build trust as we go, but that it's more important to start the work together.

I've made a commitment to show up for those conversations in as open a way as I can and be open to hearing the challenges, and helping navigate the challenges in the most generous and productive way possible. That could sound like deflecting the problem, or kicking the ball down the road, but I don't really know how else to do it other than start the work, and figure out how we want and need to work together through the work. I think you've got to find the partners and I'm feeling really good about the colleagues who have raised their hands to help lead this work.

Chris: I applaud you for that. I think a lot of leaders don't even think about when they set up a council or an alliance, or what the power dynamic will be, or how they might mitigate that. I think the formation of the group is not a means to an end. And it's not, "well, we have the group to do this work," and the burden shifts over there. I appreciate the fact that you're cognizant of it, and that you're not letting the perfect get in the way of the good, but also you will mitigate that as it comes up.

Kelly: I guess for me it is about building that relationship with the people who sign up to co-lead this work with us. I need to be really clear that I don't have all the answers and I don't have a pre-baked plan. But, I do have a pretty good idea of where I think we need to go, and it's going to take us a long time to get there. The amount of work it takes to change an organization and its relationship with its community is daunting, so start now, and start anywhere, and keep going.

Cinnamon: I'd like to shift back to you as a leader, and to think about who you are as a leader. Authentic leadership is characterized by vulnerability and transparency. Is there a catalyzing moment when you learned that you were an inclusive leader, or that maybe you needed to evolve?

Kelly: I think it was my experience of working in art museums that had me think, "there's got to be something better than this." Don't get me wrong, I love art museums, I really love them in their imperfect selves. I've spent most of my career working in big encyclopedic art museums. And, I happened to work in one that really wanted to be different, to be more community centric and relevant, and made a place for me at the senior table as a director of education and interpretation to really shape "the what and the why" of the organization. It was so incredibly hard to shift a large art museum to be more focused on people than the stuff, to reference Steven Weil[3] and bastardize his quote more than a little.

Working at the Art Gallery of Ontario (AGO), I was given a lot of latitude to shape a different kind of visitor experience. We were building a new museum; we wanted to relate differently to the people who lived in Toronto, one of the most diverse cities in the world. I wanted to think about what it would mean if all the people in Toronto actually saw real personal value in their public art museum, and felt a real connection to it. We did so much to change how we created meaning and connection between the public and works of art: opportunities for hands-on learning, inclusion of community voices and multiple points of view, experimental display techniques, interdisciplinary collections and themes, and so on. But ultimately, those interpretive techniques as pathways to greater relevance and inclusion could only ever go so far because curatorial and collection-based interests and priorities always prevailed in exhibition and gallery decisions. Experimenting with imaginative and authentic community engagement and maintaining scholarly and collection excellence were seen as mutually exclusive. I didn't have the power or the authority to hold the exhibition teams accountable for grappling with excellence in both realms.

I realized I was not going to be able to make change with just a seat at the table. I needed to go to an organization that shared my belief in the power and potential of museums to serve communities. That's what propelled me to go to Oakland. I had crossed paths with the director, Lori Fogarty, at various conferences over the years. Her ideas and work in Oakland resonated with me. I could see that the museum was really committed to figuring out what it would take and what it would mean to be truly beloved and of use to its whole community. I wanted to see if and how it worked. I wanted to be at a museum where the needs and interests of people were considered first, and those of the collection second, and that wasn't considered anti-intellectual, or museum heresy. I care deeply about collections. But, I care more about why we hold these collections in public trust and to whose and what benefit.

Chris: How do you think that shows up in your leadership style now?

Kelly: In no particular order, the way it shows up for me is, or has showed up for so far is, being really clear about what I stand for, what I value, why I do this work, and what I believe is the power and potential of museums. I look for places in the organization where I see reflections of these same values and beliefs, and start by building a connection with the people that have been doing that work.

I also start by painting a clear picture of what is possible, and inviting people into conversation about those possibilities, the urgency and need to picture new possibilities, and how we might begin to get there. That's going to take place for us through the strategic planning process. Quite frankly, that planning horizon got quickly and dramatically altered through the pandemic. The three-to-five-year planning horizon I envisioned when I started in January became a six-month horizon ten weeks later as we had to navigate financial survival and ongoing service through museum closure, and then reopening under a whole new world order.

The principle still stands that you paint a picture of where we need to go and why, and ensure people that we have a plan to get there. The destination and path forward needs to be even more clear when people are scared by it because they don't think they can do it or have the resources to do it, or afraid of their job [because of the potential exposure to the coronavirus]. This big soup of anxiety we're in with this pandemic is daunting, and it makes it tough to think about the future. I now have to paint a more near-term horizon, with enough clarity that I can confidently help people build the path forward, even with all the unknowns.

Chris: You went through this learning journey in art museums and then Oakland, how does your style manifest when you're in the top seat?

Kelly: I try to be disciplined and intentional about staying at the right altitude and engaging in the right way at the right time. This manifests in asking myself if this is a decision I need to make, is this a direction I need to set? Is this the most strategic use of my time and skills? Is there someone else or a group of stakeholders that are better equipped to make this decision? If so, how do I create the conditions for other people to shape the direction, or make that decision? What do I need to do to ensure they have enough clarity on strategic direction and desired outcomes to take the lead?

The pandemic on top of being a new CEO has challenged me in so many ways. How do I give people the hope and confidence that we'll get through this pandemic when I barely know them and the organization, and have to dig deep every day for my own sense of confidence? Where I've landed is to be radically transparent with everyone about the realities we're facing, and crystal clear about how, when, and who will be making key decisions and communicating them. This has then allowed me to lay out how to move forward with confidence, to put teams to work on planning, which I think in turn has given the staff confidence that we can navigate the challenges and get there.

Chris: I'm hearing a lot about clarity; I'm hearing a lot about openness, collaboration, transparency, and I think those are all qualities to be found throughout this book.

Kelly: I also want to add that I learned a powerful leadership lesson from Lori Fogarty when I worked at OMCA that I find myself coming back to over and over in my new role. That is the ability and willingness to have your mind changed. This is such a powerful thing for a leader to be able to do, and not something I'd experienced in other contexts. Being open to influence, new inputs, and different solutions creates an environment of trust and inclusion, nurtures leadership, and inspires people to really invest in the work. I learned that shifting course, changing one's mind, and letting go of the need to be right were actually examples of strength in leadership, not weakness. I want to be that kind of leader, and cultivate that kind of team, that is able and willing to put aside personal pride and ego to do what needs to be done to get to that shared destination.

Chris: I hear you. That was one of my big frustrations at my last museum job. I would hear, "Well, the budget is set for the year." And, I'm like, "Yeah, but the work I do, we get opportunities that come out of the blue, and we may only get one chance at that opportunity. If we say no, that particular community group may not come back." If we don't have that flexibility, we may be passing up opportunities that may not come back. I think about the work that Melanie Adams[4] did in St. Louis after Michael Brown was murdered in Ferguson, Missouri. She invited in community to talk about the issues immediately in the wake of his murder. If you say no to that or you say it's not in the budget or in our plan for the year, that's a lost opportunity.

Cinnamon: You have been doing inclusive work before AAM got into the DEAI realm, so your feet are more than wet. But, for a leader who is just facing this for the first time, and maybe has received an open letter from a disgruntled employee, or has been taken to task with protests, or showing up on Change the Museum on Instagram.[5] What advice would you give?

Kelly: Get a coach. Being a CEO is lonely and difficult work. And I can only begin to imagine how lonely and challenging it is when you're getting beaten up in the public realm. So, I'd say get a coach. Maybe even a team of coaches. Surround yourself with people who know more about the issues and solutions than you do and ask for help. Be really open and clear about the fact that harm has been done, and you can and will do it better. Invite people in to help you make it better. Make a plan and start anywhere.

Notes

1. This initiative is designed to help the museum community develop a more inclusive future by addressing board structures, accreditation, and staff practices.
2. Lori Fogarty authored chapter 25 in this book, "Building Inclusivity with and within the Board."
3. The late Steven Weil wrote back in 1999 about how museums need to be less about something, the objects/the collections, and more about being for somebody, the audience/our communities.
4. Melanie Adams is the director of the Smithsonian Anacostia Museum. Prior she served in leadership roles at the Minnesota Historical Society and Missouri Historical Society and is a scholar and community engagement specialist.
5. Launched in June 2020, this Instagram campaign (@changethemuseum) is spotlighting racist and exclusive behavior in American art museums.

ACTIVITY

The Johari Window

Self-awareness is a critical skill for inclusive leaders. Conscious knowledge of your own character, beliefs, skills, and biases can help you work to be a bridge across cultural differences. The Johari Window, invented by psychologists Joseph Luft and Harry Ingham, is a tool that uses four quadrants to help you assess your self-awareness and work to intentionally increase or decrease particular quadrants. When working across cultural difference, we can experience misalignment between how we present ourselves and how others perceive us. Increased self-awareness can be helpful to realign our perceptions and others' experience.

In the model, there are four quadrants that appear the same size (see figure 10.1). In practice, these quadrants all exist, but are various sizes. We can also intentionally change the size of each quadrant. As we begin to increase our self-awareness, we will see the Blind Spot quadrant decrease in size. When we begin to build trust and feel safe disclosing more information about ourselves, we can begin to decrease our Mask quadrant. The size of the Unconscious quadrant changes as we engage in self-discovery, shared discovery, and the observations of others.

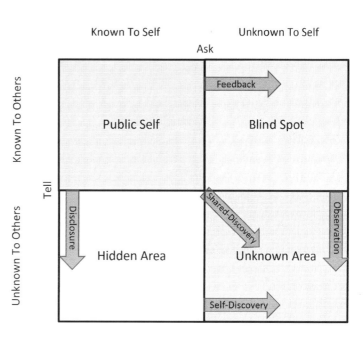

Figure 10.1. The Johari Window. Graphic by Chris Taylor

Blind Spots are attributes that others experience when interacting with us that we may not see or intend for others to experience. Increasing our self-awareness includes understanding which of our actions (intended or otherwise) have a negative impact on others.

Decreasing your Blind Spots: You can decrease your blind spots by seeking out and listening to feedback from others. As mentioned earlier, at times there can be a disconnect between how you present yourself and how others perceive you. Asking for (and authentically receiving) feedback can be a powerful way for you to decrease your blind spot. When others share feedback, you will begin to know traits, characteristics, skills, tendencies, beliefs, and attitudes that others see that you may have difficulty seeing yourself.

Note: If you currently don't have relationships that cross cultural differences, you first need to cultivate relationships that have trust as the foundation. It is in these relationships that feedback from cultural perspectives different than your own will be the most honest and helpful.

The **Hidden Area** is information that you intentionally keep hidden from others. This could be private information, but it can also consist of feelings, ambitions, and opinions that are withheld from the group.

Decreasing your Hidden Area: As a leader, decreasing your Hidden Area can cause some anxiety. Authentic leaders are aware of the strengths, as well as their limitations, and are able to be transparent and open with staff. Showing more of yourself as a leader can work to engender trust with your staff. Showing more of your authentic self can work to decrease the size of your Hidden Area.

The **Unknown Area** is where skills, behaviors, attitudes, and other attributes that are unknown to ourselves and unknown to others are located. As these characteristics are yet to be discovered, we often are not pushed to decrease this quadrant unless we face some type of challenge or disorienting experience. For example, leading during a pandemic can often present challenges that push us beyond our current known boundaries. Disorientation can often come from feedback that is contrary to how we may perceive our presence in a given situation.

Decreasing your Unknown Area: There are three ways you can decrease the size of your Unknown Area. The first is self-discovery. Learning more about yourself utilizing tools such as the Implicit Association Test or taking an assessment like the Intercultural Development Inventory gives you critical information about your ability to work across cultural differences and understand your biases. Second, you can decrease your Unknown Area through others' observation. This hinges on asking for feedback and ultimately creating an environment where feedback is built into the operating norms of your relationships. The third way to decrease your Unknown Area is through shared discovery. Shared discovery comes through sharing experiences with those who are culturally different from you, inviting feedback, and engaging in reflective discussion with others.

Self-awareness is a journey where we find great things about ourselves, but we may also find things that are hard for us to internalize. Regardless, self-awareness is critical to inclusive leadership. Remember, you are awesome. Do the work. Let your public self shine!

Part Three
Inclusive Leadership

Chapter 11

Dear White Colleague

Thoughts on Inclusive Museum Leadership from a Colleague of Color

Lisa Sasaki

Dear Colleague, let me start by saying that although I am a leader of color—specifically an Asian American, female-identifying museum professional whose current position is the director of the Smithsonian Asian Pacific American Center—that does not automatically make me an expert in inclusive leadership. I wish that I was, but, like many of you, I am a product of a museum field that I both deeply love and yet know can be deeply flawed. I started my museum career as an unpaid volunteer, knowing it was the only way into a world that rarely welcomed outsiders. I struggled through unrepentant hierarchies, first as an entry-level staff person making less than a living wage before gaining enough experiences to work my way up a ladder of positions with titles like assistant, supervisor, manager, and director. Over twenty-five years, I have seen the museum field attempt to come to terms, time and time again, with its lack of diversity even as I personally hit a series of glass and bamboo ceilings. Yet, I recognize the privilege and platform my title brings and that as part of the 16 percent of non-White curators, conservators, educators, and leaders currently in the field,[1] I do have unique insights into inclusion, exclusion, and what leaders at every level can do to develop skills that move us toward more inclusive museums.

Dear White Colleague . . .

For three consecutive years (2017–2019), I facilitated—along with my brilliant colleagues Veronica Alvarez, Megan Dickerson, Ben Garcia, Jaclyn M. Roessel, and Ariel Weintraub—a series of sessions during the Western Museums Association's annual meetings that attempted to examine racism in the museum field. *Undoing Institutional Racism: The Role of Ally and Gatekeeper in Museums* was the hardest but most eye-opening series of sessions I have led in more than fifteen years of being a speaker, moderator, or panelist at national, regional, and state museum conferences. The task of examining topics like oppression, allyship, bias, and tokenism within the confines of a seventy-five-minute session was daunting, but the need for these discussions within a professional conference setting was simply too acute to ignore. The sessions were frequently the talk of the conference as we introduced participants to concepts like microaggression, asked them to examine their privilege, and took on what I consider to be the hardest part of addressing inequities within a professional context, interpersonal interactions. How do we communicate with one another across differences, especially around sensitive topics like race and inequity?

It was during the workshop on interpersonal interactions that we developed an activity called "Dear White Colleague/Dear Colleague of Color," inspired by artist Chris Johnson's powerful project *Question Bridge*. The activity asked participants to anonymously pose a question to their Colleague of Color or their White Colleague, and to include why they were asking the question. For example, from a Colleague of Color to a White Colleague:

> Dear White Colleague . . . Why are you asking me to join your diversity task force? By asking me to join a task force, or any kind of effort to "diversify" the museum, you are asking me to take on additional work and emotional labor. When you invite me to join, are you also going to take on more work? It is common knowledge that diversity task forces ask people of color to "train" or "teach" White staff about diversity issues. These task forces dangerously reinforce the idea of White colleagues "bestowing agency" upon us to teach them about ourselves, as if we didn't have agency to begin with.

Or from a White Colleague to a Colleague of Color:

> Dear Colleague of Color . . . When I ask or say something while discussing inequities that I recognize has done harm to you, what can I do? Sometimes I am so hellbent on fixing problems that I am now recognizing that I do not stop to think about the fact that you have to live with these inequities. In that moment, my need for solutions trumped your humanity.

The honest and oftentimes raw questions posed during the activity and the facilitated discussion that followed highlighted two things for me: (1) the genuine desire that colleagues have to understand one another, especially between those who have started their journey toward recognizing their own privilege and those who experienced exclusion and oppression in the museum field; and (2) if we hope to address that which divides us, we need to find ways to communicate more directly with one another so that we can safely share how we feel, learn from each other, and ultimately find a path forward toward museums that are truly inclusive of their staff, visitors, boards, volunteers, and communities.

So, in the spirit of direct communication, it is my intention to share some thoughts for my White Colleagues on inclusive museum leadership, while acknowledging that addressing racial difference is just one dimension of inclusive practice. The areas discussed below can and should equally be addressed to Abled Colleagues, Academic Colleagues, Christian Colleagues, Cisgender Colleagues, Heterosexual Colleagues, and others, by adjusting the framing and some of the supporting topics. These inequities are very real; however, unlike some of the advances that the field has recently taken in recognizing certain disparities, like in the area of gender, stark racial inequities in museums have been clearly documented for decades with little or no movement in the statistics. National organizations like the American Alliance of Museums have recognized what Dr. Martin Luther King Jr. called the "fierce urgency of now" to call for serious work in DEAI (diversity, equity, accessibility, and inclusion) even as we, as a nation, face the deaths of George Floyd, Breonna Taylor, Ahmaud Arbery, Tamir Rice, and countless others, galvanizing an uprising that has not been seen in a generation. If we cannot make movement toward racial equity and inclusion now, then we will likely be stuck here for decades to come.

These thoughts therefore center on what role White leaders at different levels can play in creating more inclusive environments for BIPOC (Black, Indigenous, and People of Color), knowing that as professionals we are not necessarily taught the skills that we need to lead the diverse, socially conscious, and interconnected organizations of the future. And, for my Colleagues of Color, I hope I do justice to the struggles that you face every day and the countless hours of labor you have put into making museums a better place for all of us.

* * *

Dear White Colleague, you don't just have a "diversity problem"; you have an "inclusion problem."

If I had a dollar for every time a colleague lamented their "diversity problem" and asked me for a recommendation—usually around how to get diverse candidates into their applicant or board pools—I would be a rich woman. I would be even richer if I got another dollar for every time the same colleague became bewildered when I asked about their inclusion practices instead of giving them access to a mythical rolodex of museum professionals of color or the secret formula to a perfectly diverse recruitment or hiring strategy. These colleagues miss the simple fact that, without an environment where candidates feel welcomed, included, and empowered, there is no hope of engaging and retaining the diversity of backgrounds, thought, and experiences that can help an organization flourish. To reiterate the famous quote by Vernā Myers, "Diversity is being invited to the party. Inclusion is being asked to dance."

Diversity leader and inclusion trainer Daniel Juday has pointed out that this quote, while accurate as an easy way for people to understand the critical difference between two words that they often think are synonymous, fails to capture that true inclusion changes the power dynamics of who is controlling the party so no one is left waiting for an invitation to dance that might never come. Instead, he proposed this revision to the quote: "Diversity is going to the party; inclusion is being a member of the party planning committee."[2] Juday's point is well taken—not only do we need to consider the factors within our organizations that exclude certain people, but we must also examine who gets to control the music, who gets to go out on the dance floor, and who gets to tell us when or if there is even a party to begin with. We cannot continue to invite BIPOC into the organization, fail to listen to their ideas, relegate them to support positions without influence or decision-making authority, chastise them when they "make trouble" by challenging the status quo, and then still expect them to remain devoted to "the work."

To fix our inclusion problem, we must first acknowledge that the problem exists, and that the solution to the problem is not attempting to hire more BIPOC staff to mend it for us when they are the ones being systematically excluded. Instead, it is up to inclusive leaders to demonstrate their commitment to moving beyond surface inclusion efforts. I have seen many leaders jump into a series of predetermined and formulaic solutions when attempting to improve diversity and inclusion in their organizations: Diversity Task Force, check! Diversity and inclusion training, check! New hiring practices, check! While these are not bad first steps, the inclusive leader needs to dig deeper and help their museum get to the next steps, or risk continuous cycles of regression that erode staff confidence and impede organizational change. Here are some questions for these leaders to consider:

- Have I sat through a task force meeting or a BIPOC-led staff meeting without speaking? What have I heard to be the main issues? What am I willing to do to address these issues?

- Have I put myself into the same uncomfortable position that I have asked of my BIPOC colleagues and staff?
- How safe is it for BIPOC to share their truths? What must I do to ensure safety and trust while addressing difficult topics?
- What authority have I given BIPOC staff, both within a task force and outside of it, to help set policy, budget, and protocol for the organization?
- Am I holding everyone equally accountable toward the creation of an inclusive work environment?

⋆　⋆　⋆

Dear White Colleague, if you are uncomfortable with addressing oppression within your institution, just wait until you have to face your own role in perpetuating these inequities.

As difficult as it might be to face an organization's lack of inclusion, it is even harder to recognize the personal role each of us plays on a daily basis in the overt or covert oppression of others. The dictionary definition of the word *oppression* is the state of being subjected to unfair treatment or control, but oppression also occurs when a group or individual in a position of power—intentionally or unintentionally—silences, marginalizes, disadvantages, and/or disempowers others. This is a good moment to also note that internalized oppression also exists, which gives rise to things like the model minority myth and racism perpetrated by BIPOC against other BIPOC. There are numerous resources that look at how oppression, power, racism, bias, and privilege interact and manifest; however, I find the National Equity Project's work on the Lens of Systemic Oppression (figure 11.1) to be a useful way of understanding the overlapping and interconnected nature of individual and systemic oppression.[3]

Their metaphor of the lens also reminds us that, unlike some popular thought that makes us victims to the racist systems in which we are indoctrinated, we can learn to recognize the type of oppression at play and even circumvent it, because the decisions that we make every day have real impact on the visitors that we serve and the staff that we lead:

> We make dozens of decisions each day that impact those we serve. . . . As leaders for equity, our primary concern is to interrupt those rules that serve, either implicitly or explicitly, to perpetuate opportunity gaps for vulnerable students. To become agents of change who make strategic and courageous decisions, we must learn to run a set of filters, or lenses, that shift our vantage point and uncover what the "naked eye" cannot see.[4]

Inclusive leaders develop the skill of being able to discern between the personal, interpersonal, and institutional structures of oppression and understand that different phenomena require different strategies to address—not a one-size-fits-all solution.

Inclusive leaders also can see how each area affects the other, starting from how a person's individual beliefs and actions can perpetuate the very racist and oppressive systems we are trying to change. These beliefs—whether conscious or unconscious—manifest in the interpersonal discourse that we have with others, influence the decisions we make on institutional policies and practices, and frame our understanding of structural and societal issues. Therefore, because of our positions of power within an organization, it is vital that we as leaders first put on the lens of the individual, deeply examine our own beliefs and biases, and face how they may oppress others as a result.

THE LENS OF SYSTEMIC OPPRESSION

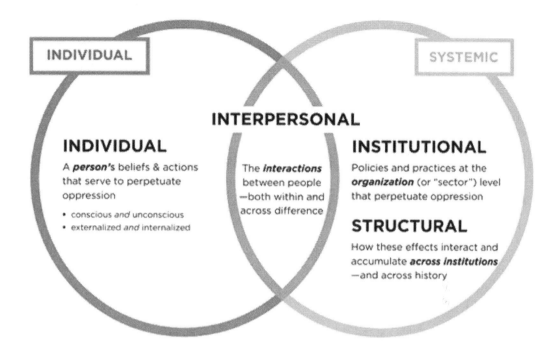

INDIVIDUAL

SYSTEMIC

INTERPERSONAL

INDIVIDUAL

A *person's* beliefs & actions that serve to perpetuate oppression

- conscious *and* unconscious
- externalized *and* internalized

The *interactions* between people —both within and across difference

INSTITUTIONAL

Policies and practices at the *organization* (or "sector") level that perpetuate oppression

STRUCTURAL

How these effects interact and accumulate *across institutions* —and across history

Some phenomena playing out at each level

INDIVIDUAL	INTERPERSONAL	INSTITUTIONAL	STRUCTURAL
• Identity and difference	• Reproductive discourse ("Discourse 1")	• Biased policies and practices (e.g. in hiring, teaching, discipline, parent-family engagement)	• Systems of advantage and disadvantage
• Individual advantage and disadvantage	• Microaggressions		• Opportunity structures
• Explicit bias	• Racist interactions	• Disproportional (e.g. racialized) outcomes and experiences	• Societal history of oppressive practices and policies
• Implicit bias	• Transferred oppression		
• Stereotype threat			
• Internalized oppression			

Figure 11.1 Graphic of Lens of Systemic Oppression and Chart of Phenomena at Play. Graphic courtesy of the National Equity Project

To be clear, this is a deeply uncomfortable process. When done correctly, this examination can strip away decades of learned "professionalism" meant to keep the status quo intact. Take, for example, the special something that we all look for in an interview called "fit"; that quality you actually cannot describe but will, nine times out of ten, make a hiring decision upon. Who gets to decide what "fit" is and why after sixty minutes—or less—are you so sure that a candidate would or would not fit into your team or organization? How many of your daily decisions might be influenced by personal beliefs that could be based upon implicit bias, unfounded assumptions, and a desire to maintain being in control? Here are some additional questions for inclusive leaders to consider when developing skills around this type of personal work:

- Who do I feel most comfortable working with? Why?
- Who do I feel most uncomfortable working with? Why?
- When have I felt oppressed? Have I unknowingly placed others in similar situations?
- What do I feel passionately about? How might those passions influence my decisions when it comes to the policies and practices of my organization? Do those practices then disadvantage others as a result?

⋆   ⋆   ⋆

Dear White Colleague, please do not make me a token gesture in your quest to be inclusive.

I have heard numerous White colleagues, leaders, and board members offer to "step down" to "make room at the table" for a BIPOC candidate or team member. This offer is always well-meaning, done in the name of diversity, inclusion, and equity . . . and demonstrates a lack of understanding about privilege, power, and tokenism. Let me explain. Those who can voluntarily give up positions of power are by definition privileged as BIPOC cannot afford to lose their spot at the metaphorical table. Having a spot at the table seldom guarantees a commensurate amount of authority and power as the privileged person departing the table; and power—not to be confused with authority—cannot be bestowed upon someone like a gift, no matter how well intended someone might be. Without power, the BIPOC is often a token representative eternally forced either to be the dissenting voice or to conform to the existing majority. Finally, while we understand the need for—and at times even appreciate—professional affirmative action, no one wants to get an invite to a table not because they merited it, but simply because they checked a box. As a result, "giving up your spot" is not required nor is it effective.

What might then appear to be a quandary—how can you increase diversity and encourage inclusion if you cannot step aside for BIPOC participants without making them into a token?—has an obvious, but not easy, solution. Instead of "stepping aside" to encourage diversity, those with racial power and privilege need to both share power and authority with those who have historically and consistently been without it *and* use their power to elevate the voices of those who are underrepresented without appropriating them. To do this requires active skill building because the authentic sharing of power is not something that comes naturally. While inclusive leadership is all of the key traits listed by Juliet Bourke and Andrea Espedido in the *Harvard Business Review* in March 2020—visible commitment, humility, awareness of bias, curiosity about others, cultural intelligence, and effective collaboration[5]—I would argue that *the* key trait is missing: the ability to share power and authority. The model of "command and control" leadership has been so embedded within us that it can feel paradoxical or uncomfortable to most leaders, especially those who have fought their way into their positions or invested decades into the advancement of their careers, to relinquish power to others.

Museums have already created several successful models for shared curatorial and exhibition authority, like the Oakland Museum of California and the Wing Luke Museum of the Asian Pacific American Experience. The cocreation of content and the inclusion of community members in the development of exhibitions, collections, and programs are all good places to start a practice of shared power. Extending those same tenets of collaboration, listening, cocreation, and representation into our organization's operations, staffing, and governance is the next step for inclusive museum leaders. Here are some additional questions for inclusive leaders to consider when developing skills around the sharing of authority and power:

- When have I successfully cocreated a project, policy, strategy, or plan with someone? What were the power dynamics that were at play? Have I ever genuinely cocreated with someone when there is an imbalance of power?
- How do I advocate for BIPOC or other underrepresented voices? What might be problematic with the way that I support BIPOC?
- Am I always representing the work of BIPOC internally and externally, or am I allowing the members to speak for themselves and represent their own ideas and progress? Do I recognize when I am needed to validate their work and when I am appropriating it?

*   *   *

Dear White Colleague, practice makes perfect.

The hardest thing about inclusive leadership is that it is something that we will need to work on forever. I understand within my own growth as a leader that I will not be able to take a single training and declare myself inclusive. I will need to dig deeper, question my own motivations and beliefs, speak up and use my accumulated power when I see inequity and oppression occurring, and at times be profoundly uncomfortable along the way. I know that I will likely make mistakes, and I am grateful for the colleagues who have in the past and who will in the future call me on them so I do not repeat those mistakes going forward. Finally, I recognize that inclusion is a constant and deliberate effort where I may fail as many times as I succeed. Because, Dear Colleague—whether you are White, BIPOC, or any other identity that has been either included or excluded—inclusion is the work.

Notes

1. Roger Schonfeld, Mariët Westermann, and Liam Sweeney, *The Andrew W. Mellon Foundation: Art Museum Staff Demographic Survey* (New York: Andrew W. Mellon Foundation, 2015).
2. Daniel Juday, "Inclusion Isn't Being Asked to Dance," LinkedIn, May 3, 2017, https://www.linkedin.com/pulse/inclusion-isnt-being-asked-dance-daniel-juday/.
3. National Equity Project, "Lens of Systemic Oppression," https://www.nationalequityproject.org/frameworks/lens-of-systemic-oppression#:~:text=The%20lens%20of%20systemic%20oppression%20is%20a%20lens%20we%20intentionally,and%2Dfor%20preventing%20individual%20or.
4. National Equity Project, "Lens of Systemic Oppression."
5. Juliet Bourke and Andrea Espedido, "The Key to Inclusive Leadership," *Harvard Business Review*, March 6, 2020, https://hbr.org/2020/03/the-key-to-inclusive-leadership.

Bibliography

Andrew W. Mellon Foundation. *Art Museum Staff Demographic Survey*. New York: Andrew W. Mellon Foundation, 2015.

Bourke, Juliet, and Andrea Espedido. "The Key to Inclusive Leadership." *Harvard Business Review*, March 6, 2020. https://hbr.org/2020/03/the-key-to-inclusive-leadership.

Juday, Daniel. "Inclusion Isn't Being Asked to Dance." LinkedIn, May 3, 2017. https://www.linkedin.com/pulse/inclusion-isnt-being-asked-dance-daniel-juday/.

National Equity Project. "The Lens of Systemic Oppression." https://www.nationalequityproject .org/frameworks/lens-of-systemic-oppression#:~:text=The%20lens%20of%20systemic %20oppression%20is%20a%20lens%20we%20intentionally,and%2For%20prevent ing%20individual%20or.

Schonfeld, Roger, Mariët Westermann, and Liam Sweeney. *The Andrew W. Mellon Foundation: Art Museum Staff Demographic Survey*. New York: Andrew W. Mellon Foundation, 2015.

Chapter 12

Beyond a Scarcity Mind-Set

My Path toward Inclusive Leadership

Ashley Rogers

I'll start by saying that I don't know how I got here. It's reasonable, of course, to ask a thirty-seven-year-old woman why she is the executive director of a museum that is, at least to some degree, nationally known. I get asked this question with decreasing frequency, usually politely, usually with a bit of good-natured curiosity. "How did you get into this?" people ask me, "What's your background?" If I'm walking around the museum and they don't know my role, they're more likely to ask different questions: "Are you a history major?" "Did you study this in school?"

It's funny to be mistaken for a college student, of course, but I've always felt there was something bigger than just the fact that I look young lurking behind those questions. We're all inundated with images in media and real examples from our world that teach us what to expect. You probably have a pretty clear idea of what a firefighter looks like, or a teacher, or a cop, or a doctor—and that image will change, individually, based on your own background, the community you live in, and what you saw growing up.

We also have in our minds an idea of what "the boss" looks like—it's a composite of the supervisors and leaders we have seen in our lifetimes. For many people, the prototypical boss is a middle-aged White man. Within the female-dominated museum field, among our peers who make the decisions to hire leaders, that idea might be collapsed to just "White." When I walk in the room, a five-foot-tall young(ish) woman with a baby face, I'm not usually what people have in mind when they imagine who's in charge. I see the surprise register on their faces while they're scanning the room looking for someone taller, more authoritative, more male. At the same time, as a White person, I absolutely fit the bill. So if one lesson from the peculiar way people react to me is that we should challenge our own ideas of who "looks like" they're in charge, another is that as leaders we must recognize how much we have benefited from those underlying assumptions. If we didn't look like someone's definition of a leader, would we have gotten an interview?

Though people often imagine I'm younger than I am, I'll concede that my career trajectory is unusual, which is why, to return to the beginning, I don't know precisely how I got here. I state that I'm baffled by my own quick ascent to leadership not to undercut my abilities but to emphasize the degree to which there's a good bit of happenstance, luck, and bias in someone like me being trusted with the keys. I can look back on my life and find examples of being attracted to leadership positions from a very young age, of frequently seeming like the type of person that teachers and supervisors could trust. At the same time, I know for certain that the fact of my Whiteness has mattered in job interviews and in an unspoken rapport with supervisors, stakeholders, and colleagues. There's a comfort level that people have with you when they think you come from a similar background. They're more natural; they can be themselves. The hiring team might think "I really liked that person" but not know precisely why. They might think, "this person seems like they fit."

I think it's important that as leaders we recognize the ways this type of bias benefited us, just as much as we work to break that pattern for new generations of leaders. One of our most important duties is to cultivate new leaders and serve as examples. It's critical that we take that role seriously, and that for White leaders like myself, we don't repeat the biases that got us here in the first place. There are overt and covert ways that we create barriers for people who do not look like us, thereby ensuring not only that our own positions will be held mostly by White people but also that most positions in our organizations will as well. My own experiences, feeling like I'm not the right type of person to lead, combined with the research and work I do about social justice and race, have taught me that inclusivity is about holding open the door for people who don't normally get in the building, and taking them seriously once they arrive.

Because my own transition from emerging museum professional to museum director happened relatively quickly—less than four years after graduating from my MA program—I experienced a bit of professional whiplash. I could acutely feel the change when I got into a position of leadership at a museum people were interested in. Suddenly, people listened to me. It was jarring, because I was the same me, actually. I had the same ideas when I was an early career professional in a very small museum that most people had never heard of. Many of those ideas were nascent and undeveloped, but my brain worked the same way. As soon as I had the credentials—that is, as soon as someone else had validated me by giving me an Important Position with a Weighty Title—leaders in my field (including higher-ups at my former job) seemed to take me seriously for the first time. It felt like people were paying attention to my job, not me. In my new role, I was treated as an expert. In the role immediately preceding that role, I worked at the front desk and was treated as a bathroom attendant. How do you reconcile those two experiences?

This bizarre transition had an indelible effect on me as a leader. People at all levels of our organizations are creative, interesting people who have things to share that could strengthen both leaders as individuals and the institution as a whole. Too often, we trust the authority of credentials more than the knowledge of individuals. I will take a quick pause here to say that I am guilty of this too—who wouldn't be excited about meeting, say, Lonnie Bunch? Would I rather have a coffee with the secretary of the Smithsonian or a grad student I've never heard of? None of us are perfect; credentials do in fact matter; but leaders are by definition gatekeepers. We decide who gets in. So it's worth investigating what we think makes one person qualified, interesting, and intelligent and what makes another person invisible.

I have tried, in my few years as a leader, to actively work against the assumption that only a certain type of person can work in any given role. At Whitney Plantation, I have made a practice of hiring people without prior experience in the museum field. I also prefer, when possible, to move people up in the organization instead of making external hires. This means that on paper, our employees' previous work experiences rarely match their job roles. What they lack in previous experience, our employees make up for in creativity, intellect, and capacity. The right person for any job at Whitney is curious and compassionate, loves learning and sharing knowledge, and cares deeply about social justice.

Some of this philosophy, I'll freely admit, is a function of running a museum surrounded by sugar-cane fields an hour from any major city. Not all of it, though. Working at Whitney can be taxing—we ask people to engage at a deep level daily with strangers about the darkest aspects of our nation's history: slavery, racism, poverty, and violence. This is why it's critical to find people whose hearts and minds match our mission. When I describe how difficult it is to find the right people to work at the museum, I usually hear from colleagues that I should turn to the local universities. There are several universities within a fifty-mile radius around the museum. They tell me I should build partnerships with history departments and I should recruit students for internships and summer jobs. I don't disagree that this pretty traditional way of recruiting museum workers can be effective and that these departments are sources of great talent. We have had some of these students apply and work out beautifully, and I'd never turn down a beneficial partnership. At the same time, I've found incredible commitment, passion, and longevity by hiring people based on their minds instead of their resumes.

What this strategy has meant for our organization is that we have an incredibly diverse staff in terms of race, age, skill set, and education. Some of our staff members have advanced degrees in history. Others come from a background of hospitality, education, or factory work. They are Sunday school teachers, janitors, IT workers, actors, secretaries, hairstylists, fast food employees, and coaches. Multiple members of the staff at all levels are direct descendants of people who were once enslaved at the plantation. This unconventional way of hiring sometimes means we have to work a bit harder to train those people who have no background in history nor any education beyond high school. It also fairly well ensures that we will have diverse perspectives represented in our operations and interpretation. In the management team as well as the front line, I welcome the variety of voices and experiences that make Whitney the special museum that it is. I love learning from the staff and hearing their ideas about how to make things work. I am absolutely thrilled every time that someone's unique background means they see a solution plain as day that I would have never even considered. Time and again, being inclusive has paid dividends.

I was not always an inclusive leader. I was not even always an effective employee! I've had more than one sit-down with a supervisor who let me know I was "almost fired." I never quite crossed the line, but I sure came close. Getting to where I am now, which is still far from perfect, took a lot of painful self-realization. For years, I was territorial, exclusionary, and conflict-averse. I was not empathetic to people's needs, even when I had all the reason in the world to identify with them. It has taken time and reflection to recognize that I was subjecting the people who worked closest to me to the types of trials I had been subjected to. I found myself saying things like, "young museum workers need to earn their stripes—I did!" I accepted, unquestioningly, the culture that was passed down in the broader field, even as I found myself bristling against it over and over. Of course young professionals should expect to get out of school and make little more than minimum wage—I did! Don't they know that this is a field you get into because you love it, not because you're going to get rich? It's normal to take work home, to work long hours, to work through lunch, to pick up all the slack. It's normal to work without recognition; you'll get recognized when you've done more work. If you expect an easy job with good pay, you won't find it in a museum!

In the museum field, we often take low starting pay, long hours, and compounding responsibilities for granted. We imagine that in your first years out of school, you should expect that you may have to work for free for a while. But after my first couple years at Whitney, after I had spent time crafting nationwide best practices with organizations like MASS Action, I thought: Wait. Who said the museum field has to be this way?

I sometimes tell people that if there ever was such a thing as a natural-born museum professional, it's me. I got my first gig as an interpreter just after I learned to walk. Short on childcare options, my mother toted me to her job as an interpreter at Lincoln Log Cabin in Illinois when I was a toddler. It was a living history farm, and she made our costumes by hand based on nineteenth-century patterns. I wasn't allowed modern toys, so I played with wooden marbles and a homemade doll (which was the subject of a meeting with her supervisor—was it appropriate for this time period?). One of my earliest memories is of being inside a crib in the museum, where my mom used to lie me down for naps while she worked the hearth fire. I remember I fit so perfectly inside this crib, and I would lie there nodding off while visitors walked through the room peering over me as if I were one of the artifacts. My mother continued to work as an employee and later an independent contractor in museums in Illinois and North Carolina, and I was almost always her assistant. As a result, I share memories with a rural child born 150 years before me—I learned to cook on a hearth fire; I learned to braid hair in a hay loft. I accompanied her to classrooms, museums, and historic sites for most of my childhood, teaching other kids to make candles and dye fabric and singing mourning songs for the rousing temperance addresses she used to deliver at the North Carolina Museum of History.

With this upbringing, in hindsight, it makes perfect sense that I ended up in the museum field, although in reality the journey was somewhat more circuitous. When I finally figured out, a couple years after graduating with a BA in history, that I wanted to become a public historian, I had a wealth of people I could ask about the field—all my mom's old colleagues from the state history organizations where she worked. I sent an inquisitive e-mail to one of her good friends and received back an e-mail that seemed like a warning: *There aren't that many jobs. The pay is bad. Only do this if you really want to.*

I plowed forward after that e-mail, unwilling to let good advice dissuade me. In retrospect, she was right, and she was trying to temper my expectations and maybe protect me. At the time, I felt certain I could prove her wrong. It took being rejected for a string of minimum-wage, entry-level museum jobs before I decided to work for free. I was "hired" as a volunteer tour guide at a small house museum in Denver in 2009, where I used to come in for shifts on my off days between jobs working as a waitress and a baker. Double shifts from six a.m. to eleven p.m. on most days left me only a few spare hours to come in and work a volunteer shift, and no days off, but I was hungry. I filled shifts, I did extra work, and I ingratiated myself to the management. In my down time, I studied for the GRE and applied to grad school, because I felt absolutely certain that a BA was not enough to get a paying job in the museum field. It seemed I had to get an MA to be qualified for the tour guide positions that paid money.

I got into Colorado State University, and I quit my job as a waitress when I moved an hour and a half north to Fort Collins, but I kept my job volunteering at the museum. Twice a month or so, I would drive three hours round-trip to work for free. It was a great opportunity; I didn't want to lose the chance to advance my career. When it came time to fulfill my internship requirement, I decided to invent my own internship at my house museum. I did research, gave tours, helped build new interpretive materials, and learned all about how the museum worked. By the time I was done with my internship and one semester away from graduating, the assistant director suddenly moved to London and I applied for her job and got it. For years afterward, drawing on this incredible experience of getting hired to be the assistant director of a museum before I was done with grad school, I would tell young people in the field: volunteer at museums! It counts as work! Put it on your resume! It worked for me.

Throughout my first years as a paid museum professional, I took the lesson of all that hustle and sacrifice with me. In my first few months on the job, after working a string of late-night events that meant I was regularly working fifty or sixty hours per week, I piped up and said it would be nice to share responsibilities so that I didn't continue working all day and all night when we had special events. I thought that leaving waitressing meant those days were behind me. In response, I was told by a supervisor, "Nobody ever said this was a forty-hour-per-week job." Even if I didn't yet have the language to explain why that was wrong, I knew it didn't feel good to hear. And yet, in some ways, it lined up with all the work experiences I'd had up to that point. *Maybe it is asking too much not to work overtime without compensation*, I thought, *things get busy, and everyone has to chip in from time to time*. So I internalized that message. I imagined that I was proving something by working hard; that there was something bigger and better waiting for me and I had to go through trials to earn it. When that came to fruition a couple years later in the form of a big important job, it only validated this idea. So the lesson became: you have to suffer for a little while to get where you want to be. Keep your head down, don't ask for help, and above all, work hard.

I thought that finally getting a real job would be a panacea; that I would no longer feel restless and unsatisfied. Instead, it didn't take long for me to begin burning out, especially when I realized that the salary I thought was pretty respectable turned out to be little more than what I had made as a waitress. To make ends meet, I became a guinea pig for market research and medical studies. I started writing articles for the local newspaper at $25 a pop. I picked up shifts on the weekend at my old restaurant. They always needed help, and an extra $100 here and there helped pay the bills that my regular pay wouldn't cover. It didn't matter, though. Saddled with student loan debt I had racked up to get the MA that I believed was so necessary, and with an aging Subaru that needed constant repairs, I had to make some tough choices. I decided to sell my car and commute to work on a 1980s ten-speed I bought on Craigslist for $75. Living without a car is cool in Denver! It's the eco-friendly choice! Sure, public transit was a little unreliable and getting groceries was somewhat challenging, but I was exercising *and* saving the planet, how about that! I also just could not afford to have a car on a museum professional's salary.

My first years in the field shortly followed the crash of 2009, and the organization I worked for was under strict budgetary restrictions that meant no one received raises, so performance reviews were somewhat pro forma. At least I wasn't taking mandatory furlough days like my predecessor. If I think about the psychological impact that these financial problems had on me, compounded with the workplace expectation to work hard without promise of reward or recognition, it's easy to understand why I was usually in a foul mood. Everyone complained about me—visitors, staff members, volunteers. My supervisor told me repeatedly in performance reviews to "be nice." I internalized all of that too, creating a narrative about myself that I am mean and rude, that the problem is me. I would snap at people and then feel guilty for weeks afterward, but I was seemingly unable to keep my attitude in check. I see now that I was living permanently in a scarcity mind-set. I had so little, I was fighting to keep the little scraps that were in front of me. Nobody took me seriously, I had no real power, and nobody listened to me, so I became small and twisted up with stress and anxiety. I felt profoundly lonely.

The curious thing about these experiences is that they aren't curious at all in the museum field, or many other fields. Many, if not most, early-career professionals are experiencing similar hardships. What makes no sense is why after going through this myself I did not immediately recognize that this is a major problem in our field. I accepted it. The first advice I got about working in museums, after all, was *there is no money in this. It's not for everyone.* It's strange to admit that I had so thoroughly been indoctrinated to this mind-set that when I first heard of Museum Workers Speak, the group of museum workers pushing for better pay and working conditions, I did not identify with them. Instead I thought, *what are they complaining about? They haven't been in the field long enough to demand more money.*

I do not believe that poor people are poor through any shortcoming or fault of their own. I know that structural racism and inequality are pervasive and poverty passes through generations, making it difficult for people to get out. I do not come from a wealthy background and I knew that my family was smart and good and capable, but that sometimes life deals you a bad hand. So why did I think that young museum workers should bootstrap themselves into the middle classes and stop complaining?

Even stranger, why did I so wholeheartedly accept the idea that working for no money was necessary? I suppose, because I saw the examples all around me: you get jobs through internships, and internships do not pay. A girl in my graduate program had interned at the Smithsonian, and I was so impressed and jealous. I thought, she really has a leg up in the field. I remember looking at those internships too, and one in particular that I desperately wanted. But it was in Washington, DC, and it paid no money. I couldn't even consider it. My mother couldn't afford to help me; I didn't have any way to pay for living expenses or even the flight to get there. When other people in my MA program spent their summers with the National Park Service or at archives, I went back to waiting tables. How else would I pay the rent? It felt like I was missing something. Just who were these internships intended for? Who could afford this? That was my real experience with unpaid internships—of feeling like I was on the other side of a giant wall built to keep me out. Yet when I got my first job, I touted my unpaid labor as the reason I was hired, and I was probably right.

The idea that this field isn't for everyone, that you have to really love it, that you have to suffer, that it is acceptable to work for free, is the exact reason that the field is overwhelmingly White and female. The people who can afford a master's degree that costs $30,000 or more, who can work for free, are disproportionately White. I also reflect often on the messages that women receive in our society that make us so willing to undervalue our own labor. Women still earn less than men in the United States, in part because we dominate professions like museum work that pay less—and we typically do not demand that pay structures change. At the same time, the museum field has changed drastically in the last twenty years. Museum work was at one time less professional, and women volunteered as a public service because they could afford to—they were retired, independently wealthy, or supported by their spouses. When I was looking for and failing to find a museum job in 2006, the problem I was bumping up against was one that plagues our field today: increasing expectations of education with the proliferation of museum studies programs means that those volunteer jobs are no longer being held exclusively by wealthy women and retirees—young MA candidates need them to get a foot in the door. I did not need a master's degree for the first job I had in this field, and although it's expanded my knowledge, I don't really need it now. I was not wrong, though, that it seemed necessary. If everyone else on the market has an MA, then you need one too.

In the first two years that I hired and supervised museum workers, I unknowingly passed these unrealistic expectations on to them. I continued to work very long hours because we were opening a new museum, and I expected the same of my staff. I thought that everyone must be able to read the room and see that these are extraordinary times, and that we should expect lower pay and longer hours while we're getting the museum up and running. When I ended up hiring a young woman very much like myself, I started to see patterns, but I couldn't recognize them for what they were. I was in the position of my old supervisor now, trying to explain to a young woman who was overworked and whose talents were underutilized why she should try harder to be nice to visitors and coworkers. I thought, we must have pretty similar personalities. I did not think, this field was toxic for me and I made it toxic for her.

In my first job, I supervised forty volunteers, so I had plenty of management experience in terms of the day-to-day. But supervising employees is entirely different. When I struggled with it at the beginning, I assumed I just was not cut out for it. I failed to see that I had a whole crew of people who were not indoctrinated to the privations of museum work who were rightfully wondering why they were being asked to do three people's jobs and work long hours. To make matters more complicated, I was one of very few White employees. The mostly African American staff assumed that work was demanding there because I was White, not because I was unable to see the bigger picture and advocate for change.

My awakening came slowly. After opening Whitney Plantation, I started attending conferences and began to meet museum professionals who were different from everyone I'd met before. These people not only saw the problems I had felt as a young professional, but thought they were wrong and took steps to address them. I began to hear about people making noise for an end to unpaid internships, and I started to recognize that the fact that I worked for free for two years wasn't a badge of honor—it was a shame on our field. I gradually began to uncoil from my scarcity mind-set, and I started to relax. It became easier to meet people where they were, to see their unique skills and talents. In 2016, Chris Taylor asked me to be among the cohort of fifty museum workers who wrote the MASS Action toolkit. Over two days in Minneapolis, Minnesota, I met dozens of other people who worked in museums and did radical work. In the months that followed, we worked together and wrote a guidebook to doing inclusive, social justice–minded work in museums. I started to understand that it was OK to be angry about the state of our field, and to demand that we do better. I started to feel like I was part of a community, and that support allowed me to turn inward and recognize that I had the ability to change things in my own little corner of the museum world.

Whitney Plantation was founded and funded by John Cummings, a wealthy lawyer who believed that slavery was our nation's original sin, and who felt it was necessary that people learn about it to better understand the world we live in today. He is sharp and spry, but having opened the museum at nearly eighty years old, he and his family knew that something must be done to ensure the museum's survival and continuity. About the same time that I came back from Minneapolis, we began a three-year process to build the museum's first Board of Directors and convert the museum into a nonprofit, allowing him to donate the property and all its assets and step away entirely.

I took all the rich conversations I had with my radical museum community into the search for board members and writing the draft of the museum's first strategic plan. With my own experiences as a backdrop, I took the history of our site seriously and recognized that our museum was uniquely positioned to take a stance with regard to labor. Whitney Plantation was a site of stolen labor for more than two hundred years, first in slavery and later in wage work and debt peonage. Recognizing the historical trauma of the site, along with the wider movement in the museum field, I made the decision to disallow any unpaid internships or volunteer work at the site, which I wrote into our strategic plan. By 2018, I had begun to work hard to make sure that jobs had realistic titles and responsibilities and began to raise salaries. I stopped basing my expectations on what I had experienced in the past and started working toward what was equitable and what we could afford. I began to build a deeper trust with my closest reports, creating a work environment that allows them to bring blind spots to my attention, especially when they concern race. This is not always easy; in fact, it's often incredibly painful. But it's necessary work.

In recruiting board members, I especially felt it was crucial to find people who were deeply committed to our mission, and not to follow a pay-to-play model. I heard colleagues complaining across the field about the fact that boards were dominated by White men who donated large sums of money, whose goals were often at odds with the movement toward racial justice in the field. I emphatically argued that board members should not be required to contribute to the organization annually, already uncomfortable that they were the only class of people being asked to work for free at the organization. After a two-year search that involved expanding our networks and looking for candidates we did not already know, our first Board of Directors began service on December 4, 2019. They are majority female, and majority African American. They come from diverse backgrounds in the arts, historic preservation, the law, and philanthropy, and they all feel driven to support and uphold our mission. They are people who, like our staff, came to us with a calling to contribute their voice to our message.

As I've become more comfortable with my own beliefs—and come to trust my own voice—doing this work has gotten easier. I often feel that the shortest path between two points is the one that's most equitable. I'm more apt now to bring employees into my decision making and ask what they think is fair. My guiding philosophy is that people should be allowed to bring their whole authentic selves to work. They might not always be happy, because they are also allowed to be frustrated or angry or upset—but they should feel, at the most fundamental level, supported and heard. I used to have a baseline of anxiety, peppered by bursts of happiness at work. I don't want anyone who works for me to feel that way. The other great benefit of people being able to show up and be themselves is that they freely display their skills and strengths instead of guarding them. It's easy to identify people who can move up and grow in the organization when you're listening to them and taking their ideas seriously.

Leaders often remark on how it's lonely at the top. You don't have any coworkers, only people who report to you. It's necessary to maintain a certain distance from your employees, which I agree with. But it's a funny thing about being more inclusive and equitable: I don't feel so alone anymore. I have everyone else in the room here with me.

Chapter 13

Diary of a WOKE Latina Leader

Susana Smith Bautista

I am not used to talking about my personal thoughts and feelings in a public forum. I do so easily with good friends and colleagues over a cup of coffee or a glass of something stronger. However, in thinking about inclusive leadership, I began to wonder if I really am an inclusive leader, and if so, when, and how did this happen? Diversity, inclusion, equity, access; these are issues that are personal, not just to me, but they affect every institution and individual in different ways that are often challenging and traumatic, precisely because they are so personal. For this reason, I could not write about this topic objectively in the third person. So instead, I write my own experience of how I became *WOKE* as a Latina leader, which, for me, is also when I became an inclusive leader, in the hopes of providing insight into how a person of color approaches and experiences both leadership and inclusion. Another reason why I separate being a Latina and being inclusive is because it is so important *not* to assume that every BIPOC (Black, Indigenous, and People of Color) leader is automatically an inclusive leader.

Although I now self-identify as a Latina, I really am multiethnic. My mother was born in Chihuahua, Mexico, and emigrated to the United States around the age of eighteen with her family. My father was born in Montreal, Canada, and drove down Route 66 straight to Los Angeles in his late twenties, at the urging of a good friend from Montreal who had already settled happily in sunny California. After living in an apartment in now trendy Los Feliz, my parents bought their first house in Whittier, a Latino residential community in East Los Angeles. And then for some reason, they decided to move to the very White, affluent community of Pasadena just before I was born. The house was in the San Rafael area, near a very good public elementary school within walking distance. Everything was perfect, until 1970 when federal courts ordered Pasadena to desegregate its public school system and implement mandatory busing. Up until that point, Pasadena was clearly divided by the freeway to the north (African Americans and Latinos) and the south (all White upper middle and upper classes). My parents had moved into the south, which meant that for my first year in kindergarten I would be bused up north. The federal courts lifted their order ten years later, and schools had indeed become more integrated, but it was a very tough decade for Pasadena families. My parents did what many others did if they could afford to—they sent me to private schools in Pasadena all through high school. I write all this to acknowledge that

I have a privileged background, but also to demonstrate why this Latina needed to wake up, and as a reminder that people of color come from all different kinds of backgrounds.

I did experience discrimination at my private elementary school, and I remember being called names like "beaner" by other kids, but I did not really understand what it meant. I just knew that the other kids were mean. Despite my very White name (Susie Smith) and the school uniform, I was darker skinned than the other kids and had long brown hair, and I guess that made me Mexican. My parents tried to talk to the teachers, but nothing changed, so they put me in another private school, all girls, which was better, but mostly I think because it was now sixth grade and the other kids were growing up.

Figure 13.1 Susie Smith in school uniform, 7th grade. Photograph courtesy of Susana Smith Bautista

At the time, there were no Latinx affinity groups at school, no diversity director, no Latino Heritage Month celebrations, no Multicultural Parent Collaborative, and nothing for the other ethnic and racial groups. There was a surprisingly good diversity of Asians, African Americans, and Latina girls in my class, as well as good socioeconomic diversity. We all got along somehow. At home, I recall spending more time with my mother's side of the family than my father's, mostly because Mexicans always find an excuse to get together and have great food and conversations. We spoke English at home, but I remember hearing my mother speak Spanish with her family, wishing that I could understand. I chose to take Spanish at school (instead of Latin or French) with an Anglo teacher, and I must admit that school is where I really learned the language. Basically, I just lived a normal teenage life with normal teenage issues, homework, going to church, my dog, boys, piano lessons, reading science fiction books, and no sense of identity other than that. Until I had to write my college entrance essay. That's when I first started to open one eye. I remember that the essay was all about my name—Susan Elizabeth Smith—which I argued was misleading because such a common name didn't reveal the complexity of my background, my thoughts, and my ambitions. Success! I was accepted into Pomona College in Claremont for my undergraduate studies, which was a pretty similar demographic environment like Pasadena, only about thirty miles away.

First day moving into the dorm and I meet my new roommate. They had paired me up with a Mexican. Hmmm, interesting. We are unpacking our things in our room when we are visited by the local Chicano student group asking us to join (I can't recall if it was MECha[1] or some other organization). My roommate and I just stare at each other, as if, who are they looking for? She certainly didn't identify as a Chicana, and I didn't either (I was not even aware of what this was). You see, I would soon learn that she came from one of the wealthiest families in Mexico and had been in boarding school in California. We became close friends, took trips to Mexico together to her family's beach homes and ranches, and traveled to Europe and visited museums, but we never really discussed identity issues. I was more interested in opening my mind to the world and learning about art. This led to a study abroad program in Athens, Greece, during my junior year and, after graduating college, a short time in Hamburg living with a German boyfriend and then a move to New York City.

Living in New York, I had three jobs, and my mom helped pay the rent in a Manhattan loft, only because it had a doorman that she thought would be safer. I worked in an Upper East Side art gallery some weekends, I checked coats some nights at a trendy Italian restaurant in Soho (just for tips and good food), and my day job was working at INTAR (International Arts Relations Inc.), a Puerto Rican–run Hispanic theater and gallery space on West Forty-Second Street. I was basically the secretary, but I convinced the gallery director to let me help her, which was an amazing experience. Inverna Lockpez was a force of nature. We did studio visits together, looked at slide registries, painted the gallery a different color for each exhibition, and even distributed condoms at adult theaters in the area and joined in an ACT UP demonstration. It was my first introduction to Latino and Latin American artists. I was hooked.

Fast forward ten years. I left New York, went back to live in Athens, Greece, for eight years (got married, opened a Mexican bar called La Tequila Loca and a tortilla factory called El Sabor, became an art critic, and worked with the artist Takis), then returned to Los Angeles. I decided to pursue a master's degree in museum studies/art history at the University of Southern California because I wanted to focus more on curatorial work in museums. I immediately threw myself into the local Latino/Chicano art scene, visiting studios and organizing exhibitions on my own wherever I could. I was now fully *WOKE* as a proud Latina.[2] In fact, I even came back to Los Angeles with a new name, Susana Bautista. In Greece I had started to use my mother's last name Bautista (Smith didn't seem very appropriate for the owner of two Mexican businesses), and Susana was just what the Greeks called me. As others saw me as "the Mexican" (who taught Polish cooks to make refried beans and convinced Greek men to buy a whole bottle of mezcal just to get the worm at the bottom), I began to fully embrace that role.

In Los Angeles, I soon embarked upon the path to becoming a Latina leader. I completed my master's degree and graduated with honors; worked in local art museums and galleries still promoting Latino and Chicano artists; was executive director of the Mexican Cultural Institute; was on the board of the Latino Museum of History, Art and Culture and advisory boards where they needed a Latina voice; was editorial director of www.LatinArt.com; and independently curated two important exhibitions of Chicano/Latino art in the late 1990s. I even got a PhD and wrote a book, published by Rowman & Littlefield in 2013. At that point, my idea of inclusion was limited to Chicanos, Latinos, Mexicans, and Latin Americans. You see, at the Latino Museum of History, Art and Culture I was not Chicana enough, and at the Mexican Cultural Institute I was not Mexican enough. I married a Colombian, and when we visited his beautiful family in Medellin, I was introduced as *la novia gringa* (which is what Mexicans call White people in the United States). I was a proud Latina.

So, when did I become an *inclusive* Latina leader? I want to go back for a moment to Pasadena in the 1970s and 1980s, to recall what it was like growing up as Susie Smith in a private all-girls school (not Catholic), where the only Latino connection that I had was with my mother's family. These years taught me to navigate different cultural worlds, Canada and Mexico, East Los Angeles and Pasadena, upper class and middle class, Spanish and English, and Christmas with tamales and English pudding. Today some people refer to this as *code switching*, which is when you learn to talk and act differently depending on the situation. This was not my case, however, because I really felt like the same person in all these situations, which helped me seek professional opportunities and friendships that were both Latino and mainstream.

There were four distinct professional experiences that I can say contributed to my becoming an inclusive leader. These four leadership positions gave me the valuable opportunity to be included and, in the process, to recognize my own duty to in turn increase opportunities to enhance inclusion, equity, access, and diversity for those coming after me. I felt grateful and I felt responsible. I had become an inclusive leader.

Four Inclusive Experiences

1. The first is in 2011 when I joined the Board of Directors of my private all-girls school, Westridge. I would serve three full terms for a total of nine years, but it took me five years to finally find the right moment. The board decided it needed to create a Transgender Policy, and as chair of the School Committee it fell upon my shoulders. After an incredibly divisive and emotional year, working with outside consultants, lawyers, and even students who came out, we passed a policy that would not ask any student to leave the school based on changes in their gender or sexual status, understanding that it remains an all-girls school. It was difficult maintaining a neutral position when faced with such extreme viewpoints, but I earned the respect of the entire board by listening to different voices and focusing on the school's mission and history. I was so proud of that achievement. Because I know that change happens at the top, I proposed that the board create a new position of diversity chair, and I would be the first one. The following year I made sure it was changed in the board bylaws as a permanent position, and that it would always serve on the executive committee. And when I left the board, I recruited another Latino to take my place and made sure that he was not the only Latinx on the board. What I learned from this experience was to recognize opportunities and seize them, then work twice or three times as hard to be successful, and to also maintain a delicate balance between being confident with your personal feelings and opinions, and being open and respectful to others. Another lesson was an awareness of the importance of creating pathways and spaces for other Latinx leaders; a transference of power as I make room for others.

2. The second experience is when I worked at the USC Pacific Asia Museum (see figure 13.2) in Pasadena in 2014, first as interim deputy director and then as director of public engagement. This was a very difficult experience because I was responsible for helping with the transition/takeover by the University of Southern California (USC), and because the museum had its own shaky history with authenticity and inclusion for over forty years. The Pacific Asia Museum was founded by Anglos, always led by Anglos, housed in a replica Chinese imperial palace that was built by Anglo architects and owned by Grace Nicholson who traveled alone from Philadelphia to Pasadena in 1901. She later became a dealer of Native American and Asian art. Together with the first Asian director of the museum, and within the context of a university structure, we tried to create an engaging space for both Asians and Anglos from all generations. Certain Asian groups had been prioritized over others, in terms of exhibitions, programming, and leadership. This was also a reflection of the local demographics (largely Chinese, Japanese, and Korean). There were three groups that I worked very diligently to support and make more prominent at the museum: Filipinos, Pakistanis, and Pacific Islanders. Looking back, I think that as a Latina I was in a neutral position to best bring everyone together and try to create new beginnings, which included the academic community of USC. A doctoral degree was very helpful in working with the faculty, especially since my two graduate degrees were from USC. I polished the skill of relationship building by genuinely listening, absorbing, and sharing. Many people talk about Pasadena *politeness*, much like Midwestern *nice*, which I recognized (and appreciated) only after I had left Pasadena and returned as an adult.

3. The third is when I became the executive director of the Pasadena Museum of California Art in 2017, its first Latinx director. There, my initial act was to expand the museum's scope to include Indigenous, Spanish, and Mexican inhabitants in California prior to 1850 when it became a US state, which was limited by its mission statement: *The Pasadena Museum of California Art (PMCA) is dedicated to the exhibition of California art, architecture, and design from 1850 to the present.* This set the tone for my tenure at the museum. Soon after I started, we had a preplanned exhibition of Chicano artist Eduardo Carrillo from Central California, organized by the Crocker Museum in Sacramento. I created a community advisory group to help bring Latino and Chicano audiences to the museum (which was much needed), I corrected much of the didactic text about Chicanos that had been written by Anglo museum staff, and I found a way to exhibit a massive mural painted by Carrillo and three other prominent Chicano artists (*Chicano History*, 1970) that had not been publicly viewed since 1990 at the UCLA Chicano Studies Research Center (see figure 13.3).

figure 13.2 The author and her husband at a Pakistan Arts Council event, USC Pacific Asia Museum. Photograph by Annie Athar.

Figure 13.3 Chicano History mural exhibited at the Pasadena Museum of California Art in 2018. Photograph courtesy of Susana Smith Bautista

I then asked our curatorial staff to diversify early California art, mostly known for Anglo or European immigrant male artists, landscape and plein air painting. We decided on Grafton Tyler Brown (1841–1918), the first African American artist working in California, who came to San Francisco from Philadelphia a free man in the 1850s and built his business of lithography, graphics, and maps. It was quickly assembled on a small budget with an African American guest curator and with great press reviews after opening. The museum staff (which were fairly diverse) were the most supportive of my intention to diversify programming, exhibitions, and building our audience. There was little or no opposition from internal stakeholders. The opposition came mostly from funders and collectors who were not comfortable with expanding the traditional notion of early California art. While the board was perhaps wary of the changes initially, they were thrilled to see an increased number of visitors, and they say that they never had an opening quite as lively as the Carrillo exhibition. I learned to appreciate small successes that can be widely publicized, to build partnerships with diverse individuals and organizations based on common goals, to always look for opportunities to be more inclusive (even at the expense of the canon), and to make sure that staff and board play a part in both the decisions and the victories.

4. The fourth is when I joined the board of the American Alliance of Museums (AAM) in 2018. I was fortunate to join just as AAM launched its Facing Change initiative to support diversity, equity, access, and inclusion in museums. This is the only example where I am still in the midst of the experience (in my third year on the board), so I can write about this in the present. As one of two Latinos on the board (and the only Latina) out of twenty-one, I feel a responsibility to Latinx museums and Latinx museum professionals. I serve on the inaugural Diversity Committee of the board, support AAM's Latino Professional Network, forge Latinx connections with the biennial Conference of the Americas, helped choose the inaugural senior fellows for Facing Change, and was program chair for AAMVirtual 2020. Serving on a national platform (and global given AAM's reach into Latin America, Canada, and the United Kingdom) definitely raises the bar as far as having to work twice as hard to demonstrate, in real ways, my contribution to the board. There is greater visibility and so much pressure to succeed, feeling that I represent all Latinas. A board colleague (Anglo) said to me recently, as we discussed matters of diversity, that I had a conversational style she appreciated because she always learned something. I have reflected on that comment, which took me by surprise. As a leader within an organization, I can clearly articulate my leadership style as being transparent, inclusive, decisive, open-minded, and collaborative. But I have never really thought of my leadership style in other aspects of my life. It may be gender stereotypical, but I do find that I tackle difficult situations best as a conversation: listening to other voices, expressing mine, and, in the process, becoming familiar with other people and, in some cases, making enduring friendships. Conversations can become heated and even adversarial because of deeply felt passions on all sides. That is fine, as long as there remains respect and professionalism.

It is noteworthy that these four experiences were all mainstream and not Latinx centric. I can confidently say that I am comfortable in almost any situation, whether sitting in boardrooms or grassroots community spaces, talking with CEOs or security guards, and delivering presentations in Spanish and English all around the world, but this is only because I am comfortable with discomfort. My upbringing prepared me well for my profession in museums and the arts because I am often the only Latina or person of color in the room. Yes, I accept that I can be the token Latina, which is OK, because I always consider that it comes with opportunities to make a difference—not only by what I can accomplish but also by what I represent with all my achievements.

I have to also admit one thing that helped me tremendously to reach this point was pursuing my PhD. I knew that the museum field was competitive, especially at the director level, which often requires a PhD, but I had no idea how important it would be for a *Latina* to have a PhD. It does really open doors, it gets people to listen and pay attention more, and it commands respect (of course backed by hard work and true merit).

This is not the end of the story. The road forward will be just as bumpy as the road that led to this point. Eventually I went back to working with two Latino organizations—LA Plaza de Cultura y Artes (a Latino museum in Los Angeles) and AltaMed Health Services (as director and chief curator of its Latino art collection). It is truly empowering to work with so many smart Latinx professionals under one roof; still, I see a need for diversity, equity, and inclusion in the forms of gender, sexual preference, age, religion, socioeconomic status, and more. And there still exists such a great need for the larger ecosystem of museums and other arts organizations to have inclusion and equity with more Latino art and culture. The truth is that—whether I work in a Latino or mainstream institution—I will remain steadfast in my commitment to being an inclusive Latina leader. Though I continue to welcome uncomfortable situations, I recognize that they may present opportunities to make a difference and to have those difficult conversations in order to find ways to improve equity, inclusion, diversity, and access whenever possible.

I do not want to say that with age comes more confidence, because it's really not about age. It's the total lived and accumulated experience of triumphs large and small that provide such personal sense of accomplishment; having faced numerous obstacles and confrontations and come out with both my professional reputation and my optimistic outlook solidly in place. Along the way, these experiences have further rewarded me with many valuable relationships, both personal and professional, that give me the support and encouragement that I need to keep pushing forward because a big part of being *WOKE* and inclusive is knowing that you are not alone. I have taken the place of many wonderful mentors, I proudly serve alongside other inclusive leaders, and I continue to make space for the many others still out there.

Notes

1. Movimiento Estudiantil Chicano de Aztlán.
2. It is important to clarify that I have never identified as Chicana, even though I will acknowledge that I am Mexican American (half Mexican born in the United States). I have tremendous respect for Chicano/as who grew up during the difficult years of the civil rights movement in the 1960s and 1970s fighting for the rights of Chicanos, Latinos, and all underserved groups, as well as for those Chicano/as in the later years and continuing through today who grew up with a heightened awareness of social, political, economic, racial, and cultural issues and also strive for equity and inclusion. This was not my upbringing. While I share and support many of the Chicano principles today at this stage in my life, it would be insincere of me to assume that identity.

ACTIVITY

Developing Self-Awareness

To complete this activity, you'll need paper or a journal, your favorite pen, and access to the internet or texting.

As a follow-up to "The Johari Window Activity" in part 2, it's time to dig a bit deeper and examine how you are perceived at certain times in your life. This exercise will help you get a sense of yourself and to see where your values rest and now manifest.

This activity is designed to help you understand yourself better as a whole person so that you can welcome your teams in, warmly and with heart.

1. Select a small group of people (three to five) who have known you for a very long time. This could be people as far back as high school and college or people who knew you when you were in your first job. You pick the group but try to go back as far as you can into early adulthood.

2. Separately, ask them each these two questions:

   a. Can you use three words to describe me as a younger person?

   b. While you may or may not have seen me in action as a museum leader, what kind of leader do you imagine I am today?

3. You can ask these questions in person, by e-mail, or text. What works really well is to send a text to one individual asking permission to ask them a couple of questions. When they agree, send the first question. When they send that answer, then ask the second question. Repeat this same activity with each interviewee.

4. Were there consistencies between the responses you received? If there weren't, why do you think that is?

5. Would you say the words used to describe you reflect the intention of your leadership? What is the impact of that intention?

Take time to record the responses in a journal and write about questions 4 and 5. If you are finding misalignment, revisit the values exercise in part 2 and consider what you need to do to clarify your values and start living into them.

In case you don't know this, you were a wonderful person when you were younger and you still are today. Keep that knowledge close to your heart.

Chapter 14

Motion Sickness

Care, Compassion, and the Future of Museums

Esme Ward

This is tough. As I write this, the pandemic still rages, deeply ingrained inequalities surface, so much of the society I hold dear is fighting for survival, and the climate crisis looms larger than ever. I am impatient for change. I am exhausted one moment, energized the next. I am worried about our future. We are in motion.

So, I should start on solid ground. Or as I call it, Manchester, in northwest England. Museums in my city have always pioneered inclusion. In 1886, Manchester Art Museum (figure 14.1) opened in Ancoats[1] (known as Manchester's dirtiest, dreariest neighborhood). Established by philanthropist Thomas Coglan Horsfall, it was a social, educational, and civic experiment. Located close to people's homes, open until ten at night so working people could visit, activities included a resident Poor Man's Lawyer, provided by a team called the Associates offering legal advice to visitors in the museum each week; an outreach program for disabled children; and a Juvenile Employment Exchange.

I often draw upon my city's heritage and radical past to build my confidence, courage, and capacity to lead change. There are strong foundations, compelling stories, and wisdom to be found there.

Fast forward to 2016, and I'm feeling emotional and hugely proud, having recently helped rebuild and transform a much-loved Manchester institution, the Whitworth Art Gallery. But after twenty years working in art museum education and community engagement, I finally acknowledge my frustration with the curatorial-driven model of working and the paralysis of perfection it all too often necessitates. I'm ready for a change.

There has been no single "aha" moment, no revelatory or defining experience that has shifted my understanding and commitment to inclusive leadership. Instead there has been and continues to be a series of catalyzing experiences and encounters, not least my time in public health.

Figure 14.1 Manchester Art Museum in 1886. Courtesy of Manchester Museum

One for All; All for One . . .

Ready for change, I undertake a secondment, becoming part of my city-region's public health team, riding the heady waves of a unique devolution deal that decentralizes decision making and budgets. Through collaboration across public and private sectors and academia, and through the empowerment of citizens, my region, Greater Manchester, is pioneering a new approach to addressing the health and social care needs of 2.8 million people. The widely recognized challenge is that the region will not realize its potential until people realize theirs.

> For us, the starting point for our NHS (National Health Service) was not the establishment of a service but the confirmation of a promise. A promise made by, and on behalf of every citizen that we will care for each other. As Bevan stated, "health by collective action . . . was a commitment to solidarity through a social model: one for all, all for one."[2]

The reform program reimagines services across the whole care system, adopting a life-course, asset-based approach that encourages and promotes self-care and mutual care across communities and stages. The challenge we set ourselves is to rewrite the story of old age, from a narrative of loss and deficit to one of aspiration and growth. My secondment explores how to embed arts and culture within the strategic, practice- and policy-based priorities for aging and population health. This makes it sound dry and hands off. It's not.

For more than a decade, I'd worked closely across the aging and arts sectors to support a shift to a citizen-based approach, with the focus toward programs that were led by older people as active citizens. This is people-powered work. The Culture Champions (figure 14.2) is a large-scale creative and cultural voluntary program for older people (or as I prefer to say, the enriched, deeply experienced, later-lifers). They participate in, advocate for, develop, and lead cultural activities in organizations and communities. Over the last decade, it had gone from a handful (an alliance of the willing) to hundreds; from the city center to six boroughs. In my experience, they are the very best of us.

Figure 14.2 Culture Champions programme in action. Courtesy of Manchester Museum

I'd been part of this work for many years and built strong networks, friendships, and alliances. But until my secondment, I hadn't put institutional ego aside and engaged fully with codesign; how to build asset-based and community-level approaches with deep listening and lived experience at their core. Community organizers know this already and do it wholeheartedly. But in UK museums, community engagement can come with a lot of strings attached.

It dawned on me just how much of my work in museums had been on the institution's terms and timescales—with the veneer of inclusion. Despite plenty of good intentions, we rarely invested the time and care where it mattered most (beyond the museum, always beyond the museum) or for the long term. My time in public health showed me that too few museums and heritage bodies were working collaboratively for the long term with communities, other organizations, and funders to understand a place, its assets, priorities, idiosyncrasies, and ambitions.

Paul McGarry, a pioneer in urban aging who leads the Greater Manchester Ageing Hub, has done more to transform the lives of older people than anyone I know. Through his inclusive leadership, he brings together sectors, citizens, underrepresented groups, researchers, and policy makers to understand, challenge, and improve the experience of aging in the city. It is through my work with him that I realized for the first time that museums could and should be playing a significant role in a shared agenda of tackling inequalities and reimagining public health in the city—but only if we understand the need and what is at stake.

In 2018, I was appointed director of Manchester Museum, the United Kingdom's largest university museum with a strong civic mission to build understanding between cultures and a sustainable world. I'd been recruited to lead change and build the most inclusive, imaginative, and caring museum you might encounter.

Figure 14.3 Traditional owners Donald Bob and Magubadijarri Yanner in museum storage. Courtesy of Manchester Museum

Since then, I've actively encouraged new forms of research, partnerships, and coworking—with charities and voluntary organizations that share our values and mission, such as the specialist creative college Project Inc., leaders in alternative mainstream education for youth and young adults aged sixteen to twenty-five, who operate a creative learning studio, based on the museum's top floor. Interdisciplinary, cross-sector working is fertile ground. The networks are messy and powerful (and you will always need a bigger room). We have a shared post with the public health team. I continue to work as strategic lead for culture at the Greater Manchester Ageing Hub. Together we've recently launched CADA, a new national Creative Ageing Development Agency, focused on creating a powerful national community led by older people to tackle ageism, underrepresentation, and the right to culture and creativity in later life.

Matters of Care

My colleagues in public health valued museums and the arts for their ability to bring people together, to confer agency and autonomy, as spaces for expression, emotion, empathy, delight, awe, ambiguity, and vulnerability. These are their words. Meanwhile, at museum conference after conference, grim dehumanizing terms like *target*, *hard to reach* and *diversified* audiences are drowning out the language of possibility and connectedness.

Until my secondment, I hadn't realized how much I'd been editing myself. I'd always shown passion but rarely emotion or vulnerability—concerned people would think I was naïve, embarrassing, or unprofessional, or that those who hold the purse strings might not take our work or my leadership seriously. Since then, I've committed to making space for bringing the language of emotion to my work. "In public conversations around race, politics, ecology, we can't leave out our emotions—like grief, sadness, anger, shame—because they are key to action. We can't explore and achieve equality without them."[3]

Care and compassion are widely acknowledged as important attributes of healthy communities, on all scales. Author and economist Peter Block[4] highlighted how we've marginalized compassion in the public conversation, and he's probably right—just look at our leaders and the dire state of political discourse. But the first months of the pandemic shifted the tone of the conversation, and the generosity, empathy, mutual aid, and solidarity we witnessed across communities in lockdown showed us what might yet be possible. As Rebecca Solnit implored, "it should be regarded as a treasure, a light and an energy source that can drive a better society, if it is recognised and encouraged."[5]

Increasingly, I believe a commitment to care and compassion is foundational to the future of inclusive museums and my leadership. This commitment to care starts, not with the collections, but with staff. With the support of a range of partners (psychologists, researchers, charities, and health partners), we are developing a culture of mutual care and support, including a dedicated staff well-being program, most recently with one-on-one art therapy sessions available for staff during lockdown.

Encouraging a culture of collaboration and distributive leadership, I convene the Museum Cabinet, a monthly group with members drawn from every part of the museum's work, to guide decision making and strategic planning. A cross-museum social justice group shapes strategic thinking and practice. Before the pandemic, we no longer were sitting in teams or departments; curators sat next to conservators, educators, and commercial team members. Each month, all staff spent time with our visitors on the museum floor—the full breadth of expertise held across the museum acknowledged and valued.

The sad reality is that in the last month, more than 150 years of cumulative experience and expertise has left our museum. We have 20 percent less staff this year than last. We are diminished. At one stage, I was e-mailing thanks and farewell on a weekly basis, a hugely inadequate gesture to those who had taken voluntary redundancy or whose contracts had ended. Valued colleagues and friends were leaving way too soon and on terms none of us would have chosen. Being as kind and transparent as possible is the only way through this—and it's far from over. Now more than ever, it's time to imagine a new ethics of care for the museum sector, extending beyond collections to people (including the museum workforce), ideas, beliefs, and relationships.

It should be so simple—objects and people are inextricably linked. But, as one of my colleagues in Manchester summarized, "the Western processes and protocols established to catalogue, preserve and analyse objects and specimens in isolation from traditional owners, countries of origin and diaspora communities, continues to inflict loss, trauma and exclusion on those people most closely connected with collections."[6] More people than ever are questioning the legitimacy of institutional knowledge, calling for deepening levels of inclusivity, and promoting solidarity. There is an existential crisis in universal museums. The inability to fully acknowledge, interrogate, and address the impact and complexities of Empire on the one hand, and the limits of our wholehearted and transparent engagement with the things people really care about on the other, have been laid bare these last few months. My fear is that museums are ill equipped for the task ahead. Even pre-COVID-19, the traditional museum model was broken.

Linda Tuhiwai Smith wrote, "The intellectual project of decolonizing has to set out ways to proceed through a colonizing world. It needs a radical compassion that reaches out, that seeks collaboration, and that is open to possibilities that can only be imagined as other things fall into place."[7] What does this mean for museums, and how can we show a new or renewed commitment to inclusion, healing, and care?

Last year, in partnership with the Australian Institute of Aboriginal and Torres Strait Islander Studies (AIATSIS) and traditional owners, Manchester Museum began the process of unconditionally returning forty-three cultural objects to four Aboriginal communities (figure 14.3). We were the first (and to date, only) European museum to undertake such a return.[8] The University of Manchester's commitment to academic freedom and social responsibility sets a powerful context; its students represent the next generation of global citizens making changes in the world, and actions such as this are a positive example that reflect our common humanity. The university's Board of Governors was unanimous in its decision for support.

This repatriation will have a profound, positive impact upon the practice, presentation, and development of culture, language, and traditions for the Aranda, Gangalidda Garawa, Nyamal, and Yawuru peoples for years to come. But it will also have a significant, enriching, and enduring impact upon our institution, Manchester, and its communities. Mangubadijarri Yanner, one of the Gangalidda Garawa Traditional Owners said at the handover ceremony, "we share a dark history—but its moments like this, when we come together as one, united by our desire to do better, to be better and to right the wrongs of the past, that we start to heal spiritual hurts and the intergenerational trauma that still exists today."[9]

Repatriation requires sensitivity, emotional intelligence, and patience. It cannot be rushed. Museum staff spent many hours talking, researching, listening, waiting. Colleagues have spoken about being moved, personally and professionally, by the process: "it sometimes took me by surprise . . . to make change, one has to move through resistance . . . not only other people's but my own conditioned beliefs and habitual thinking. Now, I want to encourage a fearlessness in facing up to where we are, what we have, how it got here and how to respond" (Gillian Smithson, registrar).[10]

If museums are to reflect the complexity of the human condition and people's understanding of the world and each other, we must find space for the spiritual and emotional. Yet so much of our work takes place on the grounds staked out by Western rationalism. We deny the laws, realities, and belief systems of Indigenous peoples. In Manchester, as we recruit a new role of curator of Indigenous perspectives, we seek to build on this moment and generate changes to museum protocols, interpretation, language, and collections.

Doing Our Thinking in Public

Most of my conversations about repatriation with other museum directors have happened behind closed doors. This cannot be right. We need to open up the conversation, do more of our thinking in public, and invite new voices, perspectives, energy, accountability, and urgency. It's why we livestreamed the handover ceremony and an event in Manchester exploring the process. It's why, in partnership with AIATSIS, we have just published the methodology and impact case study.

My commitment to "do the right thing" has never wavered. My colleagues in Manchester feel the same. It has been a humbling and profound experience, and I believe acts like repatriation shift the processes, language, and thinking of the past toward a context of possibility and action for the future. As the news of the decision broke, I'd spent almost three months recuperating at home after a serious mountain biking accident and was feeling strangely disconnected from the turmoil it seemingly created in our sector. My peers (other directors), with some notable and thankful exceptions, were mostly silent. However, more than one commented on my nontraditional background (i.e., non-curator) and relative inexperience in the role. I was criticized for not keeping other directors "in the loop" with our plans. This was a catalyzing moment for me. I'd heard leadership could be lonely and exposing, but until that moment, I had never experienced it. I learned, with the support of fellow travelers and critical friends, to acknowledge this (if not accept it) and draw upon the "courage of one's convictions" and speak up. In part, it's why I wrote an open letter to the museum sector reflecting on the experience of repatriation.[11]

Lost in Translation

We want to engage in citywide conversations about the future of collections and conceptualize those collections as stories and relationships as well as shared cultural heritage. But this openness and curiosity isn't what we show the world. Museums love to control the narrative—curators and educators spend hours writing text to go on the walls, in books, and on screens. The institutional voice, one of authority and expertise, dominates (particularly in a university context). The words just sit there, waiting to be improved, challenged, and enriched, yet we all too rarely redraft, update, or amend.

While more museum leaders and professionals are starting to embrace more iterative and inclusive approaches (from proto-typing to co-curation), the systems and processes we operate in have yet to catch up. I'm caught right in the middle of this, and it can be a frustrating, energy-sapping place to be.

I've inherited a significant capital project that includes a South Asia Gallery—a flagship partnership with the British Museum funded by central government, trusts, foundations, and philanthropists. Eleven percent of Greater Manchester's population is of South Asian descent, but barely 3 percent were visiting museums. The new South Asia Gallery would address this and be a professionally curated space (with a predominantly White-British curatorial team)—featuring a chronological display of South Asian history with a performance space at its heart for diaspora communities. There had been widespread consultation—truckloads of it.

So much about the process felt off—many key people weren't represented or part of the development. Of course, it's exactly what the RIBA (Royal Institute of British Architects) and exhibition design processes encourage, and the neat list of objects was close to completion. The designers were on stand-by. This project had the potential to become deeply and widely loved. Done right, it could become the United Kingdom's first permanent gallery dedicated to South Asian diaspora experience and contribution, and one of the UK's most inclusive museum spaces. Only a few weeks into my time as director, I nervously pressed pause on the project.

Many of the staff who were working on the project were relieved, sharing my concerns. We gathered together one hundred or so people—South Asian diaspora artists, educators, faith-leaders, researchers, business and community leaders, an alliance of the willing—for a fabulous meal at a South Asian fusion restaurant in east Manchester. The invitation made it clear that the South Asia Gallery now sought to be a creative, collective, and social endeavor. I welcomed everyone with the question we should have asked long ago (and always my first question), "What do you really care about? What matters to you?" We asked people to come on a journey with us, to explore what really matters.

It's taken us to places and partnerships we'd never have imagined, locally and globally. The work and relationships have grown. We have new members of staff, insights, expertise, and experience. We are becoming a multilingual museum. Funding has followed for youth programs, fellowships, research, and international partnerships. It's changing and enriching us. What has developed over nearly two years is a fascinating, energizing, and challenging anthology approach to the gallery, where lived experience and world class collections will come together. It will, we hope, be like alchemy. The South Asia Collective, composed of twenty-eight people with a wide range of backgrounds and interests, supported by the museum, are co-curating the space, which is due to open in August 2022.

But pausing and adapting the process delayed the program by at least six months and has added many tens of thousands of pounds to the budget. I've accepted that I'm going to be fundraising for a very long time. I have become a determined, bloody-minded storyteller, articulating the dreams and imaginative potential of the project, responding to and held aloft on the shoulders of the Collective and South Asia Gallery team. What I'm learning from numerous conversations with funders, stakeholders, and philanthropists is that the idea that "you reap what you sow" (and the momentum it builds) is compelling. But it can be exhausting. Our desire to be less transactional at every turn has collided with procurement processes. We eventually parted ways with our original exhibition designers who struggled with our approach. The South Asia Collective, young people, partners, and museum colleagues all participated in the new recruitment process, via Zoom. We've finally appointed a talented new young design consortium; we fell in love with their collaborative spirit and clean lines. They have experience in codesign but limited experience in museums.

Our commitment to enduring relationships, inclusion, coproduction, and greater collaboration, for me, speaks to the future of museums and the city we are in. The reality is that this comes at significant risk, not least financial risk, and challenges the mechanisms and realities of large-scale capital infrastructure, timetables, and processes. There will be compromises ahead, but there is also serious work to do with funders to address the systemic change that supports meaningful and longer-term commitment to co-curation and inclusion.

Co-curating essentially means caring together. We've spent a lot of time across the city building trust and connections, making lots of mistakes, and learning. We have started to understand and respond more effectively to a wider range of people's cares and concerns. Our team and our visitors are now more diverse than ever, and we are starting to reflect the communities we serve.

It has become crystal clear that if we want a deeper sense of emotional and communal engagement, belonging, and ownership for everyone, we have to create the conditions that enable and encourage that.

Iftar at the Museum

In 2019, we held the first ever Iftar at the Museum (figure 14.4), open to all faiths and none. This event was in partnership with Manchester's University Muslim Chaplain, a local restaurant that provided the food, and the charity Human Relief Foundation who provided the dates to break the fast. In the spirit of the month of Ramadan, the month of hospitality and sharing, more than four hundred people gathered for an evening of food, friendship, and dialogue across faiths and cultures. The call to prayer and prayers in congregation were performed in the heart of the museum. Many staff had never been to an Iftar, while others are practicing Muslims. We're learning how to do this together—and cannot wait to bring people together in this way again.

Our civic mission seeks to build a culture of creativity, inclusion, and care; everyone is welcome, all faiths and none. We need to unpack the notion that public shows of religiosity are not the way we do things—as often the hypocrisy of the Eurocentric lens is called out—that is, on the one hand, nuns in habits are rightly respected while, on the other hand, women in hijabs are mocked or caricatured.

The Iftar shifted relationships and expectations of the museum (within the university and Muslim communities) and foreshadows what might be possible. "Now I know I am safe here and belong," a visitor told us, "it means so much that you've done this." We were thanked for refusing to bow to Islamophobia and told it was "very brave, a great display of cultural intelligence." We had only two negative responses . . . a comment on the night, "Is there really a need for all public spaces to engage in this multifaith idealism?" We responded

Figure 14.4 Iftar at the Museum in 2019. Courtesy of Manchester Museum

that we are in Manchester and this is multifaith reality—not idealism. And via Twitter someone responded, "FFS what are you doing?" to which we replied, "Hosting an Iftar. You're welcome." The people we work so closely with on the Iftar and South Asia Gallery have been disproportionately affected by COVID-19. The gallery has become a catalyst for sharing the stories that matter most, a space committed to ensuring their heritage and experiences are valued in the context of their city, more so than ever before.

A growing sense of urgency has been a powerful undercurrent in my work in the last few months. I've tried to resist its pull. I find myself increasingly impatient. If not now, born out of the devastating multiple impacts of COVID-19 and the momentum of Black Lives Matter, when will we change and accelerate our thinking?

For all the political and civic discussion of "green and just recovery," I see little action. We've been meeting with activists from Climate Emergency Manchester, ecologists, and environmental educators to understand how to support their work, build more sustainable futures, and inspire cooperation and change in our city. This is beyond urgent—the climate emergency is a cultural and social justice issue, and more than 20 percent of Manchester's carbon budget for the twenty-first century has been used up in the last two years. Throughout summer 2020, I've prioritized deep listening and building collaborations focused on new narratives of hope and belonging. As a leading university natural history gallery with an award-winning Vivarium (live animal) team, the museum is a critical part of the research and environmental education infrastructure. As you might expect, we're now reimagining education for future survival.

Time and again, when we asked those leading change what more was needed and how we could help, they asked us to step into our convening power and encourage greater connectedness and a sense of shared purpose. In response and supported by them, we've started building a directory or ecological registry of green practitioners across the city—ecologists, educators, community groups, researchers, campaigners, artists, activists—geotagged and skills focused, to encourage connectedness, shared purpose, and hyper-local action toward greater biodiversity and a zero carbon city. It won't be comprehensive, and it will never be completed. It's not the usual work of a museum, but it's sorely needed and these are not usual times. We will get to know our city better, and we currently have the skills, people, and the will to make it happen. In a workshop last year, the value of "deep ecology" emerged as the primary shared value among staff and volunteers. We have committed to be caretakers of this citywide resource for a generation. The stories and exhibitions will come, but they are no longer enough.

The pandemic still rages. I am impatient for change. I have always believed that in caring for the past, museums are essentially staking a claim on what matters in the future. Inclusion matters. So much of the society I hold dear is fighting for survival, and the climate crisis looms larger than ever.

I am exhausted one moment, energized the next. I am worried about our future. We are in motion. We have to hold on . . .

Notes

1. Stuart Eagles, "Thomas Coglan Horsfall and Manchester Art Museum and University Settlement," in *The Encyclopaedia of Informal Education*, 2009, www.infed.org/settlements/manchester_art_museum _and_university_settlement.htm.
2. Jon Rouse, "Taking Charge? Learning from Health and Social Care Devolution in Greater Manchester," Teddy Chester Lecture, Greater Manchester Health and Social Care Partnership, November 29, 2017, http://www.gmhsc.org.uk/wp-content/uploads/2018/04/Teddy-Chester-Lecture-Jon-Rouse-291117 .pdf.
3. Tessa McWatt, *Shame on Me: An Anatomy of Race and Belonging* (London: Scribe, 2019), p. 135.
4. Peter Block, *Community: The Structure of Belonging* (Oakland, CA: Berrett-Koehler, 2018).
5. Rebecca Solnit, "'The Way We Get through This Together': The Rise of Mutual Aid under Coronavirus," *Guardian*, May 14, 2020.
6. Esme Ward, *The Tide of Change: Open letter from Esme Ward*, accessed March 14, 2021, https://mu seum-id.com/the-tide-of-change-open-letter-from-esme-ward/.
7. Linda Tuhiwai Smith, *Decolonizing Methodologies: Research and Indigenous Peoples* (London: Zed Books, 1999), Foreword, p. xii.
8. Illinois State Museum, in the United States, had been the first museum to return cultural heritage material weeks before.
9. Mangubadijarri Yanner, Handover Ceremony at Australia House, London, November 22, 2019.
10. Personal communication, in the form of email correspondence from Gillian Smithson to Esme Ward, reflecting upon the process of repatriation, Monday 14 September 2020 at 08:56, email.
11. Esme Ward, "The Tide of Change: Open Letter from Esme Ward," Museum-ID, November 26, 2019, https://museum-id.com/the-tide-of-change-open-letter-from-esme-ward/.

Bibliography

Block, Peter. *Community: The Structure of Belonging.* Oakland, CA: Berrett-Koehler, 2018.

Eagles, Stuart. "Thomas Coglan Horsfall and Manchester Art Museum and University Settlement." In *The Encyclopaedia of Informal Education*. 2009. www.infed.org/settlements/manchester _art_museum_and_university_settlement.htm.

McWatt, Tessa. *Shame on Me: An Anatomy of Race and Belonging.* London: Scribe, 2019.

Rouse, Jon. "Taking Charge? Learning from Health and Social Care Devolution in Greater Manchester." Teddy Chester Lecture, Greater Manchester Health and Social Care Partnership, November 29, 2017. http://www.gmhsc.org.uk/wp-content/uploads/2018/04/Teddy-Chester-Lecture-Jon-Rouse-291117.pdf.

Smith, Linda Tuhiwai. *Decolonizing Methodologies: Research and Indigenous Peoples.* London: Zed Books, 1999.

Solnit, Rebecca. "'The Way We Get through This Together': The Rise of Mutual Aid under Coronavirus." *Guardian*, May 14, 2020.

Ward, Esme. "The Tide of Change: Open Letter from Esme Ward." Museum-ID, November 26, 2019. https://museum-id.com/the-tide-of-change-open-letter-from-esme-ward/.

Chapter 15

8:46:40

Devon M. Akmon

It is often said that September 11, 2001, was the day that changed the world. Most Americans alive at that time can vividly recall the details of that horrific day. The recollections of where we were, who we were with, and the feelings that subsumed us are now etched in our minds and define both our individual and collective memories. And, in many ways, those acts of terrorism unified a majority of Americans as the nation sought to heal and respond to the trauma. However, for others, the events ushered in a new era of suspicion, surveillance, and marginalization that arguably continues to this day. This is especially true for Arab and Muslim Americans. In fact, 9/11 remains a day of multiple traumas for many Arab and Muslim Americans: one marked by the grief of the tragedy and the subsequent traumas associated with sharing a likeness to those responsible for the horrors. For me, as a relatively young, third-generation Arab American, the day would serve as a defining moment that would have a profound impact on my identity and outlook that continues to this day.

Throughout my life, I have been able to reap the rewards of White privilege. My family immigrated to the United States from Lebanon in the early twentieth century. Despite the myriad challenges of being immigrants, including being defined as "dark" on census papers and perceived as Other, they sought to quickly assimilate and become "American." Externally, this process of identity shedding included speaking English, concealing the use of their native Arabic, and giving their children Anglicized names. Moreover, they sought citizenship as Whites despite immigrating from a region known geopolitically as the Middle East. By the time I was a child, my complexion, name, and religion were enough to mask my ethnic identity and afford me great privileges. While we worshiped in a Maronite (Eastern Catholic) church and retained many of our customs, such as large extended family gatherings each Sunday that included a sumptuous meal with the foods that define our culture, most people had no idea we were Arab Americans.

Things changed after September 11, 2001. For the first time in my life, I began to experience the adverse impacts of a marginalization based on identity. I was dismayed to learn of family members getting detained while trying to board a flight or cross the border, by car, into neighboring Canada from Detroit. On a more macro level, it was a particularly challenging new era in metropolitan Detroit. Southeast Michigan is home to the largest concentration of Arab Americans in our nation. Diverse by religion, place of origin, and time of immigration, the Arab American communities that comprise the region were often perceived as a monolith and potential threats to the American way of life. The diverse characteristics that define Arab American communities, along with their histories and contributions to our nation for generations, was seemingly of little concern to most during the initial years of the war on terror. Instead, fear and misinformation fueled suspicion and negative perceptions.

I spent the early years after 9/11 trying to figure out my place in the world. I pursued a graduate degree and found love, but I struggled with how best to push back on harmful stereotypes and hostilities pointed at people who shared my cultural heritage. This all changed as I was completing my advanced degree. As graduation approached, I became aware of a new museum on the verge of opening in Dearborn, Michigan. This cultural institution, the Arab American National Museum (AANM), would become the first and only museum in the nation dedicated to documenting, preserving, and presenting the history, culture, and contributions of Arab Americans. As luck would have it, the new institution was in the midst of hiring personnel as the museum was being prepared for a public opening. The timing was fortuitous and, on a whim, I applied for the position of curator of community history. Given my academic training (a bachelor's degree in psychology, followed by a master's degree in historic preservation planning) and limited experiences working in a university museum as an undergraduate, I had little hope of actually landing the job. However, I secured the position and joined the museum just before the opening on May 5, 2005. In hindsight, founding director Dr. Anan Ameri's hiring strategy was clear: hire staff based on their activism and passion for preserving Arab American culture and thwarting the harmful stereotypes that malign our communities. This would become a seminal lesson for my own leadership style: specialized knowledge and aptitudes are important, but even more critical is passion and drive to build community through culture. This inclusive approach to building a staff continues to define my hiring philosophy to this day.

Conceived prior to, but developed after 9/11, the AANM was truly a first of its kind. The AANM filled a critical void in the landscape of American museums. For the first time, Arab Americans would have a cultural venue of their own. This was immensely empowering: a place for Arab Americans to have agency in documenting and sharing their diverse histories and experiences. Prior to this, the Arab American story was either ignored altogether or told primarily by those who were not of Arab heritage. Now, Arab American communities would have the ability to tell their own stories in a safe and welcoming space.

Since its inception, the AANM has played a critical role in enriching and broadening the spectrum of cultural institutions in the United States. As the singular museum in our nation dedicated to documenting and preserving Arab American history and culture, the AANM strives to dispel stereotypes and misconceptions while building greater cohesion among Arab Americans. The museum has worked since its inception to shed light on the diversity of the Arab American communities. This diversity is reflected in a number of ways, including through religion, place of origin, era of immigration, settlement within the United States, political affiliation, and much more. In short, Arab Americans are far from being a monolith, and the museum's success required us to develop an inclusive platform for all Arab Americans to feel pride and see a reflection on their story in this groundbreaking institution.

I spent my first few years at the AANM in the curatorial department. This work included helping to build the museum's nascent collection and launching a robust temporary exhibition program with my colleagues. Much of our work was done in collaboration with members from across Arab

American communities near and far. Through these efforts, I began to see firsthand the positive benefits of working with our constituents to cocreate and present museum content: it fostered community empowerment and ownership. What's more, the work of the museum began to resonate with people who had a limited history of engaging with cultural institutions within our nation.

The community-based museum work we sought to implement required a great deal of flexibility. To engage with community means working outside the normal nine-to-five business hours. It means going outside the museum to engage with constituents where they are. The Wing Luke Museum of the Asian Pacific American Experience best describes the nature of this work in their values statement:

> People give us meaning and purpose. Relationships are our foundation. We desire community empowerment and ownership. To do this, we have found the following: The work is labor intensive. The work requires flexibility. We willingly relinquish control.[1]

In addition to working in an inclusive manner with the communities we were to represent with our exhibition and programs, it was also critical for us to partner with other, non-Arab communities. After all, we strived to be an ethically specific, not ethnocentric, museum. If we expected others to learn about our history and customs, then it was paramount that we reach outside to collaborate with other communities, both to learn about them and to celebrate the diversity of our nation.

During those instrumental early years, the staff of the AANM learned immensely from colleagues at other ethnically specific museums. We respected—and often sought to emulate—the pioneering work of Ron Chew and the team at the Wing Luke Museum to form a community-based model of exhibition development. From Irene Hirano and her team at the Japanese American National Museum we learned the importance of building coalition and developing timely and responsive programming. These museums, along with the Charles H. Wright Museum of African American History, National Museum of Mexican Fine Art, and the Birmingham Civil Rights Institute, demonstrated to us the value of building an institution that was people focused and rooted deeply in the communities we serve—lessons that proved instrumental to building a fledgling institution.

The staff at the AANM began forming numerous community-based committees to advise and consult the museum on its work. This included a collections committee, an exhibitions committee, a National Advisory Board, and many program-specific steering committees. In doing so, we more firmly rooted the museum within the communities it served while also building a shared sense of ownership: work that was simultaneously incredibly challenging and rewarding. While facilitating conversations around complex and often divergent viewpoints, staff worked to mediate a range of ideas and opinions in a way that both supported the objectives of the museum while also working to build more cohesion within the diverse Arab American communities it represented. Again, staff who were both technically competent and able to genuinely engage with the communities were instrumental for positioning the museum to be both welcoming and authentic.

My role evolved as the AANM became more established. After over four years serving as a curator, I was promoted first to deputy director and then, when our founding director retired, as the second director of the museum. During my tenure as director, our team sought to further expand and evolve our community-based work. This manifested in several ways. First, we began to explore how we could design and implement programming outside the physical walls of the museum. One of the museum's greatest assets was its location within the heart of a heavily populated Arab American community. The museum sought to capitalize on this in a way that would bring the local residents in closer contact with the museum while providing visitors with a unique and informative experience. As we conceived ideas, the United States was also grappling with growing Islamophobia, and Dearborn was often wrongly perceived as governed by Sharia law and home to fundamentalist behavior. For the museum, it was of vital importance to push back on these harmful misconceptions and to humanize the experiences of the communities we sought to serve. In this regard, the museum served as both educator and facilitator.

The *Yalla Eat!* program best exemplifies this role. Similar to other ethnic communities, food is a vital cornerstone of Arab American culture. The role of food as a manifestation of culture is reflected in the museum's permanent exhibits, but the museum is also located at the epicenter of scores of Arab American food businesses. We began to imagine the possibilities of collaborating with local food-based business to share our educators' and docents' knowledge of the nuances of food as culture. And, with that a novel idea came to fruition. Working in partnership with bakers, butchers, restauranteurs, and other food purveyors, the museum designed and implemented a culinary walking tour that involved the community in sharing its history, culture, and presence in the United States through food. While in the past a museum educator might explain the idea of halal food to a museum guest, now guests could learn directly from a butcher about food preparation that adheres to Islamic law. Through this inclusive work, we were able to immerse museum guests in the local community while directly involving Arab Americans in sharing their stories and culture. The *Yalla Eat!* program proved to be one of the most popular and successful programs during my tenure as director.

In addition to collaborating with community, the AANM also sought to provide space for its constituent communities. Early on, it became apparent that our local communities needed a safe space to gather and create. I vividly recall an early conversation with an Iraqi American actor about his desire to use the museum's auditorium as a space to craft a play about the Iraq War. It sounded like a promising project, and we were more than happy to support this creative endeavor. However, he worked on the line during the day at a local automotive plant and wanted to use the museum in the evening, after hours. Unfortunately, we did not have the resources to keep staff working late and the building open. Moreover, as an accredited museum, we couldn't let members of the public into our facility after hours without ensuring the safety and care of our collections. Sadly, we were unable to support this playwright with his endeavor.

A few short years later, however, during the Great Recession, the museum was able to secure two neighboring buildings. In the years that followed, we developed a new space, called the Annex, immediately adjacent to the museum. This space was purposely designed to be minimal and physically separated from the museum so that it was highly flexible and could be used before, during, and after normal museum hours. We wanted the space to serve as a critical piece of social infrastructure in the community.

Much has been written on the importance and worrying decline of social infrastructure. Robert Putman, the Peter and Isabel Malkin Professor of Public Policy at the Harvard University John F. Kennedy School of Government, chronicled the decline of the "third place" in his book *Bowling Alone: The Collapse and Revival of American Community*.[2] More recently, Eric Klinenberg, professor of sociology, public policy, and media, culture, and communication at New York University, explored the importance and urgent need for more social infrastructure in working to solve inequities in our society.[3] Dearborn had a robust patchwork of religious institutions, social clubs, and cafés that served as a nexus for social interaction. However, there were few spaces that were nonreligious, accessible to all, and nurturing the creative spirit of the local Arab American community.

As we sought to activate the Annex, we began to explore new ways of working with the community to best utilize the space. This manifested in numerous ways and typically took place above and beyond normal museum hours. For example, the National Arab Orchestra, based in Dearborn, began to conduct rehearsals in the evening at the Annex. Further, the orchestra's founder and music director conducted music lessons in this new space. Arabic language lessons, which were typically taught at religious institutions, were designed and led by members of the community in the Annex. Additionally, we began to serve the community in ways we had not anticipated, but welcomed. The Annex was used by members of the community to organize politically, to host election return watch parties, and as a place to gather to find solace during times of grief.

In 2016, I had the privilege of hearing Reverend Starsky D. Wilson, president and CEO of Deaconess Foundation and cochair of the Ferguson Commission, speak as the keynote at the Institute for Museum and Library Services Catalyst Town Hall Meeting in Philadelphia. Reverend Wilson implored those in attendance to contemplate the role of museums as places of sanctuary.[4] This idea resonated as we recently had done just that at the AANM. In the days following the horrific mass shootings at the Pulse nightclub in Orlando, Florida, the staff of the AANM opened the Annex as a protected space for our local LGBTQ community to process the trauma and grieve in peace. In other words, our museum had become a nonreligious sanctuary for healing.

In many ways, the examples I've just shared were experiments in working to build a more inclusive and equitable institution. We sought to explore where we activated museum programs, how we included members of the community in cocreating programs, and how we leveraged our assets to provide much-needed space in a timely and responsive manner. This work was never fixed or finished; instead, it was constantly in flux and required continuously working in tandem with constituent communities.

As I reflect on the past, I'm overwhelmed by how one horrific day had such an impact on my profession and the manner in which I lead nonprofit organizations. The tragic events of September 11, 2001, put in motion a personal journey that continues to this day. I remain committed to the important roles that art and culture play in both empowering and building communities. To build a community-focused and inclusive organization requires hiring staff with shared values, committing to the hard and rewarding work of collaborating with constituent communities, and often sharing power in reaching mutually rewarding goals. Since departing the AANM in 2018, I served as a senior consultant with the DeVos Institute of Arts Management at the University of Maryland. It was there, working with dozens of cultural institutions across the nation, that I truly began to understand the importance of inclusive, community-based cultural work and its implications for a wide range of cultural institutions. As I settle into a new role as the director of Science Gallery Detroit, transitioning an organization from a start-up amid a global pandemic and push for greater social justice, the lessons learned as a leader during the formative years of the AANM serve as my North Star.

Notes

1. Wing Luke Museum, "About Us," accessed October 4, 2020, http://www.wingluke.org/about-us/.
2. Robert David Putnam, *Bowling Alone: The Collapse and Revival of American Community* (New York: Simon & Schuster, 2000).

3. Eric Klinenberg, *Palaces for the People: How Social Infrastructure Can Help Fight Inequality, Polarization, and the Decline of Civic Life* (New York: Crown, 2018).

4. Institute of Museum and Library Services, "Rev. Starsky D. Wilson Speaks at IMLS Catalyst Town Hall Meeting," September 23, 2016, YouTube video, 33:15, https://youtu.be/904kLBDny9c.

Bibliography

Institute of Museum and Library Services. "Rev. Starsky D. Wilson Speaks at IMLS Catalyst Town Hall Meeting." September 23, 2016. YouTube video, 33:15. https://youtu.be/904kLBDny9c.

Klinenberg, Eric. *Palaces for the People: How Social Infrastructure Can Help Fight Inequality, Polarization, and the Decline of Civic Life*. New York: Crown, 2018.

Putnam, Robert David. *Bowling Alone: The Collapse and Revival of American Community*. New York: Simon & Schuster, 2000.

Wing Luke Museum. "About Us." Accessed October 4, 2020. http://www.wingluke.org/about-us/.

Chapter 16

Grounded in Community

A Conversation with Stacey Halfmoon

The following conversation was recorded in October 2020 as construction was close to completion at the new Choctaw Cultural Center in Durant, Oklahoma, during the coronavirus emergency. Stacey led the creation of the American Indian Relations Division at the Ohio History Connection before returning home to lead the Cultural Center in 2019.

Stacey Halfmoon: I find myself working in museums due to two things. One would be my family. I was lucky enough to spend a lot of time with both my grandparents, Hubert and Corinne Halfmoon (figure 16.1). My grandfather was half Delaware and half Caddo and one of those people who could do it all. He was a national archery champion. He was a national boxing champion. He had a degree in business and accounting. He was the tribal chairman. He was fluent in the tribal language and sat at the drum. He was a great person, and funny, and kind. My grandmother was Choctaw who also has an impressive list of accomplishments including the Oklahoma City Indian Clinic being named after her—she served on their Board of Directors for over twenty years.

I think those family experiences, interwoven with the Oklahoma experience, were important influences on my life. There are thirty-nine federally recognized Tribal Nations in Oklahoma, and when you grow up in that realm, you're born in the middle of a diverse and culturally rich environment. Although I didn't realize it at the time, it set an important tone for the rest of my life. I grew up going to an Indian Baptist church where our pastor was Seminole and Creek, and our song leader was Kiowa and there were Caddo people and other Tribes in the church. On any given Sunday you might hear beautiful Caddo hymns, or Kiowa songs. This created in me an inherent interest and respect for other cultures, and opened my mind to the idea that there existed many different languages, different beliefs and people out there in the world, even at the time I couldn't process it the way I do today. I just knew there were all kinds of wonderful people: people of color; people who maybe didn't look Native yet were fluent speakers. That personal backdrop of my family and my tribal heritage and being from Oklahoma definitely influenced me.

Figure 16.1 Hubert and Corinne Halfmoon, Stacey Halfmoon's grandparents. Source: Stacey Halfmoon

Then when I got to college and I took my first anthropology class, I fell in love and I changed my major immediately when I figured out that I could officially study cultures of the world!

I thought, "sign me up!" Studying anthropology is the second path that led me to museum work. Soon after graduating, I was lucky enough to go to work for the Caddo Nation. This was just after the Native American Graves Protection and Repatriation Act (NAGPRA)[1] had been signed into law. The Caddo tribe was the first tribe in the state of Oklahoma to apply for and receive a NAGPRA grant,[2] and they were looking for staff to help implement the grant project. Working on NAGPRA was where my journey working with cultural resources, working in tribal relations and with tribal governments, and [working in] repatriation truly began. I loved working with my Tribe. That's when partnerships with other museum and museum professionals began. I had the opportunity to travel to other museums, see how they cared for collections, and I remember being shocked that there were so many Caddo human remains in those collections.

Now I work with the Choctaw Nation of Oklahoma, in Durant, Oklahoma. I'm the senior director of the Choctaw Cultural Center, which is the Choctaw Nation's first cultural center and has a full collections facility and archive, as well as living cultural elements for programming.

Chris Taylor: In thinking about your museum journey, how do you define inclusion and how do you incorporate it into your leadership style?

Stacey: It's so interesting to step outside your own mind-set a little bit and think about my leadership style in these terms. Obviously, part of the reason I have this background is because it's where my mind is, an American Indian perspective. I come from the perspective of always asking if Native voices are being included. In a way it has been a defining element of my career . . . asking if tribal people are being consulted. When you come from that mind-set, it's your whole driving force. It is easier to think about inclusivity as a whole—and being able to come into any work environment or organization and immediately notice how inclusive it is. If there are voices that are not being heard, it also reflects the role of inclusivity at the leadership level.

Defining inclusion, to me, is answered in a simple question—are we working with anybody that would be impacted by either our work, by our collections, or by how we're interpreting information? Inclusion is that basic question. Are we leaving anybody out? What are the stories we're trying to tell, and who should be at the table? It's funny because it seems so simple, but honestly, in a lot of work environments, it's either overlooked or the staff operate using borrowed authority. That can happen within organizations that aren't diverse internally or who have never worked with diverse populations. You will see staff using borrowed authority to make decisions on behalf of other communities or people who are not present; often not stopping to ask, "Who should be included in this conversation?"

Inclusivity is about asking, "Who should be included?" And you can apply that simple question to collections—exhibitions and care. You can apply to your Board of Trustees. You can apply it to the staff leadership team at the organization, and you can also apply it to the communities where your organization is located. "Who have we excluded from these conversations?" In my experience, in the museum world, this question often relates to interpretation because museums/programs/exhibitions are interpreting histories. Articles are being written, text panels are being written, content for the web is being created—and that involves interpreting the history of people or communities who aren't included in the process. We should be asking, "Whose history are we interpreting? Have we talked to those communities?"

Inclusivity is almost that simple in thought, but it's not as simple in an action. A recent example I can share is stems from working with a board that wasn't overly diverse. It was an organization and board using the somewhat traditional process of recruiting "upstanding citizens, well-known/established citizens or wealthy citizens," While it creates a giving board, it can easily result in a board that lacks representation from minorities or underrepresented populations. This creates a top-down effect, which reinforces exclusiveness. Fortunately, I was working with an executive director who was supportive of my idea to propose to change the board constitution to allow for federally recognized American Indian Tribal Nation leaders or representatives. And not just local community representatives, but representatives of the Tribal Nations who were Indigenous to that state. Because it was a state organization, and this could involve Tribal Nations who were no longer in that state due to Indian Removal policies, it made it even more challenging. We had to secure membership approval and pass a constitutional amendment.

That's how we approached it, and it was ultimately voted upon and approved/adopted. Now that board has its first Tribal leader who is participating as a board member, from out of state.

Being strategically drive and action oriented, I tend to focus on the path to solutions. "How can we fix this? Let's try this." Sometimes it is challenging because you run into people who don't want change, don't see the need for change, or they can feel threated by what they perceive as a critique. It can also create cultural dissonance when educating staff or others related to American Indian history. Because the need for more inclusion and the history of the United States are intertwined—especially for American Indian tribes.

This can require a lot of education and explanation to leadership about why inclusion is needed, what it would look like to be more inclusive (capacity-wise, financially, etc.), and what they might have to risk. But, in my opinion, my example includes a story of a true leader because he was willing to do that. He was willing to go out on a limb and be the one to represent that constitutional amendment to the entire organization and all of the membership. The board backed it because they believed in moving in that path, too, and because of their trust in that leader and the staff, I imagine. That certainly isn't the only thing that the organization had done, but that was one area where I was directly able to participate.

Cinnamon Catlin-Legutko: You've led initiatives across this large organization, the Ohio History Connection, and now you're at the helm of a museum that is set to open around spring of 2021. As the leader of this new Choctaw Cultural Center, what intentions are you setting for yourself? Because you've described a kind of default position in support of inclusion, how do you set an intention from that space? How do you demonstrate that moving forward? What systems may you put in place? What conversations may you have? How are you thinking about that?

Stacey: You're right, it's a completely different environment I'm working in now. It's a completely different world. Honestly, you almost couldn't get more opposite. Where I worked before, I was the only American Indian person on staff, and now I work for the second-largest federally recognized Tribal Nation in the United States. Choctaw Nation is extremely impressive. Not only did they have the cultural grounding and strength to withstand a horrific removal, but they have rebuilt a strong government and created successful economic development endeavors.

It's a completely different governing structure than a traditional museum. It's tribal and my highest-level supervisor is Chief Gary Batton and Assistant Chief Jack Austin Jr. There's the Choctaw Nation Tribal Council, and there's a solid business structure in place for employees of the Choctaw Nation. Choctaw Nation has both a government arm and a commerce arm. The commerce side manages their businesses and economic development ventures. The Choctaw Cultural Center is on the government side. It's a different level of learning how the leadership works, understanding what the community wants. The lens of inclusivity for Choctaw citizens— and I would say broadly for Native people—is inherent in all work we undertake.

A lot of the groundwork had been laid as far as the design of the cultural center—it's truly beautiful. The Cultural Committee did a fantastic job, even visiting tribal cultural centers nationwide to see how other tribal cultural centers were operating. There was an impressive team as far as the architects, landscape architects, exhibits, and media. I still wake up every day and pinch myself. Being a part of the opening of this Cultural Center is a tremendous opportunity and responsibility.

The real challenges come into play once the doors open, as far as operations, guest relations, community value and of course, financials.

One area I feel is integral to the success of this Cultural Center is related to the Tribal community and asking ourselves what we can do to be sure community values the center. The center will be open to the public as well as Choctaw people, and both audiences are important. But if we are not serving the community, serving our audience, the Choctaw people, that would be recognized when a Choctaw citizen walks in the doors. When we do serve the community well and meet their needs, it will have a ripple effect that will impact visitation. It will have an impact that will be felt all the way up to the Tribal Council if they hear positive things from community. It will even impact the authenticity that you would expect to feel and experience from a tribal cultural center. It needs to be a living cultural center where when you walk in, you see Choctaw people, hear the language, learn the history from the Choctaw perspective, and eat traditional foods. Authenticity is the quality that not only draws people into any museum or cultural center, but brings them back.

Community engagement was also important during the construction of the center. When possible, Choctaw artisans and other professionals were engaged as part of the project. There were community members who contributed to making clothing for the life casts in the exhibits, and others whose faces and features were molded to create the life casts themselves. When Choctaw people walk in, they will see Choctaw people throughout the exhibits.

Once we're open, I think my intention has to focus on maintaining that community connection while, at the same time, making sure that anyone who walks in should feel like they are valued, that they're respected, and that they are there to learn. We will be interpreting for them, and they'll be able to learn about Choctaw people. To me, that's of utmost importance. One of the ways to meet this intention is to hire a strong leadership team for the Choctaw Cultural Center—positions like director of education, facilities manager, and public programs manager. We are seeking Choctaw people for these important roles and will continue as all other positions get filled. So far, the majority of positions have been filled by Choctaw people with great talent and experience. In other cases, other tribally affiliated staff or non-tribal staff are rounding out the staffing and also bring their talent and skill.

The other leadership intention I'm setting is around the value of partnerships. There's a university nearby in Durant; the Choctaw Nation itself has over ten thousand employees. We'd like to restart a certification program in Choctaw culture and history. The Cultural Center will be a center for cultural education. Through partnerships with universities, and even other Tribal Nations closely related to the Choctaw, it will help with relationship building and will help reach broader audiences.

Chris: As you talk about your leadership strategies, I hear values represented in the museum. How does that translate into behaviors? And when it's a tribal museum that prioritizes Choctaw first, what does that mean for inclusive behaviors in the museum? How do you engage Choctaw and non-Choctaw people in inclusive ways?

Stacey: Everything the Choctaw Nation does is about faith, family, and culture. We talk about it a lot. Chief Batton talks about it. It is embedded on the lobby wall as you enter the Cultural Center— "Faith, Family, and Culture." These are strong tribal values that have existed for thousands of years. Another value is servant leadership. This is about getting in there and rolling your sleeves up and doing the work along with everybody else. Being a servant leader is about valuing leadership that is demonstrated by service to others. This is an active value in Choctaw Nation. Staff go out of their way to help you. This connects to customer service. Faith, family, and culture are also described through the Cultural Center exhibits. We define how faith, how ancestral spirituality and beliefs have translated over time and during removal. What does faith look like today? The second, family, is about balancing your work life with your family life. Our families and even our broader Tribal families are to be treasured. And then culture—in my opinion it is the foundation on which we stand. Cultural practices and traditions are what define Choctaw identity. These values are translated into exhibits through a series of films where you hear from the community. They are featured in all of our films, talking about what it means to be Choctaw.

At the Choctaw Nation, there is a group we refer to as the Choctaw Proud, and those are people who may or may not be Choctaw, but they're our allies. They might be business partners or they might be colleagues and they're familiar with the Nation. They're familiar with the values, and they're invested in Choctaw people. The Choctaw Proud is an important audience for the Choctaw Cultural Center, and it is an opportunity to share our values and know that others embody them and support those same values. These are our partners and allies and we see the important role they play. No culture exists in a vacuum—cultures exchange ideas, they trade, they share beliefs. Recognizing the Choctaw Proud and the role they play is important.

These values not only translate in the Cultural Center, but also in how we interact with others and how we teach. All staff will be trained around these values, and it will be about respect. Hospitality is a big deal—not only to Choctaw people, but to many, many tribes. I used to lecture the staff at my former employer because coming from a Native environment, you are taught that if someone walks in your house, first thing you ask is "Are you comfortable? Would you like a glass of water? Have you eaten? Do you need to use the restroom?" Basic human necessities. Always meet those first. In tribal consultation, we talk about how it's better to begin a consultation with somebody when it's not an emergency. Take time to build a relationship especially when you've never met them before. It's much better to reach out ahead of time and introduce yourself. Maybe you have lunch or at least coffee.

I wasn't seeing the value of hospitality in this particular situation. I'll never forget the scenario . . . I was flown out to interview for a position. They had set up a full day of interviews and meetings. Our day started in the morning and I met with one group of staff, and then on to another interview with a different group, etc. That entire time I was never asked if I needed to use the restroom, or if I needed a drink of water or something to eat. I paused a meeting to ask for a couple of those things. I did accept that position and later, after I knew the staff a little better, I told them that story and essentially lectured them about the importance of hospitality. It really is important in the Indian world. Hospitality needs to translate to everything we do at the Cultural Center. It needs to begin in the parking lot and continue at the restaurant. Everything we do needs to reflect that value of hospitality. It's deeply rooted, and I feel that in my role, it's vital to make sure Choctaw values are actively embodied in operations at the Cultural Center.

Cinnamon: I'm inspired by hospitality as a thinking system, a way of acting, but also the way you show up and create space for others. As a leadership style, I would suggest that it aligns with inclusive practice. Is that a fair assessment? Is that a way that you see cultural values showing up in your leadership style?

Stacey: Cultural values absolutely show up in my leadership style, and yes, I would say those values align with inclusivity practices. Values like respect and authenticity go hand in hand with inclusivity. I would say that authenticity informs my style. I've worked for other leaders and everyone has different style, but some leaders choose to separate themselves from staff. They believe perhaps that to lead they have to be seen as apart or at a higher level than others. For me, it's about being authentic. It's about treating others the way you want to be treated. I also find humor vital to a successful workplace. We can do amazing work and have fun at the same time. I don't care how far you've gone in your career, you better be able to laugh at yourself and not take yourself too seriously. I find it challenging to think about "my" leadership style because I rarely think of it in those terms. I think of it as responsibility—to my staff, to my leadership, to our constituents. We are all on the same team, but we have different roles. Mine is no higher or lower. But as a leader I have to make decisions. I have to be aware of how decisions can or will impact outcomes. Leaders have to take risks and be willing to fight for something they believe is right. They have to take full responsibility for any and all actions that take place under their lead—whether those are positive or negative.

Something I enjoy is nurturing talent. I love to know what people's passions are because, in the workplace, finding that passion can make all the difference in an employee's performance. I have seen a lot of passion as people are applying to join the Cultural Center team. There are a lot of very passionate people in the museum field, in general! I think nurturing talent and passion is repaid twicefold in dedicated and fulfilled staff.

Cinnamon: I think the way you answered my question further defines servant leadership. You really embody it.

Chris: When you consider changes museums need to make in the US and across the globe, what are some of the most important decision points that museum leaders need to make? What do leaders need to spend their time changing?

Stacey: Every museum is so different. What is so wonderful about the museum field is the diversity—we have banjo museums, memorial museums, rock and roll museums, art museums, tribal cultural centers, you name it, we have it here in the United States. Some museums have massive collections that stem from our country's colonial history. Others have a specialized focus and a small collection that was perhaps donated by one person. But whether their museum is small or large, museum leaders should spend time thinking about who is being left out of the museum's interpretations/projects/collections. They should spend time finding out how (or if) the museum is valued by the community and for what reasons. The answer to the first question can lead to changing the answer to the second question.

For some of those larger museums, it's all about the collections. It's about how you're interpreting the collections. In my personal experience, those are the museums that have the biggest challenge because it's a responsibility to care for all of those items that came from cultures and people. Interpreting those histories is a huge responsibility on top of the liability that comes with caring for collections and also the fact that ancestors are being held in museums and there is legal requirement in many cases to work with tribes.

Those in leadership positions who aren't afraid to do the work can help facilitate significant change. Museum leaders should focus on asking how they can serve the community. How can we serve not only the communities we live in and establish partnerships with those communities, but also how can we serve the community that represents the collections we have? When you begin to ask the hard questions and undertake the work, that's when it gets interesting! That's when partnerships are born and doors open. People begin to not feel so threatened.

Museum leaders should encourage transparency. It's OK for people to know what's in your collection. It's OK for people to know that you have human remains. Let people know you're working on those issues or that you aren't sure how to begin that work and you need help. Transparency goes a long way toward building trust. And being transparent, being honest about where you are in the process, is what can open a lot of doors.

We all know that nobody's perfect. Many people are aware there's an ugly history related to collection. Be aware that it's a painful history for those populations who were colonized or have been/are being oppressed. I think people are more willing to accept that and work with you if you are being transparent and you're making an effort.

I learned a phrase a long time ago that really resonated. Procedural justice—it's the idea that if you are engaging in a process and you feel like you're being treated fairly throughout the process, even if you don't get the exact outcome you wanted, you are much more likely to abide by the decision because you felt you were treated fairly in the process. You were invited to the table, you heard the discussion, and you shared your opinion. When the final decision is made, you're more likely to agree to the outcome because the process was fair and transparent.

To museum leaders I would say open your doors, share your strengths, share your weaknesses, invite people in (virtually or otherwise!), and get creative. There may be people you've never engaged with who are interested in or impacted by your mission. When those doors start opening and you invite people in and you're having these conversations, that's when partnerships start, connections are made. Relationships can start with one conversation.

Cinnamon: What will be asked of museum leaders in future? Can we move from where your vantage point is, see new trends emerging? Or is it still murky? Because we're at the cusp of change. I know I've been trying to diagnose where we're at. Are we right in the middle of it and we're completely blinded by all the chaos, or are we on this edge of something exciting? And if we hold on, the change will happen. What do you see from your vantage point?

Stacey: I think so much of it will depend on us/museums showing our value. If a museum hasn't been active in community and acts behind closed doors, who is experiencing the value? Is it an exclusive group? We have to engage with what's happening in the world. I like to think of cultural organizations and museums as the keepers of the stories. If we're not doing a good job of sharing the stories, and people don't see the value, we will be seen as irrelevant.

Many of us have walked into a museum and not felt welcome. That's no fun, and you don't really want to go back. The question is, *how* can we activate our collections, our missions, our programs within community? We need to be able to react when shifts are happening in the world; museums can be the organizations that remind society of the histories we've lived through, remind us why art and history matter, why banjos matter!, remind us all that we are connected as humans—with stories of our accomplishments, artifacts of our societies, art that proves our capabilities. But if we lose that relevancy right now as the world is shifting, we're going to be in trouble.

Notes

1. Passed as 1990, the Native American Graves Protection and Repatriation Act (NAGPRA) is human rights legislation that requires museums, universities, local governments, and state agencies that receive federal funding to repatriate ancestral remains, their belongings, and objects of community significance. You can learn more here: https://www.nps.gov/subjects/nagpra/index.htm.
2. To assist with repatriation efforts, there is federal grant funding through the National NAPGRA office.

ACTIVITY

The Ladder of Inference

To complete this activity, you'll need paper or a journal and your favorite pen or pencil.

The Ladder of Inference is a tool that can help us understand how our assumptions influence our actions. First articulated by management theorist Chris Argyris, the Ladder of Influence maps out a thinking process where we observe information, attach meaning, make assumptions, and ultimately act on those assumptions.

Each rung of the ladder can be seen as a step in the process (see figure 16.2). As we take in information through our various senses, we select data that we feel is most relevant. We then add meaning to that data and make assumptions based on those meanings. We then draw conclusions, adopt beliefs, and take action. All of these steps are impacted by our biases, particularly the steps where we select data, add meaning, make assumptions, and draw conclusions.

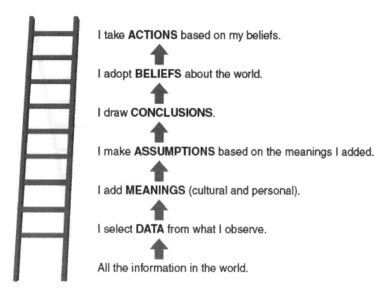

I take **ACTIONS** based on my beliefs.

I adopt **BELIEFS** about the world.

I draw **CONCLUSIONS**.

I make **ASSUMPTIONS** based on the meanings I added.

I add **MEANINGS** (cultural and personal).

I select **DATA** from what I observe.

All the information in the world.

Figure 16.2 Graphic of Ladder.

Think of a time when you *acted* on an assumption, only to find out your assumption was wrong. Think about the outcome of that situation. Use the Ladder of Inference to help you understand how your actions were influenced by how you see the world.

- What assumptions did you make?

- What information did you draw on that led to your assumption?

- What information did you ignore?

How might you use the Ladder of Inference to understand how you could have made different choices in the same situation?

We are all human, and we all make assumptions. You can do this. Use the tool to develop new habits.

Source: Peter M. Senge, *The Fifth Discipline: The Art and Practice of the Learning Organization* (New York: Currency Doubleday, 1994).

The Ladder of Inference Activity

Part Four

Values and Action

Chapter 17

Inclusive Design Centers Disabled People's Agency

Beth Ziebarth

The demands of the moment require museum leaders to acknowledge that we do not have all the answers on inclusion. We need to listen carefully to each other, our audiences, and our staff on how they define diversity, equity, accessibility, and inclusion. What we learn by listening must lead to actions that commit resources to critical examination of museum collections, programs, digital content, and design ideas by self-advocates who become museum staff.

As a person with a disability acquired when I was sixteen years old, I wanted to "pass" as someone not that different from a person without a disability. One of the many moments in my life that made me realize the rest of the world didn't see things the same way was when, as a newly married young woman passing through the courtyard of my apartment complex, a young man, gathered on a balcony with his friends, looked down at me and said loudly, "Oh look. It's one of Jerry's kids," referring to Jerry Lewis and his telethon for the Muscular Dystrophy Association. I was mortified, hurt, and angry. I am a strong, independent woman who happens to have a spinal cord injury and uses a wheelchair. I am not an object of pity, charity, or derision.

The diverse community of disabled people are keenly aware of the distinction between possessing a disability and identifying as part of the disability community with its rich history, culture, and politics. I did not begin identifying as disabled until my early thirties when I learned to be proud of my community. Disability is an essential part of who I am; my desire to change inaccessible environments, confront perceptions of the abilities of people who are disabled, and claim our human dignity impassions me in my life and position as director of Access Smithsonian at the Smithsonian Institution in Washington, DC. I have the responsibility and opportunity to challenge the museum field to value the inclusion of people with disabilities: in the design of architecture, exhibitions, programs, and digital experiences; as cocreators of museum experiences; by accurately representing disability in the past, present, and future; and by diversifying museum and affiliated staff with people who have the lived experience of disability.

I cannot do justice to a whole body of study on disability and ableism in this short chapter. However, there are certain aspects of disability and accessibility the reader should know in order to understand what influenced me to promote inclusive design at the Smithsonian. First, disability is common, and the number of individuals with a disability is increasing worldwide. It is currently estimated that sixty-one million Americans have a disability—nearly one in four adults.[1] For the first time in US history, older adults (ages sixty-five plus) are projected to outnumber children by 2034.[2] On the other end of the age scale, one in six children ages three to seventeen have a developmental disability with steady increases in ADHD (attention deficit hyperactivity disorder), autism, and intellectual disabilities reported over the past two decades.[3]

Second, we need to consider how individuals with disabilities think about themselves and how disability is perceived by society. Within the last century, the term *disabled* came to refer to a distinct class of people. There are various conceptual frameworks used by individuals, activists, scholars, and policy makers to describe disability. The two most commonly used are the social and human rights models. The focus of the social model is disabled people, whereas the focus of the human rights model is disability policy.[4]

In the social model, people with a range of body/mind traits are disabled by their interaction with various environments: physical, communication, information, social, and policy.[5] Disability is a socially produced injustice that is possible to challenge and eliminate through social change.[6] The human rights model focuses on the inherent dignity of the human being regardless of the person's medical characteristics. It affirms the agency and autonomy of disabled people. The human rights model also locates the "problem" in society, not the disabled person.[7] To operate effectively, the human rights model must work alongside the social model. It is therefore complementary to the social model and not an improvement upon it.[8]

The social model and human rights model of disability are the basis for US civil rights accessibility laws including the Architectural Barriers Act, Rehabilitation Act of 1973, Individuals with Disabilities Education Act, and the Americans with Disabilities Act, as well as the human rights UN Convention on the Rights of Persons with Disabilities (CRPD). The CRPD promulgates the right of disabled people to take equal part in community life. In the case of museums, they also provide for participation in cultural life. Disabled people refuse to be excluded from accessing, understanding, and making culture. At a recent meeting of disability advocates, Nefertiti Matos, who is blind, imparted her experience of growing up in a family that didn't understand the value of a person who is blind going to museums. Recalling her first museum field trip to New York's Museum of Modern Art, she said: "It woke up this feeling in me like, 'I do belong here.' Since then, I've made it my business to go to everything: museums, theater, dance. I can't imagine my life without those experiences."

The Path to Inclusion at the Smithsonian

At the Smithsonian, early accessibility efforts at the National Air and Space Museum by a staff member who was blind were taking place in the 1970s. In the 1980s, accessibility services like sign language interpretation or special touch exhibitions were provided for school children or adults visiting the museums. Museum educators and docents were primarily responsible for the inclusion of people with disabilities in programming. In addition, facilities staff were applying federal accessibility standards to new and renovated building projects.

At the end of the 1980s and beginning of the 1990s, two major events pushed the Smithsonian to create a new central administration office dedicated to accessibility, the Accessibility Program: the passage of the Americans with Disabilities Act (ADA); and an institution-wide Inspector General (IG) audit of accessibility for staff and visitors. Janice Majewski became the institution's first accessibility coordinator and assumed responsibility for addressing the issues impacting visitors specified in the audit. I joined the office in 1995, and Jan became an invaluable mentor to me.

A policy on accessibility for people with disabilities was adopted. More extensive audits of facilities and programming including exhibitions, public programs, and publications were executed and analyzed for priority remediation. Key responsibilities for the office were established, including facility and exhibition reviews, technical assistance on legal requirements, staff and volunteer training, fulfillment of visitor accessibility service requests, and sustained connections with the disability community and other cultural arts organizations.

After several years of development, in 1996, the Smithsonian created its own design guidelines to implement the accessibility policy, working with exhibit designers across the institution. The Smithsonian Guidelines for Accessible Exhibition Design (SGAED) are based on the 1991 ADA Accessibility Standards, exhibition design practice, and interviews with hundreds of people with disabilities. The guidelines became one of the foundational documents for the museum field in understanding how to apply the federal accessibility standards to exhibitions. The core accessibility goals in the guidelines remain true to this day. A revised version that reflects updates to ADA standards is planned.

In 2001, I became director of the Accessibility Program, which was renamed Access Smithsonian in 2018. The same core responsibilities continue and are shared by all staff. We advocated and provided infrastructure for institution-wide programs designed by consulting with disabled people, museum staff, and external stakeholders. Best practices in the cultural arts also informed program design. Grounded in our intent to "meet people where they are," our signature programs do just that: you come to us, and we provide an environment and a program adapted for you and your needs.

A flourishing example of such a signature program is Morning at the Museum (MATM), now in its tenth year. MATM uses the principles of inclusive design to create an appropriate environment for children with brain-based disabilities and their families. Educators across the institution told us that parents of children with disabilities were calling their museums to ask if they had accommodation strategies for their kids. They wanted to visit, but many families reported they felt uncomfortable in crowded spaces that may induce sensory overload and potentially trigger behaviors in their children that other people judge as negative. We started looking at children's museums and were impressed that staff were working with parents and autism services organizations to develop and present programming. We invited self-advocates, occupational therapists, parents, and special education teachers to join Smithsonian educators on an advisory committee to develop a program. After we began MATM, families embraced the program with great enthusiasm. We also realized that children with disabilities other than autism would benefit from our program structure and broadened participation. We have gone from a half dozen families in our pilot program to thousands of participants throughout the year at every Smithsonian museum. We share what we learned by consulting with, presenting to, and training museum colleagues nationally and internationally on adapting our Morning at the Museum model and implementing it in their organizations. Our next step is to offer a version of MATM online to families.

Another established program—now in its eighth year—is Project SEARCH Smithsonian. A Smithsonian colleague whose son has a disability heard about Project SEARCH, a national program that offers young adults with developmental or intellectual disabilities job training through internships. We researched what being a host site would involve, and we then sought approval from senior administration to start our own program. We formed a collaboration with external local partners who were successfully implementing Project SEARCH in their own organizations including the National Institutes of Health. Since 2013, departments ranging from the Smithsonian Archives to the Zoo Commissary have hosted sixty-seven interns in positions including museum technicians, facilities management workers, data entry specialists, library and archive technicians, gardeners, and office automation specialists. Supervisors work with educators and job coaches to adapt the duties of each position following our model of person-centered inclusive design. My office colleague who manages Project SEARCH Smithsonian says our annual graduation celebration is the happiest day of the year, and senior administration, supervisors, interns, and their families agree. To date, the Smithsonian has hired thirty-two graduates of Project SEARCH. The Smithsonian is proud to be the first Project SEARCH site in the world to host interns in a museum workplace.

Access Smithsonian also sponsors a User Expert Group in collaboration with the Institute for Human Centered Design. Individuals in this advisory group use their lived experiences to help inform us on what works or does not work for accessing museum content. We have recruited roughly forty people from across the community representing a range of disabilities and needs. User Experts help us test new apps or evaluate touch screens and other interactives. They may participate in a focus group, and their inputs will help us shape our program offerings. Currently, User Experts are testing exhibition media for the National Air and Space Museum. User Experts may start as advisors but can become codesigners, participating as stakeholders in designing a usable product that meets the needs of visitors with disabilities. User Expert sessions not only produce recommendations for our clients but also inform design for similar projects. The compiled documentation will be used to update our guidelines.

A relatively new program, See Me (At the Smithsonian) began three years ago. This signature program uses inclusive design to create content engagement appropriate for adults with dementia and Alzheimer's and for their care partners. The need for this type of program is great—and expected to increase along with an aging population. During a See Me program, a museum educator, often with a docent, facilitates small group conversations about some of the Smithsonian's most beloved objects.

The Smithsonian received a grant to expand the See Me program. Specifically, the grant provides resources to increase the number of Smithsonian museums participating in See Me, expand programming out into the local communities, offer programming in Spanish (in addition to English), and introduce and promote the adoption of the See Me model at other museums. The expansion and increased diversification of See Me will help the Smithsonian achieve a major goal of its current strategic plan: understanding and having an impact on twenty-first-century audiences. See Me programming is a socially responsive role for museums to embrace. The programs are now being offered online. Participants appreciate being able to join in from their home or congregate living facility. In fact, more people are participating online as they don't have to worry about transportation, parking, or mobility in a museum. A participant who regularly attends See Me programs said recently, "In this time of isolation where we can't be with people in person, it's just lovely to be with people through the screen. Still nice that we get to share things."

Access Smithsonian will continue to stress the broad application of inclusive design. In 2018, a three-year strategic plan by the staff-initiated and voluntary Freer and Sackler Galleries Accessibility Task Force was so well received by their director that he shared it with the secretary and suggested a renewal of commitment by the institution to accessibility. Smithsonian senior management responded with the creation of the Smithsonian Accessibility Innovations Fund, managed by Access Smithsonian. Annually $250,000 is available to Smithsonian museums and research centers in support of their efforts to develop innovative accessibility solutions for visitors with disabilities. Since 2018, we have awarded funds to twenty-five projects. Among the successful proposals was a planning grant to investigate an innovative virtual haptic device, "Feeling Virtually: Using Technology to Create Virtual Tactile Experiences," to facilitate complementary virtual tactile experiences, exhibition browsing, visual descriptions, and more.

Our commitment to the disability community is further evidenced by frequent collaborations with Katherine Ott, a curator in the Medial Science Division of the National Museum of American History, who researches, collects, publishes, and exhibits on disability and universal design history in addition to a number of other critical topics. The programs, online exhibitions, and physical exhibitions we worked on together gave us additional means to involve and learn from people with disabilities, including a conference on disability and the practice of public history; an ADA tenth anniversary physical and online exhibition; the 2005 "Whatever Happened to Polio?" exhibition; "Every Body: An Artifact History of Disability in America," an online exhibition; a multifaceted ADA twenty-fifth anniversary celebration; an exhibition on the Special Olympics; and joint supervision and mentoring of many interns and fellows through the years working on disability and accessibility topics. The connections we make and sustain with disability community members are invaluable for our work.

We are pleased by the response to our signature programs and the connections to our audiences they afford. We look forward to expanding and sustaining them. However, it must be noted that a key principle of accessibility is that signature programs cannot replace inclusive design. Some organizations have fallen into the trap of presenting only special programs for people with disabilities, rather than addressing the core activities being offered. How Smithsonian staff work to have accessibility and inclusive design as a central element of daily operations is discussed below.

Broadening Accessibility to Inclusive Design

Design philosophies and practices in architecture and programming worldwide have evolved as accessibility standards, universal design principles, and the practice of inclusive design benefit people with and without disabilities. Inclusive design is a framework for the design of places, things, information, communication and policy that focuses on the user, on the widest range of people operating in the widest range of situations without special or separate design.[9]

The Smithsonian strives to build upon the foundation of accessibility and expand it through inclusive design so all visitors can meaningfully participate in and engage with our content and programs. Human variation is the norm, not the exception. Every day we welcome people to our museums who have a right to expect our facilities, exhibitions, and programs are accessible to all. And we want to be able to serve people throughout their life spans so that they, like everyone else, have the opportunity to be lifelong learners.

I envision three inclusive design pillars that we are constructing at the Smithsonian—exhibitions/programs, digital experiences, and facilities. Access Smithsonian is directly involved with exhibitions/programs and acts as an advisor for inclusive digital design and facilities design. We are investing in a new position within our office that will have responsibility for developing a curriculum based on the principles of inclusive design for Smithsonian staff, in particular those staff who are responsible for exhibition design and fabrication, including digital interactives, or public program design and execution. Our staff member will lead training based on the curriculum, bringing in experts from the field to add to our practices. Additionally, they will manage the User Expert Group and the Smithsonian Accessibility Innovations Fund. Tying these roles together will be an effective way to further progress in inclusive design.

From its establishment, our office used a combination of rationales for why the Smithsonian should be inclusive of people with disabilities—legal requirements, the business case, organizational mission, moral imperative ("It's the right thing to do!"), and visitors demand it. Our initial work was to build the accessibility foundation and then start layering universal design and inclusive design on it. We have always relied on relationship building both within the Smithsonian and externally with community stakeholders to achieve our goals. We use training as a means to reach a wide variety of staff and volunteers at all levels within the organization to familiarize them with who we are serving, why we do it, and how we can make what the institution offers accessible and inclusive. We invite people with disabilities in the broader community to help us design programs and facilities to meet their needs. As we say, "Nothing about us without us."

The Smithsonian has made commendable strides in inclusive design for people with disabilities in the last five years. I credit the progress to the shared social justice vision of my own staff and staff working in many departments. Access Smithsonian's mission to be "a catalyst for consistent and integrated inclusive design that provides meaningful access to museum content for visitors with disabilities" cannot be achieved by my office's three staff members alone. Everyone at the Smithsonian, by policy and practice, shares responsibility for accessibility. We have an internal-to-the-Smithsonian grassroots effort gaining momentum with staff forming accessibility task forces and developing accessibility strategic plans that they present to senior administration. The Smithsonian Accessibility Network, Project Mangers Forum, and the Promoting Excellence among Exhibit Professionals at the Smithsonian group host programs on accessibility and inclusive design topics. Directors are hiring accessibility coordinators for their museums. Access Smithsonian provides the infrastructure for signature programs that are carried out by museum and zoo educators and docents. Staff believe that the "A" in the diversity, equity, accessibility, and inclusion acronym, DEAI, is essential for the institution. There is a perceptible culture shift of inclusion.

It is exciting to work on exhibition teams that want to bake inclusion into the design from the beginning of a project. Two examples stand out. The National Air and Space Museum's redesign of their exhibitions as their building is renovated and the Smithsonian Latino Center's Molina Family Latino Gallery housed in the National Museum of American History. At the National Air and Space Museum, Beatrice Mowry, department chair of the Exhibits Design Division, started the redesign projects off by stating expectations for accessibility and inclusive design in their contracts. The Institute for Human Centered Design was hired to work with the various exhibition and media design firms from concept through construction. For the Molina Family Latino Gallery, Eduardo Diaz, director of the Smithsonian Latino Center (SLC), committed to inclusive design from the beginning to amplify the center's work to "truly reflect the rich tapestry of humanity."[10] In order to ensure that all team members have a shared understanding of inclusive design, everyone—architects, SLC staff, media designers, User Experts, and Access Smithsonian and Institute for Human Centered Design staff—participates in charrettes as the design progresses.

We continue to develop resources on inclusive design for the benefit of the museum field. Digital interactives were not yet an integral part of the museum experience in the early 1990s nor part of the 1996 Smithsonian Guidelines for Accessible Exhibition Design. The Smithsonian recently collaborated with the Institute for Human Centered Design and MuseWeb on a digital interactives e-book. The press release for the e-book states:

> Inclusive Digital Interactives: Best Practices + Research is about new ways to design museum digital interactives so that the broadest range of visitors can use them easily and confidently. This collection of sixteen articles examines the theory and practice behind making inclusive digital interactive programs for museum visitors and staff, with and without disabilities, and of all ages and cultures. The articles are written by a diverse group of designers, educators, evaluators, and technology experts from six countries around the world who work with museums large and small. The connecting thread of all of the chapters is the powerful emphasis on the importance of co-designing, developing, and testing interactives with end users who have varied abilities, breaking down the paradigm of "us" designing for "them" and establishing a practice of "all of us designing for all of us."[11]

Now, as museums begin to reopen during the "new normal" created by the pandemic, my hope is that we build on the progress of the past decades rather than retreat from those efforts. It's more important than ever to invite people with disabilities to be part of the planning and protocols being put into place as we reopen our doors. In the words of Ray Bloomer of the National Park Service, "People with disabilities were the last ones in. Let's make sure they aren't the first ones out."[12]

Concurrently, as we grapple with reopening strategies and the "new normal" for museums, the museum field is urgently working to dismantle systemic racism in our organizations, and DEAI is even more of a priority. If museums intend to purposely include people with disabilities in DEAI, we need to articulate the difference between accessibility (the functional limitations imposed by poorly designed environments) and the systemic discrimination against and systematic persecution of people with disabilities evidenced by a history of eugenics, institutionalization, sterilization, denial of access to education, housing, employment, and participation in community life.

I noted at the beginning of this chapter my own journey in identifying with disability. Valuing the whole of a disabled person's identity demonstrates respect for their human difference and individual dignity. Mia Mingus, who identifies as a queer, disabled woman of color, says, "Disability is not monolithic. Ableism plays out very differently for wheelchair users, deaf people or people who have mental, psychiatric and cognitive disabilities. None of these are mutually exclusive, and are all complicated by race, class, gender, immigration, sexuality, welfare status, incarceration, age and geographic location."[13] The intersectionality of disability with other identities is a natural part of being human. If museums are to be socially responsive and reflect the people they do and could serve, they also need to address intersectionality in collections, exhibitions, public programs, digital experiences, publications, business ventures, hiring practices, and intern and volunteer recruitment. There is no human endeavor, whether it is in history, art, culture, or science, that does not include a disability perspective or story. Museum visitors with disabilities want to access narratives and interpretations about people who have a similar lived experience. Their stories need to be present or their absence explained, but they also need to be available in an accessible and inclusive way.

Twenty-first-century museums have the responsibility of addressing social justice issues, including the health and well-being of the people in their local communities. The Smithsonian Institution's vision is "to engage and inspire more people, where they are, with greater impact."[14] Access Smithsonian is committed to revolutionizing inclusion of disabled people in museums with the help of Smithsonian staff and valued partners to further solidify the institution's position at the forefront of encouraging diversity, equity, access, and inclusion for all visitors.

Notes

1. Centers for Disease Control, "1 in 4 U.S. Adults Live with a Disability," CDC Online Newsroom Press Release, August 16, 2018, https://www.cdc.gov/media/releases/2018/p0816-disability.html.
2. US Census Bureau, "Older People Projected to Outnumber Children for First Time in U.S. History," press release no. CB18-41, March 13, 2018, https://www.census.gov/newsroom/press-releases/2018/cb18-41-population-projections.html.
3. Melissa Jenco, "Study: 1 in 6 Children Has Developmental Disability," *AAP News*, September 26, 2019, https://www.aappublications.org/news/2019/09/26/disabilities092619.
4. Anna Lawson and Angharad E. Beckett, "The Social and Human Rights Models of Disability: Towards a Complementarity Thesis," *International Journal of Human Rights* 25, no. 2 (2021): 348–79, https://doi.org/10.1080/13642987.2020.1783533.
5. World Health Organization and World Bank, eds., *World Report on Disability* (Geneva: WHO Press, 2011), 4, https://www.who.int/disabilities/world_report/2011/report.pdf.
6. Lawson and Beckett, "The Social and Human Rights Models of Disability."
7. Gerard Quinn and Theresia Degener, "The Moral Authority for Change: Human Rights Values and the World Wide Process of Disability Reform," in *Human Rights and Disability: The Current Use and Future Potential of Human Rights Instruments in the Context of Disability*, ed. Gerard Quinn and Theresia Degener (New York and Geneva: United Nations, 2002), 13, 14.
8. Lawson and Beckett, "The Social and Human Rights Models of Disability."
9. Institute for Human Centered Design, "Inclusive Design Cheat Sheet," accessed October 8, 2020, https://ihcd-api.s3.amazonaws.com/s3fs-public/file+downloads/Inclusive+Design+Cheat+Sheet+6+18.pdf.
10. *Natural Resources Committee/Subcommittee on National Parks, Forests, and Public Lands, U.S. House of Representatives, Hearings on H.R. 2420* (October 17, 2019) (statement of Eduardo Díaz, Director, Smithsonian Institution Latino Center), https://www.congress.gov/116/meeting/house/110081/witnesses/HHRG-116-II10-Wstate-DazE-20191017.pdf.
11. Smithsonian Institution, "New Publication Shares Ways for Museums To Be Accessible and Inclusive Features Case Studies on Digital Interactives From Around the World," news release no. SI-306-2020, October 15, 2020, accessed November 27, 2020, https://www.si.edu/newsdesk/releases/new-publication-shares-ways-museums-be-accessible-and-inclusive.
12. Ray Bloomer, "Keeping Museum Tactile Experiences Safe and Viable" (webinar, Accessibility + New Normal Talks, hosted by the Institute for Human Centered Design, Access Smithsonian, and the Theater Development Fund, July 7, 2020).
13. Mia Mingus, "Changing the Framework: Disability Justice," *Leaving Evidence* (blog), February 12, 2011, https://leavingevidence.wordpress.com/2011/02/12/changing-the-framework-disability-justice/.
14. Smithsonian Institution, Annual Performance Plan Fiscal Year 2021, https://www.si.edu/sites/default/files/about/fy2021-performance-plan.pdf

Bibliography

Bloomer, Ray. "Keeping Museum Tactile Experiences Safe and Viable." Webinar panel hosted by the Institute for Human Centered Design, Access Smithsonian, and the Theater Development Fund, July 7, 2020.

Centers for Disease Control. "CDC: 1 in 4 US Adults Live with a Disability." CDC Online Newsroom Press Release, August 16, 2018. https://www.cdc.gov/media/releases/2018/p0816-disability.html.

Díaz, Eduardo. "Written Statement of Eduardo Diaz." October 17, 2019. https://www.congress.gov/116/meeting/house/110081/witnesses/HHRG-116-II10-Wstate-DazE-20191017.pdf.

Institute for Human Centered Design. "Inclusive Design Cheat Sheet." Accessed October 8, 2020. https://ihcd-api.s3.amazonaws.com/s3fs-public/file+downloads/Inclusive+Design +Cheat+Sheet+6+18.pdf.

Jenco, Melissa. "Study: 1 in 6 Children Has Developmental Disability." *AAP News*, September 26, 2019. https://www.aappublications.org/news/2019/09/26/disabilities092619.

Lawson, Anna, and Angharad E. Beckett. "The Social and Human Rights Models of Disability: Towards a Complementarity Thesis." *International Journal of Human Rights* 25, no. 2 (2021): 348–79. https://doi.org/10.1080/13642987.2020.1783533.

Mingus, Mia. "Changing the Framework: Disability Justice." *Leaving Evidence* (blog), February 12, 2011. https://leavingevidence.wordpress.com/2011/02/12/changing-the-framework-disabil ity-justice/.

Quinn, Gerard, and Theresia Degener. "The Moral Authority for Change: Human Rights Values and the World Wide Process of Disability Reform." In *Human Rights and Disability: The Current Use and Future Potential of Human Rights Instruments in the Context of Disability*, edited by Gerard Quinn and Theresia Degener, 13–28. New York and Geneva: United Nations, 2002. https:// www.ohchr.org/Documents/Publications/HRDisabilityen.pdf.

Smithsonian Institution. Annual Peformance Plan Fiscal Year 2021. https://www.si.edu/sites /default/files/about/fy2021-performance-plan.pdf.

Smithsonian Institution. "New Publication Shares Ways for Museums To Be Accessible and Inclusive Features Case Studies on Digital Interactives From Around the World." Smithsonian Institution. Accessed November 27, 2020. https://www.si.edu/newsdesk/releases/new-pub lication-shares-ways-museums-be-accessible-and-inclusive.

US Census Bureau. "Older People Projected to Outnumber Children for First Time in U.S. History." Press release no. CB18-41, March 13, 2018. https://www.census.gov/newsroom/press -releases/2018/cb18-41-population-projections.html.

World Health Organization, and World Bank, eds. *World Report on Disability*. Geneva: WHO Press, 2011.

Chapter 18

Begin with the End in Mind

Inclusion as a Core Museum Practice

LaNesha DeBardelaben

You instinctively know when you feel as if you belong in a place. You experience comfort and ease. You sense that you are valued and that your presence matters. You feel welcomed, respected, and supported. Museums are in the business of making people feel this way. As social spaces that create meaningful opportunities for personal introspection, social interaction, and collective impact, museums can be one of the more accessible and equitable places in a community. Inclusive museums offer visitors affections of belonging, thus making museum going enjoyable and enriching in personal, interpersonal, and collective ways. Museums play a significant role in society and, thus, have a responsibility to ensure they are welcoming, accommodating, and cultivating a sense of belonging to all.

From their internal operations to their external engagement, museums have long evolved from their earlier iterations of being cabinets of curiosity and crystal palaces. Museums were formerly perceived as institutions that were aloof from the reach and interest of community. Mainstream museums were accustomed to catering to middle- and upper-class or wealth-privileged visitors. Labels were written to accommodate them. Programming was centered on their interests. Non-diverse people staffed museums, led tours as docents, and filled board seats. They were both the forward-facing and behind-the-scenes actors of museums. Museums were accustomed to accommodating and replicating historical legacies of inequality. Twenty-first-century museums, on the contrary, march to a different tune. Modern museums that are committed to authentic inclusion cultivate a sense of belonging for all. The International Council of Museums declared the theme for its 2020 International Museum Day as "Museums of Equality: Diversity and Inclusion."[1]

The American Alliance of Museums (AAM) chose "Radical Reimagining" as its theme for its 2020 virtual conference, stating that "envisioning a new future requires us to ask what decisions we can make that will not only help us overcome the immediate threat, but help us to rebuild a more sustainable, inclusive, and powerful museum field."[2]

Inclusion has full momentum in the museum field. In 2017, the AAM established the Diversity, Equity, Accessibility, and Inclusion Working Group to build awareness in the field around the essentialness of inclusion. The working group's published report noted, "Unconscious bias matters to museums because it affects our decisions about who belongs in museum leadership and how we reach out to audiences. It influences how we set salaries, craft job descriptions, promote employees, and design interior and exterior spaces. Learning to identify our biases can help us to think again."[3] The report further called for there to be a repositioning of inclusion in museums, noting, "By prioritizing inclusion in their core operations, museums can ensure that progress is not just cosmetic or temporary but embedded into the systems that make them function."[4] AAM's report placed a national spotlight on the role of museums to foster a sense of belonging as a core practice.

The Road to Inclusion

Like any endeavor of growth, making a museum an inclusive space is a process. Inclusive museums build belonging into their institutional priorities, practices, policies, programming, personnel, processes, and partnerships. They are constantly measuring success, checking power and privilege, and maintaining an orientation toward active listening. They strategically, efficiently, and promptly work on the areas that need attention.

Inclusive museums act. They assert an intentional, ongoing effort to ensure that all individuals can fully participate in all accessible aspects of the museum experience. They demonstrate that they value all. Inclusive museums are magnetic and attractive, buzzing with energy and good vibes. They consistently ask themselves in self-reflective ways what they must change structurally to be more inclusive. Inclusion is on their institutional mind, discussed frequently, measured, and evaluated.

I have witnessed museums engage in turnaround practices concerning inclusion. One museum had a long-standing reputation as being socially cold with poor engagement. A new president/CEO came with a commitment to inclusion and shifted the priorities of practice. Soon, the energy of the museum was elevated. Visitors began to feel valued, heard, and appreciated. Staff began to think in visitor-centered ways, and those team members who did not were repositioned out. The museum intentionally wove inclusion into their core practice, and it saved the life and sustainability of the museum. The museum turned its orientation for inclusion around by prioritizing it in their daily practice. The museum has since won awards and been recognized for the stellar way it serves as an open and inviting space for community. This happened because the museum intentionally placed inclusion as a priority and adjusted its practices, one by one. Regardless of where they are on the spectrum of inclusive practice, museums can adapt, become open and accessible, and thrive as an equitable resource for good in their communities.

Likewise, I have seen museums effective at inclusion move their practices even further along. In St. Louis, for instance, the Missouri Historical Society featured a youth-based curriculum project called "In the Eyes of a Child" that made the museum fully accessible, relevant, and meaningful to all youth. Students with special needs such as autism and hearing impairments as well as wealth-impoverished youth and their families were all fully engaged in and empowered by the museum through this program. Similarly, the St. Louis Science Center's Youth Exploring Science program structured radical inclusion into the center's programming. The staffing of this program reflected the diversity of the youth the program embraced.

Museums like these demonstrate that programmatic practices of inclusion that are thoughtful and authentic make a difference. Inclusive museums target the questions of *who, what, how, when, where,* and *so what,* with the aim of making inclusion a central, consistent, and ubiquitous practice in all it does always. Inclusionary practices include consistently featuring sign language service during all public events as a considerate way to practice inclusion. Ensuring that all video content shown in the museum and conversations on virtual platform programs are closed captioned is another practical way to embrace all.

Inclusion takes place in personnel matters as well. Inclusive museums have distinctively thoughtful ways of growing their teams, from equitable recruitment and identification of diverse talent to onboarding and orienting team members. Inclusive personnel practices include eliminating traditional use of pronouns in written job descriptions and investing in less polished but high potential interns to create new opportunities for those who typically would not have them in the museum field. Cultivating an organizational culture of inclusion requires adjusting traditional human resource planning and actions. It requires advancing a visionary institution-wide philosophy of belonging that is communicated consistently and clearly.

Partnerships and collaborations are the driving ethos of inclusive museums. Partnerships build bridges and create new roads where none existed. Partnerships broaden the reach and impact of museums while collaborations deconstruct social and programmatic silos. Inclusionary practices like these require risk, reflection, and sometimes failure, which turn into valuable lessons, as well as time.

The first step museums take to move toward a more inclusive organizational culture is to say yes. View a move toward being radically inclusive as an essential and beneficial step for the sustainability of your museum. Cancel out fears, reservations, and doubts. Be bold and visionary. Thoughtfully create a plan of inclusion and execute. Integrate it into the current strategic plan and business plan if it is not yet present in those guiding documents. Train staff and team members so that the mind-set of the organization will be consistently inclusive. Associate with other inclusive museums to share successes and exchange best practices. Structure inclusion at every level of operation in your institution, and the traditional ways of exclusionary practice will eventually evolve into remarkable, mission-focused practices that embrace and respect all.

Inclusionary Practices and African American Museums

African American museums have generally maintained a legacy of inclusionary practice. The first African American museum in the United States was established in 1868 at the Hampton Normal and Agricultural Institute in Virginia.[5] A century later during the 1960s, the Black museum movement was launched by community-minded African Americans such as Margaret Burroughs of Chicago, Charles Wright of Detroit, and John Kinard of Washington, DC, among others. Historian Fath Davis Ruffin notes, "the founding directors and pioneers of the Black museum movement saw their institutions as a way to fight the internalized feelings of individuals, particularly young people, and to empower their communities."[6] Museum administrator Juanita Moore further asserts, "The founders [of Black museums] created a culture of connectedness and commitment."[7] Black museums were founded as vibrant educational resources to serve the sociocultural needs of communities and to bring awareness around Black life, history, and art. By informing, inspiring, and igniting uplift while bringing people together with the ultimate aim of educating all, Black museums were built on the premise of radical inclusion. The Association of African American

Museums, established in 1978, gathers the Black museums field for its annual conference where it affirms inclusion as a premise of Black museums.

Community, therefore, has always been at the center of Black museums, rather than objects and artifacts. From making youth summer camps free and accessible as exemplified by the Camp Africa program at the Charles H. Wright Museum of African American History in Detroit to creating life-transforming and career-shaping youth internships at the National Civil Rights Museum in Memphis to facilitating the collection of COVID-19 stories of impact upon Black lives by the Mosaic Templars Cultural Center in Little Rock, Arkansas, inclusion is a bedrock in Black museums. Historian and museum administrator John Fleming eloquently notes, "The Black community has come to learn and appreciate that museums are rewarding spaces for understanding who we are as a people, repositories for what we wish to remember about our past, and the values we hope to pass on to our descendants."[8] Black museums are spaces *for* people.

The Northwest African American Museum (NAAM) in Seattle, Washington, has served the greater Seattle community since it opened its doors in 2008. NAAM upholds a steadfast commitment to centering the needs of people and ensuring that the immediate community thrives around the museum as the community fights against injustice, racism, gentrification, and other compounded oppressions. NAAM advances inclusion across its operations.

Public programs, outreach initiatives, and events complement exhibitions at NAAM and create opportunities for intergenerational, multicultural audiences to engage in meaningful conversations. NAAM is one of the leading spaces in the Puget Sound region for racial equity and social justice empowerment and cross racial dialogue. Programs and events promote educational empowerment, informed activism, and community connection.

Making museum programs affordable is an inclusionary effort practiced at NAAM. Since 2018, for instance, NAAM has partnered with the Seattle Opera and Seattle Symphony in producing and hosting a series of opera and symphony programs that focus on the Black presence in those musical genres. A notable Black opera performer took to the stage at NAAM for a Black-centric, spirited, and accessible opera performance open to and enjoyed by a diverse audience. One audience member noted that, for the first time in his life, he felt that he could finally access opera because the program was tailored for him culturally and that he looks forward to subsequently enjoying opera. In similar fashion, to commemorate Black music month and Juneteenth, NAAM partnered with the Seattle Symphony for an organ recital featuring an acclaimed Black organist. The program was community focused, accessible, and rewarding for all. These have been fruitful partnerships built upon the core practice of inclusion.

Inclusionary practice takes museum experiences beyond the four walls of the building, like NAAM's Knowledge Is Power Book Giveaway program. The program is designed to make all children welcome to read Black literature. With continued school and library closures due to the COVID-19 global pandemic, NAAM gives away thousands of new books to local K–12 children that teach all children the rich history of Black Americans through family-friendly events within the region. These books center, reflect, and affirm Black children and are written and illustrated by Black authors and artists. Similarly, NAAM has taken its genealogy program into a local prison so that the incarcerated can be tooled with the essential resources to trace their ancestry. These kinds of projects aim to lift an entire community and advances opportunities to engage the intersectional dimensions of identity.

Furthermore, NAAM facilitates community-rooted conversations about relevant and timely issues and discussions that inspire collective unity and action. It Takes a Village is one such series that highlights voices and ideas from across the Black diaspora on important topics that inform the individual and collective Black experience, including performing artists, mental health professionals, nutritionists, writers, authors, and more from across the Pacific Northwest. Interrupting Privilege (IP) is another program that focuses on intergenerational skills building and cultivating an antiracism space of dialogue.[9] Based at NAAM, the program is built around cross-generational dialogue and radical listening that aims to interrupt current structures of power. It brings together high school and college students coupled with community members and elders for conversations about race and racism. Both a program and a philosophy aimed at combating racism and privilege, Interrupting Privilege pairs youth leadership with a commitment to critique-in-action. The program serves as a safe space to share and hear racial hurt. By offering careful training modules, Interrupting Privilege fosters discussions about how individual behaviors and biases as well as systemic and structural racism maintain racial inequality. The program uses dialogue and research as tools to change existing systems. The program inspires activism at the personal and community level.[10]

One of the most memorable occasions of inclusionary practice in action took place during a "Write On" author series event. NAAM cohosted a book talk featuring Black feminist scholar Brittney Cooper discussing her book *Eloquent Rage: A Black Feminist Discovers Her Superpower.* One audience member, an older White male, was behaving in ways that asserted his Whiteness and maleness. Cooper, however, handled the disruptions masterfully, leading the man to have a change of mind about Blackness and feminism as a result. An inclusive environment can cultivate growth, evolution, and maturity of thought. It requires that museums listen. During that program, NAAM listened and saw the need of some audience members who harbored bias to be given graceful opportunity and space to grow beyond their biases. NAAM also learned to be patient with the process and offer grace. It was not comfortable to see a bigoted man attempt to disrupt a public program. NAAM demonstrated that transformation can take place when inclusion is practiced.

Furthermore, at the Northwest African American Museum, inclusion can be seen through the museum's diverse array of programming and exhibitions featuring productions by and for people who center QTBIPOC (Queer Trans Black Indigenous People of Color). One such program is the MixxedFit aerobics series, which is taught by a Black nonbinary Transfemme instructor. NAAM's partnerships, programmatic offerings, audiences, and teams are reflective of the diverse, multifaceted community of which the museum is part. This commitment to inclusion strengthens the museum's engagement, connection, and relevance to community. Visitors clearly see themselves in the museum's initiatives, and the museum sees itself in community. That is the truest sense of belonging, when there are no barriers.

Inclusive museums continuously do the internal institutional work of being a part of and deeply committed to equitable people-centered actions and activities. Inclusive museums create social spaces for people to experience joy and healing, tap into hope, reflect, remember, see and renew themselves, where they can be their full selves and be fully valued. Inclusive museums are attentive to language. When museums become radically inclusive, the conversations in them and around them change. If the museum field is going to engage in helping to liberate our society from the inequities that have had us bound, it will take museums being spaces that are listening, learning, and leading on matters of inclusion. When museums are radically inclusive, communities can thrive, minds can be opened, and the quality of lives can be elevated. Museums are central to our communities and society becoming more equitable spaces for all.

Poet Maya Angelou famously stated, "People will forget what you said, people will forget what you did, but people will never forget how you made them feel."[11] As a child growing up in urban poverty, I found that my local museum was not inclusive. There was a myriad of barriers, culturally and socioeconomically. I experienced acceptance and access at the local public library that was located immediately next door to the town museum. But as a Black girl, I did not feel as if the museum was *for* me or valued me. Decades later, the barriers to that local museum have finally come down, and the museum has listened, learned, and is striving to be a leader on inclusive programming and operations by bringing on a more diverse board, staff, and volunteers. It took an organizational and generational shift to change the culture and orientation of that museum. No matter their size and location, how museums like that one make all people feel matters.

Inclusive museums serve as anchors for their visitors and communities, as spaces that help people navigate the uncertainty and challenges of our times. These museums adapt themselves to meet the evolving needs of those around them. Inclusive museums continuously elevate and expand their platform to always make space for more. With a sense of accountability and laser focus, inclusive museums uphold and fulfill their mission of service in equitable ways that give rise to accessibility. Inclusive museums have a practice of taking action and starting with the end in mind. Museums that foster inclusion and access are needed now more than ever.

Notes

1. International Council of Museums Committee for University Museums and Collections, "International Museum Day 2020 #IMD2020," accessed September 23, 2020, http://umac.icom.museum/international-museum-day-2020/.
2. American Alliance of Museums, "About#AAMvirtual," accessed September 23, 2020, https://annualmeeting.aam-us.org/.
3. American Alliance of Museums, "Facing Change: Insights from the American Alliance of Museums' Diversity, Equity, Inclusion, and Accessibility Working Group," 7, accessed September 24, 2020, https://www.aam-us.org/wp-content/uploads/2018/04/AAM-DEAI-Working-Group-Full-Report-2018.pdf.
4. American Alliance of Museums, "Facing Change."
5. Hampton University Museum, "About Us," accessed September 29, 2020, http://wp.hamptonu.edu/msm/about-us/.
6. Fath Davis Ruffins, "Building Homes for Black History: Museum Founders, Founding Directors, and Pioneers, 1915–95," *Public Historian* 40, no. 3 (August 2018): 13.
7. Juanita Moore, "Transitions in Time: Leadership and Governance in African American Museums," *Public Historian* 40, no. 3 (August 2018): 82.
8. John E. Fleming, "The Impact of Social Movements on the Development of African American Museums," *Public Historian* 40, no. 3 (August 2018): 72.
9. Interrupting Privilege is led by University of Washington communications professor and Mellon scholar Ralina Joseph.
10. Interrupting Privilege project description on Northwest African American Museum website, accessed September 29, 2020, www.naamnw.org.
11. LaTrisha McIntosh and LaTasha Taylor, "A Conversation with Dr. Maya Angelou," BSM, last modified July 4, 2012, http://bsmandmedia.com/a-conversation-with-dr-maya-angelou/.

Bibliography

American Alliance of Museums. "About#AAMvirtual." Accessed September 23, 2020. https://annualmeeting.aam-us.org/.

———. "Facing Change: Insights from the American Alliance of Museums' Diversity, Equity, Inclusion, and Accessibility Working Group." Accessed September 27, 2020. https://www.aam-us.org/wp-content/uploads/2018/04/AAM-DEAI-Working-Group-Full-Report-2018.pdf.

Fleming, John E. "The Impact of Social Movements on the Development of African American Museums." *Public Historian* 40, no. 3 (August 2018): 72.

Hampton University Museum. "About Us." Accessed September 29, 2020. http://wp.hamptonu.edu/msm/about-us/.

International Council of Museums Committee for University Museums and Collections. "International Museum Day 2020 #IMD2020." Accessed September 23, 2020. http://umac.icom.museum/international-museum-day-2020/.

Moore, Juanita. "Transitions in Time: Leadership and Governance in African American Museums." *Public Historian* 40, no. 3 (August 2018): 82.

Northwest African American Museum. "Interrupting Privilege." Accessed September 29, 2020. https://www.naamnw.org.

Ruffins, Fath Davis. "Building Homes for Black History: Museum Founders, Founding Directors, and Pioneers, 1915–95." *Public Historian* 40, no. 3 (August 2018): 13.

Chapter 19

Museum Leaders as Allies for Queer Inclusion

Margaret Middleton

This chapter is based on The Queer Inclusive Museum *exhibition, fall 2017.*

Traditionally in museums, the hierarchy is clear: Leaders are situated at the highest ranks of the museum, the executive level. Anecdotally, however, the queer inclusion efforts I see in museums are frequently spearheaded by people occupying lower ranks: queer-identified museum professionals, often from the education department, one of the most diverse departments in the museum. Queerness is defined by the rejection of binaries and subversion of patriarchal roles and expectations, so it might be expected that queer leadership would undermine hierarchy. These queer museum workers may not be leaders according to the org chart but they lead anyway.

As part of a minority population, queer communities have benefited from the support of straight and cisgender allies who lend the power of their privilege to the fight for queer rights. By building systems of support, those in director-level positions in the museum can work as allies, helping queer instigators to do their work effectively and without fear, and to enable and encourage all staff in every department and at every level to contribute to a culture of queer inclusion. I recognize that some of these roles are already occupied by queer people, so in this chapter I do not use the term *ally* to imply a straight and cisgender person but, rather, a person with the privilege of institutional status. Queer directors also have an opportunity to lend their privilege to the cause. This chapter will explore how the intentional allyship of museum leaders can support more meaningful and longer lasting interventions in museums. By avoiding tokenistic attempts at queer inclusion, shaping consistently queer-positive visitor experiences, and putting in place support structures for staff, museum leaders can leverage their privilege as allies to help create the queer-inclusive museum of the future.

Why Queer Inclusion

Queer practitioners leading queer-inclusive efforts face challenges like legacy ("we've never done that before"), bureaucracy ("this isn't what we hired you to do"), allocated funds ("we can't afford it"), and elaborate approval systems that seem designed to make would-be change makers change their minds. Sara Ahmed describes this as "wall work": when practitioners experience the institution as resistance and begin to feel as though they are banging their heads against the wall.[1] And yet, despite the best efforts of the institutions they serve, these leaders of queer inclusion succeed in the face of precarity and low wages by finding avenues of influence within their museum, seeking outside partnerships, and even using their own resources.

Why do they persist? Research supports what queer museum professionals know from experience: queer museum visitors are negatively impacted by not seeing their identities and experiences reflected in museum content.[2] Queer representation can also help build empathy in straight and cisgender visitors. According to Wilkening Consulting, which has conducted extensive studies on the role of the museum in American society, one in five regular museumgoers (described as visiting museums three or more times a year) report that visiting museums has given them a greater awareness of others.[3]

In a society in which people are assumed straight and cisgender until proven otherwise, museums that omit or ignore queerness support a heteronormative, cis-centric dominant narrative.[4] Museums have an opportunity and a responsibility to counter that dominant narrative—to choose queer inclusion. Commitment to queer inclusion is demonstrated by an expression of institutional values through words and actions over time. Without institutional support, leaders of queer initiatives get burned out and discouraged, and their thoughtful and genuine interventions become isolated events that come across to the public and to staff as disingenuous and tokenistic.

Avoiding Tokenism

Visitors experience tokenism when targeted audience events are singular, one-off efforts that are disconnected from the rest of the museum. Staff experience tokenism when minoritized practitioners are expected to create content based on their identities and burdened with inclusion work when it is not part of their job description.[5] Avoiding tokenism in queer inclusion requires an institutional framework that connects queer inclusive moments with a queer positive mission and recognizes and honors queer expertise with institutional support including monetary support.

Some of the most innovative queer content happens in programming. Unlike exhibitions, which are usually more time and budget intensive, programming can often be developed by fewer people and achieved with a small budget. Programs also do not always require director-level approval, so educators can use programs to experiment with content and take more risks. Unfortunately, the low visibility that makes programming such a ripe place for innovation also makes it less accessible to the average visitor.

Without queer-inclusive context, programming is an isolated moment for a select group of people. For example, the Huntington Library, Art Collections, and Botanical Gardens in the Greater Los Angeles Area hosted its fourth annual "Evening among the Roses" in 2017, a "celebration of the LGBTQ+ community."[6] A visitor who did not attend the $110 event would likely have not been aware of the institution's interest in the queer community. Especially if they attended the concurrent exhibition *Octavia E. Butler: Telling My Stories*, in which a large portion of the award-winning science fiction author's story was omitted: the fact that she was a lesbian.

In recent years since the passage of marriage equality laws and other advances in queer rights, many museums in the United States and the United Kingdom have begun to fly Pride flags, rainbow-ize their logos, and offer special queer-themed tours in the month of June. In 2019, museums across the United States and around the world took part in Stonewall 50, going beyond branding and launching comprehensive queer-focused exhibits and programming in commemoration of the 1969 Stonewall uprising. Though these efforts do help to diversify museum narratives and build queer visitorship, representation and rainbows alone do not amount to inclusion. When queer content is limited to temporary exhibitions during Pride Month or relegated to after-hours programming, it suggests that queer content is a niche interest, unimportant to the "normal" visitor. As Museum of Transology founder E-J Scott puts it, "The problem with pop-up exhibitions is that they pop down. And the problem with anniversary-led programming is that it passes."[7]

If queer representation in the museum begins and ends with a singular, temporary exhibition, it can suggest to visitors (and staff) that queerness is only appropriate to discuss in an exhibition about queerness itself. As Porchia Moore writes, "All culture is connected. We must be cautious to not send the message that minority visitors are merely niche or annual visitors."[8] At the Smithsonian Institution's National Museum of African American History and Culture in Washington, DC, curator Aaron Bryant describes their interpretive strategy regarding queer stories this way:

> The lives and contributions of LGBT communities are an integral part of the larger story we tell. These stories aren't isolated or segregated from the larger narrative, but are a natural and intrinsic part of the broader story we're sharing regarding the broad contributions of African Americans to American history and culture.[9]

By including queer narratives throughout the museum experience, queer history can be integrated into the broader narrative. This approach also helps show queerness together with other identities, including gender, race, class, ethnicity, and immigration status, moving beyond one-dimensional interpretation to show visitors a diversity of queer stories. Museum leaders can exercise their allyship by actively promoting this integration across their museum's offerings through a network of support within the institution to help ensure that queer content is not presented in isolation and that the creation and maintenance of that content is not left to any one individual.

Supporting Visitors

Special programs, new exhibits, and targeted marketing may successfully bring queer visitors to the museum, but what happens once they are in the building? A truly queer inclusive museum experience involves thoughtfully chosen language, policies, and facilities. This effort spans across departments and that requires coordination from allies in leadership roles to create a consistent visitor experience.

Membership forms must be flexible enough to serve families that do not fit an expectation of one mom and one dad residing in the same household. Program signups must serve family members who do not share a surname. Development forms that ask for honorifics must offer "opt out" or the gender-inclusive "Mx." Visitor services staff should be trained to use family-inclusive language in interactions with visitors and avoid gendering visitors with words like *ma'am* and *sir*. All staff should receive professional development training about gender and sexuality so they can contribute to a uniformly inclusive voice across all communication platforms including signage, social media, and the museum website.

The voice of the institution is not just expressed in words, it also is expressed in the built environment of the museum. Every restroom in a museum should be accessible for all genders as well as all abilities. While in the process of updating outdated gendered facilities, signage can help communicate that visitors are welcome to use the bathroom that best matches their identity. Sanitary products and disposals must be available in all bathrooms. Infant care rooms must be welcoming and comfortable for caregivers of all genders.

By cultivating a consistent voice and facility that reflects that voice, the allyship of museum leaders can help ensure queer visitors are accommodated and included in every aspect of their visit. The Perelman Building at the Philadelphia Museum of Art shows families of all kinds they are welcome by referring to caregivers as "grown-ups" instead of "moms and dads" (figure 19.1) and also offering all-gender restrooms.

Figure 19.1 A sandwich board directing visitors to the Perelman Building on the Philadelphia Museum of Art campus. The sign uses family inclusive language to encourage visitors to cross the street safely. Source: Margaret Middleton

Supporting Staff

For staff to be empowered and supported in developing queer content and creating queer-positive visitor experiences, queer inclusion must also take into consideration the museum workplace. Museum leaders have an opportunity to be allies for their queer colleagues. Hire queer staff members into director-level positions and make sure the museum's non-discrimination clause includes sexual orientation and gender identity. Staff restrooms and changing rooms should be all-gender facilities. Staff health benefits should grant leave for non-gestational and adoptive parents and should include mental health and health care for transgender staff members; additionally, health care benefits should be extended to nonmarried partners. Make gendered dress codes a thing of the past. Monterey Bay Aquarium's recently revamped dress code is a great example of a gender-friendly policy, shown in figure 19.2.

Queer museum professionals, especially those involved in inclusion work, need emotional support, too. The Field Museum of Natural History in Chicago has an employee resource group for queer staff members called the Outfielders, whose mission is to "create a safe, welcoming place at The Field Museum dedicated to promoting the inclusion of people of all genders and sexual orientations."[10] Notably, in the wake of pandemic-related layoffs, this group's roster has been decimated.

As with all diversity and inclusion efforts, the work of queer inclusion is never done. The Victoria and Albert Museum in London established an LGBTQ Working Group in 2006 to "[unearth] previously hidden or unknown LGBTQ histories in the collections and aims to facilitate understanding of LGBTQ identities and histories through research, events, discussion and debate."[11] Dan Vo, founder of the V&A's LGBTQ Tour, explains how the LGBTQ Working Group supports his work: "the LGBTQ Working Group clearly provides precedent for our volunteer activities, provides us with ongoing support and resources, connects us with a wider network of supporters and mentors, and helps to bring in new objects and ways of thinking that in turn enable us to constantly improve, or to put it differently, helps future-proof our work."[12]

The Queer-Inclusive Museum of the Future

The queer-inclusive museum strives for representation, communication, and accommodation for queer people and narratives across the institution, all year round. For true queer inclusion to take hold, it must be underpinned by broad institutional commitment. This means writing queer inclusion into the values statement of the institution, recruiting queer board members, and updating the collections policy. This also means making money available and accessible for programs and exhibits with queer content. Because of its foundational nature, this deep, institutional work is most effectively achieved by director-level museum leaders.

The LGBTQ welcoming guidelines[13] created by the American Alliance of Museum's LGBTQ Alliance shows a path forward. One of the stated standards of excellence offered in the guidelines is Public Accountability and Trust:

Figure 19.2 A graphic used to communicate the gender-free dress code at Monterey Bay Aquarium. Note that natural hair is expressly allowed which protects some people of color from discrimination, but facial tattoos are prohibited which could discriminate against some Indigenous workers. Source: Monterey Bay Aquarium

In order for LGBTQ persons to trust, attend and support museums generally, we need to see that institutions exhibit and obey ethical standards for making choices that are respectful to LGBTQ persons, families and interests. This demonstrates that the museum puts the interests of the public ahead of the interests of the institution or of any affiliated individual and encourages conduct that merits LGBTQ confidence.

Modeled on the AAM Standards of Excellence for Museums, these guidelines can be used as an assessment tool for current practice and help prioritize next steps. The guidelines are organized by department so every staff member will find something relevant to their work.

Queer museum practitioners are already innovating exciting new queer-positive offerings to help queer visitors feel welcome in the museum, often despite their own institutions. Museum leaders have a responsibility and an opportunity to lend their privilege as allies to bolster these practitioners and leverage their efforts through systems of support that extend across departments and systems that make queer-inclusive practice the standard on which all museum work is based.

Notes

1. Sara Ahmed, *On Being Included* (Durham, NC, and London: Duke University Press, 2012), 26.
2. J. Heimlich and J. Koke, "Gay and Lesbian Visitors and Cultural Institutions: Do They Come? Do They Care? A Pilot Study," *Museums and Social Issues* 3, no. 1 (2009): 93–104.
3. Conversation with Susie Wilkening, evaluator and founder of Wilkening Consulting, July 2017.
4. Chrys Ingraham, "Thinking Straight, Acting Bent," in *Handbook of Gender and Women's Studies*, ed. Kathy Davis, Mary Evans, and Judith Lorber (London: Sage, 2006), 307.
5. Museums as a Site for Social Action, MASS Action Toolkit, September 2017, 92, https://www.museum action.org/resources.
6. See The Huntington, "An Evening among the Roses," accessed July 22, 2017, http://www.huntington .org/amongtheroses/.
7. E-J Scott, "Where Can Trans People Call Home in History?" October 1, 2019, https://www.museums association.org/museums-journal/opinion/2018/10/01102018-where-can-trans-call-home-in-history/.
8. Porchia Moore, "The Danger of the D Word: Museums and Diversity," *The Incluseum* (blog), January 20, 2014, https://incluseum.com/2014/01/20/the-danger-of-the-d-word-museums-and-diversity/.
9. Clarence J. Fluker, "New Smithsonian Places African American LGBT Community in Full View," Center for Black Equity, August 21, 2016, http://centerforblackequity.org/new-smithsonian-places-african -american-lgbt-community-in-full-view/.
10. See Field Museum, "The Outfielders," accessed July 22, 2017, https://www.fieldmuseum.org/about /employee-groups/outfielders.
11. V&A, "LGBTQ," accessed March 14, 2021, https://www.vam.ac.uk/info/lgbtq.
12. Conversation with Dan Vo, freelance museum consultant and project manager of the Queer Heritage and Collections Network supported by Art Fund, August 2017.
13. See American Alliance of Museums, "Welcoming Guidelines for Museums, May 2016, http://ww2 .aam-us.org/docs/default-source/professional-networks/lgbtq_welcome_guide.pdf?sfvrsn=8.

Bibliography

Ahmed, Sara. *On Being Included*. Durham, NC, and London: Duke University Press, 2012.

American Alliance of Museums. "Welcoming Guidelines for Museums." May 2016. http:// aam-us.org/docs/default-source/professional-networks/lgbtq_welcome_guide.pdf.

Field Museum. "The Outfielders." Accessed July 22, 2017. https://www.fieldmuseum.org/about /employee-groups/outfielders.

Fluker, Clarence J. "New Smithsonian Places African American LGBT Community in Full View." Center for Black Equity, August 21, 2016. http://centerforblackequity.org/new-smithsonian -places-african-american-lgbt-community-in-full-view/.

Heimlich, J., and J. Koke. "Gay and Lesbian Visitors and Cultural Institutions: Do They Come? Do They Care? A Pilot Study." *Museums and Social Issues* 3, no. 1 (2009): 93–104.

The Huntington. "An Evening among the Roses." Accessed July 22, 2017. http://www.huntington .org/amongtheroses/.

Ingraham, Chrys. "Thinking Straight, Acting Bent." In *Handbook of Gender and Women's Studies*, edited by Kathy Davis, Mary Evans, and Judith Lorber, 307–21. London: Sage, 2006.

Moore, Porchia. "The Danger of the D Word: Museums and Diversity." *The Incluseum* (blog), January 20, 2014. https://incluseum.com/2014/01/20/the-danger-of-the-d-word-museums-and-diversity/.

Museums as a Site for Social Action. MASS Action Toolkit, 92. September 2017. https://www.museumaction.org/resources.

Scott, E-J. "Where Can Trans People Call Home in History?" October 1, 2019. https://www.museumsassociation.org/museums-journal/opinion/2018/10/01102018-where-can-trans-call-home-in-history/.

V&A, "LGBTQ," accessed March 14, 2021, https://www.vam.ac.uk/info/lgbtq.

Chapter 20

Leading Change at the Speed of Trust[1]

A Conversation with Ben Garcia

As the deputy executive director and chief learning officer of the Ohio History Connection, Ben Garcia brings with him a career focused on organizational change and inclusive museum practice. As coeditors for The Inclusive Museum Leader, we interviewed Ben in October 2020, just over a year into his new role. Ben shared how his vision and experience will shape the future of the Ohio History Connection and the early strategies he's employing to lay the groundwork for inclusive change and practice.

Chris Taylor: Trace your career path for us. I understand that you started out in the social services sector and entered the museum field as an educator.

Ben Garcia: Before working in museums I worked with mental health and law enforcement practitioners to counter burnout by developing a personal creative practice. Making art, creative writing, and music provided means for people who work with victims of violence to process the weight of that work. My first museum job was as an educator at the Getty Museum in Los Angeles. My social services background was viewed as a benefit at that time because they were thinking about museums as spaces for personal discovery. I was really motivated in that period by Lois Silverman, and her book *The Social Work of Museums*. Also by Ray Williams who works to counter burnout in the medical field using museum-based teaching. This background directly informed my commitment to equity and inclusion today as I work toward a larger context for museums as sites of healing.

Fast forward. After earning a master's degree from Bank Street College, I went to work at the Skirball Cultural Center in LA, which roots itself in the Jewish American experience and is committed to welcoming new waves of immigrants into a US context and helping them find a place and a home in LA. After a wonderful professional experience learning from a great inclusive leader, Sheri Bernstein, I moved on in pursuit of a new challenge.

I went from the Skirball to the Phoebe A. Hearst Museum of Anthropology at the University of California–Berkeley. That was pivotal moment in my life because it was there that I first understood the degree to which museums have participated in the disenfranchisement of Indigenous communities. I learned how anthropology, history, and natural history museums were actively separating American Indians from their Ancestors, cultural patrimony, and from the possibility of cultural continuity in numerous ways.

I went through an interview process, including a collections tour, and somehow didn't know at the end of that process that they were holding human remains. And so my first day there, I was having lunch with my boss, the director of the museum, and I, like a good new employee asked, "What's the first thing that we need to address together?" And she said, "We are holding the bodies of ten thousand American Indians in a storage facility underneath a hundred-year-old swimming pool that has no seismic protection. They're in a really precarious situation. And we need to move them into a better storage facility." It was one of those moments where I understood each word that was coming out of her mouth, but I couldn't quite process what she was saying. I was in shock, I think.

Two days later, I went into this storage area and for the first time saw what more than ten thousand human skeletal remains looked like. They were being stored as scientific specimens, not as individuals. Their crania were separated from the rest of their bodies; there were piles of bone on open shelves and sticking out of drawers. And when I walked in there, the dissonance between the way I was processing what I was seeing, and what the people working there were doing as museum employees was really hard for me to bridge. I felt like I was walking into a mass grave, a site of enormous tragedy. Everyone else was acting like this was just perfectly normal. This was when I first really understood that museums were not simply sites where external injustices could be explored and healed (which was how I thought about my work at the Getty and Skirball), but that museums were perpetrators too.

I managed to stay for about three years and made some gains, but ultimately knew I needed to move to a place where I could effect change and facilitate the return of the Ancestors and their belongings. That's when the opportunity at San Diego Museum of Man, now Museum of Us, developed. I shared with the director that I would only consider stepping into the role of deputy director if he had a commitment and the board had a commitment to repatriation of all the ancestral remains that are at the museum. He indicated that this made sense to him, he didn't know how to do it, and that he would leave that to me. It really felt like one of those moments when God closes the door somewhere, they open a window. It was there that we were able to create a context for decolonizing practices for collections and for the Ancestors. It gave me hope and helped me understand that there is a way forward, even when the museum community doesn't understand the issues yet.

Cinnamon Catlin-Legutko: As you consider the museum field in 2020, how do you situate the changes underway?

Ben: Our field, like many others, is reckoning with and recognizing the disparities and assumptions that were sown into it from its inception during the age of exploration and industrial expansion. Every age had its champions for equity and inclusion, and every age had its understanding of what those concepts meant. Today the roles of systemic racism and colonization in the formation of museums, their contemporary practices, and workplace cultures have risen to prominence in our internal conversations.

I hope we are at a tipping point. Time will tell if the recent focus on more inclusive practices in many museums is part of a flare-up—time-limited and ignited by the larger context of racial justice advocacy in our communities. I am hopeful that we are in the early phases of a new period when inclusive leaders at all levels of our institutions, and those working in related areas, are actually repairing and re-setting museums so that they can model the values and practices required for humans (and all beings) to prosper.

What is needed is a community of practice. Success is amplified by relationships. By the inclination of so many practitioners to share and invite and cede and seed. Noelle Kahanu, a museum practitioner and professor of museum studies at the University of Hawai'i, Manoa, called the work of inclusion "seeding authority." Any success I have experienced in leading inclusive museum practice was seeded by others. If I started naming the museum practitioners who taught, and teach, me how to do this and who cocreated pathways for shared authority and inclusion, I would fill a page at least. It would be the longest "acknowledgments" section of a book ever. I literally do not know where my ideas start or end as I carry with me the ideas and brilliance of literally hundreds of people with whom I have worked, learned from, listened to, and watched in action.

Cinnamon: You are a leader at a new museum, and you're someone who actively works on your personal journey of inclusion. How do you manage the dynamic between getting to know your staff and understanding their motivations, and finding out where they are on their journey? How do you lead and manage staff while being authentic and vulnerable at the same time?

Ben: There's a point that you reach in your personal and professional development where you realize that not being authentic, not bringing your real self to work and life is just a waste of everyone's time and energy. During the search process for my current position, in every conversation I had, I talked about what was compelling to me about this opportunity: returning the Ancestors to their communities and supporting the creation of contexts of equity and inclusion. I was very open about what drives and motivates me and why I think museums are important. It helps people understand. It gives them a chance to really think about how aligned they are with the things that I am bringing forward.

When I arrived at the Ohio History Connection, I was lucky to walk into a situation where I had five incredibly strong direct reports, many of whom had been working to center inclusion and equity in the organization. The work of building relationships with American Indian tribes whose Ancestors lived in the lands called Ohio was well underway, led by Stacey Halfmoon, who was director of American Indian relations, and Burt Logan, the CEO (and with lots of participation by staff across the organization). But in other instances, the work of equity and inclusion was still being addressed by my colleagues like a skunkworks project, acknowledged by leadership, but not yet fully centered as a priority. I think at some level, by hiring me, the organization was committing to fully centering it.

It's very difficult to walk in as a new leader in an organization and have people show you their authentic selves. There's either deference or hostility to hierarchy in systems. Neither is great. Deference needs to morph into understanding and acceptance of why decisions cannot all be collective, and hostility needs to become courageous and compassionate truth-telling. For either of those changes to occur, trust is required, and trust has to be earned. So my ability to lead authentically will happen at the speed of trust.

The Ohio History Connection is an organization of about two hundred people right now. I know probably 10 percent of them very well and then another 10 percent fairly well. That's about forty. Then there's probably 160 staff members with whom I have friendly interactions, but it will take time to get to know them. To connect with people quickly, I have to prioritize. Job number one is making sure that the people who are directly reporting to me, the people who are the leadership of the organization, are set up to be successful leaders and that they have the information that they need to be able to contribute.

What I've primarily done in year one is work to create a context for shared leadership. We went from being an organization where most of the organizational decisions being made by a cohort of two to five people to them now being made by a cohort of twenty people. And the consensus seems to be that we make much better decisions as a result.

And I also watch and I listen. I notice the people who I think are going to be essential to the future of the organization. If the organization is going to be a truly inclusive organization in the way that Lisa Sasaki[2] talks about, I look for where power and authority is truly being broken down and shared. I notice these people and I talk to them about their vision. Because I am not bringing a lot of new ideas to this team, mostly, I am just working to elevate and center the people and ideas that are already here but just needed a path-clearer.

Chris: Thinking about the ethos of the institution, it seems like they were looking for an inclusive leader. So how did DEAI [diversity, equity, accessibility, and inclusion] show up in the search process? What kind of questions and concerns did the search committee have regarding inclusion? What did they want to know that you were bringing to the table?

Ben: I think that when your professional reputation is rooted in equity and inclusion, or decolonization work, when you become a finalist for a job, you know that this reputation is one of the motivators for the search committee. I have regularly presented at conferences and participated in national conversations. There's a lot of documentation about the work that I like to do. It's interesting for me to think about how much was being asked of me versus how much I was checking out that they, in fact, really wanted what I was offering.

My initial conversations were just with the CEO, and I think before he brought someone to the rest of the team, he wanted to make sure this felt like someone who made sense from where he and the team were heading. Burt came out to San Diego to see the work that had been accomplished under my leadership there. He did a lot of due diligence to see how we installed the exhibit *Race: Are We So Different?*[3] and some of the other exhibitions we'd done. He also wanted to see the decolonizing work we were doing, in particular our commitment to the Ancestors and with collections.

This was followed up with an opportunity for me to meet with a larger group of people where I was primarily asked about leadership and emotional intelligence. I think people were more trying to understand what kind of leader I would be, and how I would complement Burt's leadership style, than they were specifically asking about DEAI stuff. And I think, really, that's because I just came with that as a known skill set.

Chris: In a way this is an even better situation because the institution knew what it was looking for and had they not been looking for someone like you, you never would have wanted to be a finalist.

Cinnamon: Are you finding a way that you can manage up and do DEAI work with the board? How do you set a tone for them for the institution? Are you finding good synergy around what the board would like to see? Are you finding a pathway together?

Ben: There are eighteen trustees on the board and also about a dozen ex-offico members representing various state agencies. The governor appoints nine of the eighteen. The rest are either member or board selected. I mostly work with the gubernatorial appointees and those who are member or board elected.

Our board generally reflects the political mix in the state, but we work to remain nonpartisan. Ohioans generally understand that because it's really a 50/50 state politically, you need to stay pretty close to the center. Therefore, finding ways to talk about equity and inclusion that are nonpartisan is important in our organization. The board is committed to becoming more representative and has supported the steps toward including American Indian stakeholders at all levels of the organization with a new American Indian Policy (drafted by Stacey Halfmoon when she worked here). As I try to move issues of equity and inclusion forward, the way that it's most effective to do that is to talk about the aspects of the work that are additive. The ways in which we want to bring a greater diversity of histories and stories to bear. We want Ohioans to understand how multifaceted its towns and communities were in the past, and that there are histories that haven't been centered in the organization.

We just completed a strategic planning process over the summer and our strategic priorities are sustainability, equity, and relationship building. Throughout we made sure that the trustees were seeing every draft of it; they had a chance to give feedback. I did moderate my language so that it worked for a number of trustees who were concerned about politically charged terms and phrases. We talked a lot about inclusive history, and I think the strategic plan is one that will allow us to make progress, especially for many of us who need to see reparative work happen.

I remember very distinctly in my interview process, a senior staff person said to me that there is a "right way" to talk about equity and inclusion in Ohio. For example, if you use the term *decolonization*, you're not even going to get through the door with a lot of people in Ohio. He recommended that I not to use the language of academia or critical race theory for this work and instead talk about it in plain language and frame it as including people who should have been part of decision making all along, but who weren't in the past.

I've really taken that advice to heart and so appreciate it. I'm a pretty pragmatic leader around this work, and I want to see it move forward. For me, I'm OK if I need to avoid using a particular term as long as we can make the change that that term describes. Because I come from California, because my name is Garcia, because of the work that I've done, there may be assumptions that my new colleagues or community have about me. I'm aware that some think that I move a bit too quickly. Or that I sometimes approach things in a way that works for California, but doesn't work for Ohio. I spend a lot of time working to demonstrate that I am not going to undermine our success with a pace that's too fast, but rather that I'm here to celebrate the strengths of Ohio's particular qualities, and that I respect the Ohio way.

I think the nice thing about this work is that, in museums, if you have a really clear understanding of the change you want to effect, being flexible about how to manifest that change is going to serve you. This is especially true if you are more invested in seeing the change happen than you are in proving a point.

Chris: When you consider the changes museums need to make in the US and around the globe, what are the most important decisions museum leaders need to make in your opinion?

Ben: I think that revisiting the traditional hierarchies that exist in our organizations, and changing the way leaders are held accountable is the most important thing we can do. Currently in most of our institutions, the influence of the CEO is disproportionately large and that does not always contribute to creating sustainable change. You can have a group of people at all levels of the organization steadily moving toward inclusivity and equity and if the next CEO doesn't buy in, all that work can be swept away quickly. It was one thing when CEOs usually remained in organizations for fifteen to thirty years, but with the top job rotating in many institutions every five years or so, this issue is becoming more pronounced.

Yes, a CEO needs to have a vision (and that vision will hopefully be influenced by others in the organization). And yes, the CEO needs to keep the organization pointed at that vision. But the CEO is not the only person devoting their life to the organization, and so they need to find ways to work with the board and staff to ensure that when they move on, the work of equity and inclusion can continue. And they need to figure out systems that can do this effectively. By codifying a distributed power structure, or inclusive decision-making process, for example, so that the next CEO inherits it and needs to work within it. And by codifying practices of equity and inclusion through policies written into the by-laws to ensure a more lasting legacy for these values.

Another essential decision leaders need to make today is to prioritize economic equity in museums in several ways. First, we need to set some standards for how many resources go to serving internal needs versus the needs of our communities and customers. Having a values-driven process for determining the scale of investment in capital projects or collections is crucial. So when museums commit tens of millions of dollars to new buildings, they also commit equally to the financial security of their staff and communities. Second, we need to all aim for compensating the lowest-paid staff with a minimum living wage, tied to the cost of living, rather than paying minimum wage. And third, income disparity has grown in our nonprofit field as it has grown in the private sector. I believe that the CEO of a museum should earn no more than about five times the amount of the lowest-paid person. It is reasonable for a CEO to advocate for a competitive salary, and for boards to want to reward good work. But let's ensure that an investment in the CEO's compensation will also require an investment in all the staff, as their success did not occur in a vacuum.

It helps me to remember that *museums* aren't inclusive and *museums* aren't equitable—*people* are those things. Museums are only as inclusive as the people who run them. Inclusion is a practice of individuals, and museums reflect the cultures of people who staff them.

Chris: In my experience, board members often don't know enough about museums to hold museums or the CEO accountable. What needs to shift with board governance and recruitment? How do these structures need to evolve?

Ben: Boards are essential partners in changing the way leaders are held accountable, and boards need to do more to hold the CEO accountable for equity in the organization, and generally for workplace culture. In my experience, museum boards often see delving into workplace culture issues as a bright line they should not cross (except in extreme circumstances), and so the CEO needs to ask and expect this of the trustees.

Generally, the only staff member trustees know well is the CEO. They often know some of the staff who report to the CEO but rarely connect with levels further down in the organization. I am certainly guilty of this in the boards on which I serve. While this is standard nonprofit practice, it is not conducive to equity and inclusion. Too much depends on the CEO being an extremely self-aware gatekeeper. There are few mechanisms for addressing unconscious bias or blind spots in that individual.

When thinking about board recruitment, the CEO needs to explicitly talk with prospects about how they are part of the checks and balance structure. To be an inclusive museum and one committed to equity, trustees and staff at all levels of the organization need to find ways to work directly together, develop relationships, and trust each other so that the CEO isn't the sole go-between. I feel like this is an essential step to changing the dynamic and making institutions (and not just people) equitable. In grad school, a visiting lecturer posited that the director sits at the neck of the hourglass between the board and the staff. That is too much power for one individual to have. We need organizations to be tube-shaped, not hourglasses.

I think it's important to have some people on the board who really know the museum industry—but not just from the leadership seat—as a way to keep the CEO honest. I worked with a board president, George Ramirez, who said that a good rule of thumb is to have three of any category on a board if you want them to have a real voice and not be tokenized. What if three of the trustees on museum boards were staff members from other museums in entry- or mid-management-level roles? They would immediately sniff out the things that are getting swept under the rug. They would have the radar for that. They'd know the questions to ask about how the staff are doing and how the executive director is doing in relationship to workplace culture and morale.

Cinnamon: You've already noted that your leadership team is much larger. You've gone from the smaller, more traditional format to twenty plus folx. Can you talk a little more about how that gets formed? How did you determine the folx who really needed to be in that decision-making group?

Ben: I observed from the start that as the deputy executive director, I oversaw five division directors and when all of their respective staffs are combined, it adds up to 85 percent of the staff. There's no way I can understand the work of 85 percent of the organization and represent that to the leadership team. Yet in the initial structure, that was the expectation. An equivalent position exists in many nonprofit executive teams. I knew that I was going to make some bad decisions, because on a good day, I understand maybe 25 percent of what is going on. So for the interest of the organization, I proposed this larger leadership team.

Not every single manager in the organization is part of the leadership team, but every chief officer, every division head, and every director is on it. We also have necessary administrative staff on the team to help it run smoothly. In the end, 10 percent of our organization is on the leadership team. I wonder if that is potentially a good rule of thumb for other museums.

Proportionally bigger leadership teams are better because it's really easy to make a decision that can ruin the work lives of a whole segment of your staff simply because you didn't have the necessary information or perspective at the table. You only need to do that once to know you want the right people at the table the next time around.

Chris: This is interesting because I've experienced the opposite where we had a leadership team of about twenty-two, and we went to a leadership team of eight. It was tough to navigate that change. It became even smaller while I was there. In the end, there was one person in charge of finance and HR and then one person in charge of exhibits, collections, sites, and education. That's essentially 90 percent of what the museum does.

Ben: I think we find that in most places. When I arrived at Ohio History Connection, most decisions were made by a team of five: the chief financial officer, chief development officer, chief marketing officer, the deputy director (me) and the CEO. This meant that finance and development were disproportionately weighted in decisions that ultimately impacted not just the vast majority of staff but also most of the external stakeholders. We all recognized that expanding the set of voices around the table was necessary and so changed the structure.

Chris: I think you hit on something that is really key: the institution is driven by money. When you give that equal weight as core mission work, so many voices are lost. This makes me think about risk. When you seek to create change, how do you determine the acceptable amount of risk involved in pushing for that change? When would you walk away from a change initiative if it feels too risky? What are those factors for you?

Ben: I think what helps me is my education background. One of the first concepts you learn as an educator is that you meet people where they are. If you think about Paulo Freire's *Pedagogy of the Oppressed*, the way people learn most effectively is by starting with the context in which they live. The way Friere taught adults to become literate in weeks was by basing the language and the lessons of literacy around their professional and lived contexts. I think the rate at which you can make change is directly connected to your ability as an organization, as an individual, to meet someone where they are and to help them recognize a new opportunity from where they started. It's about showing, not telling. You have to model the way forward; no one wants to be told what they should do.

Generally, I think that if 10 percent of the people think you're moving too fast and 10 percent think you're not going nearly fast enough, then I think you're going about the right pace. When those percentages really shift, when 30 percent of the people think you're moving too fast or when 50 percent of people think you're moving too slow, that's when you really need to take a hard look.

When the pace gets out of whack, I know that it's time for me to not walk away, but to shift gears up or shift gears down. Our recent strategic planning process was a perfect example. There were times when I felt like I was selling out because to get to the finish line, I had to accept that we weren't going to name things like White supremacy. I chose to use the language of inclusivity rather than the language of critical race theory in order to meet our constituents where they are. And we ended up with a strategic plan that probably feels like too much for about 10 percent of the people and not nearly enough for 10 percent. But it is a plan that centers equity in ways that are unprecedented for our institution.

It requires patience, and again, at the end of the day you have to decide who are you doing this for? If you want to lead change in a way that actually has a chance to be lasting, you need to modulate it based on your context.

Chris: There is certainly a tension between radical change and knowing what radical change needs to happen but having to structure it so that it's sustainable.

Ben: Certainly. I think that we need the people who are pushing from the outside and holding institutions accountable. And we need the people who are trying to make that change happen from inside. For whatever reason, I decided that I was going to be an inside guy. You need both because those outside voices help some of your inside skeptics see that this is a direction we have to go. I think it works as an ecosystem, and both revolutionaries and evolutionaries have roles to play in creating inclusive institutions.

Chris: You have to have those people that will stay in there and work internally. But I don't fault people who have to get out of that environment. There are days when I feel like that too.

Ben: You have to wake up in the morning and get back into the fight every day for a reason. I feel like the reason that I can lead change, and process the natural frustrations, is because every morning I know why I'm going to work. I know exactly who it is that I'm going there to serve, and first and foremost, it is the Ancestors. I think often about a lesson I learned from Alutiiq elder Cheryl Potts. When I was at the Museum of Us, she regularly visited to provide care for her Ancestors whose remains were at the museum. Once when we were talking about an upcoming repatriation, I felt the need to apologize for how long it was taking. She said to me that time is a construct for the living and it works differently for the Ancestors. For the Ancestors, intention matters more than time. And so if you're doing this work with true intention, and you're moving it forward, the pace—if it's three months, if it's three years—it doesn't matter to the Ancestors. That really helped me, and I took permission around that and then more broadly around the work of equity and inclusion. As long as you know every day that you're getting up with the intention to move the work forward, if the time frame is out of your control, it doesn't matter. It's about commitment to that continual momentum.

Chris: Have you thought about where your wall is—the wall you won't be able to clear because you hate the work and can't do it anymore? As a change agent, how much time do you put into thinking about what that threshold is for you?

Ben: I have definitely put time into thinking about that. I live solidly within the protective margins of our current culture. I am queer and Latinx but also White-presenting, cisgendered, and live in a dual-income household. These facets of my identity have opened doors, professionally, and shield me from a host of threats experienced by my colleagues of color, those who are transgender or gender nonconforming, and those who are more economically vulnerable. I recognize this. And I recognize that because of this I can consider a scenario where I step back from the work.

After all, "taking a break" may be the biggest privilege of all in our field for anyone who is White or White-appearing. Walking away is a privilege that many BIPOC [Black, Indigenous, and People of Color] people don't get. Recognizing this privilege is part of what makes me say, "Just deal with it, find your way to stay in the work."

My way to stay in the work is my relationship to Spirit (my understanding of the divine). That connection to a larger context for the work I am called to do helps me a lot. I think about the work I did with folx who worked directly with victims of violence before I worked in museums, and the way a creative practice helped them stay in the work. We need to find the energy sources for hope (whether divine, creative, or other) as losing hope is what burns most people out.

But bottom line, I don't think you get to "peace out" if you're a cisgendered, White appearing, economically comfortable person in this work. I mean, of course, anyone gets to do anything they want, but I wouldn't be able to do it. *That's* my wall. I would never be able to live with myself with any sense of integrity if I did that.

Cinnamon: I'm really glad to hear that you're in this work for the long haul; the field and our colleagues have so much they can learn from your experience and perspective. Because of this, I think it's important for you to respond to what gives you joy about the future. What gives you hope about where museums are going? In addition to your sheer willpower and integrity, what else keeps you in it?

Ben: My hope for the eventual success of this work is founded on the racial justice advocacy I have had the opportunity to participate in directly with Museums & Race and Museum as Site for Social Action.[4] It comes from the (mixed) success of my own attempts at inclusive practice as I have moved into roles of expanding responsibility. Mainly, though, it comes from the community of decolonizing and antiracist museum practitioners who have been working in sites across the country to respond to, and amplify, the activism of American Indians, Native Hawai'ians, and constituencies of color—both the path-breaking labor of a prior generation of inclusive practitioners, and those of us working in a context of connected efforts today.

The other day I had this moment when I was reflecting on the University of California's new repatriation policy. Dr. Amy Lonetree, who authored the book *Decolonizing Museums*, was part of the group that wrote the policy which will address the serious issues at the Hearst Museum at UC-Berkeley.[5] All those Ancestors that I walked in on ten years ago, they all have pathway for repatriation now thanks to this policy. I was thinking about how Noelle Kahanu, Karen Kosasa, and Halena Kapuni-Reynolds at the University of Hawai'i, Manoa, brought Amy and me together (among others) to talk about decolonizing work at the Seeding Authority conference in 2018. I only knew about Amy Lonetree's work because of you, Cinnamon, and the work your team did at the Abbe. Amy talked in Hawai'i about how seeing her work manifest in Bar Harbor and San Diego expanded it in ways she never imagined. And I cannot help but think that this influenced her work with the new policy for the UC system. I think about these bright lines of connection between all of us who are doing the work. Without you, Chris and Cinnamon, without Joanne Jones-Rizzi or Veronica Alvarez, without Dina Bailey—everyone I am inspired by, how would I know how to do this work?[6]

And I will also name the generation on whose shoulders I stand as deep sources of hope. Claudine Brown, Leslie Bedford, and Laura Roberts. My museum *tías* (and graduate school instructors). Muses of integrity, wonder, and strategy. Claudine first suggested that I work where my values and the museum's are aligned. Leslie showed how to center wonder and imagination and storytelling in the work. Laura taught me how to step into leadership and also to step back. I will also name the *tías* of my path with the Ancestors, Sharon Simone, Cheryl Potts, and Deena Metzger. Guardians of revisioning. Sharon showed me to answer the call of Ancestors. Cheryl told me that for them time is meaningless, and intention is what matters. And Deena showed me a way to practice a constant undoing of my colonizing mind. I carry these lessons into my daily work.

We are this matrix of folx working to make museums inclusive along the lay lines of healing and justice. We've developed a new social capital in the field that's not based on the traditional notions of, "Where did you grow up?" "What school did you go to?" "What social club do you belong to?" We have this new social capital that's built on integrity and doing the hard work of centering equity. And that really gives me hope. Connecting with thoughtful hearts and minds gives me hope. Mainly, though, staying in the work gives me hope.

Notes

1. While many have expressed this statement in writing, adrienne maree brown in *Emergent Strategy* inspires this writing.
2. Lisa Sasaki is the director of the Smithsonian Asian Pacific Center. She also authored chapter 11 in this book.
3. This exhibit was produced by the American Anthropological Association in collaboration with the Science Museum of Minnesota. Joanne Jones-Rizzi, the author of chapter 1 in this book, was a key member of the project team. While it continues as a traveling exhibit, some museums have opted to purchase it and install it on a more permanent basis, like the Museum of Us.
4. Formed in 2015, Museums & Race is committed to challenging and transforming structural racism and oppression in museums. You can read more about their efforts at www.museumsandrace.org. MASS Action, launched in 2016, is committed to creating resources for and dialogue about museums that are aligning with equitable and inclusive practice. You can read more about this project at www.museum action.org.
5. Amy Lonetree is a renowned Ho-Chunk scholar who, among other publications, wrote *Decolonizng Museums: Representing Native America in National and Tribal Museums*. It serves as essential reading for understanding decolonizing museum practices. After many years of noncompliance and harm, in 2020 the University of California passed a sweeping policy that enforces compliance with NAGPRA (Native American Graves Protection and Repatriation Act). You can read about this policy and its significance here: https://ucop.edu/research-policy-analysis-coordination/policies-guidance/curation-and-repatria tion/index.html.
6. Claudine Brown was lovingly celebrated in chapter 1 by Joanne Jones-Rizzi. Claudine is credited with inspiring the museum careers of many while leading educational and arts initiatives at the Smithsonian and the Brooklyn Museum. Veronica Alvarez is a leading advocate for inclusive museum educational practices and Spanish-language interpretation. Dina Bailey is a facilitator and trainer who works to shape antiracist and inclusive practices for museum boards and staffs. She wrote chapter 9 in this book.

ACTIVITY

Identifying Values

To complete this activity, you will need paper or a journal, your favorite pen, and access to the internet.

1. Identify and name three personal values. You can draw upon the chapters you're reading in this book, conduct an internet search for "personal values," and/or refer to resources you turn to often for inspiration and motivation. Write these down on a piece of paper, preferably in your journal or calendar.

2. Take time to write your observations about the following:

    a. How do your personal values intersect with diversity, equity, accessibility, and inclusion? If they don't intersect, why?

    b. How do you exhibit these values in your museum? Consider moments in daily interactions, in team meetings and board meetings, and in community events/ meetings. How are you showing up as a leader?

    c. What can you do to better align your practice with your values? What can you do to build from strength so that you are leading inclusively?

3. Hold onto what you've written and continue to refer to this when you're preparing for an important presentation, engaging in difficult conversations, or needing some reminders. Also be sure to refer to this writing as you complete other activities throughout this book.

By the way, you're amazing and keep being you. Let your values guide you.

Part Five

Choosing Your Environment

Chapter 21

How to Spot an Inclusive Leader and Choose to Work for Them

Kayleigh Bryant-Greenwell

When the editors invited me to contribute to this book I was a mixed bag of feelings—honored, of course, but also petrified, intimidated, anxious, elated, and determined. I remember not too long ago, there was a time that I never hesitated to reply enthusiastically "Yes!" to every opportunity that came my way. There is power in "Yes," but I've come to realize that there's power in "No" as well. My history with "Yes" is more about the impossible easy road to success in museums than it is about my willingness to try anything. What I mean is, that for years I felt my only career option *was* to say "Yes" to everything, do everything, and overexert myself physically, mentally, and emotionally just to have a place in this field. In 2015, I was working two part-time jobs, adjunct teaching, curating four exhibitions, freelance writing, and speaking at conferences. I said "Yes" to everything. How could I not? How could I possibly say "No" to a single invitation to work in this field, while I witnessed my peers from my cripplingly expensive master's degree program intern for free for years postgraduate without a light at the end of the tunnel? No, I had to keep clawing, keep pushing, never stopping, always saying "Yes" to the next great opportunity no matter how exhausted, drained, or weary I was getting. This is not a complaint. I recognize how very privileged I am to have scaled the ladder, broken the barriers, that are so firmly cemented in this field. This little bit of context is twofold. First: this is my brief love letter to all the recent graduates and emerging professionals. Don't give up! I know it's hard, even impossible. It shouldn't be. It's not right or fair or even sustainable. Keep working, keep striving, keep demanding more of this field. You are not alone. As you see in this book there are leaders out there who are looking for you. Find them. That's what this chapter is about, how to find your inclusive leader. I would not be where I am today (or where I will be in the future) had it not been for my mentors. I am eternally grateful for my mentors—the epitome of the inclusive museum leader—who guided me along the way. I dedicate this chapter to them.

My second reason for beginning this chapter with a very personal tangent is that nothing in this field happens outside of the context of the problems within this field. We use a lot of different words to describe the crisis we find ourselves in: inclusion, diversity, equity, accessibility, antiracism, decolonization, empathy, neutrality. Without conflating one issue with another, all of these problems have a common source: power. Museums were built on oppressive and harmful systems of power. Today's museums are drunk on power. This field is designed to make those new to it— its own future leaders—feel *powerless* against a system of inequitable practices. Inclusion is the way we approach our work. Inclusion not only informs our practice, it is our practice. Inclusion in museums is the active operational strategy that seeks out and eliminates injustices. Typically when we think of inclusion we think about increasing diversity and representation. But inclusive practice engages in the dismantling of all forms of oppressive structures in museums. Nothing that happens within museums is unrelated to any and all harm levied by the field. Inclusive leadership resides within this context as well. In fact, the best examples of inclusive leadership are those who are actively working to dismantle oppressive barriers in this field. Inclusive leaders pay their interns. Inclusive leaders affirm a healthy work-life balance. Inclusive leaders support unions.

I'll add this about inclusive leadership and "Yes." Inclusive leadership is committed to "Yes." Like myself, our inclusive leaders have over-endeavored to say "Yes." Yes to leading this field into a more inclusive future. Yes to mentoring and building up the next generation. Yes to taking on the next dozen projects while already juggling an existing dozen. Yes to uncredited labor behind the scenes on someone else's project. Yes to working overtime, overtime, overtime. Yes to managing up to the directors who continue to struggle with equitable practices. Yes to leading the grass-roots movements for collective liberation.

So when you find your inclusive leader and go to work for them, be aware of all the "Yeses" they hold. And be a "Yes" that helps their cause.

Qualities of an Inclusive Leader

The business of leadership is voluminous. Consider the number of books, courses, lectures, and Hollywood dramas that teach "good leadership." We may assume that the museum directors who lead this field embody these good leadership attributes. But do we actually hire most directors for their leadership skills? The premium we place on fundraising skills—which often is more about high-monied connections than skills themselves—suggests otherwise. So when we consider the importance of leadership for field-wide progress, what are the implications of a field of leaders hired for their Rolodexes?

We often think of representation when we think of inclusion. Representation matters, of course. An inclusive workplace will reflect the diversity of our society. Though representation is a sure marker of an inclusive leader, inclusive leadership incorporates a multitude of standards. The qualities of an inclusive leader not only are reflected in the diversity of the company they keep but also define the approach and motivations to their work. Inclusivity is not achieved through diversity alone. Inclusive leadership is a constant effort. It demands equity in all facets of its environment. An inclusive leader uses their power to abolish injustice and advance collectiveness. The following is a short and incomplete compilation of the other qualities, in addition to representation, embraced by inclusive museum leaders.

Leads with Empathy

The Empathetic Museum, a collective of educators, exhibit designers, interpretive planners, and administrators consulting on institutional change, asserts, "An empathetic museum is one that, at the core of its mission and in all its outward manifestations, resonates closely with the people it serves."[1] An empathetic lens benefits an inclusive leader in framing their approach to museum

Figure 21.1 National Museum of Art in Taipei, Taiwan. Source: Kayleigh Bryant-Greenwell

work within the context of their audiences—staff, visitors, neighborhood, communities, and other stakeholders. Contrary to the way museums behave, museum work does not exist in a bubble unrelated to societal happenings. Yes, a museum can literally continue to *exist* while social unrest rages against their metaphorically closed doors. Curators can continue to curate, educators can continue to educate, but that does not mean the museum is doing its *job*. Conversely, inclusive leaders actively engage their work with social realities—police brutality, protest, human rights vulnerabilities. Inclusive leaders do not merely offer words of solidarity and condolence during civil unrest. If the museum's audiences are hurting, then the museum is hurting. This is empathy. An inclusive leader does not put up artificial barriers to "what's happening out there." An inclusive leader recalibrates the work needing to be done in relation to social realities. An empathetic lens demands leadership that is responsive and obligated to the world we actually live in.

Embraces Emotionality

Traditional leadership models that value dominance and indifference would balk at the first two qualities listed here: empathy and embracing emotionality. But inclusive leaders are decidedly nontraditional. Inclusive leadership bucks tradition not only for its out-datedness and lack of relevance today but also for its origination in oppressive, exclusive practices. Where museum status quo holds tight to archaic and obsolete tradition, inclusive museum leaders embrace new values and, thus, are creating a new way to museum, but I'm getting ahead of myself.

In the misguided effort to professionalize the museum field, human emotion has been stripped away from the workplace. Museums are not the only industry to do so; "professionalism" has long been associated with aloofness and detachment across the professional plain. But an article from the *Harvard Business Review* notes that in "interviews with executives and employees, some people have told us that their organizations lack emotion altogether. But every organization has an emotional culture, even if it's one of suppression. By not only allowing emotions into the workplace, but also understanding and consciously shaping them, leaders can better motivate their employees."[2] Just as relevance and reality cannot be divorced from museum work, neither can emotion. However, the lived experience of the "unemotional" museum workplace is very real and often falls along lines of identity.

I have personally experienced the trauma of the intolerance of emotionality in museums. Over the course of my career, I've been labeled "negative," "intimidating," and "difficult." I am a young Black, biracial woman committed to change making in museums. When I wrote earlier of the impossibility of my career trajectory, I was not giving into hyperbole. By all accounts of the impenetrable Whiteness and maleness of this field, it is impossible that I continue to be here. Even more so when you consider how my being me is distorted as negativity. As a young Black woman, I see all the cracks in our pristine museum facade. I see how we center Whiteness in our exhibition labels, how we misrepresent perspectives of people of color in our collections databases. But when I voice these shortcomings, I am being negative against the White fragility of my coworkers; I am being intimidating by holding our museum work to a higher, more equitable standard; and I am making "perfectly good" work more difficult. By nature as a Black woman who will not tolerate being treated "less than," I am emotional. And emotion is unprofessional. To say it plainly, emotionality is coded as racialized behavior, perceived as "unprofessional" or not White.

Resistance to emotionality is categorically a racialized, gendered, identity-politicized power play, so embracing emotionality is a decidedly radical act. Understanding how emotionality is weaponized against women and nonbinary people of color, inclusive museum leaders give space for emotions in the workplace. As the *Harvard Business Review* reports, inclusive museum leaders understand and utilize the power of emotions to shape workplace culture and achieve the vision of the museum itself. Whereas previous oppressive leadership models ineffectually compartmentalize and dehumanize their staff, an inclusive museum leader nurtures the entirety of personhood of their staff.

Dissolves Silos

There is certainly something to be said of the principle of holism in any workplace, but especially in museums. A holistic sensibility provides leaders with an understanding of the visitor's experience of the museum. Visitors don't necessarily easily distinguish curatorial work from interpretative work or from archival work, nor should they be required to. Our self-imposed silos do nothing toward a visitor-centric museum philosophy. This argument has been illuminated by practitioners far more experienced than I am. So while I give a nod to the spirit of holism, I want to focus on the distinctive issue of inclusion in the dissolution of silos. The continuation of siloed work threatens the viability of an inclusive museum.

According to leadership development experts, "Silo Mentality in the workplace occurs when people specifically conclude that it is not their responsibility to coordinate their activities with peers or other groups. With this mindset, people have little interest in understanding their part in the success of the organisation as a whole."[3] Siloing is so common across museum departments it's typically shrugged off as an unfortunate but inevitable norm. But siloing abuses more than just teamwork and staff morale. In a siloed museum, hierarchy reigns supreme. Siloes place certain work, often curatorial, as superior to other work, often front of house or visitor services. Siloing allowed for the massive layoffs in the wake of COVID-19 that left hordes of people of color out of work, because in considering who was "necessary" to keep employed museums disregarded whole areas of expertise not deemed worthy. Dissolving silos for inclusion disrupts these exclusive behaviors. It becomes impossible to achieve your work without the collaborative input of your coworkers. Leaders can no longer dismiss whole departments of workers because the work cannot thrive without them. Moreover, silos hurt leadership. In her groundbreaking book, *Emergent Strategy: Shaping Change, Shaping Worlds*, author and activist adrienne maree brown explains that we need to counter structures that limit connectivity and warns against "the usual model of leader isolation."[4] Inclusive leadership thrives in community with others.

An inclusive museum leader dissolves silos with urgency and intentionality. These leaders demand a change in the work itself. It's no longer acceptable to keep to your passion projects. Knowledge is shared, work is collaborative, and the museum is made the better for it.

Addresses Pay Equity and Pay Gap

Another triggering issue long held in museums but now amplified by the COVID-19 crisis is pay equity. Several journalist investigations reported on the frighteningly wide gap in pay between top leadership and entry-level staff throughout the museum sector.[5] Countless blog posts, journal entries, and Tweets hold the record of this field's entrenched pay inequities. From unpaid internships to the grueling hardship that is finding museum work that actually pays the bills to the crippling debt incurred from graduate studies required to "get ahead," the museum field has long been ensconced in a salary crisis. But the particular casualness in which scores of museum workers lost their jobs and livelihoods in the knee-jerk response to failing economic models during the COVID-19 crisis illuminates a particular deficiency of leadership. This is not to say that an inclusive leader fortified with empathy and emotional intelligence would not be forced to conduct some layoffs. But an inclusive museum leader would never prioritize their institution over their people.

This book is an effort to amplify the voices in this field that are fighting for the change we need. This book is full of rock stars and role models. I do not want to diminish the positive endeavor that this book encompasses, but sometimes it is necessary to look at the example of what *not* to do to fully hold ourselves accountable to our inclusive visions. Several museum directors made blunder after blunder as we collectively fumbled through the first wave of the COVID-19 crisis in the United States. But one particular misjudgment stood out to me. The Field Museum's CEO, Richard Lariviere, demonstrated, in my opinion, an unwillingness to lead with inclusion in his hostile approach to mitigating his museum's economic woes. According to workplace reporter Jeff Schuhrke, "Lariviere's total compensation in 2018—the most recent year with available data—was $796,000. While the presidents of the Boston Museum of Science and American Museum of Natural History have respectively taken a 50% and 25% pay cut in light of the crisis, Lariviere reportedly dismissed the idea of reducing his own compensation as 'a meaningless gesture.'"[6] As pay gaps in museums continue to become public knowledge, it is impossible to hide from scrutiny. But an inclusive leader is not motivated by public appearance, but by advancing equity throughout the field. An inclusive leader leads with courage, like Jason Porter, director of education and programs at the Museum of Pop Culture, who, when directed to, refused to make a list of staff for layoffs in the COVID-19 crisis. He resisted. He found another way, stating, "I'd urge all of us to not just accept these decisions without at least making a counter-argument, one which focuses on who will be best positioned to adapt to the new environment during and after COVID-19."[7] An inclusive museum leader uses their power to support their staff whether that is amplifying their efforts to unionize, being transparent about balancing pay cuts in a crisis, or being open to other money-saving alternatives.

Renounces Neutrality

It's hard to believe that in the twenty-first century museums are still arguing that neutrality is not only possible but a standard to attain. But still this fiction divides the field. LaTanya Autry and her partner in the #MuseumsAreNotNeutral movement, Mike Murawski, continue to provide the definitive word on museums and neutrality in their ongoing research and documentation of the field. But in summary, LaTanya notes, "As museums are cultural products that originate from colonial enterprise, they are about power. They are political constructs. Their ongoing practices also are rooted in power. The very fact that this field has a long history of excluding and marginalizing people of color in terms of selection, interpretation, and care of art and other objects, jobs, visitor services, board representation, and more indicates that museums are political spaces."[8]

An inclusive museum leader must renounce neutrality because acting in neutrality contradicts inclusive practice. A neutral approach often seeks nonconfrontational actions, which may seem benign on the surface. However, a deeper look at nonconfrontationalism in museums shows the systematic neutralization of difference. Neutrality kills diversity. Museums that embrace neutrality silence any who dissent from the status quo—often people of color. If the status quo is White, male, and privileged, then that is the legacy of the neutral museum. An inclusive museum leader invests their power in social concerns to amplify diverse voices.

Compels Corrective Storytelling

It may seem obvious, but an inclusive museum leader affirms inclusive stories. However, as many museums are built on oppressive storytelling that marginalizes and exploits certain groups and glorifies others, it takes a great effort to compel corrective storytelling. Corrective storytelling requires change. In 2020, the world witnessed the tenacity of communities fed up with false stories literally taking up space in their lives with the toppling of monuments dedicated to slave owners and historic oppressors. Inclusive museum leaders surmount the pressure of the status quo to maintain the museum's victorious stories in favor of uncomfortable truths.

Early in my career, I observed just how entrenched one-sided storytelling can be. I was working at a small historic house aiding the White woman curator in mounting an exhibition on comic books. Noticing the overwhelming Whiteness of the artists included in the checklist, I reached out to some local comic artists of color, specifically a Japanese American and an Ecuadoran American artist. I presented their samples to the curator and explained we could include them within the budget and time line for installation. With very little consideration to the artwork—I believe it was a passing glance—she immediately replied that there was no way to include them because "once you start including the Asian guy and the Hispanic guy you have to include the Black guy and the other Brown guy and it never stops." Hundreds of experiences like this are being recorded by the Instagram handle @changethemuseum. This is not an isolated event by one bad apple. The museum field is poisoned with this mind-set. An inclusive museum leader actively seeks out and diminishes the power of those who seek to uphold exclusive narratives. It's not enough to advance inclusive stories, a truly inclusive museum leader compels inclusive research by making practices like exclusion unacceptable.

Builds Collective Power

Inclusive leaders are engaged in change making across the field. The impact of inclusive leadership exceeds the immediate staff and stakeholders directly involved in the museum. Inclusive leadership is a radical act that influences the field at large. Reflecting on the need for new models of leadership, Mike Murawski writes, "Leadership is human-centered. Leadership means standing apart. Leadership is a collaborative, collective, and shared endeavor. Leadership is everywhere around us."[9] You can probably spot an inclusive leader by the company they keep. An inclusive leader builds collective power. By dissolving silos, empowering all levels of staff, listening and empowering ideas unlike their own, flattening hierarchies and creating platforms for collaboration, inclusive museum leaders change the way leadership is traditionally controlled. I recently wrote about leadership for the *Museum as Site for Social Action* blog, stating, "For far too long our field has been led exclusively by White, cisgenered [sic], male, privileged, overly educated, wealthy, elite, upperclass, heteronormative, ableist, colonist gatekeepers."[10] The differences between a gatekeeper and a collective power builder are obvious. But as museums continue to grapple with relevance in an ever-diversifying world, the principles of collective power become more imperative. An inclusive leader recognizes the strength of collective power and dismantles structures that prevent its growth.

Defining the Inclusive Museum

As previously discussed, museum leadership is an effort in shaping the museum field itself. Thus, an inclusive museum leader is engaged with the field itself. The opinions held by inclusive museum leaders about the role of museums are equally as important as the principles that guide their leadership practice. An inclusive museum leader doesn't just endeavor to make their workplace a more equitable environment, they want equity for all museum workers. The following are museum ideas upheld by inclusive museum leaders.

Museums and White Supremacy

Many of us in museums still don't know where to place museums in relation to White supremacy. But as previously discussed, inclusive leaders affirm difficult and uncomfortable truths. How can we look at "institutions whose histories are so inextricably linked with slavery, genocide and colonialism" and not call out White supremacy?[11] Notably the construct of Whiteness often distorts museums in complacency. "[O]ne of the many challenges of addressing racism and White supremacy in our workplaces is the fact that White people have constructed Whiteness to be rendered both normalized and invisible in our daily lives—a challenge that is also true for oppression more broadly."[12] But inclusion is an act of antiracism. Inclusion seeks to represent all people. Thus an inclusive museum leader is willing and able to call out the indisputable link to museums and White supremacy. If we are to change from who we are to who we want to be, we have to be authentic and critical. Inclusive museum leaders are guiding the way, setting the example of courageous truth telling and affirm museums as platforms for dismantling White supremacy.

Figure 21.2 Glenstone Museum in Potomac, Maryland. Source: Kayleigh Bryant-Greenwell

Museums Must Respond

Following the police murder of George Floyd, the United States saw an unprecedented response rate condemning the violence by individuals, corporations, and even museums. Though this moment was a much-needed first step in cultural responsiveness, many institutions seemed to waver when more than a vague solidarity statement or Black square was demanded of them. The creators of the movement #MuseumsRespondtoFerguson, Aleia Brown and Adrianne Russell can attest to how far museums still have to go to live up to their responsibility of responsiveness. The movement, started in 2014, would grow for six more years before we began to see a nation-wide uptick in responsiveness, sadly brought on by the brutal killing of another unarmed Black man. But Brown and Russell explain that museums need to do more, "As mediators of culture, all museums should commit to identifying how they can connect to relevant contemporary issues irrespective of collection, focus, or mission."[13] Inclusive museum leaders are leading this change. Where we see museums regularly engaging in issues of race and injustice, we see inclusive leadership. Where we see museums partnering in community efforts to reverse the impacts of systemic racism, we see inclusive leadership. Where we see museums offering community services beyond direct connections to their collections, we see inclusive leadership.

Museums Have a Responsibility to the Future

We are all responsible for our future, including museums. Museums with vision statements should critique their visions through the lens of creating a better future. If we're following a progressive plan to achieve some lofty goals in the future, shouldn't those goals aim to make a more equitable, inclusive future? Inclusive museum leaders understand that museums need to stop playing catch-up to the present and focus on building a future of environmental sustainability and racial equity. Goabaone Montsho, an anthropologist with the Botswana National Museum wrote for the UK-based Museum Ideas #FutureMuseums project, that "future museums will largely be concerned with the pursuit of socio-cultural developmental programs and confronting the policy issues which plague their communities. They will assume the role of pioneering social development."[14] Inclusive museum leaders are concerned about the future and are not afraid to speak out about the role museums must play in securing a better future for all.

Museums Work to Solve Issues within Their Local Community

We are already seeing a turning point in museums embracing the role of civic engagement as fundamental to our work. The next hurdle is the role of social betterment. If museums are to truly be places of civic engagement, then we must also be committed to positive change making in our communities. What is civic engagement if not an effort to make the world a better place? In an essay on civic engagement and cultural institutions, Deborah Cullinan, CEO of San Francisco's Yerba Buena Center for the Arts, explains, "culture precedes policy and cultural movement catalyzes lasting change."[15] If museums respond, if museums challenge the status quo, if museums are to be catalysts for justice, then museums are active within the issues of their communities. Inclusive museum leaders already accept this responsibility and, like Cullinan, are finding creative ways to use their power for social good.

Museum Work Is Cultural Equity Work

We can name the tension we're experiencing in museums in this moment. It is the agonizing tension of trying to be something we're not. While museum change makers struggle to get a foothold for antiracist and inclusive practice, long-outdated power structures continue to resist the inevitable. Museums are not meant to be fortresses of authoritarian power. We may have started out that way, but that's not what we're meant to be. Museum work is fundamentally cultural equity work. We need to stop pretending to be anything else. Reading mission and vision statements across the field, it is clear that museums today are committed to diversity, equity, inclusion, and accessibility like never before. Problems arise when we try to jam these principles into existing structures of oppression. Every tactic in the inclusive museum leader playbook is designed to mitigate our transformation into the cultural equity workers that we are. Dissolving our silos, building collective power, challenging White supremacy, and committing to our communities helps us realize that museum work *is* cultural equity work. The act of curating, conserving, and educating are all a part of the role of public service. Let's listen to our inclusive museum leaders when they tell us who *we* are.

Impacts of Inclusive Leadership

Now that we have an elementary understanding of what makes an inclusive museum leader and how their influence shapes the field, it's time to hone our senses to spot them in the wild. We should be able to determine the character of a leader by what they do and what they say, but there is another way to discover an inclusive museum leader. Impact speaks volumes. How a leader impacts their staff, operations, and stakeholders speaks to their effectiveness as well as their principles. Inclusive leadership that thinks beyond representation considers the factors that cause exclusivity in the first place. Inclusive leaders resolve the source of the problem, not merely treat the symptoms. Exclusionary practices are often the result of oppressive power structures.

Inclusive museum leaders work to dismantle problematic power structures within their staff and operations creating outcomes that are decidedly inclusive.

Curators Are Community Experts

Curatorial work has been at the center of countless offensive museum scandals. The act of exhibiting another culture, being an expert of someone else's experience, is inherently offensive. That's not to say that all curatorial work must come to an end. But there are best practices that continue to go ignored, causing yet another community offense. The Smithsonian's Asian Pacific American Center put it simply in the Culture Lab Manifesto, "Nothing about us without us." In other words, experts on culture come from that culture. In her book *Inclusive Curating in Contemporary Art: A Practical Guide*, Jade French discusses how she embraced change in her curator role to "devis[e] ways to support intellectually-disabled artists to have autonomy in how their work was made *and exhibited*."[16] French continues, "Curating plays a key role in how our shared culture is constructed, portrayed, and legitimized."[17] With the act of curating holding such gravitas *who* gets to curate matters.

I once had an experience with a White male curator coworker that exemplifies how fraught the power of curation has become. I had just completed a Black History Month program featuring local Black art experts. I did not invite any of the curators from my museum to participate in the talk because (1) I wanted to represent Black thought leadership and at the time we had no Black curators on staff and (2) I wanted to amplify community leadership without the interference of museum authority. One White male curator took umbrage with my decision making but hid it behind polite confusion. Once he understood my program strategy, he then went on to *educate* me with all the other Black community leaders I could've invited to speak instead. I smiled through gritted teeth and took the microaggression on the nose. I had planned to leave it at that, but the following day he cc'ed me on an e-mail to our director explaining how thrilled he was by the "good attempt" of the program and how he looks forward to including his input next year to make it "even better." I met with the head of curatorial the next day, a Latina recently promoted to her position. She listened and that's about all. Less than six months later this same White male curator is giving an all-staff presentation on the Black artists collective *Africobra*. For context, the connection to this historic artists collective was brought to our director by one of the panelists from the talk I organized. Our museum priorities didn't allow time to pursue the panelist's interests in collaboration . . . until after the national uprising following the police murder of George Floyd. Additionally, the curator in question enthusiastically announced in an e-mail thread how the museum can acquire works by artists of color at newly lower prices due to the financial fall-out for galleries and art advisors from COVID-19. *How wonderful to capitalize on Black and Brown tragedy*. People can grow. People can change. But the condensed time line of these events feels suspiciously like opportunism. I also never got an apology or even an acknowledgment of the microaggression.

An inclusive museum leader investigates trauma caused by harmful museum practices and specifically sets a standard of racial equity in curatorial practice. They recognize that curatorial expertise does not equate racial or cultural competence. They understand that not every curator is fit to preside over any and all content, especially when content is racially conscious. In *Emergent Strategy*, adrienne maree brown puts it simply, "who leads matters."[18] Inspired by the fierce Black women leaders of Octavia Butler's science fiction, brown continues, "understanding that what happens at the interpersonal level is a way to understand the whole of society."[19] As curatorial work has become a marker of a museum's willingness to change harmful practices, look to what's happening in curatorial departments when seeking out inclusive museum leaders.

Visitor Dynamics Are Transformed

Lately a frequent discussion topic at museum conferences is the idea of transformative engagement. Many museums desire transformative results but are still stuck in transactional approaches to engagement. One measurable impact of inclusive leadership is engagement that goes beyond the transactional. As discussed, inclusion is engaged in the entire system of the museum. Inclusion embraces institutional empathy and renounces neutrality, the outcome of which should be increased connection to communities. In an essay on the platform Medium, journalist Andrew DeVigal discusses how public trust in the media is at an all-time low and how this impacts journalism. He notes how journalism "needs to focus more on the relationship than the transaction. And it starts with and continues with sustained listening as engagement takes time."[20] Museums can learn a lot from the challenges and new solutions being generated by a field in flux, such as journalism. Willingness to learn from experts outside the museum industry is certainly a characteristic of inclusive leadership. But to the point, engagement is transformed under inclusive leadership. Inclusive museum leaders are dissatisfied with transactional engagement and are willing to experiment to change the dynamic. Museum strategist Seema Rao explains it clearly, "Often visitor-center work also overlaps DEAI work. . . . Inclusion is the practice of breaking/transforming barriers to include everyone."[21] An inclusive museum leader is acutely attuned to how visitor engagement is a marker of realized inclusion. So as you're honing your critical senses to find inclusive leaders, look at what's happening in visitor engagement. Visitor satisfaction surveys and social media reveal hidden depths of the principles governing the museum.

Global Questions for the Inclusive Museum Leader

As a final marker of the composition of an inclusive museum leader, I turn to questions. *New York Times* best-selling author John C. Maxwell wrote a book titled *Good Leaders Ask Great Questions*. In it he describes the irrefutable power of questions and how questions are essential to leadership.[22] As change makers, inclusive museum leaders grapple with the future of museum practice. Practice is influenced by theory, so it is pertinent that inclusive museum leaders consider the most pressing, challenging, and theoretical questions of the field. Because I believe questions are just as important as answers, and because I believe museum polemics are a global issue, the following are just three of the most provocative questions that I've encountered in various international readings and museum conferences. I believe every inclusive museum leader should carry these questions close to their practice in all that they do.

1. "Are museums irredeemable colonial projects?"—Nina Finnigan, Curator Manuscripts, Auckland War Memorial Museum, Auckland, New Zealand[23]
2. "If the museum's collection cannot interpret the world today for today's audiences, what is its usefulness?"—Joyoti Roy, Head of Strategy, CSMVS Museum, strategist, Mumbai, India[24]
3. "The question then is, rather about the degree of involvement a museum has with the present lives of the visitors and the quality, and also the ethics, with which they may intend to participate with their intimate worries and actual needs."[25]—Américo Castilla, Director Académico, Laboratorio TyPA de Gestión de Museos, Buenos Aires, Argentina

This field so desperately needs more inclusive leadership. We need leaders who see and understand the crisis of equity and power that threatens the future of museums. Poet Jamara Wakefield writes, "Museums could be one of our greatest allies in liberation struggles. They have the physical space, the means, and the public confidence to partake in a large scale social movement against colonial powers."[26] I hope this chapter illustrates that inclusive museum leadership is both practical and achievable but, more important, that is necessary for museums to realize their potential as equitable institutions. Yesomi Umolu, director and curator of the Logan Center Exhibitions at the Reva and David Logan Center for the Arts, University of Chicago, provides a call to action, "The task of the moment is not to seek to welcome the other and the excluded into these fragile spaces, i.e. filling quotas and exacting hastened inclusion policies without making any other changes to institutional culture or structure. For the violence will only worsen. The task is to commit to practices of knowing and care that critically interrogate the fraught history of museums and their contemporary form, uprooting weak foundations and rebuilding upon new, healthy ones."[27] If visiting a museum offers a way of making sense of the world around us, then our leaders carry a heavy responsibility. Inclusive museum leaders demonstrate that through a critical practice and embracing of our cultural-responsive purpose, we can exercise the power of the museum toward challenging the status quo and dismantling harm within our institutions and our communities. Inclusive museum leaders will lead the way into the next chapter of museum work as cultural equity work.

Notes

1. Gretchen Jennings et al., "The Empathetic Museum: A New Institutional Identity," *Curator: The Museum Journal* 62, no. 4 (October 2019): 6, https://doi.org/10.1111/cura.12335.
2. Sigal Barsade and Olivia A. O'Neill, "Managing Your Emotional Culture," *Harvard Business Review*, January–February 2016, 59, https://hbr.org/2016/01/manage-your-emotional-culture#.
3. PerceptionDynamics, "What Is Silo Mentality?," accessed September 12, 2020, https://www.perceptiondynamics.info/silo-mentality/how-to-remove-silo-mentality/#.
4. adrienne maree brown, *Emergent Strategy: Shaping Change, Shaping Worlds* (Chicago: AK Press, 2017), 21.
5. Tim Schneider, "The Gray Market: Why New York's Museum Pay Gap Tells a Story of American Decline (and Other Insights)," *Artnet News*, August 24, 2020, https://news.artnet.com/opinion/new-york-museum-pay-gap-1903571.
6. Jeff Schuhrke, "Field Museum Workers Say It's Time for the CEO to Start Making Sacrifices, Too," Workplace Fairness, June 12, 2020, https://www.workplacefairness.org/blog/2020/06/12/field-museum-workers-say-its-time-for-the-ceo-to-start-making-sacrifices-too/.
7. Jason Porter, "Making the Case for Museum Education in the Midst of Crisis," *Art Museum Teaching* (blog), May 14, 2020, https://artmuseumteaching.com/2020/05/14/making-the-case-for-museum-education/.
8. LaTanya Autry, "Museums Are Not Neutral," Art Stuff Matters, accessed September 12, 2020, https://artstuffmatters.wordpress.com/museums-are-not-neutral/.
9. Mike Murawski, "Upending Our Ideas about Leadership in Museums," *Art Museum Teaching* (blog), July 27, 2020, https://artmuseumteaching.com/2020/07/27/upending-leadership/.
10. Kayleigh Bryant-Greenwell, "Waking Up to Wokeness (Actually Woke Is Over It's Time to Do the Work): An Open Letter to Museum Peers," *Museum as Site for Social Action* (blog), June 12, 2020, https://www.museumaction.org/massaction-blog/2020/6/12/waking-up-to-wokeness-actually-woke-is-over-its-time-to-do-the-work.
11. nikhil trivedi, "Oppression: A Museum Primer," *The Incluseum* (blog), February 4, 2015, https://incluseum.com/2015/02/04/oppression-a-museum-primer/.
12. Hannah Heller et al., "Uncovering White Supremacy Culture in Museum Work," *The Incluseum* (blog), March 4, 2020, https://incluseum.com/2020/03/04/white-supremacy-culture-museum/.
13. Gretchen Jennings et al., "Joint Statement from Museum Bloggers and Colleagues on Ferguson and Related Events," *The Incluseum* (blog), December 22, 2014, https://incluseum.com/2014/12/22/joint-statement-from-museum-bloggers-colleagues-on-ferguson-related-events/.

14. Goabaone Montsho, "Future Museums as Key Actors in Public Policy," Museum Ideas, accessed September 12, 2020, https://museum-id.com/the-futuremuseum-project-what-will-museums-be-like-in-the-future-essay-collection/.
15. Deborah Cullinan, "Civic Engagement: Why Cultural Institutions Must Lead the Way," *Stanford Social Innovation Review*, March 22, 2017, https://ssir.org/articles/entry/civic_engagement_why_cultural_institutions_must_lead_the_way.
16. Jade French, preface to *Inclusive Curating in Contemporary Art: A Practical Guide* (Leeds: Arc Humanities Press, 2020), xi.
17. French, preface to *Inclusive Curating in Contemporary Art*, 4.
18. brown, *Emergent Strategy*, 21.
19. brown, *Emergent Strategy*, 22.
20. Andrew DeVigal, "Engagement Is Relational, Not Transactional," Medium, November 23, 2015, https://medium.com/experience-engagement/engagement-is-relational-not-transactional-6dcf8d92980f.
21. Seema Rao, "Community-Engagement, Visitor-Centered, and Other Words," Museum 2.0, October 22, 2019, http://museumtwo.blogspot.com/2019/10/community-engagement-visitor-centered.html.
22. John C. Maxwell, *Good Leaders Ask Great Questions* (New York: Center Street, 2014).
23. Finnigan, Nina, "In Search of Power and Resistance in the Archive (presentation)," *Museum Ideas 2019*, September 12, 2019, The Museum of London, London: UK.
24. Roy, Joyoti, "The Future of Co-Curation in Museums (presentation)." *Museum Ideas 2019*, September 12, 2019, The Museum of London, London: UK.
25. Américo Castilla, "From Consensus to Social Dissent: Museums of Latin America," in *Museum Ideas*, vol. 2, *Innovation in Theory and Practice*, ed. Gregory Chamberlain (England: Museum Identity, 2016), 323.
26. Jamara Wakefield, "Museums Could Be Powerful, Liberatory Spaces if They Let Go of Their Colonial Practices," RaceBaitr, May 14, 2019, https://racebaitr.com/2019/05/14/museums-could-be-powerful-liberatory-spaces-if-they-let-go-of-their-colonial-practices/.
27. Yesomi Umolu, "On the Limits of Care and Knowledge: 15 Points Museums Must Understand to Dismantle Structural Injustice," *Artnet News*, June 25, 2020, https://news.artnet.com/opinion/limits-of-care-and-knowledge-yesomi-umolu-op-ed-1889739.

Bibliography

Autry, LaTanya. "Museums Are Not Neutral." Art Stuff Matters. Accessed September 12, 2020. https://artstuffmatters.wordpress.com/museums-are-not-neutral/.

Barsade, Sigal, and Olivia A. O'Neill. "Managing Your Emotional Culture." *Harvard Business Review*, January–February 2016, 58–66. https://hbr.org/2016/01/manage-your-emotional-culture#.

brown, adrienne maree. *Emergent Strategy: Shaping Change, Shaping Worlds* (Chicago: AK Press, 2017).

Bryant-Greenwell, Kayleigh. "Waking Up to Wokeness (Actually Woke Is Over It's Time to Do the Work): An Open Letter to Museum Peers." *Museum as Site for Social Action* (blog), June 12, 2020. https://www.museumaction.org/massaction-blog/2020/6/12/waking-up-to-wokeness-actually-woke-is-over-its-time-to-do-the-work.

Castilla, Américo. "From Consensus to Social Dissent: Museums of Latin America." In *Museum Ideas*, vol. 2, *Innovation in Theory and Practice*, edited by Gregory Chamberlain, 321–27. England: Museum Identity, 2016.

Cullinan, Deborah. "Civic Engagement: Why Cultural Institutions Must Lead the Way." *Stanford Social Innovation Review*, March 22, 2017. https://ssir.org/articles/entry/civic_engagement_why_cultural_institutions_must_lead_the_way.

DeVigal, Andrew. "Engagement Is Relational, Not Transactional." Medium, November 23, 2015. https://medium.com/experience-engagement/engagement-is-relational-not-transactional-6dcf8d92980f.

French, Jade. *Inclusive Curating in Contemporary Art: A Practical Guide*. Leeds: Arc Humanities Press, 2020.

Heller, Hannah, nikhil trivedi, and Joanne Jones-Rizzi. "Uncovering White Supremacy Culture in Museum Work." *The Incluseum* (blog), March 4, 2020. https://incluseum.com/2020/03/04/white-supremacy-culture-museum/.

Jennings, Gretchen, et al. "Joint Statement from Museum Bloggers and Colleagues on Ferguson and Related Events." *The Incluseum* (blog), December 22, 2014. https://incluseum.com/2014/12/22/joint-statement-from-museum-bloggers-colleagues-on-ferguson-related-events/.

Jennings, Gretchen, Jim Cullen, Janeen Bryant, Kayleigh Bryant-Greenwell, Stacey Mann, Charlotte Hove, and Nayeli Zepeda. "The Empathetic Museum: A New Institutional Identity." *Curator: The Museum Journal* 62, no. 4 (October 2019): 505–26. https://doi.org/10.1111/cura.12335.

Maxwell, John C. *Good Leaders Ask Great Questions*. New York: Center Street, 2014.

Montsho, Goabaone. "Future Museums as Key Actors in Public Policy." Museum Ideas. Accessed September 12, 2020. https://museum-id.com/the-futuremuseum-project-what-will-museums-be-like-in-the-future-essay-collection/.

Murawski, Mike. "Upending Our Ideas about Leadership in Museums." *Art Museum Teaching* (blog), July 27, 2020. https://artmuseumteaching.com/2020/07/27/upending-leadership/.

PerceptionDynamics. "What Is Silo Mentality?" Accessed September 12, 2020. https://www.perceptiondynamics.info/silo-mentality/how-to-remove-silo-mentality/#.

Porter, Jason. "Making the Case for Museum Education in the Midst of Crisis." *Art Museum Teaching* (blog), May 14, 2020. https://artmuseumteaching.com/2020/05/14/making-the-case-for-museum-education/.

Rao, Seema. "Community-Engagement, Visitor-Centered, and Other Words." Museum 2.0, October 22, 2019. http://museumtwo.blogspot.com/2019/10/community-engagement-visitor-centered.html.

Schneider, Tim. "The Gray Market: Why New York's Museum Pay Gap Tells a Story of American Decline (and Other Insights)." *Artnet News*, August 24, 2020. https://news.artnet.com/opinion/new-york-museum-pay-gap-1903571.

Schuhrke, Jeff. "Field Museum Workers Say It's Time for the CEO to Start Making Sacrifices, Too." Workplace Fairness, June 12, 2020. https://www.workplacefairness.org/blog/2020/06/12/field-museum-workers-say-its-time-for-the-ceo-to-start-making-sacrifices-too/.

trivedi, nikhil. "Oppression: A Museum Primer." *The Incluseum* (blog), February 4, 2015. https://incluseum.com/2015/02/04/oppression-a-museum-primer/.

Umolu, Yesomi. "On the Limits of Care and Knowledge: 15 Points Museums Must Understand to Dismantle Structural Injustice." *Artnet News*, June 25, 2020. https://news.artnet.com/opinion/limits-of-care-and-knowledge-yesomi-umolu-op-ed-1889739.

Wakefield, Jamara. "Museums Could Be Powerful, Liberatory Spaces if They Let Go of Their Colonial Practices." RaceBaitr, May 14, 2019. https://racebaitr.com/2019/05/14/museums-could-be-powerful-liberatory-spaces-if-they-let-go-of-their-colonial-practices/.

Chapter 22

Teaching the Change We Want to See

A Conversation with Faculty at Museum Education Programs

The following transcript is a combination of interviews with museum professors who are committed to training the next generation of inclusive museum workers. While their curriculum and field trip experiences may differ, their focus on adult learners and their power to effect change is palpable. The following is a list of participants:

Elizabeth Kryder-Reid, Chancellor's Professor of Anthropology and Museum Studies, Director, Cultural Heritage Research Center, Director of Graduate Programs for Museum Studies, Indiana University–Purdue University Indianapolis (IUPUI)

Stacey Mann, Senior Lecturer, Museum Exhibition Planning + Design, University of the Arts

Therese Quinn, Director and Associate Professor of Museum and Exhibition Studies, University of Illinois, Chicago

Mattie Reynolds, Assistant Professor in Museum Studies and Director of the Balzer Contemporary Edge Gallery, Institute for American Indian Arts (IAIA)

Cynthia Robinson, Director, Museum Studies Program, Senior Lecturer, Education Department, Tufts University

Gretchen Sullivan Sorin, Director and Distinguished Professor, Cooperstown Graduate Program for Museum Studies

Chris Taylor: Thinking about your programs and the curriculum that you are teaching, how do you center topics such as equity, justice, inclusion, and diversity in your curriculum?

Mattie Reynolds: My first semester teaching, I actually audited a colleague's class because they had been working on this very interesting project. My colleague started the class by saying to the students, "We intend to make you dangerous." That has stuck with me for a very long time. It's not dangerous in the real definition of the word, but dangerous to the colonial status quo that we still see a lot of in museums and museum structures.

I like to prepare my students to be aggressive in the way they pursue positions within a museum that position them to tell their own narratives. That is equity, inclusion, and diversity. They are telling their own stories without the oversight of this colonial body. I want them to understand that the future of museum work involves them, including their traditional practices and life experiences. We make it clear those experiences are very important to their work and to their careers as museum professionals. We teach them necessary skills to work within a museum based on Western museum practices but also teach them to shake it up when they get in the field. There is no reason that you can't use your traditional upbringings and your cultural knowledge to make the museums more relevant to the communities that they exist in. We intend to make you dangerous.

Therese Quinn: I love that story about "We want you to be dangerous." When I talk to my students, we discuss what they want out of a work environment. They often say something about "being a professional." By that, I know they mean they want to be treated with respect. They want to earn a decent salary. They want a life that is thriving and flourishing. In fact, we all deserve that, no matter what kind of work we do. I try to help them separate those goals from what it means to be a professional, which is really about replicating the structures of power and not rocking the boat.

I try to weave into my curriculum a broader emphasis on justice and social movements. I talk with my students about cultural work as justice work, but we also learn about topics such as labor law and employee rights so they won't be completely blindsided like I was when I was employed by a museum that wanted me to sign a contract agreeing that I could be fired at any time, without any notice. I didn't think I had a right to refuse those terms, and I had no idea that those are the terms for all at-will—which is most—employees. People need to be armed with definitions and real information, and school should help with that.

I also try to provide my students with theoretical, moral, and ethical underpinnings for the work that they do in museums. There's a lot of managerial stuff that is not all that complicated, but having a moral center is complicated for a lifetime. Thinking about how that shapes your work on the ground is something we're always doing.

In terms of curriculum, I like to bring in discussions about museum work as political education or museums as places of popular education. We talk about the Brazilian educator and theorist Paolo Freire, who argued against the banking model of education, in which teachers pour knowledge into the empty vessels of their students. We talk about sociomuseology—social museology—a politically Left tradition influenced by Freire, which was fostered by the International Movement for a New Museology from the 1970s to the present and urges museums to support social movements for freedom and liberation. And we read things like Miya Tokumitsu's *Do What You Love and Other Lies about Success and Happiness*, a book which suggests questioning the idea that you should love your work and work for love, not pay, fair treatment, and so on. Should you work in a museum because you love it, even if you can't put food on the table? Well, that's a bad ideology for our students. They have to demand to be paid fairly.

Elizabeth Kryder-Reid (Liz): I think we have really embraced pressing social issues around equity, justice, and inclusion in response to our work with community partners. We collaborate with museums, but we also work with a number of grassroots groups and organizations that are interested in issues such as mass incarceration, mental health treatment, access to education, environmental justice and water quality issues, and the prison-to-school pipeline (i.e., access to higher education for formerly incarcerated people). Those conversations helped us identify opportunities in our curriculum to give students experiences and training in the core skills that they need for museum work, but do that in partnership with community in ways that address their needs and concerns.

For example, I have a colleague who teaches visual culture and curatorial practices. She is involved in a local arts group that uses art to revitalize damaged neighborhoods. She worked with students to curate an exhibit in partnership with this grassroots art group, where they took abandoned houses and turned them into art installations that speak to the assets, resources, power, and creativity of the neighborhood.

Figure 22.1   Museum studies students at Tufts University. Source: Cynthia Robinson

Cynthia Robinson: Those topics permeate our program, but particularly in the foundation course, Museums Today: Mission and Function. The course presents a broad overview of the way American museums of all types—art, history, children's, science, zoos, aquariums, etc.—have evolved over time, and how they function today. We address current issues, considering how they impact museums and how museums address them. Our goal is to enable students to participate in making museums better; more inclusive, more accessible, more democratic in their work with communities and visitors, and less authoritarian. We address equity, justice, inclusion, and diversity through assigned readings drawn from museum journals, books, and newspapers; through guest speakers; and through assignments that allow students to explore some of these issues more deeply.

Gretchen Sullivan Sorin: We have centered equity and inclusion in everything that we do, and it is not something that happened based on recent event. This I something we have been committed to for twenty-five years. We began by changing our curriculum. We have added courses to the curriculum to explore topics such as African American Art, Civil Rights History, and Migration and Community. Every student learns to conduct oral histories, something we have been doing for the more than fifty-year history of the program. We also expanded our teaching materials collection. We bought a lot of objects to supplement the traditional materials found in museum history collections. We bought a copy of *Muhammad Speaks*, objects related to the Black Panthers and the Black middle class. We have Jewish artifacts, objects related to gender, and a fabulous mailbag from a Japanese internment camp. When we're talking about museums and what they display and what they interpret, we can pull objects out of our collection that relate to these communities.

Another thing that we do is to support paid internships. We don't believe in unpaid internships. Museums have got to move in the direction of paid internships, because the only people that can afford to work without compensation are generally pretty wealthy folx. We established a fund called the rural-urban partnership to provide stipends. If a student really wants to do a museum internship at a particular place and that museum doesn't pay, we provide a stipend. That ensures that all students have an equal opportunity to gain experience no matter what their background.

Stacey Mann: When I was working in the digital interpretation side, I focused a lot on transferable skills. I was thinking about accessibility to the field and understanding that storytelling is a critical skill. Storytelling cuts across a whole host of different fields and is not unique to museums. Teaching students to leverage technology to tell compelling stories that engage audiences and think about user-centered design became the crux and center of my teaching practice. I also tend to let the students direct a lot of the conversations, because they are coming in with a lot of different questions. They are pushing us to ask questions and think about museum work in ways that maybe we haven't in the past as an industry, or if we have there has been resistance and those ideas haven't necessarily found purchase.

I tend to do a lot that is really focused on the students themselves and then, using the networks and the groups where I've been doing work, to put them in touch with the individuals who are specialists in repatriation or in decolonization of collections or programming. I try to find the people that are going to really help them think more deeply about whatever the question is that they're looking for.

Cinnamon Catlin-Legutko: How are you preparing students for the workforce? How are you situating them in the museum world so they're ready to go when they graduate?

Cynthia: In the past, students often came into the program believing that museums were perfect sanctuaries; enchanting and magical places for discovery or respite. Many thought that museums never changed. Our job was to equip them with knowledge, insight, and strategies for participating in the transformation of the nineteenth-century museum model of show-and-tell to the twenty-first-century model of audience engagement with issues that matter.

In the past two years, far more incoming students are critical of museums, ready to participate in change. It makes it easier to leap into discussions of why there are problems, and what can be done. Personally, my goal as a teacher is to help my students become self-directed learners. Self-directed learners are lifelong learners who pursue new ideas and skills because they want to, not because they have to. Self-directed learners take initiative to define and set goals, find resources to meet the goals, implement learning strategies, and assess the results.

I take a constructivist approach to teaching, believing that students learn best when they internalize and "construct" ideas for themselves. I rarely lecture, a didactic approach, and instead teach through discussion and activities, which asks students to take active roles in making meaning, individually and collectively.

Gretchen: We do a lot of case study work. And we have partnerships with a wide variety of local, regional, and even national museums. We get our students out into real communities and have them work with people. We have an active partnership with the Dyckman Farmhouse, a small museum in Manhattan that is the last farmhouse in New York City. It's a Dutch, eighteenth-century farmhouse in Inwood, New York. It's a largely minority community. Why would a largely

Figure 22.2 IUPUI Museum Studies students in a mass incarceration class tour RecycleForce, a social enterprise focused on the re-entry of returning citizens from incarceration. Source: Elizabeth Kryder-Reid

minority community care about an eighteenth-century Dutch farmhouse? There are so many of these historic sites and museums around the country that are in neighborhoods that have changed quite a bit over time. Some of them are just completely moribund, and others of them have become vibrant community centers. If you look at these case studies and you see which ones have been able to make themselves essential to their communities, you understand that sometimes you have to take on responsibilities that are not traditional museum practice as a museum professional in order to keep an organization relevant.

The Dyckman Farmhouse, for example, conducts a summer science camp for kids, and they found that some of these kids don't bring lunch because they don't have food. The museum provides them with a healthy lunch as a part of science camp, and this may be the best meal these kids get all day. You might not think of this as museum work, but we have a responsibility to our communities. People don't go to museums unless their basic needs are met. Sometimes museums need to help meet those needs. That's our responsibility. We like to immerse our students in these communities because you cannot learn to love people and learn to understand people if you don't interact with them or if you are afraid of them because you have never had a friend who was a black person or a Latinx person, for example. And in our very segregated society—with gated communities, you would be surprised how many students fall into this category. Our students now spend a week in Harlem working at the Dyckman Farmhouse, doing public programming, working with the kids, doing science camp, or whatever the museum and community need us to do. It gives our students the experience of living in the community and working with people who are different from them.

Liz: The core of our philosophy is the central question of, "Why do museums matter?" How are they relevant to audiences and to their communities? Students need to grapple with these foundational questions and be thoughtful and intentional in applying all of their critical theory and readings to their work. You mentioned Mass Action.[1] Those readings are assigned across the curriculum, and God love you for the free PDFs. Thank you.

For us, inclusion is one of our core values, and that means we value diverse perspectives, experiences, and traditions. We have two students who are very open about being on the spectrum and living with autism. One of them is passionate about how he can help museums create experiences that are accessible to people like himself. Again, that's not something our faculty has expertise in, but it's been powerful finding ways to support these students in following their passion and to create a broader, contextual, critical, reflective framework that helps them understand their place as they enter the museum field and how they can be change agents. Yes, we have our philosophy and values, but we also evolve in response to what the students and community partners teach us.

We have also had the opportunity to participate in the Humanities Action Lab (HAL),[2] which is based on a public history model of using the past in order to understand the present. HAL coordinates a number of universities working together to produce content about a theme. The HAL projects have been an opportunity to develop multicourse sequences. One semester is a research seminar on the topic, then the exhibit development and design class produced exhibit and digital content, and the final class focuses on public programs. The first, the Guantanamo Public Memory Project, included eleven universities that developed a collaboratively traveling exhibit that went around to each of the universities. We developed programming to go with the exhibit when it came to Indianapolis, and students presented in an amazing symposium when the exhibit opened in New York. That worked so well that we participated in the next one, which addressed mass incarceration and was called "States of Incarceration." The last HAL project was Climates of Inequality, looking at environmental justice and climate justice.

For our local environmental justice research, we looked at the quality of urban waterways in Indianapolis and their impact on affected communities, which were typically communities of color and low income. We worked with the grassroots organizations Groundwork Indy and the Kheprw Institute, who are both advocates for their communities and powerful, resilient forces within them. We helped tell those stories and through the exhibit mounted at the Central Library in downtown Indianapolis. Through these kinds of projects, students learn collaborative curatorial practice working with community partners. These are incredibly powerful experiences.

Chris: When you think about inclusive leaders and inclusive practice, what are some of the characteristics or skills that come to mind? How are you teaching those in your programs?

Cynthia: I define "leaders" from those at the top or those who are well known to those that have the courage and conviction to share their thinking and their work with the field. I introduce my students to a vast array of colleagues past and present who write (books, articles, blogs), present at conferences who are leaders. These leaders may not be well known, but they've taken the trouble—and the risk to contribute to the field, not just to their own careers, thus modeling the kind of active involvement that I want my students to emulate.

This fall we started the foundation course, Museum Today: Mission and Function, by asking students to listen to the American Alliance of Museums session with Lonnie Bunch III, Dr. Johnetta Cole, and Lori Fogarty, "Racism, Unrest, and the Role of the Museum Field,"[3] to address the issue of racism and museums from the get-go. We paired it with A. Andrea de Shuman's letter of resignation from the Detroit Institute of Art, "No Longer in Extremis: A Letter of Resignation & Courage,"[4] to begin the discussion of the systemic absence of cultural competence and the prevalence of resistant leadership in many museums. We added historical evidence of museum issues that have existed for a long time by asking students to read John Cotton Dana's cranky and funny diatribe, "The Gloom of the Museum."[5] We later encounter Lonnie Bunch (and other staff members) again when we explore the careful planning that resulted in the National Museum of African American History and culture, through several articles published in the *Journal of Museum Education* in 2017.[6]

Museums that we hold up as models include the Abbe Museum, with its model approach to decolonization, and the Wing Luke Museum, starting with the lovely and passionate plea from then director Ron Chew to humanize the collection.[7] The Wing Luke has a long history of inviting communities to curate their own exhibitions and continually refines the process of community -based work.

Gretchen: It is often difficult for an energetic student hoping to change the world being hired by a museum that is very slow to implement changes. Team building and managing up are important skills on which we work very hard. It helps the students understand how to be persuasive when they are at the lower levels of the institution. It involves how to make arguments that are going to be persuasive without being labeled the institutional radical. It is also important to learn how to work as a team member. Young staff members need to know how to work with every member of the staff, from the guards and docents to the marketing staff, shop staff, curators, and janitorial crew—to respect them all and to work collaboratively.

Liz: The idea of supporting self-reflective leaders for the future of museums is baked into our curriculum and pedagogy. We are clear that they need to be active listeners, they need to be self-reflective, they need to be critical thinkers about structures of power in which their museums exist. Collaboration is one of our core values. In our Museum Administration course, we ask them to be observant about the leaders that they meet and who come to speak. Cinnamon Catlin-Legutko comes and speaks about decolonization or her work in transforming institutions or why small museums matter. Aside from the important information she shares, the reason I keep asking her is because she performs leadership through her practice and her presence, and that's what students get.

Cinnamon: When I went through my grad program in museum studies, it was very traditional. I think we know now in museums that there is more we can do, need to do, and must do. I'm wondering how you encourage students to challenge this thinking.

Stacey: I teach in an exhibition planning program at an arts institute that is very much focused on skills and skill development. Many students do not fully recognize or understand what equity and inclusion work looks like in the real world. Breaking down traditions is about pulling back that veil and just making students aware of what museums are really like. Yes, you are going to be responsible for X, Y, and Z, but A, B, and C are going to be right there alongside and you need to be prepared and ready to balance those in your work life, while also creating space for your personal life, healthy boundaries, and self-care to avoid burnout.

We also have to get comfortable leaving the building and engaging with communities where they are. That means thinking very differently about what we are offering, how you are constructing the stories that you are telling, and the spaces that you're telling them in. In my prototyping and community engagement class, we are spending a lot of time looking at alternative models. We find different organizations, who may or may not even be affiliated with the museum field, to examine what creative community engagement look like.

Liz: There's a few students who come in starry eyed, romantic, "I love museums. I've always loved museums." We teach them how to be critical, and they are in a much better place to help museums reach their potential because they see them as instruments of power. For example, I'm teaching our intro. class, and last week we were at Newfields, formally the Indianapolis Museum of Art. I had them read Kelli Morgan's essay on museums as White supremacy spaces and watch a wonderful talk she gave.[8] Then students went around the galleries in small groups reflecting on how they see the spaces operating as White supremacy. A lot of what is still hanging on the walls in the American gallery is Dr. Morgan's attempt to use critical race theory to transform the American art collection into a critique of race and gender and the structures of power in American history.

Therese: Our program foregrounds our focus on social justice, which frames everything from the program structure, to the curriculum for every class, to funding we find to support students. And, I have worked hard with my colleagues over many years to make sure that the program is majority students of color, which is different than most other museum studies programs in the US. That makes a big difference to our students. They come in as a cohort, and there are many students of color in each entering class, forming a core of support, to verify each other's perceptions of cultural work and the purposes of museums, and other things like that.

I don't like the framework of curation because it's top down. I was an exhibit developer, and I like to talk about why I think that lateral teamwork is so much better for creating a cultural product. I know some of my students still want to be curators, and that is fine. I support them in that dream, but I also want them to resist curation, to be skeptical and ask critical questions about it, such as: What are our exhibits and programs teaching, beyond facts? How can we build our exhibits and programs to activate people? How can we build in the mode of activism to the products that we create? Is there a way to do that and to do it in a smart way that has some legs in the world? Those are the kinds of perspectives that I try to pose.

Mattie: I want to know what really gets them jazzed up and not always in a good way. I want to know what they do not like. I want to know what offends them. I want to know what they think is missing. As a majority Native population of students, I want to know what essential element is missing or misrepresented in Native narratives, especially in this area. I want them to really, really examine how Native ways of knowing can be integrated into museum practice.

Once they're done with their degree at IAIA, I want the students to be able to walk into a museum and say, "Hey, you've done this wrong, but I can help you fix it because here I am as an indigenous professional telling you that this is the way that it should be done. I'm coming in with all this experience to help you fix it, and it's going to be beautiful and more inclusive. It's not going to be a traumatic experience for the community that you're trying to reach with this exhibit."

We try to direct them to rethink how those Western-centric museums can be a place for them to direct their energy. At the same time, we also want these students to be able to go back to their communities and their reservations, tribal museums, and cultural centers and adapt Western-based museum practice to share with their community and share with the professionals within their tribe.

Chris: What can your students do when they leave your programs to apply the philosophy and the practice that you have taught them as leaders?

Mattie: I think it is a delicate line because, especially if it is an institution that does not have any indigenous professionals and it is very easy for them to become that token Native person that represents a huge group of people that are so culturally diverse. It is a really delicate line to walk, especially if you are the student that ends up being that first person that forges the path. But at the same time, they are basically knocking down so many obstacles for the next person to come in, making it an easier transition for them. I want them to be the aggressive squeaky wheel in those institutions, or go back home and really be able to take a tribal museum or a cultural center and make it an incredibly good tool for their community based on the skills that they've learned at IAIA. We can frame artwork now or we can create an exhibition for our artists and the community, and we can market their work on our website and sell it and help them support their families.

Gretchen: My former students of color call me, and I try to be a mentor. We chat. One of the students called me recently because she works for a major, large mainstream institution. When George Floyd was murdered, the institution went to her and said, "We want you to write the museum's statement in support of Black Lives Matter." They wanted the young African American professional who had never before been asked to provide input on diversity issues to write the institutional policy. This was a totally inappropriate request by the senior management team. Leadership is a balance. You cannot allow yourself to be taken advantage of, especially for students of color and employees of color, but at the same time, these young staff members are pushing the institution forward and helping to bring about much-needed change.

Liz: The students graduate with their two years of kickass coursework and their amazing ten-month internships. They're babies in the field. They are novices. We encourage them to be humble about what you know and respect the wisdom that is in your colleague who has been doing their job for twenty years. At the same time, they have come to us because they are committed to be change agents, and they want to fulfill the promise of what museums can be. It is a challenge to carry those two realities in tension.

To the extent to which they even have the vantage point to see this, I really encourage our students to have a lens about the ethnography of power, both within their institutions and in their communities. Many of our students go off to very small museums where they are given a lot of authority because there are maybe two people on staff. They have this opportunity to really think about what they can and cannot change, what constraints are present, what possibilities exist, and then take that knowledge and move forward with humility.

Stacey: As museum professionals and specifically those of us that work in exhibits, we are storytellers. The fact that we can be storytellers, that we can use design, we can use light, we can use texture, we can use color, we can use sound, we can use all of these elements, all these collections, objects, and layer that with honest testimony and just incredible stories to help people truly unpack and understand our history, our present, our future, and to understand one another in a more holistic way.

We know the techniques that work that allow us to marry all these design elements with this pedagogical knowledge to create spaces where we're going to set visitors up for moments of engagement, moments of inspiration and moments where they can truly take in new information and fully integrate it into their understanding of the world. Storytelling is something that takes a long time to really perfect and to understand. If we can move our students forward in being stewards of the stories, while honoring the people whose stories they're telling and showing respect and empathy for those stories, that is huge.

Therese: It is also important to acknowledge work that's happened before. There are people who have been doing social change work for a long time. We should acknowledge that they have done it and give credit. Then we pick up from where they left—we may not need to repeat things that have already been done, or relearn lessons that someone else learned.

I also talk to my students about the importance of finding a base. If they're inclined to work within existing social movements, people are already doing work they can affiliate with. They don't need to think they have to go out and do everything alone. In fact, if you see something that needs to be changed, it is likely that someone else has already noticed that a change is needed and is probably already doing that work. It might be good to look and see what is going on and affiliate with those people so you are not just out there all by yourself. It is important to have a base and to have people to back you up.

Cinnamon: What might you think the future museums and museum workers look like? What's the future holding for us?

Therese: I think the pandemic moment has shone a light on the stark disparities in society and the cultural fields. There has been a retrenchment by the powerful. People in power do not want to let go of that power. And museums are all about power through control over knowledge as well as wealth. They are not just places of entertainment; they package and transmit our national ideologies. That is why they are places the ruling elites won't be giving up easily. But museums are also increasingly sites of struggle over meaning and for justice.

For example, many unions have been organized by museum employees over the past few years, which is incredible. Increasingly, people working in museums know that there are problems and they are organizing to address those problems. That is just one indicator that the future of museums will be different than the present. Change happens over the long term.

Stacey: Museums have not changed that much. I teach "Mining the Museum,"[9] as it was a moment where we had an opportunity to see how collections could be totally flipped on their head. An opportunity for us to tell stories and have people look at them completely differently—same objects, totally different interpretation. That exhibit is held out as this incredible example, and yet there has not really been the interest, the urgency, or the courage for folx to embrace that in any sort of a real way across the board.

To me, it feels like we are approaching a tipping point. We are not there yet, but it feels like we're getting there. You have had these independent cohorts like Mass Action and Museums & Race[10] coming together, and they are finding their communities of practice and strength in numbers. That is definitely starting to push a little bit further. I am interested to see where that goes.

Mattie: I really hope we see students and professionals coming out of graduate programs that are young and hungry and want to be creative. They want to be the spark that keeps museums relevant and interesting and useful parts of their communities. I hope the pandemic teaches current professionals, emerging professionals, and students that the name of the game is flexibility and creative thinking. If you cannot adjust to a crisis situation and keep moving forward, then you might as well just stick your head in the sand and stay there.

Liz: I look to the explosion of the different dimensions of diversity and intersectionality that we are recognizing. I'm curious to see how those understandings of the divinity of lived experience will continue to shape how museums collect, the stories they want to tell, and the ways that they tell them.

Gretchen: Museums are not really about objects. They are really about people and stories. The collections are the essential tools that we use to inspire, to tell stories, to help us understand artistic expression, to know people who are different from us, and all of the other purposes we ascribe to museums. The objects and art that we collect have got to be diversified, just as the stories and the programs that are a part of the museum must represent diversity. Some people are kicking and screaming as collections change. And museums sometimes get into trouble when they try to deaccession some objects to make room to acquire a more diverse collection. People are fighting against changing the collection, but collections are changing.

I think the museum is going to become a more equitable place to work and a place where people are paid a little bit better. When the economy recovers and museums start to recover, they are going to be thinking more about caring for their employees and treating people fairly as they think about caring for their collections. The demands of museum employees all over the United States and this summer's revelations about the way that staff are treated makes this inevitable. I think that there may be more unions in museums and hopefully boards that are more sensitive to the needs of the museum's workers.

Notes

1. See Museum as Site for Social Action, https://www.museumaction.org/.
2. The Humanities Action Lab (HAL) is a coalition of universities, issue organizations, and public spaces in forty cities, and growing, led from Rutgers University–Newark, that collaborate to produce community-curated public humanities projects on urgent social issues. See https://www.humanitiesactionlab.org/about.
3. Lori Fogarty, Lonnie G. Bunch, and Johnetta Betsch Cole, "Racism, Unrest, and the Role of the Museum Field," American Alliance of Museums Annual Meeting panel session, American Alliance of Museums, May 2020.
4. A. Andrea Monteil de Shuman, "No Longer in Extremis: A Letter of Resignation & Courage," *Art Museum Teaching* (blog), June 15, 2020, https://artmuseumteaching.com/2020/06/15/no-longer-in-extremis/.
5. John Cotton Dana, "The Gloom of the Museum" (1917), in *Reinventing the Museum*, ed. Gail Anderson (Lanham, MD: AltaMira Press, 2012), 17–33.
6. *Journal of Museum Education* 42, no. 1 (2017), published online February 13, 2017, https://www.tandfonline.com/toc/rjme20/42/1.
7. Ron Chew, "Five Keys to Growing a Healthy Community-Connected Museum," Keynote speech, 48th Annual British Columbia Museums Association Conference, Nanaimo, BC, Canada, October 2004.
8. Kelli Morgan, "To Bear Witness: Real Talk about White Supremacy Culture in Art Museums Today," *Indianapolis Recorder*, June 23, 2020; Dr. Kelli Morgan, IAHI Art and Ethics Seminar, April 29, 2020. Access through the IAHI Facebook page, https://www.facebook.com/456543341040368/videos/234347274486282.
9. *Mining the Museum* is an exhibition selected and installed by Fred Wilson. Wilson was invited by The Contemporary, Baltimore, to create the exhibition using the archives and resources of the Maryland Historical Society. The exhibition, organized by The Contemporary's curator, Lisa Corrin, was installed in the society's museum in October 1992.
10. Excerpt from Museums & Race Statement of Purpose: "We are a group of museum professionals who are interested in effecting radical change in our field. We believe that it is the persistent and pervasive presence of structural racism in our institutions that is at the heart of the museum field's failure to diversify its boards, staffs, collections, members and visitors, despite over a generation of effort in this area. We also believe that coming to understand and recognize entrenched racism is a difficult and potentially contentious undertaking—but also a necessary step—if America's museums are to serve its diverse citizenry" (Museums & Race, "Statement of Purpose," https://museumsandrace.org/).

Bibliography

Bongiovanni, Domenica. "Curator Calls Newfields Culture Toxic, Discriminatory in Resignation Letter." *IndyStar*, July 18, 2020. https://www.indystar.com/story/entertainment/arts/2020/07/18/newfields-curator-says-discriminatory-workplace-toxic/5459574002/.

Chew, Ron. "Five Keys to Growing a Healthy Community-Connected Museum." Keynote speech. 48th Annual British Columbia Museums Association Conference. Nanaimo, BC, Canada, October 2004.

Dana, John Cotton. *The Gloom of the Museum*. N.p.: Sagwan Press, 2015.

———. "The Gloom of the Museum" (1917). In *Reinventing the Museum*, edited by Gail Anderson, 17–33. Lanham, MD: AltaMira Press, 2012.

Fogarty, Lori, Lonnie G. Bunch, and Johnetta Betsch Cole. "Racism, Unrest, and the Role of the Museum Field." American Alliance of Museums Annual Meeting panel session, May 2020.

Morgan, Kelli. "To Bear Witness: Real Talk about White Supremacy Culture in Art Museums Today." *Indianapolis Recorder*, June 23, 2020.

Museums & Race. "Statement of Purpose." https://museumsandrace.org/.

Shuman, A. Andrea Monteil de. "No Longer in Extremis: A Letter of Resignation & Courage." *Art Museum Teaching* (blog), June 15, 2020. https://artmuseumteaching.com/2020/06/15/no-longer-in-extremis/.

Wilson, Fred, and Halle Howard. "Mining the Museum." *Grand Street*, no. 44 (1993): 151–72.

Chapter 23

Helping Boards to See Diversity, Equity, and Inclusion Clearly

A Conversation with Naree W. S. Viner

As coeditors of The Inclusive Museum Leader, we recorded a conversation with Naree W. S. Viner in October 2020, in the midst of the coronavirus pandemic. Naree is a managing director at Koya Leadership Partners. Naree is widely regarded as one of the leading search consultants working with art museums and cultural institutions. She has placed many accomplished museum directors across the United States and has networked internationally to find potential candidates. Naree talks with us about working with boards to embed diversity, equity, and inclusion into the search process, but she recognizes that her work often is to shift the thinking of the board altogether.

Chris Taylor: Thank you for joining us today, Naree. To start off, could you tell us how you find candidates for director positions?

Naree Viner: One of my favorite sayings, which is from a friend of mine in the museum world, "Boards get the leaders they deserve." What my friend meant is that museums becoming more inclusive is about the board changing. The change has to happen at the board level in nonprofits for change to be truly significant.

Although my projects have a beginning, middle, and end, my experience working with search committees often mirrors the experience of my placements as directors, in terms of the various personalities that have to be managed and the different points of view. When I work with a search committee, I'm working with a slice of the board. My experience as a representative of the search firm is a microcosm of how the executive director or CEO ends up working with the entire board. What I experience during the search helps me understand what the candidates may experience. This is helpful information for me and for the eventual placement.

The hardest part about being a director is managing your board because they are not monolithic; they are a group of individual people. They are also all volunteers. They are all giving of their time and energy and resources, because they believe in the museum's mission. Managing those board members with a deft hand and getting the best from them, but not allowing them to move into managing the institution, can be really hard. The partnership between a board and their director, when museums are facing the pressures they are under now, is critical for survival. We all know museums are under threat with COVID and the pandemic. We all expect that not all of them are going to survive. To my mind, the places that are going to survive are the museums where there is a close partnership between the director and the board that know they are all in this together.

When I am working on a search, I begin by talking with search committee members to figure out what they are looking for. In many cases, I talk to a broader group of board members about the things that are most important to them. I ask the committee to define their top three must-have qualities. Sometimes those are about expertise or skills; for example, someone who is a good fund-raiser or a leader who can help us with the strategic planning process. Sometimes it is museum-related skills like a good curator who can help us develop good exhibitions. Other qualities have to do with the soft skills like a candidate who will treat staff humanely or someone who is not about him or herself. Other times committees really want someone who knows what to do on day one, versus someone who is learning how to be a director for the first time.

Often, our clients want to know about our track record engaging and building a diverse slate of candidates. We share how we network in the field and where we can place ads with affinity groups. Our job as recruiters is to give them interesting choices. In order to do that, we listen carefully to their top criteria.

If they don't mention diversity, that's also a data point. We have been in situations where diversity does not come up. When that happens, we make sure to engage the topic. We ask if it matters that the candidates are diverse. I have heard answers across all ends of the spectrum. There are some people saying they want the best candidates and don't mention diversity. We have also had organizations that recognize that diversity is important to their community. Every institution is different because their contexts are different. Our job is to listen very carefully and try to draw out their priorities.

As an executive recruiter, it is my job to give clients as many interesting choices as possible. It is also my job to persuade them to look at people they had not yet considered. Search committees often think they can learn about someone by Googling them or watching YouTube videos, or just reading the candidate's CV or resume. Once they engage us, we begin an interview process that allows the client to go beyond what is on paper, LinkedIn, or even on a YouTube video. When Koya identifies top candidates, we begin with what we hear the clients need the most, but we also read in between the lines to figure out what are they not telling us.

Chris: Thank you. So to follow that up, when a board indicates that they are looking for a diverse candidate, how much education of the board do you do? How do you assess what they already know and what they need to learn if they are looking to diversify the board?

Naree: I am going to tell you right now that I am probably different than a lot of recruiters, because our firm is very different. Koya Leadership Partners has diversity, equity, inclusion on our banner and as a core value. We look different. We have more women and we have more people of color within the firm. We sit in an interesting place because we can engage in conversations with board members about these very issues. Our role in educating clients about DEAI [diversity, equity, accessibility, and inclusion] is very important.

At the same time, I am also sussing out the degree to which the client is open and receptive to diverse candidates. There was a recent client to whom I introduced quite a number of candidates, several of whom were Black, Indigenous, People of Color (BIPOC). At one point, they thought about hiring a White European person as the director and one of the two BIPOC candidates as a deputy director. I helped them understand the optics are problematic if you put a European man at the top and a BIPOC woman as a number two. I am not saying that is the only thing you have to think about, but that could be problematic.

At another point, the search committee chair indicated that they did not want to worry too much about optics as the search committee. For them, finding the right person was the priority, but they did tell me to interject and tell them when they needed to be careful about the optics. That conversation only happens if I have built a relationship of trust with the search committee. There used to be this notion that executive recruiters are like these puppet masters that put people in place. Let me be clear, we never make the decision. Ever. The boards that make the decisions, however, we can open their eyes about what messages their decisions send to staff and stakeholders of their museums.

During a different search, I was sitting in when a client search committee conducted an interview with a candidate. The committee chair mentioned to the candidate that the museum had done a show about African American quilts, but mentioned that the museum struggled to get African American visitors to come to the museum in great numbers, nor had they been able to find a board member who is African American. The chair stated, "Our staff is diverse." I felt I had to challenge that statement.

During the due diligence at the start of the search process, I had only met White staff members. When I pointed this out, the search chair commented that I had only met the senior team, but that other levels of the museums were diverse, like "the security guards, facilities, and gardeners." I do not know if I would have said this at a different firm than Koya, but I said, "As the only person of color sitting in this room"—and I was—"that is not diversity. Diversity, equity, inclusion means having people of color sitting at the table, making decisions, either as part of your senior team or part of your board. Otherwise that is not diversity. That's not a diverse staff."

These examples illustrate two different levels of understanding between different search committees. The first recognized that they may have some blind spots and that I could help them see those and navigate through them. The second committee felt confident in their work around diversifying their staff, so much so that they were unable to see their blind spots.

These conversations with search committees about whether the organization is welcoming of BIPOC individuals, staff members, and audiences ha[ve] to happen before they meet actual candidates. I can find you diverse candidates, but are they going to be comfortable working in those organizations? I need them to be comfortable. It is not just about putting a body in a seat and dropping them into the middle of a very homogenous situation. If the BIPOC candidate is not feeling at all welcome, it is not an achievement. It is not just about putting somebody in a seat but about a true and authentic partnership.

When an organization takes it upon themselves to make a BIPOC leader feel welcome, I am more comfortable putting a BIPOC leader in place. However, if I detect that that person will feel isolated or alone, that is not a good place for someone BIPOC to enter because they should feel embraced by the organization and the community, then that means we either need to work with the board to understand the work needs to be done to create a welcoming atmosphere, or I cannot, in good faith, recommend that position to the candidate. I aim to be honest with candidates about the context and allow them to make the choice whether they would like to be considered, while fully informed of the situation.

Cinnamon Catlin-Legutko: I can't second that enough. What do you think about the moment we're in right now? It's this groundswell that's moved into this tsunami of "Change will happen and it's not going away," as you said earlier. Do you think something needs to change in our process to increase the pace of hiring BIPOC leaders?

Naree: The structure we have in nonprofit organizations in the US is that there are volunteer board members that support these organizations. The reality is that most museums rely on individual major donors. Until this country comes up with a different model to move away from largely private donors as the major funding source for museums, it is the system that we have in place and the system we have to work within. The fact is that most individual donors who have the means and desire to support museums are wealthy and White. With that money comes influence, which often puts them in a gatekeeping role.

I do not know what replaces the volunteer nature of boards because, in the United States, there is no equivalent to having a ministry of culture that funds arts and cultural institutions in other countries. If you look at the history of museums in this country, they were largely founded by wealthy individuals who collected and then decided to make their collection public.

I have been watching that Change the Museum Instagram account carefully. I applaud staff members for speaking out and voicing examples of microaggressions they have experienced as museum employees. The posts on the account are creating a deeper understanding of the experience of BIPOC individuals in museums. The more people know that these types of subtle acts that exclude people happen over and over on a daily basis, allows non-BIPOC staff to more deeply understand how they might be contributing to an atmosphere that is oppressive.

The responsibility of explaining and promoting inclusion should not sit on the shoulders of BIPOC people, because they have enough burden to deal with as it is. Directors need to reflect on what they can do in their roles to recognize their privilege and create more inclusive environments in their museums. Doing so can make a director an ally in the work because they can control the direction, pace, and depth of change at their museum.

There is this question about how you engage people. Everybody is in a different place of understanding the importance of diversity, the notion of systemic racism, and the burden that is put on BIPOC staff to be the catalysts for change. If we call someone a racist, I think what we do is we end the ability to dialogue about it, but if we engage with board members, we can help move them along in their understanding of their privilege.

I absolutely applaud that group of Black museum trustees that are banding together to figure out how they can have more potency and leverage to create systemic change within how boards and museums operate. They have seats at the table, and they recognize that with their seats at the table they have a bigger role to play beyond just their institution, but for any institution that brings Black members onto the board. They are using their power for good, beyond their individual institutions.

Cinnamon: What kind of characteristics are boards looking for right now, especially in this moment of significant change and flux? Are there particular words they're using that have piqued your interest to signal a change?

Naree: There are quite a few language cues that send signals to candidates. What we try to do is signal an inclusive mode, in terms of attracting candidates. Some board members talk about how candidates need to know how to diversify their audiences. We have woven that into a lot of interview questions. In some cases, there can be language that will eliminate people. If it is required to have a PhD, you are automatically going to get a less diverse candidate pool, because there are fewer BIPOC people who have PhDs. We recognize there is tension between this traditional practice and an inclusive practice. We still include an academic degree as a requirement, but in order to make it more inclusive, we phrase it as "these degrees," and list as many as possible. Then we also include language that "equivalent professional experience will be considered." We also try to use gender-neutral pronouns that will signal an openness to a broader group of candidates.

Chris: Changing academic requirements is a signal to applicants. How else do museums articulate that they want to attract diverse candidates or that they are ready to diversify their board?

Naree: There's a couple ways you can look at an organization's level of readiness. Sometimes a board member or a board search committee directly expresses they want a slate that includes diverse candidates. If not, you can try to assess what stage of implementation the museum is in for their diversity initiatives. For example, I worked with an organization where they ostensibly talked about diversity, equity, inclusion, and intersectionality being important. Then when we talked to the staff and when we met with the staff, there were very few people of color, other than people who were assistants and more junior members of the organization. The people who were higher up in the hierarchy were all White women. Our priority became to find someone who was not a White woman to run the organization because their work is about intersectionality and communities of color and the organization wanted to reflect that.

Everybody comes at it from a different place in their journey. My job as a search consultant is to find out from all the stakeholders how much buy-in there is at the board and staff level. During one search, a candidate asked for the organization's statistics on the diversity of their audience, board, and staff. I sent that request over to the board president, and he sent me not just the demographic info but also info about the DEAI work that they had engaged in that year at both the staff and board level. Do they have it done perfectly? Not yet, but the fact that one question elicited all of that information in a short time told me that they were further along than I thought.

There was one client I worked with that had very explicit Black Lives Matter statement on their website. I also worked with a client after George Floyd's murder, where the board shut down the staff's desire to make a statement because the board determined that, in that community, that they couldn't do that due to the negative impact they thought the statement would have on donors' desire to support the museum.

I know of another CEO who shared with me that his staff wanted to put out a Black Lives Matter statement, but the board members of color in the organization that felt that would be a mistake, based on the organization's standing in the community. Now that holds some weight when board members who are BIPOC do not feel that the museum should make a statement like that, compared to board members who are more worried about upsetting donors. Directors can be often caught in the middle between what their board is expecting and what their staff is expecting. Navigating through such dynamics means walking on a very fine edge.

Chris: Is that more the exception than the rule? In terms of museums having proof of their initiatives at the ready?

Naree: I'm seeing it more and more. Several large museums are hiring chief diversity officers. What remains to be seen is the relationship between the Human Resources director or chief Human Resources officer and the chief diversity officer. If you really value diversity, how do these two positions interface?

Museums are getting to this work late, and in many cases, it is because they have been taken to task for a lack of diversity within their structure. As I have said, we are all at different moments of the journey, but it is happening a lot more quickly because of external movements like Black Lives Matter and incidents such as the violence against George Floyd, Jacob Blake, and many other displays of systemic racism.

I had a candidate recently who was grateful that I called him and was in the market for his next opportunity, but recognized he is a White older male. He said, "I hope you are introducing candidates who are people of color, because I don't want to be one of a parade of White men." That's allyship, advocating for equity and recognizing that may mean a decrease in the benefits of White privilege, standing aside so that others can lead.

I am learning, in the Black history museum realm, there's a generational shift going on, too. There are similar trends in the American art museum realm, too. There are several directors stepping down and retiring now so that someone else will be able to step in.

Another focus right now with museums is "Why do museums matter?" What is the role they play in a society that is changing, that is becoming increasingly more diverse? What role does a museum play in advancing knowledge and opening people's minds? What can people learn and enjoy from that experience?

Boards appoint the directors. The boards are the volunteers. If they don't take a stand and understand what their decisions mean, in terms of the messages they are sending to their communities, it can be a problem.

Chris: Thank you for bringing up boards of directors. Change is required there, too. What are some of the traditional practices that boards employ that need to change in order for them to be successful in attracting diverse candidates, but also setting a different tone for their museums?

Naree: In an interview last year, a Black woman was being asked about fundraising. She responded that when she can get into the room with the right people, the room where it happens so to speak, she can do well. She shared that she does not always have access to that room and that the board could help her gain access. What she was talking about was privilege. She hadn't grown up meeting high-net-worth people and building networks similar to those of the board members. She knew she could fund-raise, but she needed the same access that board members had to wealthy donors. Her answer did not sit well with everybody around that table, but it was authentic, and it was accurate, and it was true.

That access extends to high-level interviews as well. When BIPOC candidates have not been through an interview process that includes search committees and a search firm, it is my role as the search consultant to inform them about the multilayered process. We share that there will be more than one interview, including some panel interviews, and eventually the committee will develop the short list. This understanding is very important so candidates will know what to expect. If you have never been in that kind of process and you are BIPOC, you might not necessarily know the expectations. People who are White tend to be more familiar with that realm. It's about the privilege piece. They become gatekeepers who determine the credentials and the background that even get you in the door.

The pipeline of people who are curators and later on director candidates are starting to diversify, but until those people are selected for leadership roles, they will not be in positions to have impact as directors. I understand looking for proven track record, but boards should also look for the capacity of someone to do the job. That capacity piece is about a candidate's potential, even if it is not yet obvious. As I said at the beginning, boards get the leaders they deserve. If I were going to do anything besides search, I would consult to boards, because the best boards get the best leaders.

Several of the BIPOC candidates that I've placed are called for everything. They often feel that they are just a number on a list, one of many in a beauty pageant, so to speak. Even though they are approached over and over, some feel that they never end up getting chosen. This can result in an initial resistance from BIPOC candidates when I am recruiting because they feel like we are just filling out the pool of candidates. I approach candidates based on their credentials, experience, and demonstrated leadership. However, because of "check the box practices," I need to explain my process to them to get past the initial skepticism. That is not how it should work.

Cinnamon: It is like you have to prove that you have good intentions when you are recruiting BIPOC staff. Thinking about the qualities that you look for, when you are recruiting, what do you see in leaders and future leaders that expresses an inclusive mind-set?

Naree: I do behavioral interviewing, which is all about eliciting examples of how someone has faced different situations. I use prompts such as, "Tell me about a time when you had to do X. What did you do? What happened?" It is much more illuminating to ask those sorts of questions because, in the way they answer, you will find out things about their style.

If they are not using the words *inclusivity*, *diversity*, *equity*, and *access* just automatically, that is a sign. I also talk to them about who they have hired, whom they inherited, and how they communicate with diverse staff members.

The other type of clue is someone who does not only need to lead from the front but also leads from behind or on the side. This type of leader is comfortable giving their team members credit. It is the notion of how they make decisions, too. Do they bring other people in? Are they collaborative?

I was doing a mock interview for a group of aspiring museum directors, and I taught them the premise of behavioral interviewing and examples. One of the questions I typically ask, "As someone who hasn't been a director and needs to step into that broader institutional role, tell me about a time when you had an idea or a project that not everybody was supporting, and you had to bring people along and get them to support your idea. What did you do first? Who did you talk to? And then what happened?" One person talked about being the chief curator. He had an opportunity to bring in an exhibition, but it would totally upend the exhibit calendar and displace a number of other projects that were already in progress. He tried to explain to each person why his exhibition was really important to the institution and convince them to move their project time lines to accommodate the exhibit. Here is the critical part, though. He shared that in his mind, it did not really matter what these other people thought, as long as he convinced the director. That spoke volumes about this person's management style much more than if you had asked, "What's your management style?" You listen for those things such whether or not they bring other people into the discussion before they make a decision. Those are signals right there. That question elicited a rather interesting insight about his style.

Cinnamon: Let's switch to a positive note. What gives you hope and enthusiasm for the museum field?

Naree: What gives me hope is when I find out that an organization that I thought was pretty homogenous and fairly privileged has been doing work on DEAI. I think that is great. I get hope from an experience I had recently when I received an e-mail that will buoy me for the rest of the year. I printed it out so I can look at it again on a dark day when I get frustrated with the search process. I had a search committee that was looking for a director. During the process, I was talking to the committee about lack of diversity in the field. We managed to surface a diverse candidate, but this diverse candidate was not going to have all the expected credentials. We also surfaced another diverse candidate, a woman candidate who also was interesting, but scale was the issue. She was not from an R1 (Research 1) university, but from a smaller institution.

Before we presented the slate, we told the search committee that they would see some variety in the candidates' identities and credentials. We pointed out to them that not everybody has access to working at an R1 university. There are people, because of the way they grew up and the opportunities they were given, who are not going to have had the pathway that you expect. We want you to be aware of that as you're looking at their backgrounds. We have interviewed these people and we believe they have the capacity to do the work.

This was before the committee selected candidates whom they were going to interview. A search committee member wrote to us to thank us for raising his awareness around the opportunities that he had as a White older male, but that other people have not. It made him look differently at the candidates. As a result, he was drawn to a candidate from a smaller institution whom he would not have initially considered, but because we helped him see his privilege and his bias, he realized that even though the candidate had not followed the traditional path, she had a lot of capacity. He told us that "as an older White male, that worked mostly during a different time and from a position of power for most of" his career, this was very important for him to hear. He shared that the lessons he learned during the search helped him see that when he raised a concern that one candidate came from such a small school, that there were issues with using that to exclude that candidate from consideration. He shared, "From our committee's discussion about a need for a candidate to be experienced and capable of functioning in a large university environment, I thought she must not be qualified. As the search continued, I could see how she may have lacked ideal experience, but she seemed to be an extraordinarily capable, proactive and innovative person." She ended up being one of the three finalists for this search.

Through this process, we were able to help this man through a paradigm shift. He wrote us this e-mail during the search: "As an older White man whose had privilege, I didn't realize and didn't think about the fact that other people didn't have the opportunities I did." That is a monumental shift. That is why we do the work. There's been a paradigm shift in how he thinks about his role as a gatekeeper. That committee had their eyes opened to something they didn't know was even there. That's the issue with systemic racism: people don't always see and recognize it.

Chapter 24

Practical Ambition

Positioning Inclusive Board Member Ethic as Basic Board Duty

Tonya M. Matthews

Many of us are grappling with this question: What does it take to be an *inclusive* board member? Perhaps we come to the question with a sense of "Finally!" as we have been waiting for a moment to have the conversation. Or perhaps we come with a sense of "So now what . . .?" as we have been pushed into the conversation by recent events or stakeholder demand.

In this chapter, I am largely grounded in diversity with respect to race, amid a smattering of nods to gender. I do not focus on race because it is most important. I focus on race because it is most difficult to deal with, most visually telling, and the hardest to ignore, while also being the easiest difference to exclude. Racial exclusion is often frustrated by vague notions of "good fit" and hidden beneath modern distractions of "diverse diversity," such as cognitive, geographic, and age diversity. Moreover, inclusion of racially diverse board members can be "justifiably" derailed and marginalized (or severely limited) by red herrings of pedigree, professional title, or proclaimed scarcity of interested individuals of required pedigree and professional titles.

In this context, I introduce you to two hats (both of which I have had the responsibility of wearing). These are the hats of the *Inclusive Board Member* and of the *Included Board Member*. I capitalize these phrases purposefully because, in the grand scheme, these are critical designations and, thus, proper nouns. An inclusive board has an inclusive culture that is deliberately and constantly seeking and welcoming "the new." If a board has successfully achieved a particular diversity goal—for example, gender diversity or even recruitment of board members from a new business sector—and achievement of that goal has not created a ripple effect across the entire spectrum of board demographics, then the board can be assumed to be noninclusive. The singular achievement of a specific metric is a measureable outcome, not a culture shift.

A board's shift to inclusive culture requires the work of the Inclusive Board Member.

Anyone on the journey to becoming an Inclusive Board Member works within a three-legged stool context. Those contexts are (1) an awareness of the disparate experience of the Included Board Member; (2) an understanding of fundamental board duties viewed through an Inclusive Board Member lens; and (3) a grasp of the promise and the pitfalls of powerful board governance and nomination structures.

The Experience of an Included Board Member

In order to authentically grapple with the challenge of being an Inclusive Board Member—let alone an inclusive board *leader*—we must first develop an awareness (and as much understanding as possible) of the disparate experience of the Included Board Member. Being an Included Board Member is not simply a privilege. It is a responsibility. The role is as much (if not more) a burden to bear as it is an opportunity that inspires gratitude. Any Included Board Member who tells you different is simply well trained for his or her role and well versed in the language and politics of this position.

The Included Board Member is often the answer to the "diversity challenge." Diversity is community specific. When considering goals for diversity on your board, the question could be broad— Who is or is not represented in our region? in our state? in our sector? Or the question could be local—Who is or is not represented on our board? on our staff leadership team? Furthermore, the question may be centered on reflection and empowerment. For example, in the museum sector, women may be overrepresented on the front lines and on the staff but underrepresented or undercompensated at the executive level. In another scenario, a particular community may decide an emerging immigrant population should be the target of diversity goals, while in other cases, a historically excluded group may be the focus.

Regardless of the specific diversity target, when power and prominence are at issue—such as with board appointments—there tends to be "a list," "a responsibility," and "a burden."

As an African American female who is well credentialed and well established in institutionalized circles, I am on "the list." Similarly yoked colleagues and I joke about this phenomenon. We tease each other and laugh that it's a list of twelve people and that our "number has come up!" every time we get the call or swap board seats or committee appointments *among ourselves*. We know we are on the list; we know why we are called; and we know the consequences of saying no—for example, one more board is allowed to remain monolithic or populated with naïve, untrained voices. I even heard award-winning poet Nikki Giovanni cite the phenomenon as one of the reasons she was invited to speak at NASA. Since when does NASA invite poets as keynotes? Since NASA is trying to appeal to a "broader community" and since it is February (Black History Month), they are going to the "B Files," she said. That said, what the folks at NASA did not know is that Nikki Giovanni is a staunch astronomy and space travel aficionado—she is fascinated by the science and the possibility, and she knew quite a bit more about NASA, the science, and the vision of space travel than most might have guessed. But she was not asked to lean on and, in fact, was lightly steered away from leaning on any of these traits and learnings.

And in this is the grand riddle of the responsibility and the burden of the Included Board Member: bringing the requested part of you to the table and navigating the inclusion of the rest of you that is, frankly, needed by the table.

An Included Board Member has the responsibility to show up regardless of the other burdens on their time and, often, regardless of their passion for the mission and vision of the organization recruiting them. More often than not, the Included Board Member—likely already representing on numerous boards—has been at the table for numerous conversations in which particular communities have been declared "uninterested" or "unqualified" because attempts at diverse recruitment and retention have failed. An Included Board Member understands that his or her rejection of an invitation to join a board has community consequences. Moreover, the Included Board Member also realizes that the responsible alternative—offering to replace their nomination with another—is often equivalent to taking on a part-time job.

It is easy to shrug and suggest that these theatrics are arguably above and beyond the duties of any board member, let alone a board recruit. However, this is *exactly* the responsibility of an Included Board Member: an Included Board Member must accept the responsibility of understanding the impact of their nomination in the larger context of an organization's work (or lack thereof) to diversify themselves. Included Board Members understand their impact and their role—even at the candidate state. In fact, recruiting diverse board members who do not understand these duties is not a good use of any of the involved persons' time.

Ultimately, becoming an Inclusive Board Member requires sensitivity and insight into these background considerations and experiences of the Included Board Member. The mind-set of an Inclusive Board Member takes into consideration the idea that not all board duties tax all board members alike. And furthermore, not all board structures support all board members alike. More important, an Inclusive Board Member translates this insight into an understanding of "diversity in action" and deliberately works not to simply eliminate these disparities, but to leverage the diversity of skills and experiences shaped by them to create a more effective board that generates and drives more sustainable, more impactful work of the organization they serve.

Board Duties Are Legal; Board Effectiveness Is Cultural

If you ever want to make a board member pause—even veteran board leaders—ask them, "So what *exactly* does a board do?"

The challenge is that among the various legal, erudite, and scripted ways of answering that question the most honest answer is this: "It depends." A board member's duties depend on the organization they are serving. A board's fundamental duties are rigorously and legally defined, but these are best executed and interpreted within the context of the specific "healths" of the organization—from financial health to structural health to community relationship health to the health of its board and organizational culture.

Generally speaking, a board—and thus any board member—has three fundamental (i.e., legal) duties: the Duty of Care, Duty of Loyalty, and Duty of Obedience.[1] There is a lot of legalese behind these pithy titles, but essentially this breaks down to (1) mind the care of the organization's money and resources; (2) mind your conflicts and your priorities—the organization you serve comes first; and (3) mind the laws, legal agreements, and mission that binds the organization you serve. These duties consistently bind the boards of *any* corporation, for-profit or nonprofit.

The challenge with these "simple" duties is that each breaks down into things a board monitors and advises upon and things a board actively does—and this is where confusion and chaos reign.

BoardSource's evaluation of this issue, based on data from their recent *Leading with Intent* report is succinct and familiar:

> "According to *Leading with Intent 2017*, boards, in general, are doing well with more fundamental board responsibilities—understanding the organization's mission and providing financial oversight. Conversely, they struggle most with external responsibilities, including fundraising, advocacy, and community-building and outreach. This lack of understanding of what is—and is not—a part of the board's essential roles can lead to a whole host of dysfunctions, such as micromanagement, rogue decision-making, lack of engagement, and more."[2]

"Micromanagement, rogue decision-making, lack of engagement, and more!" is a familiar tune of board governance challenge, but what does this have to do with being an Inclusive Board Member? An argument is now being made that such governance missteps are as much a product of lack of diversity and inclusion as they are a product of lack of understanding of authentic board duties. Meaning, boards that have monolithic composition and group think–like culture are likely to devalue all dissenting opinions, inputs, and strategies.

Compelling evidence of this is included in the American Alliance of Museums' *Museum Board Leadership 2017: A National Report.*[3] The report showed that boards of American museums are overwhelmingly White and startlingly male—regardless of size, budget, location, mission, or museum archetype; zoos, aquariums, gardens, and cultural centers, for example, are not immune to this phenomenon. On record, museum directors and board chairs state a belief that board diversity and inclusion are important to advancing their missions but acknowledge that they have failed to prioritize action steps to advance these priorities. In a bit of "chicken and egg" conundrum, this lack of prioritization of diversity and inclusion is evident in that 46 percent of museums surveyed had all White boards.

Museum boards are *exclusive*. Exclusion is a natural by-product of power, paternalism, and privilege. Desired characteristics of board members such as "helpful relationships and connections," "meaningful community standing," "political influence," and the ever-ambiguous "good fit" often have the (un)intended consequence of reinforcing—if not demanding—a culture of exclusion. The intersection of board power and *anything*—especially a mind-set of "necessary exclusion"—is a challenge to becoming an Inclusive Board Member.

Consider the following: Boards now overwhelmingly do not represent the communities they serve. Given changing national demographics, museums increasingly find themselves in more and more diverse communities. Moreover, despite lack of progress at the executive and board level, initiatives to diversify museum staff have begun to bear fruit. Thus, boards are increasingly less representative not only of the museums they govern but also the communities those museums serve. Herein lies the origin story of the challenge journey for the Inclusive Board Member who, more often than not, is not a community representative him or herself.

The challenge of the Inclusive Board Member is to manage one's legal duties and privileged seat at the table with intentional inclusion—to move his or her board beyond diversity for diversity's sake. The good news is the "duty to inclusion" is not separate from the duties of care, loyalty, and obedience. Most effectively, it overlays or is the foundation.

For example, under the Duty of Care a board member advises on and asks tough questions about the use of capital and resources. Most board members are well accustomed to asking if a return on investment is appropriate to expenditures or if the most compelling collections are being displayed and properly stewarded. An Inclusive Board Member will question the equitable distribution of resources: Which communities are being served by our investments and with what intent? or Which collections representing which communities are being displayed and restored? Encouragingly, many museum boards have begun to ask these questions under the umbrella of "community engagement" and "diversifying audiences."

The Inclusive Board Member will take these conversations one step further and probe *who* is included in decisions of captial and resource distribution. Is there an equitable distribution of the resources, the control of resources, and decision making about those how resources are controlled within the organization? Is the curatorial staff monolithic? Are the *managers and leaders* of the education design teams reflective of the "community" the organization serves? Who are the managers within the organization who control the largest budgets, the most impactful staff, and the decisions about which collections and programs move forward and for whom? Moreover, in service of Duty of Care and within the context of absence of representative staff—and thus inequitable distribution of decision making regarding museum resources—the Inclusive Board Member drives an expectation for community input–driven decision making for the organization. However, one will do this while also noting that requiring such an approach for *every* decision is inefficient, making poor use of the scarcest organizational resource of all: staff time and capacity. An Inclusive Board Member deliberately makes use of such conversations to drive home the issue that, therefore, more robust diversity and inclusion within the organization itself is a more responsible use of all resources concerned. And she or he will make a similar note about the work and composition of the board itself.

As the Inclusive Board Member stretches the exploration of Duty of Care within the context of a duty to inclusion is stretched to the topic of board composition, one recognizes that the most valuable resource at a board's disposal is the time, talent, treasure, and truth of the board members themselves. Thus, when a board grows to welcome Included Board Members, the Inclusive Board Member is as vigilant and proactive in monitoring the "use" of Included Board Members as one is of the ROI on the P&L. In the absence of Included Board Members (with respect to race), the Inclusive Board Member is watchful of the way the board deals with *any* diversities among its members—and wields their power accordingly. The Inclusive Board Member recognizes their own privilege at the table as a tool and uses tactics such as "redirecting the rooms attention" or actively cosigning thoughts of newly Included Board Members to dismantle historical nepotism or elevate nontraditional perspectives.

A similar intentional overlay of a duty to inclusion can be played across the Duty of Obedience and the Duty of Loyalty, as well as further examples in the execution of the Duty of Care. Through this approach, the commitment of the Inclusive Board Member to construct his or her "duty to inclusion" as a framework for activating their legal, mission-driven responsibilities to a board and to the organization the board serves can be transformational. The Inclusive Board Member is not striving for nextgen "group think" or seeking to disrupt board cohesion. Rather, the Inclusive Board Member is willing to grapple with the complexities of diversity of thought and experience to most effectively execute the duties of board service. This requires intentional evaluation of power, role, and voice balance in decision making, general discussion, resource control, and board leadership. Thus the truly masterful Inclusive Board Member will employ these tactics and lenses across their interactions with *all* board members while being mindful of the disparate experience of the Included Board Member.

The Promise and the Pitfalls of Powerful Governance and Nomination Structure

Modern recognition that barriers to diversity, equity, and inclusion are not simply *historical* but *institutionalized* has opened the door to more effective strategies for change. The apologist language of "that was only in our past" is giving way to an understanding that dismantling institutionalized inequities and exclusions require the institutionalization of processes *specifically intended* to dismantle inequity and exclusion. When it comes to boards, this work sits with the Nomination and Governance Committee. (Some organizations have a separate Nomination Committee and Governance Committee. The structure is not as relevant as the philosophy of approach, and this discussion applies regardless of a single or dual committee structure.)

Contrary to popular understanding and in absolute opposition to how most boards allocate time on board meeting agendas, the Nomination and Governance Committee is the most powerful committee on any board. The Nomination and Governance Committee is the gatekeeper by which all board members must pass. The Nomination and Governance Committee is often the only set of board members that surfaces new candidates and often the only group that vets, courts, and rates board candidates—even when candidates are suggested by non-committee members. Furthermore, the Nomination and Governance Committee designs board member orientation— essentially training board members in appropriate and expected action. The Nomination and Governance Committee sets the standards of "good standing," giving expectations, participation expectations, and board self-evaluation standards. In many cases, the Nomination and Governance Committee also chooses board leadership. In short, the rules and processes by which the Nomination and Governance Committee acts sets board culture and composition.

Therefore, the Inclusive Board Member recognizes nomination and governance processes as ground zero for building inclusive board culture—and recognizes his or her individual actions as an amplification of what an inclusion-minded Nomination and Governance Committee is attempting to build and maintain. Thus, every Inclusive Board Member must require board Nomination and Governance Committee work that adheres to intentionally inclusive policies and practices.

The Inclusive Board Member discerns the difference between inclusive and exclusive processes— and a *masterful* Inclusive Board Member discerns the difference without judgment. Why without judgment? Because the evaluation of institutionalized processes requires asking the question "Why are we doing this?" followed by a robust discussion of all the answers, recognition of implications and unintended consequences, and commitment to effective mitigation of unacceptable or mission-damaging consequences. (See below for an interrogation of the classic exclusive criteria: Do we require board members to donate or not?)

In some conversations, the word *inclusion* is mistaken for a simple updating of the definition of diversity. However, the ugly truth about diversity is that it is not stand-alone solution. In a recent study, DiStefano and Maznevski[4] codified this misunderstanding by measuring the overall impact of diversity on team performance. They found that when compared to homogeneous teams, diverse teams could be shown to have better *or* worse performance—with almost equal predictability—depending on the "management expertise" engaged in supporting those teams in managing diversity. In other words, diverse teams coached into navigating and leveraging differences succeed; those that are not, fail. Therefore the "why" of the Inclusive Board Member is further clarified: diverse teams—for example, boards composed of Included and Inclusive Board Members—require governance culture, process, and leadership that supports, coaches, and reinforces inclusion in order to be effective.

Given the impact of Nomination and Governance Committees and the dangers of poorly managed diverse teams, it is clear that Nomination and Governance Committees should be populated with Inclusive Board Members. However, beyond that basic composition, there are six go-to priority board nomination and governance practices that the impactful Inclusive Board Member is supported by and will champion, if not demand:

1. Eliminating use of shorthand and euphemism in descriptions of board candidate characteristics.
2. Setting solid board member expectations embedded with diverse pathways to achieve those expectations.
3. Honoring term limits and managing influence of emeritus board members.
4. Setting goals, measuring progress toward, and cultivating board talent that drives ongoing diverse board leadership.
5. Creating authentic and reflective board orientations and board retreats.
6. Radicalizing the transparency and thus raising the bar for outcome expectations of board governance and nomination processes.

The first two priorities—elimination of shorthand and euphemistic descriptions of board candidate characteristics and setting solid board member expectations with diverse ways of achieving them—are linked and reinforcing practices. One of the most common (and misguided) "shorthands" of board candidate characteristics, for example, is the use of job titles or organizational affiliations instead of explicit descriptions, characteristics, or outcomes being sought. Consider the phrase "corporate leader," a woefully unhelpful characteristic shorthand. Is that shorthand for "has money"—and is that personal capital or as a decision maker for corporate capital? Is that shorthand for "lending gravitas to your board list," or are you more interested in someone who can pick up a phone and open a door to other C-suite peers—and is that within business sector or across business sector? If you are looking for, say, a marketing executive, do you want a marketing company CEO who can assign you thirty hours of pro bono support, or do you want a brilliant practitioner who can coach communication strategy while sitting in a board meeting? When you say "Junior League" or "Jack and Jill," do you mean the socialite or soccer mom? Furthermore, define the term *diverse*. If you are not ready to say out loud, "We need more African American and Arab American board members," then it is unlikely you are ready to welcome them.

Increasing the level of specificity in board member characteristics supports conscientious alternative consideration of how standardized board member expectations can be achieved, while remaining consistent with board outcomes and values. Consider the classic conundrum of board exclusivity is: "To give or not to give—and how much is the question." The challenge with setting "give" versus "get" (i.e., personal donation versus conduit to donation source) in opposition to each other is that juxtaposition suggests we are talking just about money. Actually, we are talking about financial commitment versus time commitment—and a solidly yoked board will require both. The Inclusive Board Member does not necessarily drive conversations that shy away from big numbers, she or he drives conversation that demands multiple pathways to bringing "the number" to the table for *all* board members. A board member who brings $1 million corporate to the table but never shares a personal dime will be as much resented as the board member who annually donates $100 and never makes any introductions will be dismissed. Governance and nomination processes that maximize the impact of Inclusive and Included Board Members will be clear about *who* the board is recruiting and *what* is expected of every board member recruited while also creating practices that honor the diversity of ways board members achieve expectation with applause, not judgment.

The second two practices—honoring term limits and setting goals for diverse board leadership—are obviously linked. Refreshment of thoughts, perspectives, and people is key to the growth and sustainability of any business, especially museums. Platitudes and farewell mugs aside, if any individual board member is truly irreplaceable than neither the board nor that member has done their job of creating a healthier, more sustainable organization than the one they found on the day they arrived. Additionally, increasing board size of "member-locked boards" solely for the purpose of diversification is, at best, a temporary or starter solution and cannot continue indefinitely. Moreover, diversification one board member at a time increases both the burden and isolation of the Included Board Member and may ultimately challenge retention—which leads you back to square one. And within healthy board turnover processes, managing the shadow of emeritus board members is key. There are many powerful and necessary ways emeritus members are critical to an organization, and they are indeed due their fair share of care and feeding. That said, inclusive governance practices will not only include them but also will not allow their shadow to loom so large that it inhibits new voices and diverse perspectives.

Process-driven term limits, emeritus power balance, and diverse board member cohorts drive open the doorway to diverse board leadership. However, the Governance and Nomination Committee may be the gatekeeper, but the Inclusive Board Member is the watchdog at the gate. Thus, the classic maxim "What gets measured gets done" is even truer for cultivating and maintaining diverse leadership than it is for most things. The Inclusive Board Member studies the DEI (diversity, equity, and inclusion) dashboard ahead of every meeting (and was probably the one who asked for such a thing in the first place). He or she will ask critical questions about time lines to board diversity goals, question process that interfere with goal achievement, and make a note when diverse "leaders" consistently hit ceilings as vice chairs, cochairs, and de facto chairs of community outreach task forces, rather than progressing to the board chair role.

The fifth priority of governance practice may seem less outcome driven than its counterparts. Yet, on the contrary, authentic board practices of member orientation and board retreats are critical to building the shared language, skills, and culture required for the board to behave effectively as a diverse team. In fact, these are the practices that are also required to cultivate new Inclusive Board Members. A consistent and comprehensive board member orientation will reveal diverse appreciations for and interpretations of board practice. Clarity on what is required versus what is expected versus what is customary can protect against misunderstandings reinforcing false assumptions about fellow board members and board practices. For example, it may be customary but not required for board members to remain after meetings for coffee chat. Let's say a new board member, a high-wealth female of color, is unaware of this custom and consistently leaves promptly at meeting's end and is thus perceived as aloof and not a team player, rather than as rushing off because Thursday night is family pizza night and she brings home the pizza. As another example, consent agendas may seem efficient to some and purposefully opaque to others. Regardless of whether a board changes this practice, noting reactions to it provides critical insight for board leaders to manage mixed impressions accordingly, and perhaps even refresh explanations of the "why this practice" periodically.

If board orientation allows for level setting around board expectations, then board retreats offer opportunities for reflective conversation and skill building in managing diverse perspectives, approaches, and impacts of these expectations. Broad-audience nonprofits, such as museums, should not dismiss the necessity of this practice. If you consider your museum welcoming and engaging for "all ages" or "all communities" or "every citizen of our state/nation," then you must expect that diversity of impression and engagement to come together on your board. As noted earlier, Inclusive Board Members are masters of navigating the time, talent, treasure, and *trust* of diverse board members. Trust is a product of relationship building. Relationships among board members not only grow from engaging in expansive blue sky conversations but also from adequate time to respectfully be in conflict over ideas. Well-designed board retreats create space for these relationship-building supports. Furthermore, donation of time and talent is a product of feeling that your time and talent is well utilized—and commonly grounding diverse board members in one "big picture" supports the Inclusive Board Member in stewarding the contributions of all fellow board members. And then, of course, the treasure follows.

The last priority practice, though certainly not least, is radical transparency in governance and nomination practice. Inclusion of an Included Board Member *is not possible* within a culture of hidden governance practice and intention—and such lack of transparency will drive both Included and Inclusive Board Members away. Above and beyond best practice necessity of transparent governance and nomination practice, it should also be noted that governance of a diverse, rotating board membership across various tenures, passions, communities, and connections is a very difficult job. Particularly as a board builds toward an inclusive culture, the work of simultaneously supporting the needs of the individual and of the whole is work that needs allies. Radical transparency creates an ally of every board member, for example, when board members have full clarity on what governance and nomination processes are designed to do, they can be helpmates in achieving those outcomes and calling attention to potential missteps before they even happen. As the numbers and skill sets of Inclusive Board Members grows on a board—given all of the above—the actions, mind-set, and vigilance of the Inclusive Board Member transforms such work from tactical to cultural and is thus sustainable.

Closing Notes of Gratitude to Inclusive Board Members

Inclusive Board Members bring the commitment, stamina, and "curiosity of other" that is required for the future credibility and sustainability of museums. The masterful Inclusive Board Member knows that one is not meant to be and should not accept being an island. The goal is always to create a sustainable culture of inclusion on the boards we serve, and thus multiply.

These three ideas—acknowledging the experience of the Included Board Member; engaging with fundamental requirements of board service through an Inclusive Board Member lens; and leveraging the power of governance and nomination process in service of inclusion—are not written as a step-by-step how-to of the Inclusive Board Member for good reason. The experience of any given Inclusive Board Member is too unique for that approach. Rather, these three ideas form a comprehensive framework from which majority and minority, historically included and excluded, classically and unusually qualified Inclusive Board Members can leverage their power toward sustainable and critical transformation within the culture of our boards.

A mentor, a longtime museum and board member veteran, once noted that he had never seen an organization move farther than its board. As someone who frequently serves on boards, I had never heard anything more terrifying—or more of a marching order. Essentially, if I don't move, the organization I serve can't move. And if I'm the only one on that board who moves, the movement will be imperceptible and irrelevant. If I ever had any doubts about whether taking on the challenge of becoming an Inclusive Board Member was worth it, they were eliminated at that thought.

I acknowledge that this work is hard, isn't it? But I revel in this work because it is also invigorating, isn't it? Even marathons end eventually—and this journey of the Inclusive Board Member is surely worth the run.

Notes

1. Lee Bruder Associates, "The Three Legal Responsibilities of a Nonprofit Board of Directors," https://www.nhnonprofits.org/hh/welcome-and-meet-your-mentor; Jacqueline Leifer and Michael Glomb, *The Legal Obligations of Nonprofit Boards: A Guidebook for Board Members* (Washington, DC: National Center for Nonprofit Boards, 1997).
2. BoardSource, "Roles and Responsibilities," https://boardsource.org/fundamental-topics-of-nonprofit -board-service/roles-responsibilities/.
3. American Alliance of Museums, *Museum Board Leadership 2017: A National Report* (Washington, DC: American Alliance of Museums, 2017).
4. Joseph DiStefano and Martha Maznevski, "Creating Value with Diverse Teams in Global Management," *Organizational Dynamics* 29, no. 1 (October 2012): 45–63.

Bibliography

American Alliance of Museums. *Museum Board Leadership 2017: A National Report.* Washington, DC: American Alliance of Museums, 2017.

BoardSource. "Roles and Responsibilities." https://boardsource.org/fundamental-topics-of-non profit-board-service/roles-responsibilities/.

DiStefano, Joseph, and Martha Maznevski. "Creating Value with Diverse Teams in Global Man-agement." *Organizational Dynamics* 29, no. 1 (October 2012): 45–63.

Lee Bruder Associates. "The Three Legal Responsibilities of a Nonprofit Board of Directors." https://www.nhnonprofits.org/hh/welcome-and-meet-your-mentor.

Leifer, Jacqueline, and Michael Glomb. *The Legal Obligations of Nonprofit Boards: A Guidebook for Board Members.* Washington, DC: National Center for Nonprofit Boards, 1997.

Chapter 25

Building Inclusivity with and within the Board

Lori Fogarty

I've worked with boards of museums for more than thirty years at three museums, each with a range of board structures, processes, cultures, and ways of working. The board of the San Francisco Museum of Modern Art (SFMOMA), where I worked for twelve years, was very large—around fifty-five people. Most of the board members were modern and contemporary art enthusiasts, and many were major collectors. At the Bay Area Discovery Museum (BADM), where I served as director for five years, the trustees were largely parents of young children—active users of the museum for their families. While they were a highly accomplished group of individuals in their personal and professional lives, BADM often represented their first-time board service, and part of the long-standing role of the executive director was board education. At the Oakland Museum of California (OMCA), a multidisciplinary museum of art, history, and natural sciences, our board is much more diverse—by interest, life experience, and motivation for serving, as well as by the more visible demographic benchmarks of age, gender, sexual orientation, and race.

Despite the differences in these boards, however, the basic constructs of board service are often quite similar and are grounded in the long-standing "ways of working" of museum boards. There are standing committees and officers. There is a recruitment and nominating process. There are roles and responsibilities that include financial contributions. There are fiduciary and legal responsibilities, and all major policy and financial decisions require a vote of the board, which requires consensus. Perhaps most important for the museum director, the boards hire, evaluate, and determine compensation for the director. The museum director serves at the pleasure of the board.

So, when these are the fundamental constructs—constructs within which power and privilege are embedded—how does a board actually begin to support and advance a museum's commitment to inclusivity, equity, and even antiracism? How can boards partner with the director and with the staff to determine and then embody the values of the museum? Can museum boards, which are often responsible either directly with their own philanthropy or through the fundraising, be catalysts for inclusion? These are the questions that deeply engage the OMCA board at this time.

The work has been underway for the past several years, but there is no question that, at this moment of national reckoning around issues of race and justice, these questions and the commitment to inclusion have taken on a greater urgency. And, like many institutions, the call for action is strong and passionate among our staff, requiring that our board and staff explore together what a partnership in support of antiracism, equity, and inclusion really looks like, feels like, and means.

Over my close to fifteen years as director of OMCA, diversity has always been among the criteria for the board recruitment and nominating process. Indeed, diverse representation is the first place many museum boards begin with in a diversity, equity, inclusion, and access (DEAI) effort. As we know from a report from the American Alliance of Museums (AAM)—*Museum Board Leadership 2017: A National Report*—46 percent of museums surveyed had *no* people of color on their board.[1] For this reason, AAM's current Facing Change initiative for board diversity and inclusion—in which OMCA is one of the fifty museums across the country taking part—identifies the recruitment of two trustees of color over two years as one of the requirements for participation.

Thus, the goal for diverse representation was and remains an area of focus for the OMCA board. While that goal was always stated as a criterion, five years ago our Governance Committee set an explicit target for the composition of our board at 40 percent people of color. The committee and the full board discussed whether it was appropriate to set this kind of numerical benchmark and what the right number would be, but the committee and I agreed that, without a specific goal, we wouldn't be able to hold ourselves fully accountable. Because our board does have term limits and is in a continual process of recruiting new trustees—a prerequisite to truly achieving a diverse board—we were able to meet that target within two years and have sustained this level ever since.

Beyond representation, however, our board also began to consider a deeper connection between governance and the museum's broader commitment to diversity, equity, inclusion, access and engagement. Seven years ago, OMCA was one of fifteen arts and cultural organizations throughout California to receive a grant from the James Irvine Foundation through its New California Arts Fund (NCAF) program. This program specifically supported arts organizations in an effort to increase participation by low income communities and communities of color by placing engagement at the core of their work. The key shift with this grant initiative is that it funded training and other learning opportunities in the areas of governance, staff, organizational culture, financial sustainability, and evaluation, as well as programming and audience development. This funding was further galvanized by an active and rigorous cohort that involved workshops, conferences, and forums multiple times each year by and among the fifteen participating organizations.

One of the central areas of learning for these organizations was what we called "twenty-first-century governance"—or moving beyond the traditional mechanisms, process, and constructs of board service. During a variety of workshops and convenings, trustees and staff from the NCAF organizations examined questions such as these: What does it mean to recruit trustees for their networks and spheres of influence rather than by the specific skill sets or expertise, such as law, marketing, or finance? How can a board be truly in service to the institution rather than the other way around? And how does a board place engagement at the core of its work as well as the core of programming?

Propelled by the NCAF initiative, OMCA formed what was first a task force and now is a standing board committee, the Community Engagement Committee. Because the task force's formation was linked to the NCAF initiative focused on engagement, the committee's role encompassed external, community-focused work as well as an internal capacity building related to equity and inclusion. As stated in the Museum's Committee Purpose and Priorities document:

> The Community Engagement Committee supports the Museum's efforts to deepen engagement with the local community and to advance OMCA's social impact. To this end, the committee works to: 1) link the Board's work and priorities to community needs and connections; 2) provide support and facilitation to enhance the Board's understanding of community engagement and social impact; 3) build engagement into core Board practices such as defining Board roles and responsibilities and incorporating engagement related topics into agendas; 4) partner with the Governance Committee in ensuring Board diversity and recruiting trustees of diverse cultural and ethnic backgrounds and with strong community networks.[2]

Over the years, the committee has worked with staff to explore the concept of what "social impact" means and to create a framework focused on social cohesion—building greater trust, connection, and understanding between and among individuals and communities. It helps identify topics and themes for board meetings and retreats, as well as investigating and selecting speakers and developing plans for DEAI training. The committee partners with the Governance Committee to develop approaches to recruiting diverse candidates. A number of trustees of color who have been recruited to the board now serve on this committee.

The committee also championed practices our staff members utilize to engage community members, such as "listening circles," which are gatherings our exhibit teams lead to hear and learn from community members about exhibition topics, particularly topics that may elicit a range of perspectives and responses. For example, the committee members participated in and facilitated board listening circles for our recent exhibitions such as *All Power to the People: Black Panthers at 50*, *Altered State: Marijuana in California*, and *Queer California: Untold Stories*.

In the past year, the committee, together with board leadership, has served as the working group for OMCA's participation in the AAM Facing Change initiative. When we submitted our application to AAM, the committee identified goals and approaches that I believe truly and authentically address how boards can become leaders in equity for their institution:

- to move beyond numerical representation toward an understanding of the broader implications and imperatives of equity and inclusion;
- to fully embody and reflect the Museum's vision and values for social impact;
- to foster an internal culture of social cohesion and understanding of issues related to personal, organizational, structural and systemic inequity; and
- to apply these understandings to the specific work of OMCA.

In order to achieve these goals, the board recognized a need for continued education around key concepts related to equity and inclusion. They acknowledged the need for support for having challenging and yet constructive conversations about issues related to oppression and equity. And they identified the need to develop specific tools to operationalize equitable policies and practices within the board's work and on behalf of the institution.

Over the past year, as the board has become more deeply engaged with issues of equity and inclusion, our individual trustees themselves have recognized the importance of vulnerability and transparency—hallmarks of inclusive practices. In a Facing Change retreat in November 2019, board and staff leadership explored what shifts would be required. They noted a need to create psychological safety for new perspectives to be shared—not a typical condition for many board rooms. They noted the importance of questioning new ways of doing things—new structures, process, and ways of work. They acknowledged that we need to recruit more board members who are truly representative of our community, beyond demographics.

Our board has begun to take specific steps on this path. One simple and powerful mechanism is to simply make space for sharing of stories at board and committee meetings. For example, at a board meeting in summer 2020—at the very moment where racial justice protests in opposition to police brutality and in support of equity and justice were actively underway and demanding that cultural institutions state their intentions around Black Lives Matter—one of our trustees and the chair of the Community Engagement Committee, Dana King, shared a deeply personal story of her own upbringing.

Dana is a Black sculptor living in Oakland, but before her recent artistic career and commission of major sculptures across the country, she was a well-known television anchorwoman and journalist. Dana led off the discussion on our equity and inclusion initiative with the story of her Black father and white mother who got married at a time when interracial marriage was illegal in much of the country. She acknowledged the deeply personal sadness, rage, and pain that the current moment called for, and she described her passionate sense of responsibility to lead change, including in the institutions of which she is a part. Her vulnerability in those brief few moments changed the conversation with our board, even as it all took place over Zoom.

Our board is now plotting other specific steps to catalyze equity and inclusion at OMCA. The Governance Committee is researching different structures for recruiting board members who represent and can connect the museum to specific communities, such as the artist or education communities. The Finance and Investment Committees are beginning to develop new investment and vendor policies centering the museum's commitment to antiracism and social impact. The Community Engagement Committee is exploring additional training opportunities, particularly around implicit bias and white privilege. This fall, the board will begin in earnest the development of a Diversity, Equity, Inclusion and Access Plan, in collaboration with the staff and in fulfillment of another requirement of the Facing Change initiative. Underlying all of this work are four key themes:

- *Examining Our Structures*: We need to look critically and constructively at our practices, such as board meetings, committee meetings, and committee roles.
- *Sharing Our Personal Stories*: We need to bring all of our filters and identities into our roles and board exchanges.
- *Creating New Ways to Engage*: We need to find new ways to deepen our understanding of individual, interpersonal, and institutional systems of oppression and ways to engage in the work of equity through mechanisms for relationship and trust building.
- *Connect*: And, as a board, we need to connect more with the staff, with the community, and with the museum's mission.

For me as a museum leader, beyond the action steps and plans is a moment of deep and profound reflection for all aspects of my work, including my partnership with the board. I've often said in these last few weeks that I'm climbing the steepest learning curve of my professional life. Much of the learning I'm doing is the same kind of self-education that millions in our country, particularly white people, are pursuing related to understanding this country's history as a nation built on the oppression of enslaved and Indigenous people and the economic benefits to white people of racism. Other learnings relate to practices of antiracism and understanding the culture of white supremacy. Much of this learning is highly personal, uncomfortable, and, as a leader, it often calls into question many of the practices on which we depend, particularly during crises like the ones brought about by the COVID-19 pandemic and economic fall-out. These practices include top-down decision making, often involving financial decisions and not involving more than a few people.

So, with this self-reflection, I've had to reconsider my partnership with the board. I am very much in the process of considering the changes that need to take place and what is needed for these changes to support new models of equitable governance and leadership. First, I believe that, like any change in culture or structure, we begin with trust. That trust emanates in the relationship between the board chair and the executive director. I am so fortunate to be working with our current board chair, Quinn Delaney, who is such a model to me in so many ways of philanthropy, volunteerism, and activism. Some twenty years ago, she and her husband created a private foundation, the Akonadi Foundation, dedicated to racial justice and ending the criminalization of young people of color in our community. (Akonadi references the goddess in the Western African culture of Ghana and is associated with justice.) Quinn has a deep and demonstrated commitment to equity and antiracism, making implicit my trust in her leadership of advancing equitable governance. In turn, over many years of working together, I believe she trusts me, both in the values I hold and in giving me the space to suggest different approaches and to move in new directions.

The foundation of trust extends to the broader board as we have been on the journey of social impact, community engagement, and equity over many years. This trust has been most evident for me in just these past few months as our staff has formed cross-functional, institution-wide teams around priorities of antiracism and equity at OMCA. The teams developed written documents that are bold in their recommendations with calls to action that take on some of the most essential principles of nonprofit cultural work including philanthropy and financial integrity, recruitment and hiring, organizational structure, and representation in content and programming. In the past, I might have received these documents from staff, consolidated and synthesized them in a way that the board could more easily absorb, and then presented them in a neat and tidy presentation at a board meeting. Instead, we held "office hours" with board members and staff participants in the antiracism design process, and staff presented their recommendations directly to the board. I realized at that moment both the trust I have in our board and in our staff and the vulnerability required to step back from the typical CEO role as the primary and often exclusive pipeline of communication between the two.

I have also tapped into my own vulnerability—and the attendant practices of humility and transparency—as I consider our next steps in equity work. My default position would be to read as many resources as I can find (which I've done), put to paper an action plan with specific next steps (which I've also done), and then to roll it out for input and feedback (yes, I've done that, too). What I am working on is realizing that I don't have the answers, and, in fact, the answers will come from others, both trustees and staff. I am exploring every day the concepts of shared and distributed leadership, and, while the principles of this form of leadership are ones toward which I gravitate and believe in some ways come naturally to me, I also realize that years in the executive director role, working within the board and staff hierarchies, have ingrained habits that now need to be broken or at least adjusted.

One of the most ingrained habits is for an executive director to have a clear plan. I am accustomed to presenting to the board a clear strategic vision, with measurable objectives, and sequential tactics, all wrapped up with a nice bow in a balanced budget. There are no nicely packaged plans when it comes to the work of becoming an antiracist institution, and that is particularly true when that work is happening during a pandemic and economic crisis. For the first time in my career, I've drawn upon my vulnerability and the shared trust in the board to convey: I'm not sure exactly what's going to happen. I don't have the answers. We're going to have to live with some ambiguity and learn as we go. And we're going to have to be OK with that. I admit that stance causes me a lot of discomfort, *and* I believe it is fundamental to the work of undoing the practices that we have come to understand undermine equity and inclusion.

The Oakland Museum of California opened in 1969 at the height of the civil rights movement. The museum opened its doors in downtown Oakland across the street from the Alameda County Courthouse where Huey Newton, the founder of the Black Panther Party, was on trial for murder and where the "Free Huey" protests were underway. Against this backdrop, OMCA was founded as the "Museum of the People," and values of community, education, and multiculturalism are in our institutional DNA. As we now look to our next fifty years, we must again examine what it means to be a "Museum of the People," and the work that it will truly take to become an equitable, inclusive, and antiracist institution. We certainly don't have all the answers, and I am sure our continued journey won't be easy or without mistakes. I believe, though, that we need all of the players working along this continuum—board, leadership, and staff. These stakeholders must be aligned, mutually supportive, and intentional in moving toward the changes that are needed and long overdue. It is only by achieving social cohesion within our own OMCA family that we can achieve greater trust, connection, and understanding within our broader community.

Note

1. American Alliance of Museums, *Museum Board Leadership 2017: A National Report* (Washington, DC: American Alliance of Museums, 2017).
2. "Oakland Museum of California Community Engagement Committee Purpose and Priorities," working paper (Oakland: Oakland Museum of California, 2020).

Bibliography

American Alliance of Museums. *Museum Board Leadership 2017: A National Report*. Washington, DC: American Alliance of Museums, 2017.

"Oakland Museum of California Community Engagement Committee Purpose and Priorities." Working paper. Oakland: Oakland Museum of California, 2020.

ACTIVITY

Taking Inventory

How often do you stop and take stock of how diverse and inclusive your life is? Is cultural expansion part of the conversations you typically have with friends, family, and colleagues? Even if it is, try the next activity. It tends to be an eye-opener.

Diversity Inventory

For your top five friends (folks you trust the most), list each person's race, gender, religion, sexual orientation, socioeconomic status, occupation, and personality type (extrovert, introvert, etc.). How are they similar to you? How are they different from you? What else did you notice?

Cultural Inventory

Maybe you don't have opportunities to befriend new people. That's cool. You're still able to scan to expand in order to overcome bias. What you need is a cultural activity inventory:

1. List the last three books you read.

2. List the last three movies you saw.

3. List a few TV shows you watch.

4. List your favorite music artists.

5. For each of these categories, list as best you can the race, gender, religion, and sexual orientation of the musicians, authors, or main characters. How are they similar to you? How are they different from you? What else did you notice?

Some people find these activities challenging, while others find them easy. There is no correct set of responses. It is simply a tool you can use to raise your awareness about who we choose to have in our lives and the cultures we expose ourselves to. If you never stop to think about the composition of your networks or your cultural exposure, you will find that your journey may be slower than you'd like.

Knowing your patterns can help you grow. You got this. Stay in the discomfort—that is where change happens!!

Source: Tiffany Jana and Matthew Freeman, *Overcoming Bias* (Oakland, CA: Berrett-Koehler, 2016), Kindle.

Part Six

Looking Ahead

Chapter 26

What Kind of Ancestor Will I Be?

Bob Beatty

It was about November 2019 when I really began to seriously ponder the meaning of the question Richard Josey posed when he launched Collective Journeys: What Kind of Ancestor Will I Be?[1] My older daughter Ryan was seventeen, about a third of the way through her senior year of high school. Her sister Tyler was in tenth grade.

I attended a concert celebrating the Band's *Last Waltz* (look it up if you're unfamiliar). Toward the end, Lukas Nelson, Willie's son, stepped to the mic and sang, "May God bless and keep you always, may your wishes all come true," the opening lines of Bob Dylan's "Forever Young."[2]

As the band played, it hit me that that was the prayer I had for my daughters. Ryan was about to embark on the first great adventure of her adult life: college. Was she ready? What lessons did I need to impart to her before she left home? Would I still be able to guide her once she did? Did I let her know how loved and respected she was for who she was? Had I been a good role model, a good ancestor? All of these questions rolled around my mind as I listened to a gorgeous rendition of the Dylan classic.

As the song drew to a close, the guy next to me (a stranger) noticed the tears streaming down my face. He had them, too. "That was righteous," he said. I nodded in agreement, wiping my eyes.

Dylan's second verse inspired the kind of ancestor I want to be:

> May you grow up to be righteous, may you grow up to be true.
> May you always know the truth, and see the lights surrounding you.
> May you always be courageous, stand upright and be strong.
> May you stay forever young.

I want to instill in my children and their children (and so on) the importance of being righteous, truthful, courageous, and firm in conviction. More than anything, I want my descendants to live in a world that is just, and to work to make the world just for those who are not as fortunate as they are.

That my descendants learn to have courage in their convictions is the kind of ancestor I want to be.

I've gotten a lot of support to get to this point and, thus, I suppose I come by this naturally. I was incredibly fortunate to have two very stable male role models in my life: my father and my paternal grandfather. Each was the epitome of a mid-twentieth-century man. They'd served in the military and were the sole breadwinners in their families. (My grandmother and my mother were both proud to call themselves *housewives*—a term I will use here out of respect to their wishes.)

Though manifested very differently, there was definitely a sense of paternal obligation and gravitas with both men. They took their roles as family patriarchs seriously, and I learned and observed. Out of that I formed one view of who I was supposed to be as a man, one firmly grounded in my own, personal experience.

The lesson came home for me in the 1980s, when our local paper featured Dad in a column. Mom had it framed. One quote stood out. The reporter asked his personal philosophy. "Those of us in a position to help others should do so," he answered.

Use my position to help others? That's the kind of ancestor I want to be.

I'm sure Dad meant that somewhat paternalistically. It offers no excuse that I wouldn't expect him to think otherwise. This was the world Dad was raised to live in. He was a southerner in the Jim Crow era. Though he grew up on a chicken farm, he was not poor. In 1952, Dad went to the University of Florida (UF) forming a lifelong affiliation with UF and our family. It was completely lost on me that Dad's education had only been available to White women since 1947 and unavailable altogether to African American undergraduates until 1962.

I'm not sure how much Dad thought about any of that as I watched him navigate the world, but helping others through his law practice became his life's work. For Dad, the personal desire to help where he could intersected with his professional life; it is a lesson I've carried with me in my own work. I followed suit, doing it through history and museums. My younger brother Brian, who passed away in April 2020, did it through his service to people in Alcoholics Anonymous.

In this way, Dad reminded me a lot of Atticus Finch, another small-town southern attorney. Among Atticus's most famous lines is this: "You never really understand a person until you consider things from his point of view . . . until you climb into his skin and walk around in it."[3]

The quote reminds me that I want to pass down the critical life skill of empathy to the folks who come after me. I want them to be better people than I am, than my own ancestors were.

Empathetic is the kind of ancestor I want to be.

One of the first museums that resonated with me was Bok Tower in Lake Wales, Florida. Located near Dad's hometown of Babson Park, it stands on Iron Mountain. At 295 feet above sea level, it is one of the highest points in peninsular Florida, and it was an early landmark for our entire family.

Bok Tower was the brainchild of Edward Bok, most famous as editor of the *Ladies Home Journal.* Among its beautiful, Frederick Law Olmsted Jr.–designed gardens, I could feel the influence of a quote from his grandmother that inspired Bok's oasis on the sandhills of the Lake Wales Ridge, "Make you the world a bit better or more beautiful because you have lived in it."[4]

Remembered for making the world better or more beautiful is the kind of ancestor I want to be.

A few weeks ago, Ryan texted me a question that had come up in one of her classes, "Why would someone who has power (i.e., White males) relinquish that power? What is the incentive?"

This is a very good question, one that strikes at the heart of the issue I'm writing about here. My answer to her was simple. "The incentive for me," I responded, "is Jesus's Second Great Commandment, 'Love your neighbor.'" So yes, I identify as a straight, White, Christian male. I am well aware of the outside perception and internal baggage that comes with that statement, and I do my best to own every bit of it.

But know that I am in this work, our work, because of this precept. I believe we are all children of God, with unique talents and abilities, and I want to be the kind of ancestor who is kind and thoughtful and who tries to lift others up in love and in mutual respect.

Yes, it's a far-reaching goal. Yes, I've often failed mightily in my attempts to be a good ancestor to my neighbors. But it's my life's work. While there are days I feel like Sisyphus, there are also days I've celebrated victories large and small.

I'm guessing that many of you reading this feel likewise, at least I hope you do. The work we do is profoundly important and meaningful. Our dedication to history, to arts and culture, to museums, to public discourse, and the like can, and does, make the world a better place. But it only does so if we think more broadly than our own experiences.

Thus, the inclusion imperative is more than just opening access to the corridors of power to people who don't look like us or have a shared background. It also means opening our own minds to others' insights and ideas, learning from them as we build our own understanding of the world around us.

For me—and, I'm sure, for many of us—the study/understanding of history is more than just a career pursuit or a lifelong passion. History has helped provide focus to the world I inhabit, and the study of history (both formally and informally) has changed how I view the world. It has also driven in me a commitment to be better, particularly when it comes to issues of diversity and inclusion.

Though I have ancestors who fought on both sides of the Civil War (including my great-great-uncle John Buford), I grew up steeped in the glory of the Lost Cause. My paternal grandmother was a member of the United Daughters of the Confederacy, as was her mother and her mother's mother (who'd lived through the war and Reconstruction). My father was a member of the Kappa Alpha fraternity, who, through at least the 1980s, were still taking official photos in Confederate uniforms, with swords in hand, in front of the battle flag. In my adolescent years in the 1970s and 1980s, the Confederate battle flag flew over the state capitol buildings of South Carolina and Alabama and was officially part of the state flags of Georgia and Mississippi. In all cases, I thought, "How cool, they're honoring our heritage." It was not much later I learned how those flags were used in direct reaction to any number of events in the African American freedom struggle. This was an example of history being abused in the service of a political narrative. And it offended my sensibilities.

Fast-forward to 1990, when in an undergraduate History of the Old South class, Shirley Leckie (later my master's thesis advisor) declared, "Make no mistake about it, the Civil War was about slavery." Reared in the states' rights arguments of the Lost Cause, I bristled but did not challenge her. I already understood that slavery was an important cause of the war, but its primacy had remained secondary in my mind's eye. Thirty years later, Dr. Leckie's words, and my initial response, still challenge me.

In 1997, I took my first graduate class in history: the History of the New South with Kari Frederickson. The semester was among one of the most profound learning experiences of my life. Frederickson's class made abundantly clear to me something I had theretofore been able to ignore: Black people in the American South did not have the same opportunities that I had growing up and they were often terrorized when they tried to get them. I could no longer ignore that the system was fundamentally stacked against African Americans, and that I had benefited from that in ways great and small.

Dr. Frederickson's class also introduced me to the concept of the Lost Cause Mythology and sparked my nascent understanding of the effects/impacts of systemic racism and discrimination. I realized quickly I'd been duped by the stories of the glory of the Old South, and I have spent a significant part of the last two-plus decades unpacking this and building a new understanding.

It helped me realize I want to be the kind of ancestor who not only acknowledges historical wrongs but also actively works to address them.

There are multiple sides to this. One is obvious: a commitment to doing the work. If you're reading this book, you're engaged in it already. And whether or not you actively embrace the radical trust inherent in shared authority, our world is changing and will continue to change. While it's an important first step to acknowledge the role the complexities of the past play in our lives today, our communities demand we do more than just note how history favored some at the expense of others. Our staff and colleagues deserve that same respect.

Over the years, I've noticed this is one place the discussion often gets stuck. "Where does one's personal responsibility begin and end?" I've struggled with this question my entire adult life.

I first heard the term *White privilege* in a 2000 workshop of the National Conference of Community and Justice (NCCJ). I can't remember exactly how they posed the definition, but this was my main takeaway: I was privileged because my skin color did not necessarily place barriers on me the way skin color does for people of color. Likewise, I enjoyed privilege as a straight, White, middle-class, Christian male.

Acknowledging that I have privilege as a White man doesn't mean I haven't gone through hardships, nor did it condemn me for reaching the level of success I had at that point. All I know is this: my chances for success were as preordained as they could be. I grew up in a household with two parents who each had college degrees. My father was an attorney. I have never gone hungry of anything but my own accord. I lived in a nice neighborhood of well-manicured lawns and went to great public schools. I matriculated to college with a full-ride academic scholarship, despite my relatively minimal academic achievements. (In fact, it was until my younger siblings didn't finish or go to college that I realized I had a choice not to go to college.) At age thirteen and continuing for much of his life, my younger brother Brian was in and out of trouble with the law, but he only spent a night or two in jail at most.

These factors offered me advantages that others didn't necessarily have. Yes, I took advantage of opportunities. But I also acknowledge that I had some of those opportunities because of who I was, not necessarily because of what I'd accomplished to that point. That 2000 NCCJ workshop, and the two three-day Building an Inclusive Community workshops altered the course of my life. They provided me a way to reconsider who I am in the world and how I got there, and they framed for me a new understanding going forward. In short, to be a good ancestor and fight against historical injustice required me to rethink my world considerably. No, I wasn't "Born on third base and thought I hit a triple," but I did have a ticket to the game. And thus, I had access to opportunity that others did not.

So let me say that again for the people in the back: White privilege doesn't *necessarily* mean I had it easy. And it doesn't mean you did either. It just means that we didn't have to struggle *because of* our race/ethnicity, gender, sexual orientation, or ability/disability.

I need to say right now that I have failed mightily in these endeavors over the years. I'm sure there are people reading this whom I've hurt with any manner of careless talk, microaggressions, and simple ignorance. I regret those instances, both the ones I know about and, especially, the ones I don't. I cannot go relive my own past, the times I've sat on the sidelines or squashed another's ideas or opportunities. I can, however, resolve to do and to be better.

Resolving to do and be better, that's the kind of ancestor I want to be.

What does this look like inside the structures of power that we, as museum leaders, control? How can we be better? It starts with acknowledging the important role diversity plays in American communities. As Patricia Williams Lessane writes, "We need to begin from the standpoint that diversity is an American legacy and boldly proclaim it as our birthright. We are who we are because of the varied cultural and religious traditions and historical moments—good and bad—that have shaped American history and thus our collective identity. By embracing the premise that our collective history is storied, complex, colorful, inspiring, and yes, sometimes ugly and difficult to accept, we free ourselves from the albatross of race, and thus empower ourselves to see ourselves and the world through new eyes."[5]

Embracing diversity as an American legacy and boldly proclaiming it as our birthright. That's the kind of ancestor I want to be.

But diversity is just a passive pursuit. To me it means some acknowledgment of a wide variety of opinions, audiences, and such. It takes two forms in museum practice. The first is the most obvious, in terms of the people/places/things that an institution represents or interprets. Historically, American museums have been very top down, focusing on a monied group of people, traditionally White and protestant.

The second is in a museum's audience. The New Social History of the 1960s had a great impact on this in diversifying the stories and voices that museums told. This has been on the radar of the profession for the past fifty years and has included efforts to engage/interpret more women, communities of color, the LGBT community, and the disabled, among others.

This is a good thing—a very good thing—for two reasons:

1. It's the right thing to do.
2. It helps museums be more engaging in their communities.

Our colleagues and our stakeholders have told us, repeatedly, that this is not enough. I've had more discussions than I care to about this, and while I love a good philosophical argument as much as anyone (and I've spent a significant part of my life and no small amount of tuition) honing my skills in this arena, talk is just that. I'm more action oriented when it comes to our work.

Issues of diversity and inclusion are again at the forefront in American discourse right now. I'm not a futurist, but I really do think we are at a tipping point of sorts. It's time those of us in museums act proactively when it comes to inclusion and representation in our institutions.

In *An American Association for State and Local History Guide to Making Public History* (2017), I wrote how Chris Taylor, this book's coeditor, forever altered my thinking, when he helped me realized that my pursuit of diversity was not enough. Diversity, he wrote, "'tends to be more about the number of programs aimed at diverse audiences and the number of diverse attendees to our programs.' This often gives institutions and history professionals cover for a field that is a vast majority White and whose exhibitions, programs, and activities have often skewed toward that demographic as well."[6]

Thus enters inclusion into the vernacular. Inclusion takes diversity a step further and seeks to actively engage people in museum initiatives—programs, exhibits, collections initiatives, staffing, volunteering, whatever. Inclusion is where American museums and history organizations have a pretty dreadful track record.

From my vantage point, what underpins all of this work is the gaping, festering wound of systemic racism and discrimination. Looking beyond just the current moment and the protests that have arisen out of the killing of Black people at the hands of the police (a very real, important issue), it's reflected in the fact that the vast majority of our visitors are White, and people of color are way underrepresented, not only in our staff but also in leadership roles.

If you are a leader and the latter fact gives you pause, think about your own team. Where are your Black, Indigenous, and People of Color (BIPOC) staff working? From my admittedly anecdotal perspective, if I see non-White staff members at a museum, they are often in customer service, custodial, and security roles. I have noticed the same thing when I meet with senior leadership teams.

In short, *we have to do better* in terms of a more diverse racial/ethnic representation in our museums. Our audiences and staffs simply do not reflect the multiculturalism of American society today. Working to solve this is our job. It's not only the right thing to do but it is also a matter of survival.

Inclusion is active. It means it is incumbent upon us to reach out and actively seek to make connections, to make people feel more a part of the work we are doing. Ultimately, as Taylor notes, inclusion signifies "feeling safe, engaged, respected, and valued."[7]

We are going to differ in how this plays out. Not every answer is right—nor is there a right answer to every question. But if history has taught us anything, it's that change is rarely smooth nor linear.

What does action oriented look like? There are lots of examples peppered throughout this book. I find examples and inspiration on social media (if you can believe that), in blog posts, in podcasts, and in documentaries.

One thing I've found is to be sincere and humble in your approach. Seek to be actively inclusive. And to be intentional. My own experiences tell me you will encounter struggles. You will have some missteps (individually and institutionally), but the payoff is worth the effort. You are helping to model a more just world, and you're using history and museums to do so. I can think of few more noble causes!

I want to make very clear that while I believe the lack of representation and the physical assaults against BIPOC communities make racial and ethnic inclusion a matter of vital importance, we must also pursue diversity and inclusion with issues of gender, sexuality, and (dis)ability. It's not an either/or. We must continually strive to be inclusive in the voices we include, in the talent we nurture, and in the stories we tell. Our job is to be responsive to our communities, and this is what they're asking for.

The issue is one of intentionality. We don't "do" diversity and inclusion for the under-engaged or underrepresented folks only for their benefit—we do it because it's most true to the field in which we work. I get just as much in an exhibit on an immigrant community, a program on women's history, or a book on African American art as a person directly from those communities.

It's important to engage members of the community and build rapport. You have to start slowly—there's a lot of well-placed mistrust in the type of institutions we represent. So you can't just come in and say, "Hi, I represent the museum! It's a new day and we're here to serve you!" They've heard that line before, as has your staff. It rings hollow without some action.

If pressed, and if they trust you, people of color will tell you they often not only feel uncomfortable in our institutions but also feel they're unwelcome. And this includes the classroom, professional associations, and the like. It is our job to fix that.

Trust is the operative word here. I have found that people are looking for you to be authentic in your interactions. And that's going to take some time and the reaction to your actions is out of your control entirely. But it's no reason to quit trying.

Ultimately, the work of history organizations and museums is built on trust. Trust is a somewhat nebulous, "I'll know it when I see it" construct. It is up to us to earn the trust of our colleagues, staff members, and our stakeholders. And we do so by being deliberately authentic, a term I use deliberately because of its many meanings in our work.

I want to be the kind of ancestor who is authentic in my interactions with others.

This isn't easy work. It involves self-reflection and self-criticism. It means changing the structures we are a part of and the systems we've carefully learned how to navigate.

Many leaders reading this have reached a certain level of success. We have carefully honed tried-and-true strategies to navigate the world around us, to lead the organizations and our teams and colleagues toward some goal in the future.

We know what works, or we think we do. But we only really know what works for us. Sure, we've been successful with it and we do have a responsibility as leaders to responsibly steward whatever we've been entrusted to care for, but that should not preclude us from being inclusive in our work.

In preparation for this chapter, I asked a number of colleagues to share thoughts about inclusive leadership. Responses varied, which is natural. But as I looked at them in toto, a couple of things stood out.

"Want to be better?" someone replied. "First, stop interrupting. Then, actually *listen*"—rather than just "hearing" what someone says. When a person of color, a woman, or someone from an identity group you do not belong to highlights structural barriers to inclusion, listen to them and work to fix it.

Shift your thinking on inclusion from a view of managing people (getting them to do something) to leading (inspiring others toward a shared vision). We can do neither if we're not inclusive.

As a leader, you must prioritize inclusion. If we truly acknowledge that history itself is inherently inclusive, I believe our personal leadership needs to reflect this principle within our organizations as well. Use your privilege to this end, in the staff you hire, in the people you mentor, in the partnerships you make and manage, and in the stories you seek and tell.

Question your own assumptions about hierarchy and how you lead. Demonstrate your commitment to inclusion in your acknowledgment that some people don't move as easily in traditional hierarchies and in creating structures where they feel included and valued. "We need to be mindful of not only creating a diverse workplace, but an equitable and supportive one as well," Joan Baldwin wrote in October 2020. "Inviting someone to the table isn't enough. Sometimes the rules are mysterious, opaque, and strange. We owe it to every creative, diverse soul who works with us to offer them the support and the path . . . to navigate the museum world."[8]

Critically examine the power dynamics at your organization. Look beyond the obvious when you are thinking about who to empower and who is ready to lead. Create leadership opportunities at all levels.

Consider this hypothetical from a colleague shared with me:

> If you are a White male leader of a nonprofit in 2020, you likely did not work as hard to get that job as your Black female receptionist worked to get hers. Are you offended? Stop for a moment. Sure, you worked hard, and you have accomplishments. You got your PhD. You are very smart. You run your organization well; your board respects you. And some part of all of that is you, yourself, your very own work. But some of it is the privilege you were born with. The expectation that you are smart enough, good enough, educated enough. The job was, likely, at least in part, yours to lose. And, all in all, you are still doing a good job. But I am asking you to be mindful that the women, people of color, and even just the young people in this day and age did not come into the workforce with the expectation that they would succeed. And many are just as smart as you are, just younger, or less advantaged. And perhaps even more important, some day one of them will, or rather should, run your organization.[9]

Remember that your privilege, and my privilege, is a fact of life to other people who don't have it. If any of the above stings a little bit, it should. This is a reality for those around us, one many of us do not see unless we look for it. That's the very definition of privilege. Arguing it doesn't exist is inauthentic.

Recognize your defensiveness and keep it in check. Instead, ask yourself, what, if anything, are you doing to ensure the next generation of museum professionals and visitors have opportunities for success?

Again, this is not easy work. When you reach a certain level of the hierarchy, you are less and less likely to hear criticism, particularly constructive criticism. Remember, just because you can't see something doesn't mean it's false. Please don't insulate yourself in an echo chamber. Seek outside voices and test them against your assumptions. Start from a position of trust, believing that the people sharing their insights with you are offering them to you out of a genuine desire to make you or your organization better.

I want to be the kind of ancestor who is inclusive in my work as a leader.

The year 2020 is no doubt a truly significant year in American history. The COVID-19 pandemic, the racial turmoil and unrest resulting from a bevy of police shootings of innocent African Americans, or the rancor of the presidential election has dominated our lives and the headlines. More than anything, it has highlighted the systemic inequalities in American life.

Historian John Hennessey recently challenged us all when he wrote about the role of the National Park Service (NPS) in social change in October 2020. He writes,

> For long stretches, America behaved as though it had a single, universal history, whose virtues the NPS faithfully emphasized and promoted. As political power has dispersed throughout our society, so have the demand that both academic historians and public historians . . . recognize aspects of the American story long overlooked, or even purposely forgotten. This is not political correctness. This is historical justice within a society built on the concept of equality and justice.[10]

I want to be an ancestor who actively works toward historical justice in a society founded on the concepts of equality and justice.

What is our response to this? I'd say it's a commitment—as individuals, as leaders, as a field, and as citizens—to inclusion. It is in our DNA. Let 2020 also be the year you commit fully to inclusion.

Here's what this looks like for me. I was deeply moved as people took to the streets in protest after a White Minneapolis police officer knelt on the neck of George Floyd, ultimately strangling him to death. I had a firsthand look at how my Black friends and colleagues reacted to Floyd's murder. It came on the heels of Breonna Taylor's death at the hands of police in Louisville, Kentucky, and the murder of jogger Ahmaud Aubrey by White supremacists in Georgia. My friends were troubled, they were scared, they were hurt, and they were angry. I just felt powerless.

The protests were both exciting and scary. I'm not a fan of destruction of property, but I understand property can be replaced, human lives cannot. People were expressing their frustration with a political and social system I am a product of. Protest is dirty and messy, and it can be destructive. It gives voice to the oppressed and forces us to listen to the cries of those suffering under the stultifying conditions of systemic racism and discrimination.

History is a long-game pursuit, that we won't truly know what any of this means for museums (or our communities) for a long time. What we did learn was that museums aren't first responders in moments like this. And this is where inclusion comes in. Throughout summer 2020, my African American colleagues, friends, and neighbors asked that I not speak on their behalf but to instead listen carefully and to amplify their voices. Your BIPOC colleagues are saying the same to you.

I took that message to heart, as I've also considered how the field might consider in deeper detail some of the lessons being shared and put them into action. In early spring, Vedet Coleman-Robinson, executive director of the Association of African American Museums, sent a message that provided me a road map in the moment, through today. These are good lessons for us all. Museums should continue doing what we do best, she wrote. They should:

- Advocate for those whose voices can no longer be heard.
- Commemorate the stories and legacies of our people.
- Denounce racism and racist ideas.
- Provide safe spaces for social activism.
- Teach lessons of the past to move the needle forward.[11]

I hope Coleman-Robinson's words ring as true for you as they do for me. These five points are simple, but they are profound. Read just the first words—advocate, commemorate, denounce, provide, teach. They are all verbs, action words. They provide for us a road map forward, if we'd only first listen.

Finally, I ask anyone reading this to make a personal commitment against racism and systemic oppression. Here is mine.

In my life and my work I will do the following:

1. Respectfully and proactively seek to better understand the experiences of BIPOC and other people who do not look or act like me.
2. Listen and hold space for the voices and perspectives of BIPOC and others who have been traditionally excluded from the corridors of power in my professional and personal spheres.
3. Carry and advocate for the experience of BIPOC and other marginalized communities of people in my job, civic life, and within my family (immediate and extended).[12]

I do not make these statements casually. They offer specific ways I can build on my commitment to love my neighbor. If I've learned anything about goals, it's that I must regularly check my progress toward them. I must be accountable to myself, and to others. I didn't write this chapter in a vacuum. I asked a number of my colleagues for their insights to ensure that the general gist of what I wrote reflects not just my own needs but also theirs. I have maintained a relationship with a White male colleague who, over the past twenty years, has served to check me on any number of issues regarding the intersections of history, race, and the present day. These same tools are available to you, too. They are not as useful if unused.

I want to be the kind of ancestor whose life and work reflects a personal commitment against racism and systemic oppression. What kind of ancestor will you be?

Written for my beautiful daughters Ryan and Tyler Beatty, may you live in a world better than the one you have inherited from me. "May you stay forever young."

Figure 26.1 Bob, Tyler, Candy, and Ryan Beatty in St. Augustine 2019. Source: Bob Beatty

Notes

1. Many thanks to Richard Josey of Collective Journeys for introducing me to this phrase, as well as his read of this draft. I am grateful for you, my brother!
2. The song inspired a playlist I made for Ryan as she went off to college; it's here if you're interested: http://bit.ly/RyanAnneForeverYoung.
3. Lee, *To Kill a Mockingbird*, 30.
4. Bok Tower Gardens, "Our History," accessed March 13, 2021, https://boktowergardens.org/our-history/.
5. Patricia Williams Lessane, "Seeking Diversity: Response," in *Zen and the Art of Local History,* ed. Carol Kammen and Bob Beatty (Lanham, MD: Rowman & Littlefield, 2014), 154.
6. Bob Beatty, *An American Association for State and Local History Guide to Making Public History* (Lanham, MD: Rowman & Littlefield, 2017), 207.
7. Beatty, *An American Association for State and Local History Guide,* 209.
8. Joan Baldwin, "Diversity without Intersectionality Is a Cart without a Horse," Leadership Matters, October 12, 2020, https://leadershipmatters1213.wordpress.com/2020/10/12/diversity-without-inter sectionality-is-a-cart-without-a-horse/.
9. Anonymous, Interview by author, Nashville, November 2020.
10. John Hennessey, "What Role Should NPS Historians Play in the Process of Social Change?" Remember-ing, October 20, 2020, https://fredericksburghistory.wordpress.com/2020/10/20/what-role-should -nps-historians-play-in-the-process-of-social-change/amp/.
11. Vedet Coleman-Robinson, "Executive Director's Corner: AAAM Continues to Stand in the Face of Social Injustice and Police Brutality," Association of African American Museums, April 1, 2020, https://black museums.org/a-special-message-to-aaam-members-and-supporters/.
12. Thanks to Salvador Acevedo for providing these phrases.

Bibliography

Baldwin, Joan. "Diversity without Intersectionality Is a Cart without a Horse." Leadership Matters, October 12, 2020. https://leadershipmatters1213.wordpress.com/2020/10/12/diversity-without-intersectionality-is-a-cart-without-a-horse/.

Beatty, Bob. *An American Association for State and Local History Guide to Making Public History.* Lanham, MD: Rowman & Littlefield, 2017.

Bok Tower Gardens. "Our History." Accessed March 13, 2021, https://boktowergardens.org/our-history/.

Coleman-Robinson, Vedet. "Executive Director's Corner: AAAM Continues to Stand in the Face of Social Injustice and Police Brutality." Association of African American Museums, April 1, 2020. https://blackmuseums.org/a-special-message-to-aaam-members-and-supporters/.

Hennessey, John. "What Role Should NPS Historians Play in the Process of Social Change?" Remembering, October 20, 2020. https://fredericksburghistory.wordpress.com/2020/10/20/what-role-should-nps-historians-play-in-the-process-of-social-change/amp/.

Lee, Harper. *To Kill a Mockingbird.* New York: McIntosh & Otis, 1988.

Lessane, Patricia Williams. "Seeking Diversity, Response." In *Zen and the Art of Local History,* edited by Carol Kammen and Bob Beatty, 152–54. Lanham, MD: Rowman & Littlefield, 2014.

Chapter 27

Stepping Out to Step In

A Conversation with nikhil trivedi

Currently working as the director of engineering at the Art Institute of Chicago, nikhil is an important voice for equity and liberation in museum spaces. His writing, "Oppression: A Museum Primer,"[1] is essential reading for college students as well as the established museum leader. This conversation was recorded in October 2020.

nikhil trivedi: I kind of ended up in museums. I wasn't a person who grew up with a strong connection to museums or ever really felt like they were a place for me as an adult. I think I probably went to field trips to museums when I was a kid, but I honestly don't remember. After high school, I got a job for the company that makes Beanie Babies, Ty. I did graphic design for them when they were getting started, and I was able to learn how to make a website while I made theirs. After working for Ty, I had my own web company while going to college, followed by a stint with a telecom company. Since I didn't pursue art in school, I started looking at jobs at the Art Institute of Chicago because I heard that you can take classes for free. I started with a temporary position fifteen years ago and I'm still here. That's why I'm working in a museum. It wasn't because of the mission or because of a long-time fondness of them.

Cinnamon Catlin-Legutko: With your perspective and life experience, what does inclusive museum leadership look like in action?

nikhil: *Inclusion* isn't the word that resonates with me most around this work. I'm not fighting as hard as I am and working as hard as I am for inclusion. Inclusion is great and I think it's important. But that's not my ultimate vision. What resonates with me more are words like *justice*. And *decolonization*, which is a concept that I'm just beginning to understand. *Justice* is the word that drives me. Inclusion is certainly one small part of it, but it's not the whole picture. I think we've limited our ability to dream big, to see the whole picture, to see the whole landscape of how hundreds of years of oppression have affected the people we interact with every day, when we just focus on only inclusion.

When in practice, inclusion as well as justice ultimately comes down to a recognition and an analysis of power. Each of us holds power whether we're formally designated that power by job title, or whether we just kind of happened to inherit it. For myself, being a man, I didn't choose male supremacy, but I certainly benefit from it. I think inclusion and justice begin with an analysis of power within our interpersonal relationships, within the organizations that we're a part of, and a critical analysis of where power lies, where should it lie, where doesn't it lie, and the recalibration of power. How we analyze one-on-one conversations, is different from how we analyze the structures of our organizations and funding—everything.

Chris Taylor: When we think about leadership, it inherently has power, if one chooses to accept it. So what would a just, or an inclusive leader look like? What kind of environment would this leader create?

nikhil: Leaders have power, period. Whether they choose to acknowledge it, whether they choose to use it, even if they actively don't use their power, they have power. Acknowledging and understanding that is important. But I want to clarify—designated leaders are given power.

But leadership can develop in different ways. There's people who are given roles that give them power, and there's people who, in many ways like myself, build their own power by just building relationships, connections, and community around them. For me, I worked as a web developer for eleven of my fifteen years in my museum. But I hadn't supervised anybody. I don't have budget responsibility. I was a one-staff person, doing a solo job at my museum. It was really siloed and hierarchical. I only talked to maybe ten people in my work over the course of an entire year, in a five-hundred-person organization. It was isolating.

The power that I built for myself started when I decided to go through the company directory and e-mail people and ask them if they want to have coffee. I just wanted to meet people. Slowly over time I ended up building a larger network of people around me. That network grew and grew with the various projects that were formally part of my formal work, as well as projects that became part of the justice-centered work that I'm doing at my museum. But what does leadership look like?

Leadership looks like a lot of listening. I see a lot of leaders around me that talk much more than they listen. Even when they do listen, they are hearing but not listening. I think listening is a skill that takes a lot of patience and practice to be able to do it well.

I think an inclusive leader is a good listener. I think compassion and vulnerability are important aspects to inclusive leadership, and we need to be able to empathize with what the people around us are struggling with. We need to be able to create time and space for the people around us to feel the benign nature of everyday work, as well as the harsh realities that we live with every day.

Equally important, we need leaders to be vulnerable and to create space for vulnerability; it is one of the most important factors for building trust. Trust is often missing in many organizations inside the museum sector, as well as outside of it. We also see a lack of trust in groups of people and families.

Cinnamon: You're connecting with many of the themes that are threaded throughout this book, and I'd like to pull a thread a little bit more. What does it look like to be vulnerable when you are in a hierarchy? When you are, let's say, a supervisor with direct reports, what level of vulnerability are you seeking? Is it a baring of emotions or is it just an acknowledgment that you don't know? I think there's this interesting line we walk as leaders about how much we can share of ourselves.

nikhil: That's a hard question to really get at . . . there's certain things that I wouldn't share with the people I supervise. I now supervise staff members and, say, if I was really struggling with writing performance evaluations because of my workload, or maybe I'm emotionally and mentally not in a space to fill out a bunch of performance evaluations while the world is crumbling around me. That's not something that I would share with the people I supervise. It's not an opportunity for vulnerability that I would take. But there are a lot of opportunities where we can find common space.

For example, with the pandemic and the racial uprisings, plus the economic collapse and all the things that we're experiencing in the world right now, these are certainly areas that are real and alive for us. People bring that hurt with them to work; sharing your feelings really demonstrates vulnerability but also supports how they feel. Just share how you're feeling in the moment. Maybe you've read an article before you started work and you're feeling really anxious and scared about the future. It's OK to say that, because likely the people you're talking to are feeling the same way. We don't have to be emotionless in order to maintain order. That's not what I'm looking for, as a leader and as someone who's led by others. Emotional vulnerability is one piece of it.

Another piece I wanted to share is transparency. Being transparent about processes and how things work is something I talk about with people. Within the museum sector, I see a pattern that's developed over 150 years of museum operations. We work on something for years and years and years until it is perfect. Then we'll release it and make it available only then. We don't really know how to share our process, and that exclusion seeps into everything our organizations do. As leaders we can push against that pattern and be transparent in our processes. We can reveal the ways we stumble while getting to a goal, and we can be radically honest about things we tried that didn't go well. That's a form of vulnerability, too, and we need to see more of it.

Chris: I'd love to hear you talk about working within a large institution to promote justice and to promote inclusive thinking to make sure they become regular practice. How do you do that? How have you worked to make that shift within a large institution?

nikhil: I feel like looking back there's probably a lot of steps to it. Some of which I am grateful for and have control over, some of which I just simply don't. I think one important step is relationship building, and building close relationships with as many people, across the entire organization, and across positions of power, across gender, class, all the identities that divide us. Building a network of relationships across difference, as wide and as varied as we can.

But there is this weird Midwestern dynamic where you don't really get legitimacy until you go out somewhere and come back. For example, many artists in Chicago move to one of the coasts because they hit a limit for how much they can actually do here in the city. When they come back, they've got everyone's attention even though nothing's really changed in their practice. For me, I started doing a lot of writing and speaking outside of my museum and building a name for myself. I was building myself outside of my organization. Once people started hearing about the work I was doing outside the organization from within the organization, there was more of an awareness of who I am and a better understanding of what I was saying.

Sharing my point of view and experience was possible through the combination of those two things—building relationships and creating space where people can listen to each other and be heard. I felt like I was only talking to ten people a year and then sending an e-mail to my director saying we need do all this stuff, but there's no context and no relationship to where my concerns and ideas were coming from. So, I ended up building this name for myself outside the organization to build relationships within the organization. Then there was context to what I was communicating and it carried a little more weight. People were more willing to hear me out.

Cinnamon: I think it's equally interesting and upsetting that you had to step out to step in. But I think there's something about being decisive about stepping out—what compelled you to do that? What was it within you to speak on a stage about these issues, and to speak to groups of people about what you're seeing and what you're concerned about?

nikhil: I want to recognize that the way that I engage with people has a big role to play in my decisions. My ability to connect with other people and be heard plays a part, too. I feel like I'm able to meet people where they're at, and I demonstrate this in my communication. I'm able to articulate my message in a way that I feel will more easily resonate with people rather than defining a brand for myself and always talking about my brand. By listening, I'm able to understand the other person's position and frame of mind. And in return, I can better articulate the things that I'm trying to say to them, by meeting them where they already are.

In thinking about stepping out and what compelled me to do that, I've always been a person who needs to be part of a community. I'm a Leo, and I really identify with lions as animals that always live in a community. I didn't realize that I was isolated at work for a long time; it was really hard. I thrive when embedded in community. What ultimately compelled me to step out and speak out was my desire to find people. Then Twitter happened, and I was able to connect with other like-minded folx on Twitter, thanks to the work of people like Aleia Brown and Adrianne Russell who founded the #MuseumsRespondtoFerguson movement. I was also regularly participating in museum technology conferences, like Museum Computer Network (MCN), which allowed me to build more relationships.

Building connections for myself outside of my organization on those other platforms in other spaces was filling me up while I was struggling to make connections at work. After a few years of connecting online with people and building the community of people around me at MCN, I was attending an MCN session where Dr. Porchia Moore[2] was speaking on her doctoral research on the visitation patterns of people of color. She found that for a large number of people of color she interviewed, they haven't visited the museum in five years. That was significantly larger than the period of time for White folx who had visited museums. I was in the audience for her presentation. That was the first time we met.

During the talk back, and while questions were being asked, one of the big issues that was nagging me about the conversation was that it was really obvious to me why people of color weren't visiting museums. I'm a person of color; I've had experiences and thoughts of my own. Plus, I had worked at a museum for quite a period of time at that point. To me, it was clear that there's a connection between colonialism, genocide, and slavery, and the reasons why people of color and my people don't go to museums. That just wasn't part of the conversation. At this time I was still new to the museum community, and still new in my career, but I felt like I just needed to say something. So I shyly raised my hand and said something like "we need to name the reasons why our institutions exist and the reasons why people of color don't visit them. Many of those reasons are the same—genocide, slavery, colonialism, and war." Porchia was silently cheering me on from the stage. I think that resonated with other people.

A year later I gave an Ignite[3] talk that folx have seen online; it's a six-minute talk where I share my thinking around an anti-oppression framework for museums and what that could look like. After giving that talk, I started connecting with many more people who were interested in hearing more of what I had to say. I then started writing more, and Porchia and I started the Visitors of Color project.[4] At some point, our posts started reaching my colleagues at the museum. I think some folx who saw my name were like, "Doesn't he work here?" By that point, I'd already been working in a museum for ten years. It was a long haul.

Cinnamon: I appreciate this conversation around building community and what it takes to do it. As you embed yourself more and more in this work and live and breathe it, you have to have community to sustain you as the pressures make it difficult to fight your way back.

Chris: Agreed. I had a similar experience working at the Minnesota Historical Society where I had to work outside of the museum to build my reputation and then all of a sudden people are like, "Oh, he works here? He could do some of this work here!" For you, how did that shift things for you at work? Did you feel like it was genuine on the part of the institution, or do you feel like it was opportunistic? How did that unfold for you at work?

nikhil: I think the opportunistic pattern for leaders is probably deeply connected to White supremacy culture. I don't really fault White leaders for defaulting to opportunism. That's how they operate, and it takes really active attention to think an alternate way. In my museum, we've been led by a new director for the past five years who came to the museum with the specific intention to address equity in ways that the museum hasn't before. I think leadership, in general, had an openness to the perspective that I was bringing. I think it was also genuine.

But a few things started happening. Once my reputation outside of the museum started coming back to the museum, it opened up lines of communication between me and folx in leadership. In some ways, I created these lines because our deputy director saw one of my posts. It gave me an opportunity to talk to her. This also coincided with the second year of the MASS Action project,[5] which was the year when museum people were invited to attend and learn about the toolkit and develop plans for change at their organizations. The alignment of these two things was serendipitous; I used this opening to talk to leadership and present the MASS Action project to them. A lot of folx hadn't heard of the project before, or maybe they had heard of it but weren't really in touch with what was happening with the project. I sent out a few e-mails to a few leaders I had started connecting with across the organization. This led to a fifteen-minute conversation with the deputy director, where I gave her a postcard about the convening, told her about my involvement, and shared that I would love for our organization to be represented there. We ended up sending six people. This turned into a series of reading groups that built a base within the staff. We reached 150 people walking through the Mass Action toolkit chapter by chapter.

It's helped others who, like me, lacked connection with other people in the museum. Because with these reading groups, one of the basic things we were able to do was simply allow people to talk to each other. It was a bonus that they were talking to each other about social justice issues. I think at the core, we were creating space for people to talk to each other in an environment that lacked opportunities for this. That project ended up building a much larger community, a much larger base of people who now had a common language. A space to start thinking about transformation and change and what that could look like. The connectedness of folx across the organization was critical because there was only so much I would be able to do alone, sitting at my desk and chair.

Having a few hundred people at the organization who are now connected with each other, who know each other and know of each other, creates a richer opportunity for change. Leadership was interested in change. A year or two into our staff engagement around MASS Action, leadership started bringing in equity consultants to take stock of the equity projects underway at the museum. Over the course of a year, they did an organizational cultural assessment, as well as a series of two-day trainings that reached three hundred staff across the museum. Many of the staff were already part of the MASS Action project; many more weren't. The consultants helped us plan how this work can move forward at the museum and in a sustainable, ongoing way. We constructed four working groups that comprised of 140 people. When the groups launched in December 2019, they had a direct line of communication with leadership, and it was sanctioned by leadership and given authority.

MASS Action was a grassroots project at the Art Institute, building power from the ground up while leadership was creating these structures and mechanisms for transformative work to move forward. I don't think either initiative could have taken off and made change alone. Coming back to your initial question, Chris, about if my experience over the past few years with my colleagues was genuine or opportunistic, I think it was genuine. I don't think leadership's efforts could have succeeded if there wasn't already a massive group of people across our organization already invested in moving this work forward. I think it's a good moment for my organization where change is happening at all levels, and I don't think it's an accident. I think it's just taken a lot of hard work, like an exhausting amount of hard work. It's no accident.

When I think of these two parallels, I think of the movie *Selma* a lot. I feel like that movie showed us two forces in action: Martin Luther King Jr. and the huge movement he was creating and Lyndon B. Johnson and the changes he was trying to make happen at the government level. Both of those two things needed to be happening at the same time. If it wasn't clear that there was a huge groundswell of people demanding it, Lyndon B. Johnson, or anyone in his position, wouldn't have been willing or able to get buy-in to create transformative policy. When people are demanding change, they have a really hard time if leadership isn't ready to listen and to enact those changes. That's when leadership gets removed and replaced with folx who are willing to make those changes. Those two things need to exist, and then happen at the same time for change to quickly move forward.

Cinnamon: I want to flip the example a little bit and ask you, do you think there's the same opportunity for equity to move forward if it starts at the leadership level first, and it takes a while for the rest of the staff to react?

nikhil: It's like a chicken or egg question. Should the grassroots come first or should leadership's intentions come first? I think it probably depends on the organization. I think there's a lot of organizations where an equity leadership initiative is met with a lot of skepticism, but that doesn't mean it shouldn't happen. If it's an environment where that grassroots work hasn't taken shape yet, I don't think that means that leadership shouldn't do anything. It just means it'll take a lot of time and it'll just take much longer. That's time that needs to happen. I think leadership should still be transparent, should still communicate, and it should still be honest about their intentions—about where they're at and their thinking—as imperfect as it likely will be. It is going to be messy, and it's going to take a lot of time, but it needs to happen. Equity needs to move forward.

Chris: You speak directly about the incredible amount of hard work and emotional work this requires, and that takes a toll on a person. I think there's often times when we want to step back, but we can't. How are you taking care of yourself, feeding yourself, while you are leading these initiatives?

nikhil: I haven't been perfect at self-care. I think it's hard for anyone to be, and I'm not going to be hard on myself about that. But I'm an emotionally open person. I let myself cry in front of other people; I don't hold that back. Being open helps, and therapy helps. I'm a big advocate for therapy for all people at all levels. It's a space that I appreciate. I've done different forms of therapy from one-on-one therapy with a formally trained provider to engaging with peer counseling communities. Therapy has been really amazing in its own way. Therapy can look a lot of different ways. I'm a big advocate for creating space for that in your life. It doesn't have to be expensive either.

I really enjoy having fun and creating fun in any space that I'm in, and I don't want to wait until I'm done with the work to have fun. Even if it's telling corny jokes before a Zoom meeting kicks off or playing with virtual backgrounds. Finding fun in any moment is something that I try to do. I'm also a musician, and I play music as much as I can. During the pandemic, I've turned to cooking a lot. Working from home has given me an extra two hours of my day to just be home. That's been really therapeutic in its own way.

Programming and software development is eight hours of problem solving. I like digging in, taking things apart, and putting them back together over and over and over again. That's what the work of software development is. And cooking feels like that process, too. I've used this pandemic as an opportunity to learn how to cook the foods of my ancestors. I've tried to do this a few different times in my life, and for some reason during this pandemic it has just sort of taken hold more than it has in the past.

Cinnamon: I want to ask a futuristic question that is also situated in where we're at right now. What's your hope for the next ten to twelve years in the museum industry? Are we threatened to lose our place in society? Is there's something different down the road? What's your hope?

nikhil: Should museums exist? When we think about keeping our place in society, should we even have a place? That question probably has a different answer for different organizations. Over the next ten years, I think there will continue to be a reevaluation of the plight of our institutions. An institution by its definition is a socially agreed upon solution to a problem. If the conditions of those problems have changed, should the institution still exist? Perhaps at their inception, museums were places to preserve ideas. We do this by caring for objects that represent ideas and human accomplishments. Today, is that still a problem that museums need to solve? We give a lot of importance to physical objects, but at their heart, museums collect stories and ideas. There's a lot of different ways that that could happen.

I think the vehicle by which we've been doing museum work for the past 150 years might not be the same vehicle we need today. It makes me sad to think about museums closing. It makes me sad to think about workers losing the institutions that they have dedicated decades of their lives to. I'm not really sure how to reconcile these two ideas that I hold in my head. But I'm not sure if museums should hold their place in society anymore.

I resonate with the word *abolition* when it comes to museums. I think the abolition of museums isn't about shutting it all down. It's about taking a critical analysis of the needs that museums meet and creating the space for those needs to be met in a myriad of ways, not just the one that we figured out so far.

Notes

1. nikhil trivedi, "Oppression: A Museum Primer," *The Incluseum* (blog), February 4, 2015, https://incluseum.com/2015/02/04/oppression-a-museum-primer/?blogsub=confirming#blog_subscription-2.
2. Porchia Moore (@PorchiaMuseM) is a scholar and museum activist; she is an assistant professor of museum studies in the School of Art and Art History at the University of Florida. She is also a member of the teaching faculty at Johns Hopkins University in the Museum Studies Program.
3. You can watch nikhil's talk here: https://www.youtube.com/watch?v=WicEkXGqv8Q (accessed November 21, 2020).
4. See Visitors of Color, https://visitorsofcolor.tumblr.com/.
5. See Museum as Site for Social Action, https://www.museumaction.org.

Chapter 28

A Call to Action

Putting Inclusion to Work

Robert (Bert) Davis

Diversity, equity, accessibility, and inclusion must be woven into the fabric of every for-profit and nonprofit organization henceforth.

There is no singular approach to building a diverse organization; it is multifaceted. It does start at the board level and then works its way into the mission and vision of the nonprofit. It should percolate from the nonsupervisory and supervisory staff as well. To further the museum field, the American Alliance of Museums has embarked on a bold project that has been supported by the Walton, Ford, and Mellon foundations to build diverse nonprofit boards.[1] The African American Association of Museums[2] can also be a source of reference on organizations whose missions are based on combating social injustice and racism. The tools for making change are taking shape; it is now up to the individuals who will take up these tools to use their power to transform museums.

In the face of a pandemic, recession, and national civil unrest, leadership is of utmost importance in both for-profit and nonprofit organizations. The actions that the leaders take must be strategic, purposeful, pragmatic, clear, and yet concise. In a crisis, everyone is looking to the leader for direction.

Communication is the very first strategy to employ on this journey. You must listen, and you must share your ideas, thoughts, and concerns. Your audience is segmented although you are speaking with them simultaneously and, in most scenarios, giving them the same information but in different ways. Assure your staff, board, donors, constituents, and community that you are in control regardless of the crisis.

To be frank, people have lost the art of shutting up and simply listening. I quote Bryant McGill, "One of the most sincere forms of respect is actually listening to what another has to say." A great leader is not only a great visionary, innovator, thought provoker, and incessant worker . . . they are the best listeners!

In the end, the journey of leadership in our nonprofit and museum field is ever changing and evolving. We must be aware of the constant concerns and impacts on nonprofit fundraising during a crisis, board governance during and post-crisis, how our nonprofits and museums have a role in being leaders during this crisis, and how we position ourselves during these times of racial and social unrest. We must ultimately realize that, in fact, no crisis should go to waste. Tough times can ultimately be good ones as well.

The innovative and bold ideas you and your staff have dreamed of can be supported by the board and your community constituency during these uncertain times. Be bold! Be brave! Be innovative! Now is the time to seize the moments and lead not through these crises . . . but *beyond* them.

The first area of concern is your finances. I had a former board member say to me once, "All roads lead to money." The status of your organization's budget is extremely important. Transparent discussions with your staff leadership and your board on your financial status will ultimately govern all fiscal decisions that you will make.

Use partners, peers, and external experts as resources when developing your strategy for dealing with your finances during a crisis. Too many business leaders fail to utilize external experts and peer groups. Over the years, I have sought advice from outside experts, hired people with different skill sets, and tapped peer groups and other business leaders for their expertise.

We have seen that, during a crisis, leaders have been able to renegotiate the terms of grants originally designated for specific programs so that they can be converted to funds for general operations to help support survival of their institutions. Do not be afraid to ask.

After you have created your financial strategy, be certain to share your plans with your key donors and community leaders as well.

Your next focus, of course, is your staff. People trust leaders who are honest, and they will quickly lose faith if they don't trust the information they are given. It's critical to learn the truth and be transparent in sharing it. You may sometimes be tempted to protect people by withholding information or sharing only part of what you know. But in times of crisis, people are in search of truth. They will quickly lose trust if they sense you are hiding information.

Employees often leave their personal beliefs and ideals out of the workplace for fear of crossing professional lines. This is most true for people of color and for women. But if their personal practices and principles help them stay healthy, organized, composed in stressful situations, and even motivated, omitting them from their work life means losing a critical part of who they are. That, in turn, can limit your ability to lead effectively. The team must lean into the museum's core values and engage with others who share them. Don't dismiss positive personal ideals and standards, especially in the face of a crisis.

Even when things are going well, we don't always take time to get to know each other. Because different personalities and work styles can clash, especially in stressful and uncertain situations, it's important to make connections. The best leaders take responsibility for meeting people where they are and try to communicate with them in ways they understand. That means understanding different work styles, preferences, and attitudes.

As leaders best prepare for dealing with a crisis across the board for their institutions, having a clear and consistent communications plan with your board, donors, staff, and supporters in tandem with a sound financial strategy will set the foundation for all other operations.

As you navigate a crisis like the COVID-19 pandemic, leaders and employees alike will need to make sacrifices to ensure business continuity. Whether this means working more hours, taking a pay cut, or doing tasks that are outside the job description to fill needed services, you'll likely be asking people to do more. Incentivize and reward those who make sacrifices to help the team and the organization succeed.

The good news is that a crisis will eventually pass. Your employees need the truth, no matter how challenging, and they need optimism and hope to make it through this crisis. You must keep a positive outlook and focus on the possibilities. You may not always feel optimistic, but keeping your eye on a better future gives people a goal to work toward and makes you a stronger leader.

As we best prepare for the crisis that will not end soon or without strenuous work on all individuals, the civil unrest and the social consciousness around the loss of so many men and women of color has shaken this world to its core. How do we start to deal with this and ultimately embrace it?

The deaths of George Floyd and so many others have catapulted issues of day-to-day Jim Crow practices, police violence, race, ethnic misinterpretations/differences, and socioeconomic and health disparities exacerbated by COVID-19 to the forefront of Americans'—and the world's—psyches.

Figure 28.1 The author. Source: Robert Davis

I dare to say that we have not seen a confluence of critical issues affecting the entire world, most especially the United States, ever in our history.

As museum leaders, our organizations serve as educational entities and not advocacy groups. Now we are grappling with what our roles are and should be in the future with all that is occurring in the world today. I believe we start with honest, open dialogue, preferably at our nonprofits and museums. We must also communicate via technology.

Although we must stay true to our missions and not take any political stances, I do believe as museum leaders that we must stand with the families of George Floyd, Ahmaud Arbery, Breonna Taylor, and with all of those families whose loved ones have been violently taken from them. The unrelenting outrage, pain, and sadness that so many of us from around the world are feeling in this moment has been long held by the black community. With the taking of Indigenous land and the genocide of Indigenous people, from centuries of chattel slavery to generations of race-based terror and lynching and through the countless racially motivated killings, this history persists today.

Despite a global pandemic, people of all ethnic groups, races, ages, abilities, and cultural backgrounds gather in solidarity to bear witness and, to once and for all, denounce these horrific acts. Our museums must ensure that the truth about the American experiment be told in a compelling and inspiring manner.

There have been detailed discussions regarding how preexisting health conditions make certain populations more vulnerable to viral outbreaks and how it disproportionately affects people of color. We must also focus our programming and messaging on the long-standing issues of discrimination, wealth inequality, and the unjust disparities in employment, health care, housing, and education.

So, now the question is, what do we do in the face of these glaring inequities? In these extremely challenging times, we look to the words of Dr. James Cameron (figure 28.2), the founder of America's Black Holocaust Museum (ABHM):

> In 1930 I became sick with hatred. Hatred is a disease that eats into the core of the whole body and destroys it from within. But if you have love in your heart, you can blossom as the sun shines every day.[3]

Dr. Cameron is known as one of the only individuals in American history to survive a public lynching, which took place in Marion, Indiana, in 1930. He was only sixteen years old when his life was nearly taken. He then spent the rest of his ninety-two years sharing his story and those of African Americans from pre-captivity to the

Figure 28.2 Dr. James Cameron, founder of the America's Black Holocaust Museum. Source: Robert Davis

present day. He is the only person to write a book about his life experiences and to open a museum that chronicles American history through the lens of a Black man.

As we preserve the legacy of our history, as leaders of museums, we must be poised to continue to serve as an educator and convener of these incredibly painful and difficult issues and the conversations that we must have to resolve them.

In closing, I must once again reiterate the importance of American museums as accurate promulgaters of the history and cultures of this great place we call the United States. This nation is at a very serious crossroad as it relates to race relations, civil and social unrest, and the pernicious racial divide that has consumed us all. It is incumbent that our museums that focus and highlight the history of the Indigenous peoples of this land, and all of the underrepresented cultures and races of immigrants, take a leadership role in sharing our important stories that make the United States a true promised land.

Museums, especially those that tell the narratives of people of color and women, play a vital role in being a resource for those change agents in our society to draw from and create positive social action and ultimate social change.

Notes

1. To read about this initiative, see American Alliance of Museums, https://www.aam-us.org.
2. You can learn more about AAAM at African American Association of Museums, https://www.black museums.org.
3. Cameron, James, *Sweet Messenger*, interview, 2006, https://www.abhmuseum.org/about/dr-cameron -founder-lynching-survivor/.

ACTIVITY

Developing Your Leadership Philosophy

To complete this activity, you will need paper or a journal and your favorite pen.

Throughout this book, you have heard from many powerful leaders within the museum field. Strong leaders are often guided by a leadership philosophy. Articulating your leadership philosophy is important for many reasons, but paramount is clarity for those that you lead. When you are clear about your philosophy, it brings consistency and transparency to your leadership style. Those that you lead understand why and how you make decisions and feel a sense of transparency that is helpful and appreciated. Generally, a leadership philosophy includes a theory, attitudes, values, and behaviors. We hope that the chapters and the exercises in this book have helped stimulate your thinking about your own leadership philosophy. Now it is your turn.

First, think about leaders that you feel are strong leaders. There are examples throughout this book. What stands out to you about their leadership? What makes them a good leader?

- How do they make decisions?

- How do they interact with staff?

- Can you discern their values from their behaviors?

- How might they recognize and mitigate their weaknesses?

Next, it is time to articulate your theory, attitude, values, and behavior.

- Theory: We hope that inclusion, equity, and justice are at the root of your leadership theory, but there are many theories out there. Some potential theories that could be helpful are Transformational, Authentic, or Servant leadership.[1] Understand that no single theory may be the complete fit for you, but as you understand different leadership theories, you can develop your own that takes elements of different theories.

- Attitude: How do you generally show up in the workplace? What is your approach? Are you optimistic? Are you a problem solver? Or maybe you seek to empower those around you. Whatever it is, you should articulate your attitude as part of your leadership philosophy.

a. What might you take from the authors in this book? What did you learn? What examples have been provided to help you articulate what type of attitude fits best for your leadership philosophy?

b. What did you learn through the other exercises in this book that may help you articulate your attitude? Look back at what you found out about yourself in the Johari Window, Implicit Association Test, and Self-Awareness exercises.

- Values: You have completed your values exercise earlier in the book. Use that exercise to further refine your values.

- Behaviors: It is time to articulate specific behaviors that will support your leadership philosophy. What will people experience? What will you do to live your philosophy? You should use what you have learned through the Johari Window exercise, particularly the feedback you receive from others about how they experience you. You can also look at the Inventory exercises and the Self-Awareness exercise.

Now, it is time to write. *Write, write, write*!!!!! Take what you have learned about inclusive leadership and yourself as a leader and write out your philosophy. Writing it out helps you come to clarity about your philosophy and can bring specificity to how you want to show up as a leader in your organization. Writing also helps create a sense of accountability for you. You can always come back to your philosophy to see how you are doing.

You are set and you have the tools. Write out your philosophy and put it into practice! You are an incredible asset to your organization.

Note

1. Peter Northouse, *Leadership: Theory and Practice* (Thousand Oaks, CA: Sage, 2019).

Epilogue

Dear Museum Leader,

In her prescient writing, *Emergent Strategy*, adrienne maree brown makes the case that "[w]hat we practice at the small scale sets the patterns for the whole system."[1] Leaders have the power to make radical organizational change through relatively small changes.

You can start today or tomorrow by working past your tendencies to put this book on the shelf and fall back into your own habits. Name something that you are going to change. It can be big or small, but it has to be something different. What did you learn in the book? What examples did you see that might apply to your work? What did you discover about yourself through the activities? Now, take this learning and apply it. Begin (or continue) your practice of self-reflection by focusing on what you learned in this book and how you will walk into work tomorrow and do something different, something inclusive.

We hope that you've taken our advice and conscripted a journal and have started writing your observations and ideas as you worked your way through this book. The activities are designed for you. We know the work of museum leadership is difficult and some days it's all you can do to get home and have a meal with loved ones. Or there are days where everything went sideways and you're not sure what the next few days will bring. Boy oh boy, do we know how that feels.

Here's some truth, though. If you want it to be easy, you shouldn't be a designated leader. Much like 2020 brought us challenges we have never faced before, the next crisis will bring new challenges. It will be a whole new experience and conditions to understand. Take time now to fortify your intentions and dive deep into inclusive change systems and personal learning. You'll be more ready next time.

It is our intention with this letter to acknowledge you and the waters you need to cross. We are filling your sails with wind so you have the power to continue your journey. Stay on course with care and self-awareness, and be sure to find people to travel with . . . there's no need to do this alone.

In solidarity,

Cinnamon and Chris

Note

1. adrienne maree brown, *Emergent Strategy: Shaping Change, Changing Worlds* (Chicago: AK Press, 2017), 13.

Index

About the Contributors and Editors

Devon M. Akmon

Devon M. Akmon is the director of Science Gallery Detroit. He believes in the power of cultural organizations to inform and transform communities. Devon brings to Science Gallery Detroit more than fifteen years of experience in nonprofit management, as well as extensive expertise in arts administration, curatorial practice, and community building through the arts. Previously, Devon served as a senior consultant with the DeVos Institute of Arts Management and as director of the Arab American National Museum (AANM). As director of AANM, Devon established new relationships with individuals and organizations that resulted in the expansion of the museum's mission and programming throughout the nation. At present, Devon is a board member of the American Alliance of Museums, Artspace, and CultureSource. In 2013, he was named one of *Crain's Detroit Business* magazine's "40 under 40" business leaders. In 2016, Devon was named one of twelve American Express NGen Fellows with Independent Sector.

Dina A. Bailey

Dina Bailey is the CEO of Mountain Top Vision, a consulting firm that generates systemic change within organizations so that they can more positively impact their communities and, so, impact the world. Using a unique approach that combines research in empathy, bias, diversity, equity, and inclusion with strategies and techniques from the fields of education, anthropology, and transitional justice, Mountain Top Vision specializes in supporting organizations as they transform themselves into places that consistently center inclusion in decision making and action. Dina has more than fifteen years of experience in formal and informal education. For ten years of that time she focused on building deep, authentic community relationships through various dialogic formats at both the National Underground Railroad Freedom Center as well as the National Center for Civil and Human Rights. Those organizations' missions tied the past, present, and future together through the topics of enslavement and civil rights, respectively. Dina spent the remaining five years in consulting with organizations who more often than not need support in having difficult conversations, about topics that center or intersect with race, with members of their staff and communities.

Bob Beatty

Bob Beatty is founder and president of the Lyndhurst Group, a history, museum, and nonprofit consulting firm. From 2007 to 2018, Bob served the American Association for State and Local

History, and from 1999 to 2007, he directed the education department at the Orange County Regional History Center in Orlando.

He holds a BA in liberal studies and an MA in history from the University of Central Florida and a PhD in public history from Middle Tennessee State University. In addition to the forthcoming book *"Sure Has Been a Fine Weekend": At Fillmore East and the Legacy of Duane Allman*, he is author of *Florida's Highwaymen: Legendary Landscapes, Zen and the Art of Local History* and *An American Association for State and Local History Guide to Making Public History*.

Kayleigh Bryant-Greenwell

Kayleigh Bryant-Greenwell is a cultural equity strategist with more than ten years of museum and nonprofit experience at the intersections of social justice and racial equity. She contributes to the Museum as Site for Social Action and Empathetic Museum movements. As head of public programs with the Smithsonian American Art Museum and the Renwick Gallery, she is responsible for leading new outreach and inclusion initiatives toward developing new audiences and cultivating public engagement. In the wake of COVID-19, she was appointed to organize a museum internal taskforce toward reopening planning and strategies. In 2020, she served on a six-month term detail with the Smithsonian's Anacostia Community Museum to develop a new initiative on race and community. She has previously worked with the Smithsonian's National Museum of African American History and Culture, National Museum of Women in the Arts, and the David C. Driskell Center for the Study of Visual Arts and Culture of African Americans and the African Diaspora. She has developed college-level art history curricula for the study of art by African Americans and the art of social justice movements for Trinity Washington University. She serves on the board of Washington Project for the Arts and on the Artist Selection Committee of Halcyon Arts Lab and VisArts in Rockville, Maryland. Additionally, she leads the Strategy Committee of Museum as Site for Social Action and has been a member of the Empathetic Museum since 2017. She received her BA in art history from the University of Maryland, College Park, and MA in museum studies from George Washington University. She is a graduate of the 2020 Museum Leadership Institute with Claremont University (formerly The Getty).

Cinnamon Catlin-Legutko

Working in museums for more than twenty years, Cinnamon Catlin-Legutko believes they have the power to change lives, inspire movements, and challenge authority. A museum director since 2001, Cinnamon is a frequent presenter at national museum meetings and is often asked to comment on national museum issues. As the president/CEO of the Abbe Museum (Bar Harbor) from 2009 to 2019, she was the motivational leader behind the museum's decolonization initiative, working with the Native communities in Maine to develop policies and protocols to ensure collaboration and cooperation with Wabanaki people. Prior to joining the Abbe in 2009, Cinnamon was the director of the General Lew Wallace Study & Museum in Crawfordsville, Indiana, where she led the organization to the National Medal for Museum Service in 2008. In 2019, Cinnamon became the director of the Illinois State Museum. Cinnamon holds a BA in anthropology and art history from Purdue University, and she is a graduate of the University of Arkansas (Fayetteville) MA program in anthropology with a specialization in museum studies.

In 2016, Cinnamon gave her first TEDx talk, *We Must Decolonize Our Museums* (www.tedxdirigo .com), and she's been featured on the Museopunks podcast series. She's the author of *Museum*

Administration 2.0, The Art of Healing: The Wishard Art Collection (2004), and coeditor of the *Small Museum Toolkit* (2012).

Robert (Bert) Davis

Dr. Robert (Bert) Davis of America's Black Holocaust Museum, Milwaukee, Wisconsin, has more than twenty-nine years of zoo, aquarium, museum, and nonprofit leadership experience. Since 2017 he has served as the principal of DRMD Strategies LLC. From 2016 to 2017, he was the president and CEO of the Dubuque County Historical Society and the National Mississippi River Museum & Aquarium. Prior to that, Dr. Davis served for ten and a half years as the president and CEO of the Zoological Society of Milwaukee. His previous leadership roles also include vice president of education at Lincoln Park Zoo in Chicago, director of education and external affairs at Zoo Atlanta, and supervisory veterinary medical officer at the Smithsonian's National Zoological Park in Washington, DC.

Dr. Davis earned a BS degree in animal and poultry sciences and completed two years of graduate study in cytogenetics at Tuskegee University. He then entered Tuskegee University's School of Veterinary Medicine from which he received a DVM degree.

LaNesha DeBardelaben

LaNesha DeBardelaben has spent her career in education and museum work. She is executive director of the Northwest African American Museum (NAAM) in Seattle, Washington. Prior to re-locating to Seattle, LaNesha was senior vice president of education and exhibitions at the Charles H. Wright Museum of African American History in Detroit, Michigan. Her career in museums of more than fifteen years began at the National Museum of Kenya in Africa, and she has studied museums and libraries internationally in Ghana, South Africa, England, Germany, and Israel.

LaNesha is national president of the Association of African American Museums (AAAM) Board of Directors. LaNesha has served on the national Executive Council of the Association for the Study of African American Life and History (ASALH) and Seattle Metropolitan Chamber of Commerce. She is a member of the International Women's Forum and Seattle's Community Development Roundtable.

Omar Eaton-Martinez

Omar Eaton-Martinez leads the Prince George's County Historical Resources, which include historical house museums, an aviation museum, the Black History Program, and archaeological parks. He oversees the programming of those sites with an emphasis placed on preserving, sustaining, and enhancing these resources as well as engaging and building communities through education, outreach, and innovation. He has recently worked at the Smithsonian's National Museum of American History, National Park Service, the Office of the National Museum of the American Latino Commission, and NASA, and he also was a K–12 teacher in New York City and Washington, DC.

He has had leading roles in racial equity organizations like Museums & Race: Transformation and Justice, and Museum Hue, and he contributed to the Museum as Site for Social Action project. His research interests are Afro Latinx identity in museum exhibitions; diversity and inclusion in museums and cultural institutions; and hip-hop history, culture, and education. Moreover, he has supported public history projects centering on blackness in Puerto Rico.

In 2019, Omar was selected to be an American Alliance of Museums Diversity, Equity, Accessibility, and Inclusion (DEAI) Senior Fellow, which is dedicated to diversifying museum boards, and he is a gubernatorial appointee to the Maryland Lynching Truth and Reconciliation Commission. In 2020, he was elected to the Board of Directors for the Association of African American Museums. He holds a BA in African American studies from the University of Maryland, College Park (1996) and a master's degree in educational leadership from the American Intercontinental University (2009). He currently is a part-time PhD student in American studies at the University of Maryland, College Park.

Lori Fogarty

Lori Fogarty is the director and CEO of the Oakland Museum of California (OMCA), a multidisciplinary museum that brings together collections of art, history, and natural sciences to tell the extraordinary stories of California and its people. Since 2006, Lori has worked to oversee and guide all the museum's programmatic and administrative operations and has transitioned OMCA from a public/private cultural institution supported by the City of Oakland and the Oakland Museum of California Foundation to an independent nonprofit organization with an innovative new organizational structure. Lori also led the museum's $63 million "Museum of California" campaign and building renovation project, which has included the reinstallation of 90,000 square feet of gallery space as well as the first major enhancement to the museum's landmark building. She is currently leading the "All In: Campaign for OMCA," an $85 million comprehensive campaign to support programs and operations, endowment and investment fund growth, and capital improvements to the museum's seven-acre campus. Lori has spearheaded OMCA's efforts to place the visitor at the center of the museum experience and to focus the institution's efforts on community engagement and social impact. She received major recognition in the museum and nonprofit field as the recipient of the John Cotton Dana Award for Leadership from the American Alliance of Museums and the Hank Russo Outstanding Fundraising Professional Award from the Association of Fundraising Professionals. Prior to her current position, Lori was executive director of the Bay Area Discovery Museum and was senior deputy director of the San Francisco Museum of Modern Art. Lori is on the board of the Association of Art Museum Directors.

Terri Lee Freeman

Terri Lee Freeman was appointed president of the Reginald F. Lewis Museum of Maryland African American History and Culture in December 2020. The seventh director of the State's largest museum devoted to African American history, Freeman is responsible for providing strategic leadership in furthering the museum's mission as an educational and cultural institution.

Freeman served as president of the National Civil Rights Museum from 2014 through 2020. Prior to joining the museum, Ms. Freeman served as president of the Greater Washington Community Foundation for eighteen years. Her intense passion for the nonprofit sector and community was nurtured while serving as the founding executive director of the Freddie Mac Foundation, which at the time, was one of the five largest corporate foundations in the metropolitan Washington region.

Freeman has served on a variety of nonprofit boards including the Community Foundation for Greater Memphis; The Orpheum Theatre Group; the Greater Memphis Chamber of Commerce; the Memphis Brand Initiative; Urban Teachers; and the Southeastern Council of Foundations. In 2020, she was named Memphian of the Year by Memphis magazine. In 2019, she was named a Superwoman of Business and a member of the Power 100 by the Memphis Business Journal. Freeman received a BA in journalism/communication arts from the University of Dayton and a master's degree in organizational communication management from Howard University

Ben Garcia

Ben Garcia is deputy executive director and chief learning officer at the Ohio History Connection. There he leads special projects and oversees six divisions. His prior museum experience includes tenures in the Education Department at the J. Paul Getty Museum, as associate director of education at the Skirball Cultural Center, as head of interpretation and operations at the Phoebe A. Hearst Museum of Anthropology at UC Berkeley, and as deputy director at the San Diego Museum of Man (now, Museum of Us). Ben serves on the boards of Equality Ohio and the Association of Midwestern Museums.

Stacey Halfmoon

Stacey Halfmoon is Caddo, Choctaw, and Delaware. She has twenty-five years of professional experience in cultural preservation, tribal liaison work, tribal consultation, cultural resource law, and museum leadership. She has a BA from the University of Oklahoma in anthropology as well as certificates, training, and coursework in museum studies, cultural resource law, and consultation practices.

Stacey's career began in earnest in 1995 when she started working for the Caddo Nation immediately after college, where for a decade she helped develop a comprehensive cultural preservation program. In 2001, Stacey was recruited by and served the U.S. Defense Department as the senior tribal liaison in the Office of the Deputy Under Secretary of Defense for Installations and Environment. She helped manage the Native American Lands Environmental Mitigation Program (NALEMP) and implementation of the Defense Department's first American Indian Policy. In 2007, back in Oklahoma, she began what would be eight years as the director of outreach and museum programs for the State of Oklahoma—American Indian Cultural Center and Museum. In 2015, Stacey's work took her to Columbus, Ohio, where she served as the inaugural director of American Indian relations for the Ohio History Connection. In 2019, Stacey returned to Oklahoma to begin serving the Choctaw Nation as the senior director of the Choctaw Cultural Center near the Tribal Headquarters in Durant, Oklahoma. Stacey is also the owner/operator of Halfmoon Consulting LLC.

Joanne Jones-Rizzi

Joanne Jones-Rizzi currently serves as the vice president of science, equity, and education at the Science Museum of Minnesota, where she leads the Science Museum's science and education initiatives, ensuring that they achieve maximum impact and are equitably accessible for all audiences. Jones-Rizzi has a decades-long career working on systemic, ecological change within museums, specializing in expanding meaningful access through exhibitions relevant to audiences who do not yet think of museums as their cultural institutions. She advises museums nationally and internationally on culture, identity, antiracism, exhibition development, and community engagement.

Elizabeth Kryder-Reid

Elizabeth Kryder-Reid is Chancellor's Professor of Anthropology and Museum Studies at Indiana University–Purdue University Indianapolis (IUPUI) where she also directs the Cultural Heritage Research Center. She directed the Museum Studies Program from 1998 to 2013 and from 2016 to 2020. Her interdisciplinary research investigates cultural heritage focusing on intersections of landscapes and power, and the contestation of social inequality. Her publications include *California Mission Landscapes: Race, Power, and the Politics of Heritage* (2016) and *Keywords in American Landscape Design* (2010). Her current research is on toxic heritage.

Lisa Yun Lee

Lisa Yun Lee (BA, Bryn Mawr College; PhD, Duke University) is a cultural activist and the executive director of the National Public Housing Museum, an associate professor in art history and gender and women's studies at the University of Illinois at Chicago, and teaching faculty with the Prison Neighborhood Art & Education Project. Lisa has worked as the director of the Jane Addams Hull-House Museum, and she has published books and articles about aesthetics and politics, public art, public housing, and the potential of museums as radical sites of resistance and for participatory democracy. She served as a cochair of Mayor Lori Lightfoot's Arts & Culture Transition Team and on the Mayor's Committee for the evaluation of monuments, memorials, and historical reckoning.

Stacey Mann

Stacey Mann is a learning experience designer and interpretive strategist who consults with educators, designers, and technologists on how best to engage audiences both onsite and online. She advocates social action through inclusive storytelling, civic literacy, and empathy. Early work with the Exploratorium provided the foundation for an inquiry-based and user-centered design methodology that she applies to award-winning digital media interaction design, exhibition development, interpretive planning, and visitor evaluation. In her role as a strategic consultant with museums and cultural institutions, she facilitates dialogue and planning efforts around questions of representation, accessibility, and community engagement. Stacey is on the Museum Exhibition Planning and Design faculty at University of the Arts, and she previously served on the editorial board of *Exhibition: The Journal of Museum Exhibition* for the National Association of Museum Exhibition. She is a founding member of The Empathetic Museum, a steering committee member of Museums & Race, and strategic advisor to UNSILENCE, a human rights education and advocacy nonprofit.

Tonya M. Matthews

Tonya M. Matthews, PhD, served as president and CEO of the Michigan Science Center (MiSci), rebuilding and reclaiming Detroit's science center legacy after the closure of the Detroit Science Center. During her tenure, Matthews founded the STEMinista Project and led MiSci to become a STEM Hub for the state of Michigan. Previously, Matthews served as vice president of Museums for Cincinnati Museum Center, stewarding the community, education, and research footprints of three museums and two research centers, and prior to that, she served as BodyLink director for the Maryland Science Center. Currently, Matthews is associate provost for inclusive workforce development and director of the STEM Learning Innovation Center at Wayne State University

(WSU). In this role, Dr. Matthews is part of the WSU leadership team setting a vision to address the challenge of an inclusive STEM student success pipeline and pathway from "preK-to-Gray."

Known as a thought-leader in the intersectionality of formal and informal education in STEM, STEM equity, institutionalized inclusion, and social entrepreneurship, Matthews has been recognized as one of the Most Influential Women in Michigan by *Crain's Detroit Business* (2016) and honored as a Trailblazer by *Career Mastered Magazine* (2017). Matthews is also a published and performing poet and was included in the first edition of *100 Best African-American Poems* (2010), edited by Nikki Giovanni. Matthews received a PhD in biomedical engineering from Johns Hopkins University and a BSE in biomedical and electrical engineering from Duke University.

Matthews has served on numerous boards, including the American Alliance of Museums, Chatfield College, Detroit Public Television, First Independence Bank, and the National Academy of Sciences Board on Science Education.

Kelly McKinley

Kelly is the CEO of the Bay Area Discovery Museum. She was most recently the deputy director of the Oakland Museum of California (OMCA) where she oversaw collections, conservation, curatorial, interpretation, exhibition design and production, and evaluation and visitor research. Prior to OMCA, she served as executive director of education and public programming at the Art Gallery of Ontario in Toronto, Canada. She serves on the board of the American Alliance of Museums and the editorial board of *Curator: The Museum Journal*.

Margaret Middleton

Margaret Middleton is an independent exhibit designer working at the intersection of design and social justice. Middleton has a degree in industrial design from the Rhode Island School of Design and more than fifteen years of experience in the museum field.

Middleton developed the Family Inclusive Language Chart and consults with museums on implementing family-inclusive practice. Their writing has been published in the *Journal of Museum Education*; *Exhibition* (National Association for Museum Exhibition); *Dimensions* (Association of Science and Technology Centers); and *Museum* magazine (American Alliance of Museums).

Armando Perla

Armando Perla is an activist and independent curator based in Montreal, Canada. He is one of the main organizers behind the #CMHRStopLying social media campaign, which looks to hold the Canadian Museum for Human Rights accountable for exposing current and former employees to different degrees of racism, homophobia, transphobia, sexism, sexual harassment, and other forms of oppression. Armando has been part of the founding teams for the Canadian Museum for Human Rights in Winnipeg, Canada, and the Swedish Museum of Movements in Malmo, Sweden. Armando is a board member for ICOM's International Committee on Ethical Dilemmas and an international advisor on museums, human rights, and social inclusion for the City of Medellin in Colombia. Armando works nationally and internationally with diverse cultural organizations with issues such as DEAI, ethics, community engagement, and participatory museological practices.

Armando has been associate professor at the University of Winnipeg and the faculty of law at the University of Manitoba. He has worked in different capacities for Casa Alianza Guatemala, Lunds University Commissioned Education in Sweden, the Manitoba Interfaith Immigration Council in Canada, and the Center for Justice and International Law in Washington, DC. Armando holds an LLB from l'Université Laval in Canada and an LLM in international human rights law from Lund University in Sweden. He is currently pursuing a PhD in art history and museology at the University of Montreal, where he is researching the impacts of institutional racism in the museum sector in Canada and the United States.

Therese Quinn

Therese Quinn, associate professor and director of museum and exhibition studies at the University of Illinois at Chicago, has worked as an exhibit researcher, developer, and evaluator for the Field Museum of Natural History, the Chicago Children's Museum, the California Academy of the Sciences, and other cultural institutions. Dr. Quinn has received National Endowment for the Humanities (2018, 2017) and Fulbright (Finland, 2009) awards and is an elected representative of her faculty union. Her most recent books are *School: Questions about Museums, Culture and Justice to Explore in Your Classroom* (2020) and *Teaching toward Democracy: Educators as Agents of Change* (2nd ed., 2016), and she has published articles and other writings widely, including in *American Quarterly*, the *Journal of Critical Military Studies*, the *Journal of Museum Education*, the *International Journal of Qualitative Studies in Education*, the *Journal of Gay and Lesbian Issues in Education*, and *Rethinking Schools*.

Mattie Reynolds

Mattie Reynolds (Choctaw Nation of Oklahoma) received her MS in arts management with a graduate certificate in museum studies from the University of Oregon, where her research focused on the implementation and issues of the Native American Graves Protection and Repatriation Act. Previously, Mattie was the preparator and exhibition coordinator at the Institute of American Indian Arts (IAIA) Museum of Contemporary Native Arts where she worked closely with students and alumni to install visionary contemporary Native art exhibitions. Currently, Mattie is the director of the IAIA Balzer Contemporary Edge Gallery, a community-wide educational and exploratory venue, and an assistant professor in the IAIA Museum Studies Department.

Cynthia Robinson

Cynthia Robinson is the director of museum studies and senior lecturer at Tufts University, where she specializes in museum education. She spent twenty-five years working in and with museums and has extensive experience in developing programs, curricula, and exhibitions, as well as in museum management and administration. Cynthia received the 2017 John Cotton Dana Award for Leadership, presented by the Education Committee of the American Alliance of Museums. The award recognizes individuals outside the field of museum education who exhibit outstanding leadership and promote the educational responsibility and capacity of museums. It has only been awarded nine times in the past thirty-two years. Robinson has also served as the editor in chief of the *Journal of Museum Education* since 2010.

Ashley Rogers

Ashley Rogers is the executive director of the Whitney Plantation, a museum and memorial in South Louisiana dedicated to the interpretation of slavery. Ashley has led the museum since its opening in 2014. She is an advocate for inclusive and social justice–informed museum practice, and she is a contributing writer to the MASS Action toolkit; the *Inclusive Historian's Handbook*; Montpelier's Engaging Descendant Communities rubric; and *The Inclusive Museum Leader*. Ashley is a PhD candidate in the Department of History at Louisiana State University (LSU), where her research focuses on labor, sugar plantations, and the petrochemical industry in the twentieth century. In addition to her work at Whitney Plantation and LSU, Ashley serves on the Board of Directors for the Southern Mutual Help Association, a rural community development organization based in New Iberia, Louisiana.

Lisa Sasaki

Lisa Sasaki is the director of the Smithsonian Asian Pacific American Center (APAC), which brings Asian Pacific American history, art, and culture to communities through innovative museum experiences online and throughout the United States. Previously she was the director of the Audience and Civic Engagement Center at the Oakland Museum of California and the director of program development at the Japanese American National Museum. Sasaki has served as president of the Western Museums Association's Board of Directors; as a member of the American Alliance of Museums' Diversity, Equity, Accessibility, and Inclusion working group; and as an advisor on the Advisory Council for the Council of Jewish American Museums. She is a frequent guest lecturer for museum studies programs and has also lectured internationally for organizations like International Council of Museums and the Museums and Galleries of Queensland.

Susana Smith Bautista

Dr. Susana Smith Bautista is a museum advisor and administrator, art historian, and curator in Chicanx/Latinx and Latin American Art. She received a PhD in communication from the University of Southern California (USC) and a master's degree in art history/museum studies with honors (Phi Kappa Phi). Susana wrote a book on *Museums in the Digital Age: Changing Meanings of Place, Community, and Culture* (2013) and taught at USC Annenberg School of Communication and Claremont Graduate University Arts Management Program. Her leadership experience includes the Mexican Cultural Institute of Los Angeles, USC Pacific Asia Museum, Pasadena Museum of California Art, LatinArt.com, LA Plaza de Cultura y Artes, and Arts and Culture Commissioner for the City of Pasadena. Susana is currently director and chief curator of the AltaMed Art Collection, her book on *How to Close a Museum* will be published early 2021, and she serves on the Board of Trustees of the American Alliance of Museums.

Gretchen Sullivan Sorin

Gretchen Sullivan Sorin is director and Distinguished Service Professor at the Cooperstown Graduate Program, a training program for museum professionals that is part of the State University of New York College at Oneonta. Dr. Sorin writes and lectures frequently on museum practice, diversity and inclusion, and African American history. Her books include *Touring Historic Harlem, Four Walks in Northern Manhattan* with architectural historian Andrew Dolkart, *In the Spirit of Martin: The Living Legacy of Dr. Martin Luther King, Jr.* for the Smithsonian Institution Traveling Exhibition Service, *Through the Eyes of Others: African Americans and Identity in American Art*, and *Case Studies in Cultural Entrepreneurship: How to Create Relevant and Sustainable Institutions*. She is the author of *Driving While Black: African American Travel and the Road to Civil Rights* (2020). Sorin is also cowriter and senior historian working with filmmaker Ric Burns on the PBS documentary film *Driving While Black: Race, Space and Mobility*.

Chris Taylor

Chris Taylor spent fifteen years working in museums, primarily at the Minnesota Historical Society. He began his career as an educator but quickly saw the power that history can have on an individual's identity. Through the stories they elevate (or suppress), museums have the power to either fortify or disrupt the status quo, but Chris came to understand that this must be an intentional choice. He began teaching undergraduate courses at the University of Minnesota on "Diversity in the Museum Field" as part of a museum fellowship program designed to increase the diversity of museum professionals. At the Minnesota Historical Society, he successfully created the Department of Inclusion and Community Engagement to steward the museum's systemic efforts for inclusion and equity. He also became the first chief inclusion officer in the museum field, a role he occupied for four years. Museums around the country sought out Chris as a consultant for their inclusion and equity efforts. In 2019, Chris Taylor was recruited to become the chief inclusion officer for the State of Minnesota, one of only two states to have such a position. There he leads the development and implementation of a statewide strategy for inclusion and equity across more than twenty state agencies. He has authored numerous articles including two chapters of the MASS Action toolkit.

nikhil trivedi

nikhil trivedi is the director of engineering at the Art Institute of Chicago as well as a facilitator, educator, and community builder. His experience planning and executing complex web projects has also brought him to work with institutions to create concrete plans around the healing and accountability from historic traumas like colonialism, slavery, genocide, and war. He's a regular contributor at Incluseum and is a project advisor for MASS Action. His writing has been featured in the *Journal for Museum Education*, *Fwd: Museums*, and *Model View Culture*.

Naree W. S. Viner

Naree W. S. Viner has deep experience in executive recruiting with an exclusive focus on mission-driven clients. She is widely regarded as one of the leading search consultants focused on finding leaders for museums and other cultural institutions. She is a managing director at Koya Partners and previously worked at global executive search firms Korn Ferry and Heidrick & Struggles, and she started her career in search at a boutique firm. Before going into search, she worked at the J. Paul Getty Trust, in the dot-com world, and at a social service organization. She earned her MA from the University of Washington and BA from Williams College, both in art history.

Esme Ward

Esme Ward is director of Manchester Museum, the United Kingdom's largest university museum, a role she has held since April 2018. She is the first female director in its 130-year history. Esme is leading a transformative capital project, "hello future," renewing the creative and civic mission of the organization. She is the strategic lead for culture and aging in Greater Manchester and the city's cultural lead for sustainability and climate action. She is also chair of the national Culture, Health & Wellbeing Alliance. Last year, Esme was awarded an Honorary Professorship (Heritage Futures) at the University of Manchester.

Beth Ziebarth

Beth Ziebarth has a personal interest and professional responsibility in advocacy for people with disabilities. She currently serves as the director of Access Smithsonian. In her position, Beth develops and implements accessibility policy and guidelines for the institution's nineteen museums, the National Zoo, and nine research centers, ensuring that the Smithsonian's thirty million annual visitors experience a welcoming environment that accommodates individuals of all ages and abilities. Her work includes staff training on accessibility and disability topics, facility and program technical assistance, direct accessibility services, outreach and collaboration, and five signature programs for people with disabilities.